OASIS and OBQI

A Guide for Education and Implementation

Sperling, Randa L.
OASIS and OBQI

5/6/99

OASIS and OBQI

A Guide for Education and Implementation

Randa L. Sperling, MSN, RN C

President
Randa Sperling Consulting
Boonville, Indiana

Carolyn J. Humphrey, MS, RN

Editor
Home Healthcare Nurse
& Home Healthcare Nurse Manager

President
C.J. Humphrey Associates
Louisville, Kentucky

Lippincott

Philadelphia • New York • Baltimore

Acquisitions Editor: Susan M. Glover, RN, MSN
Assistant Editor: Bridget Blatteau
Production Editor: Virginia Barishek
Senior Production Manager: Helen Ewan
Production Service: Shepherd, Inc.
Printer/Binder: Victor Graphics
Cover Designer: Larry Didona
Cover Printer: Lehigh Press

9 8 7 6 5 4 3 2 1

Library of Congress Cataloging-in-Publication Data

Sperling, Randa L.
  OASIS and OBQI : a guide for education and implementation / Randa
L. Sperling, Carolyn J. Humphrey.
    p.   cm.
  Includes bibliographical references and index.
  ISBN 0-7817-1955-0 (alk. paper)
  1. Home care services—Quality control.   2. Home care services-
-Documentation.   3. Outcome assessment (Medical care)—Methodology.
4. Home care services—Data processing.   I. Humphrey, Carolyn J.,
1947- . II. Title.
  [DNLM: 1. Home Care Services—standards.   2. Outcome Assessment
(Health Care)   3. Quality Assurance, Health Care.   4. Quality
Indicators, Health Care.   5. Data Collection.   WY 115S749o   1998]
RA645.3.S67 1998
362.1'2'021873—dc21
DNLM/DLC
for Library of Congress   98-36724
                                                               CIP

Care has been taken to confirm the accuracy of the information presented and to describe generally accepted practices. However, the authors, editors, and publisher are not responsible for errors or omissions or for any consequences from application of the information in this book and make no warranty, express or implied, with respect to the contents of the publication.

The authors, editors and publisher have exerted every effort to ensure that drug selection and dosage set forth in this text are in accordance with current recommendations and practice at the time of publication. However, in view of ongoing research, changes in government regulations, and the constant flow of information relating to drug therapy and drug reactions, the reader is urged to check the package insert for each drug for any change in indications and dosage and for added warnings and precautions. This is particularly important when the recommended agent is a new or infrequently employed drug.

Some drugs and medical devices presented in this publication have Food and Drug Administration (FDA) clearance for limited use in restricted research settings. It is the responsibility of the health care provider to ascertain the FDA status of each drug or device planned for use in their clinical practice.

New Medicare Conditions of Participation (COPs) which govern all home health agencies that provide home care services under the Medicare program were to be put in regulatory force in 1998. These regulations will require Medicare certified home health agencies to collect data and determine outcomes of care provided using the Outcome Assessment and Information Set (OASIS) and develop their entire OBQI (Outcome-Based Quality Improvement) program around this data set. Using this data system is complex in that it requires a total organizational change that impacts computerization, documentation forms, staff and management roles and functions as well as a total revamping of the organization's quality improvement (QI) program.

The mandatory implementation of OBQI and the collection of OASIS information has sparked an industry of its own. It has certainly created a "buyer beware" market for home care professionals, managers and administrators who are looking for accurate information to learn about the process and publications they can use to teach staff. To create an accurate database there *must* be accurate data collected or else the remainder of the activities are worthless. The term "garbage in–garbage out" has never been more meaningful than it is when used in the context of learning how to collect OASIS data and implement OBQI as it *was intended*. To assure that the *most reliable and valid* information is collected during patient assessments using the OASIS data set, everyone working with the system must understand the data set *just as it was created*.

The OASIS data set and the analysis of outcomes using the mandated OBQI process has only been strictly tested by the agencies in the demonstration project conducted through the Center for Health Policy Research through the University of Colorado, Denver (The Center). Therefore, the information in this book is based on the research project and its use by several demonstration agencies. This is not to say that many home healthcare organizations aren't using OASIS and OBQI correctly, however, by our review of material and discussions with several agencies, there are several indications many people are using this information *incorrectly*, and many products on the market have errors in implementation. We wanted to write this book for many reasons, the main ones being:

♦ Randa wanted to share her real life experiences in using OASIS and OBQI *just as it is written* to develop the content of the book. She has been responsible for initializing an agency's involvement with the Center, coordinating the implementation of the project in one of the demonstration agencies, participating in all of the educational and evaluative sessions held at the Center, and is currently working as a consultant while maintaining contact with the Center. She has seen many people easily get confused about OASIS and OBQI and felt strongly that there should be information provided for those implementing the system in their own agencies that will help them learn it the correct way.

♦ Carolyn's many years of experience as a home care administrator, educator, author, editor and practitioner in the home care field have always led her to want to provide information to practicing nurses, managers and professionals who work in the home care field every day. She was also concerned that this information should be presented in the most concise, clear way so that staff who are collecting the data and those that are analyzing and interpreting it can soundly learn the basics first before implementing it in their own organizations. She brought her expertise in format and writing to the project and has helped produce a user-friendly book for learning OASIS and OBQI.

The book is organized to give the reader the rationale and background of OASIS and OBQI **first** to be used as a foundation for learning *how* to implement and analyze the results. Just as when teaching patients the nurse must teach in the affective domain of learning (**why** they need to know the information), then in the cognitive domain (what they need to know), and often then in the psycho-motor domain (how to go about making it happen) before a change in behavior can take place, so it is with learning about OASIS and OBQI. We strongly believe that everyone involved with OASIS must first understand the background and purpose of this change in focus to outcomes and then they can learn how to collect the information, score the questions and analyze the data.

- ◆ In general, the objectives of this book are to:
  - ◆ Provide an overview of the entire OBQI Process as mandated by the Medicare COPs and its impact on the organization and staff.
  - ◆ Explain the process necessary to integrate OASIS items into existing forms from a management and staff perspective.
  - ◆ Present training strategies and techniques to assure the collection of accurate, meaningful data.
  - ◆ Identify specific approaches and formats for integrating the material and data into an agency's forms, computer systems, and quality improvement program.
  - ◆ Present information on how to choose the most meaningful outcomes for remediation or reinforcement. The process of care review and audits will be demonstrated and explained through case studies and hypothetical examples, using aggregate data.

The book is organized in three sections. The first, **OASIS and OBQI in Home Health** gives the reader an overview of the evolution of OASIS and OBQI based on the research project funded by HCFA. A discussion of how the collection and interpretation of the OASIS interfaces with the Medicare Conditions of Participation, an agency's performance improvement activities, accrediting bodies, consumers and managed care is included. Additionally in this section are the suggested steps a home health organization can take to incorporate OASIS into their daily operations.

The second section, **Training Staff to Use OASIS,** is for the nurses and therapists who will be collecting the OASIS information at various timepoints. We call these professionals assessors since they are the front-line information gatherers, without whom the information would

not be accurate. This section presents several ways to learn about the OASIS questions presented in a conversational, easy to understand way. Especially helpful are the two sections, "What Exactly Am I Looking For?" and "Learning OASIS by the Functional Assessment Approach." This material walks the assessor through each of the MO numbers and gives them guidance on exactly what the question is looking for as well as helps them differentiate between choices based on the patient's functional ability.

In the third section, **Data Interpretation and Measurement of Outcomes,** the reader is presented with an overview of what happens to the data, once it is collected and presented in various reports. Examples of reports and determinations of how outcomes are used to reinforce or remediate care behaviors are explained based on examples from current data collection companies and information from the Center. Additionally, numerous Appendices elaborate on the content to show the reader examples of assessment forms, frequently asked questions and terms used in OBQI and OASIS.

We have made every effort to be as accurate and descriptive about OASIS and OBQI as possible. All material presented in this book is based on the way the demonstration project was conducted and anticipated changes in the Conditions of Participation (COPs). This route was chosen since the MEQA project is a research study and much care has been taken in the study to approach the development and refinement of the OASIS data set as well as the outcome reports from a research focus. We feel it is critically important that this same focus remain intact through the HCFA regulations. Although the study won't be completed until 1999, the information coming from the Center has shown the validity and reliability of the data set and so should be rigorously followed when implemented through the country.

We recommend thorough review of all materials from this book and the Center before purchasing any computerized or manual forms and systems for collecting OASIS and OBQI information. Readers are encouraged to keep up with the changes in the Medicare Conditions of Participation (COPs), through the Health Care Financing Administration (HCFA) regulations and state and national home care association publications and seminars and professional journals. We have found the materials published by the Center for Health Policy and Research extremely helpful. Everyone at the Center, especially Peter Shaughnessy and Kathryn Crisler, has always been open to responses and questions from all who call for assistance. They can be reached at:

Center for Health Policy Research
1355 W. Colorado Boulevard
Suite 306
Denver, CO 80222
Phone: 303-756-8350
Fax: 303-759-8196

Although the OASIS and OBQI project is still in its infancy and has some limitations, the objectives of the program—to measure home care patient outcomes in a valid and reliable way on a national basis—is well on its way to being reached. We support this effort to validate home care services through a scientific, research-based approach and look forward to continuing our work in this area. We hope this book assists agencies in implementing and refining their expertise in the collection of performance improvement data using OASIS and OBQI.

Randa L. Sperling, MSN, RN, C
Carolyn J. Humphrey, MS, RN

Acknowledgments

We first want to thank all the demonstration agencies that kindly shared with us their experiences in using OASIS. They not only helped form the section on "Suggestions from Agencies Who Have Made It Work" in Chapter 3, but assisted us in the overall approach to this book.

We also want to thank Dr. Leslie Jean Neal PhD, RN, C, CRRN, Rehabilitation Clinical Nurse Specialist, Inova VNA Home Health in Springfield, VA, a wonderful colleague who brought her expertise in home care and rehabilitation nursing as the author of Chapter 5, "Learning OASIS by the Functional Assessment Approach." She has provided the learner with a creative approach to combining functional assessment knowledge with the collection of OASIS data.

Special thanks also go to Kathryn Crisler at the Center for Health Services and Policy Research at the University of Colorado whose openness and enthusiasm for outcomes is contagious. She has always been willing to share her ideas and thoughts as well as be available for questions and encouragement in the past and during the process of writing this book.

Our thanks to our publishers and editors at Lippincott Williams & Wilkins who shared in our vision of presenting the basic information on OASIS and OBQI to home health providers everywhere. Their support of our educational mission and their willingness to quickly get the book in print as well as explore other learning tools that can assist home care providers in learning about OASIS, makes clear their commitment to the entire home health industry. In addition, thanks to Patricia Carr, RN, Jane G. Frankenfield, RN, BSN, CPHQ, and Nina M. Smith, RN C, MedEd, who reviewed the proposal and provided input about ways to improve our initial outline and create the most comprehensive OASIS and OBQI manual on the market.

And now, a word to our friends and families. Thanks to Mike and Jill Conner for providing the equipment and moral support I needed to begin this project. Michael, I promised I'd dedicate my first book to you! A heartfelt Thank You goes to my parents, Randall and Joyce Ann Ferguson, for always saying "You can do it!" and making me believe it. Thanks and love to my husband, John, and children Jon, Matt, and Bobbie, for having patience with me when I needed to "work on the book" and to Faith Heritage Christian School in Evansville, Indiana, for all the prayers offered that I would finish this book!

I especially want to thank Carolyn for being my mentor as well as my friend. Without her patience, guidance, and expertise in writing, this book would probably never have happened. She opened her home and heart, and gave up time with her family to drag me through the process of writing this book. Carolyn, you're a wonderful role model.

My major thanks go to Randa, whose knowledge and experiences of OASIS and OBQI taught me so much that I kept saying, "You should write a book about this!" She decided to work with me on this project and give me the opportunity to help others learn from her experience and down-to-earth approach. I heartfully thank my family, Fred and Jonathan, as well as my staff, Ruffles and Mikey who have gone on with many activities while I was working and always share in my accomplishments by letting me know how special I am to them.

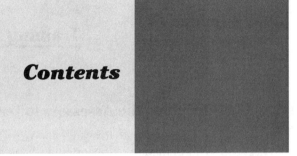

Contents

Part I

OASIS and OBQI in Home Health

Part II

Training Staff to Use OASIS

Part III

Data Interpretation and Measurement of Outcomes

Appendices

Part I

OASIS and OBQI in Home Health

History and Purpose of the Outcome and Assessment Information Set (OASIS) and Outcome-Based Quality Improvement (OBQI)

1

Introduction

◆ What is wrong with the way we're currently doing things?

◆ What is so important about Outcome-Based Quality Improvement?

◆ Why OASIS?

◆ Why now?

◆ What are Outcomes?

This first chapter addresses these questions so the reader can understand the underlying issues that are driving the home health industry to implement and put high value on Outcome-Based Quality Improvement (OBQI) and The Outcome and Assessment Information Set (OASIS). Although hardly an academic outline for a dialogue, these questions are being asked by direct providers and reimbursers of home care throughout the United States and therefore demand discussion to frame the content of the remainder of this book.

Front-line home care professionals, predominantly nurses, are responsible for collecting patient information through the use of the OASIS data set. The main components of outcomes and outcome-based performance improvement need to be discussed first so everyone can have a clearer understanding of *why* the data set (OASIS) and the emphasis on outcomes (OBQI) are making radical changes in the way home care agencies and staff operate. After the *why* is better understood, the *hows* of implementation are easier to put into action. This, then, forms the outline of the book.

So, to answer the questions. . . .

What Is Wrong with the Way We're Currently Doing Things?

It's not so much that we have done things incorrectly or wrong in the past, it is simply that the focus of care needs to shift. In the past, home health organizations' quality improvement programs focused on the *structure* and *processes* involved in delivering services, not so much on the outcomes. For example, quality assurance programs always focused heavily on the *structure* of the organization—how many nurses, home health aides, and other personnel were needed to provide certain services and how much they cost. As a cost-reimbursed system through the Medicare program, home health evaluated these staffing numbers to assure they were reimbursed the amount it *cost* to provide the services. Essentially, home care organizations were reimbursed, within specified limits, what it cost to provide the services, and productivity and the impact on the outcome of the patient's care were not closely examined.

Additionally, when examining the *process* aspect of quality assurance, auditing records to assure that the correct blanks were complete on the clinical record or that the teaching was done by the nurse on a visit became an important activity used to measure quality. The information gathered only measured that the care was provided and that all the boxes were checked as they were supposed to be. Just looking at these processes does not give an adequate picture of the effect of care on the patient and the costs incurred. Agency record reviews often found that even though the processes were completed in a timely manner and the clinical record looked wonderful, we weren't sure how the patient was faring throughout the time on home care services. At discharge we also didn't understand how much it had cost to provide the service(s) to this patient and to all our patients as a group. So many questions arose, one of the main ones being, "What difference does home care make in a patient's recovery, rehospitalization, and long-term health status?"

National expenditures for home care, estimated at $36 million in 1996, are projected to rise well into the next century due to many factors. In the 1980s and 1990s, care delivery shifted from the institution to the home, and along with that shift increasing dollars were spent on home care services. Projected growth in the numbers of elderly, as well as improvements in technology that allow for complex procedures, diagnostic measures, and treatments to be safely implemented in the home, are increasing rapidly while consumer demand for these services also rises. To control costs, decrease the potential for fraud and abuse, and better measure the true cost benefit of home care, research and professional opinions agree that the focus of care must shift to evaluating the outcomes of home care services.

What Is So Important About OBQI?

Historically, health care has focused on the processes and tasks involved in delivering care in all settings. With a cost-reimbursed system, Medicare, as a main payer of health care costs, paid providers what it cost to deliver the service and did not evaluate to what extent patients had benefitted from the care provided. As technology and costs increased, it became more important to evaluate health care services so that payers could better understand exactly what they were getting for the money spent. Additionally, increasingly knowledgeable health care consumers want to judge health care providers not only on cost, but also on the resultant outcome of their care, and then compare them with other providers to see if they are receiving the best possible care. These two factors in the late 1990s created the need to compare the quality as well as the cost of all health care.

Outcome-based quality improvement is based on the principle that patient outcomes are central to continuous quality improvement. Traditionally, quality improvement has been centered more on staff performance than on patient outcomes. In fact, one of the limitations of quality improvement in its traditional sense is that it tends to point fingers and place blame on individuals, thus causing decreased employee morale and ultimately, worse outcomes. Remember that most of what we know about quality improvement is based on the manufacturing model, which works well for widgets and washers but is often mired down in patient–nurse relationships, learning barriers, and other hindrances to positive patient outcomes.

The quality of care provided to patients *does* need to be monitored. By no means should substandard care be rendered. On the other hand, the focal point of OBQI is, "What happens to my patients as a result of the care *I* provide?" OBQI allows everyone to ask questions like, "If quality care is provided, do outcomes become more favorable?" and "What part does the patient play in the outcomes game?"

Why OASIS?

In order to demonstrate how the care you are providing actually *affects* the end result, or outcome (i.e., increased ability to perform an activity of daily living [ADL], or a decreased or stabilized medical condition as measured by OASIS), it is necessary to use a standardized set of data elements or questions that will give you valid information for measuring outcomes from various time points. This data set has been given the acronym OASIS, for the Outcomes Assessment and Information Set. Although there will be revisions of the original data set (currently in use is OASIS-B1 (6/98)), OASIS is used in the industry and will be used consistently in this book to discuss the data set.

The Health Care Financing Administration (HCFA), the Office of Research and Demonstrations (ORD), and the Robert Wood Johnson Foundation (RWJF) began studying the possibility of assessing the cost and outcomes of home care and standardizing patient assessments. These entities developed and tested measures of home health care patient outcomes from 1988 to 1994. Data was collected and analyzed on 3,427 patients from 49 different home health agencies. The end result included a system of outcome measures described in articles and volumes. The evolution of the OASIS continued during various studies from the late 1980s to the present, with the latest version, OASIS-B1 (Appendix A). Various aspects of home care patients, agencies, and actual and potential payment programs were included. In 1994, HCFA and the ORD, with support from the RWJF, selected 50 home health agencies nationally as "beta-sites" to pilot the OASIS. These agencies were to actually carry the entire process through from integration of OASIS into current assessment forms to collecting data, reporting data, analyzing data, developing plans of action, and ultimately, implementing changes in care behaviors based on these results. It is felt these activities would lead to improved patient outcomes. This study is called the Medicare Quality Assurance Study (MEQA).

The MEQA study is not scheduled to be completed until 1999. However, all signs indicate that the Medicare Conditions of Participation including the OASIS will be approved in the final version in 1998. (Conditions of Participation [COPs] are those standards or conditions to which an agency must comply to be eligible to receive reimbursement from the Federal Government [HCFA] for services provided to patients.) The implications of this action have yet to be determined. However, it can be assumed that HCFA feels the data set has proven successful in doing what it was designed to do. How well this premise works when all Medicare-certified agencies must incorporate the OASIS and collect data remains to be seen.

Why Now?

In the cost-conscious environment of managed care, payers and consumers want to know what they are getting for their money. Accreditation and certification programs are emphasizing outcomes, and home care agen-

cies and staff want to know how care affects their patients and how they compare with other providers in their area and across the country. As in all businesses, current pressures to become more cost-effective drive the need to constantly evaluate the services and personnel needed for successful outcomes, quality care, and financially stable organizations.

Unfortunately, the impact of mutual interaction, or the responsibility of working *with* the patient, has sometimes been overlooked. The focus of home health care has often been directed toward improving the patient's physical condition based entirely upon standards set by the care provider, with little or no input from the patient or caregiver(s). In addition, the complexity of assessments and investigation into how the patient's environment, financial status, functional capacity, and personal support systems affect the outcomes of care vary from nurse to nurse based upon experience, education, and expertise. Although this is true in all areas of nursing, it exists markedly in home health.

The proposed Medicare Conditions of Participation (COPs) issued in March 1997 address the mandating of a standardized data set for collection of data to be used to determine outcomes of care. The OASIS contains items that are designed to measure changes in adult clients' health status and to statistically risk-adjust these outcomes. OASIS data is to be collected at the initiation of care (on admission), at follow-up (recertification), and at discharge to determine the effectiveness of interventions and to document outcomes.

All facets of the health care delivery system are struggling with the same issues relative to measuring outcomes of care and budget constraints. These issues lead management to increase the emphasis on productivity and cost effectiveness. This momentum leads home care organizations to know the time to act is *now* to remain competitive in this new marketplace. Due to the complex nature of home care, these issues have become difficult to totally evaluate. Creating data that focus on outcomes of care, both patient-centered and cost- and quality-centered, will help home care agencies and professional practitioners understand how to best use resources to help their patients and their communities reach the best possible outcomes. This emphasis on outcomes will not subside, nor should it. It is up to everyone involved with home care to understand and implement OBQI. The rest of this chapter, as well as the entire book, will help accomplish this goal.

What Are Outcomes?

Donabedian (1985) defined outcomes as "those changes, either favorable or adverse, in the actual or potential health status of persons, groups, or communities, that can be attributed to prior or concurrent care" (p. 256). According to Shaughnessy and Crisler (1995), an outcome is a change in patient health status between two or more time points. This change can be positive, neutral, or negative and therefore can relate to improvement, decline or no change in the patient's condition. This change in health status can be the result of the actual care provided and/or the natural progression of the disease process over time, which care cannot necessarily alter.

Many times outcomes are confused with other activities with similar names. Nurses have studied care planning, goals, objectives, and expected outcomes for many years and often tend to lump them all together without really understanding their differences. The following health care activities are *not* outcomes:

♦ Assessments done at the beginning of care in any setting are part of care delivery are NOT outcomes.
♦ Care planning is a service provided for a patient and is NOT an outcome.
♦ Health care services are the processes of care and NOT outcomes.
♦ Expected outcomes are anticipated patient goals and NOT *actual* outcomes.
♦ Critical paths have been described as "processes of care we undertake on behalf of our patients . . . they are formula-like approaches for providing home care and are tailored to a particular type of patient." (Shaughnessy & Crisler, 1995, p. 2–5) They are NOT outcomes.
♦ A patient's actual health status at a single point in time is *not* an outcome because there is no comparison to the health status at *another point in time.*

For the purposes of OBQI, the definition of outcomes as discussed previously is:

An outcome is a change in patient health status between two or more time points.

This definition is fundamental to the entire OBQI process as well as important to remember when collecting and analyzing OASIS data. Other outcomes that are listed following this section are used in the entire health care delivery system to analyze care, plan programs, and allocate resources. When using outcomes in these approaches, the time points can be based on what exactly you are looking to measure, *but* for the purpose of OASIS, the time points cannot be changed and are:

♦ Admission
♦ Reassessment (60-day recertification)

♦ Discharge. Discharge occurs at the time the home health agency care ceases because:
  ♦ The agency considers the needs of the patient met.
  ♦ The patient refuses further care.
  ♦ The patient moves from the community.
  ♦ The patient transfers to the care of another provider.

It is important to understand that if a patient is admitted to an acute care facility for 48 hours or longer, agencies have two options, as follows:

Option 1

Discharge patient and complete the appropriate OASIS items, following the designated skip patterns.

Option 2

Do not discharge patient. Agencies who choose not to discharge patients after 48 hours in an inpatient facility are required to recertify patients when they resume home health care services after an inpatient discharge (rather than formally discharging the patient and readmitting him or her). The agency must remember that specific questions must be answered when the "transfer" option is chosen on the OASIS data set, and essentially, for data collection purposes, the patient is treated as a *new* patient.

As managers and administrators determine the policy regarding discharge, the following should be considered:

1. If the patient was ill enough to be admitted to the hospital for 48 hours or longer, his presenting problem, assessment data, and/or his outcomes will undoubtedly be affected. This new patient status (assessment) is most likely best represented in developing a new plan of care and identifying more relevant outcomes.
2. Even though readmitting the patient to the agency after such a short period of time involves more paperwork by the admitting professional, the resultant care plan, outcomes, and statistical counting of the patient as a duplicated admission may better reach the agency's overall goals and outcome monitoring goals.
3. If the patient's status has changed significantly during hospitalization and requires more extensive, expensive services than previously and the patient has *not* been discharged, the agency *must* readmit the patient, since he is a carried case, incur the expense and find a way to provide the needed service(s) even though the agency may not have those services available.

The key feature of measuring outcomes is collecting data on the patient's condition at regular intervals. These data, aggregated across patients with similar diagnoses or health problems, can then be compared within the agency and externally against other agency and national statistics. This comprehensive examination of outcomes over time allows for changes in care if the outcomes are found to be poor. Then performance improvement and quality improvement activities can take place. This examination also provides the ability to emphasize care that has been exceptional or outstanding by reinforcing that care based on the documented outcomes. By looking at exceptional outcomes and outcomes that need further examination, the entire process can be easily seen as potentially positive for everyone involved.

The changes measured are inherent to the *patient;* that is, the change *must* be identified as occurring in the patient, not in the nurse's behavior. However, the patient's change may have occurred as a *result* of a change in practice by the nurse. For example, when caring for a patient with a wound, with no improvement by the estimated time point, the nurse, after consulting with the physician and an enterostomal therapist (ET), changes the wound care procedure (a change in the practice of the nurse resulting in a change in the care plan). This change then results in a positive healing process in a shorter period of time than anticipated, with the patient having a positive outcome of care.

For a patient with a behavioral health problem, the nurse's approach of open listening may not be producing the desired outcome, so a firmer style, including a specific contract outlining the patient's responsibilities is devised (a change in the practice of the nurse resulting in a change in the care plan). This change then causes the patient to realize his or her role in recovery and limited time for receiving home care services. Thus the patient becomes compliant with the medication regime, and the desired outcomes are achieved. Benson (1992) has reported that "from a clinical standpoint, outcomes are simply what happened to patients as a result of their interaction with the health care system." In other words, has there been a change in the patient's health status? Health status in this context encompasses physiological, functional, cognitive, emotional, and behavioral health.

Shaughnessy and Crisler (1995) have defined outcomes in three distinctive ways:

1. *End-result outcomes or pure outcomes.* This is the *actual change* in the patient's health status between two or more points in time as discussed previously.

2. *Intermediate-result outcomes or instrumental outcomes.* These outcomes involve a change in the patient's behavior, emotions, or knowledge level that influences the patient's end-result or pure outcomes. Changes in treatment, regimen compliance, knowledge of self-care, satisfaction with care, and motivation to improve are all examples of this form of outcome.

3. *Utilization outcomes or proxy outcomes.* These outcomes concentrate on a considerable change in a patient's health status over time. Discharges from home care due to admission to an acute or subacute care facility suggest that the patient's health status has changed substantially. The term "proxy" parallels this category of outcome because the mere change to another level of health care provision can infer a change in actual health status.

Other Types and Definitions of Outcomes

In this discussion of outcomes as they relate to OBQI and OASIS, it is important to remember that outcomes can be used in other situations. To understand the many ways outcomes can be used requires "big picture" thinking. Outcomes are often examined when doing operational studies of an organization, when evaluating the use of resources, by payers when looking at large groups of patients, and/or by program planners when determining the outcomes of a new or existing program to see if the program has accomplished its mission. When looking at the larger picture of evaluating outcomes many different types of outcomes can be examined and used. Some definitions of the various types of outcomes to consider are:

Global Outcomes

Global outcomes pertain to all patients. For example, an agency may want to analyze the readmissions to the hospital of all patients admitted to the agency during a six-month period, such as patients with congestive heart failure (CHF).

Focused Outcomes

Focused outcomes pertain to a subgroup of all patients. To compare to the example discussed in global outcomes, analyzing the change in *dyspnea* in all CHF patients over a *six-month period* would be an example of a focused outcome.

Clinical Outcomes

Clinical outcomes are designed to evaluate the *process or outcomes* of care associated with the delivery of clinical services. Clinical measures may include medication use, infection control, or items from the patient assessment. Clinical measures allow for comparisons within and across health care organizations. These measures focus on the *appropriateness* of clinical decision making and the processes for implementing those decisions.

Health Status Outcomes

Health status, in its broadest aspects, includes all of the manifestations of health, including functional status. Health measures address the functional well-being of specific populations, both in general and in relation to specific conditions, demonstrating change over time. The functional status of patients is often reflected in rehabilitation. For example, a change from dependence to independence in ADL such as walking or bathing could be called a functional status measure under the health status rubric.

Satisfaction Outcomes

Satisfaction is concerned with the *patient's perception of care* services. An important development in health care has been recognition of the patient's point of view as a legitimate measure of quality. Satisfaction measures focus on the delivery of care from the patient's/ family's/ caregiver's perspective. Some believe that satisfaction is not a valid outcome measure because it is subjective; others believe it is the only valid measure because if the patient is happy, nothing else really matters.

Utilization Outcomes

Utilization outcomes are the easiest to gather. Utilization data has to do with demographics, lengths of stay, rehospitalization rates, and/or the number of cases admitted in a specified time period. While they do not measure the effects of care on patients per se, they are a source of good information about *service trends* within an organization.

Financial Outcomes

Financial outcomes reflect the *costs of providing home care services.* They include the cost per case for a particular diagnostic category, the cost per visit or per episode, and/or the total costs of providing home health care services in any given time period.

This is by no means an exhaustive list of all possible types of outcomes, but it does encompass the major types that need to be examined by any organization to understand and analyze the relationships between many variables.

Implementing OBQI

The general steps in implementing OBQI are:

1. *Gaining an initial understanding by everyone involved of what outcomes are and how to measure them.* It is critical that all staff, from those professionals who do home visits to managers and administrators understand the basics presented in this book before going on to implement the other steps of the process.
2. *Formulating goal statements that are measurable and realistic for a select group of patients.* The selection of a group of patients who have similar characteristics is critical in making the OBQI system effective. Discussions similar to the selection of patient groups for the development of critical paths or Joint Commission on Accreditation of Healthcare Organizations (JCAHO) performance improvement activities can be helpful in choosing these patients.
3. *Specific data items then need selection with time frames (points) for the achievement of goals.* For the collection of OASIS and OBQI data mandated by Medicare in the COPs, the time points are specifically given and should be strictly adhered to. Agencies and staff must be sure they are using the definitions of recertification and readmission used throughout the country if the data produced in their agencies is to be compared with these external sources for benchmarking and evaluation purposes.
4. *Formulating the specific outcome reports for consistent reporting of data, coupled with determining appropriate data collection and forms.* In other words, determine exactly what it is you want to measure—what health attributes you want to look at, with an eye on collecting consistent information over a set period of time—and then develop the report forms that are most meaningful to everyone involved with analyzing and reporting the outcome information.
5. *Piloting and revising the forms selected and created to assure consistency and accuracy.* Since

it is imperative that the OASIS items be *integrated* into the agency's existing forms, these documents must be constantly evaluated to assure that the data is being collected accurately and consistently by all staff. Chapters 4 and 5 explain each of the OASIS questions and their meanings and can be very helpful in teaching staff this important aspect of data collection. Additionally, skip patterns inherent in many of the questions must be included in *exactly the same way* as in the OASIS data set.

An Overview of OASIS and Its Relationship to OBQI

The OASIS is a key component of Medicare's partnership with the home care industry to foster and monitor improved home health care outcomes (Crisler, Campbell, & Shaughnessy, 1997, p. iii). A large sample of home care agencies, either as part of the demonstration project or independently since 1995, has worked on developing and testing the OASIS data set in various types of agencies. The proposed rule 42CFR Part 484 of the Conditions of Participation (COPs) would require that the agencies use a standard core assessment data set (OASIS) when evaluating adult, nonmaternity patients. The purpose of this proposed regulation is to make the COPs more patient-centered and outcome-oriented and to provide home health agencies with more flexibility to operate their programs. All agencies will be required to develop, implement, and manage an outcome-based quality improvement program based on data collected by using the OASIS. It has become obvious that HCFA is very serious about including the OASIS in home care patient assessments for a long period of time. Review of the proposed COPs published in the Federal Register, Volume 62, Number 46, stated the following:

- ♦ "We intend that the OASIS become one of the most important aspects of the HHA's quality assessment and performance improvement efforts."
- ♦ "We intend to require that HHA's use the OASIS exactly as specified."
- ♦ "We plan to implement full use of the OASIS in stages."
- ♦ "We intend to publish another proposed rule that would require HHA's to report OASIS data electronically into a national database."
- ♦ "We encourage computerization as soon as it is possible to do so."

And further:

- ♦ "We do not envision how a home health organization can successfully move to a continuous quality improvement approach without developing and using a computer-based system to manage and use organizational and patient-based data."

When the final Medicare regulations relative to OBQI and OASIS are published, home health agency Medicare surveys will eventually focus not only on the methods the agency used to collect and interpret patient data but also on how the agency uses the data to provide care that will result in optimal outcomes. If an agency has several outcomes, that are consistently lower than other agencies of the same size and auspice, more detailed investigation by the surveyors may be required to determine why this has occurred. Likewise, if the agency has more than one outcome that should be addressed, the one most significant for the patient should be addressed first. Thus, not only the ability to determine outcomes but the ability to prioritize them on the basis of the patient's best interest will be required. The ultimate use of outcomes will be to develop a prospective payment system for home health services. From this overview, it is clear that it is essential for everyone in a home health agency, from professional field staff to manager to administration to learn the basics of OASIS and OBQI before higher level analysis and planning can take place.

An Overview of OASIS

The following review of the OASIS process can be helpful in understanding its history and why it has been well thought out, developed by professionals in the field, and tested for reliability and validity so that it should be implemented *exactly* as developed.

- ♦ The OASIS data set was developed and continues to be refined through the Center for Health Policy Research in Denver, Colorado.
- ♦ Involved in the process were nurses, statisticians, and economists, with input from physical, occupational, and speech therapists, a social worker, and one physician. This interdisciplinary approach has created an instrument capable of globally assessing the patient, indicating areas where referrals may be required, such as to social services or physical or occupational therapy.

- Data collected using the OASIS have proven to be a valid and reliable way to measure the quality of home care services. The specificity of the data elements assists in assessment and care planning, as staff can easily and quickly review patients' levels of ADL and instrumental ADLs (IADLs). This information will assist in determining if a patient should be recertified after the initial 60-day period of care.
- The main components of OASIS focus on the following:
  1. Medical or nursing diagnoses
  2. Requirements for particular types of care
  3. Functional limitations
  4. Patient's environment
- OASIS items, intended for assessment and care planning, describe a patient's health and functional status.
- The goal of OASIS was *not* to produce a comprehensive assessment instrument, but to provide a set of data items necessary for measuring patient outcomes and those items essential for assessment.
- The OASIS data set is intended to be integrated into the agencies' existing assessment form, not tagged on as an appendix or used as a separate, distinct form. Objective assessment information, such as vital signs, needs integration into the data set.
- The OASIS data set must be viewed as a component of the OBQI program. Collecting data over a period of time and comparing results with other agencies of similar size and auspice will allow agencies to measure the quality of care they provide. Areas in need of remediation as well as areas of practice that are exemplary can be investigated, and standards of practice developed.
- Outcome reports that come from the data are instrumental in indicating the areas for improvement and for continued monitoring of a home health agency's quality of care.
- Field nurses initially find that the OASIS data set requires more time, but once oriented and efficient in its use, they discover assessment time may not change significantly.
- OASIS needs to be a fully integrated part of the agency's operation, from both the administration and clinical perspectives. All aspects of the agency, especially administration and management, must support OASIS from the beginning.

As home care moves forward into managed care and prospective pay, the monitoring of outcomes will become increasingly important in justifying the level of care provided and in demonstrating consistent positive outcomes. Home health nurses and other professionals, by using the OASIS data elements integrated into the patient assessment, will be able to fully assess all areas that impact the patient's overall health and learn what interventions effect more positive outcomes.

Interplay Among OBQI, OASIS, the Medicare Conditions of Participation, Performance Improvement, Accreditation, and Consumers

2

Introduction

This chapter is meant to provide a "big picture" that can help staff, management, and administration better understand the *reasons* driving the current shift in focus toward a more outcome-based quality approach. Unless everyone in an organization understands the reasons behind the movement toward outcome-focused quality improvement, other factors that involve collecting information, changing agency forms and procedures, setting up systems, and analyzing results will be much more difficult. Just as patients need to know *why* before changing their behavior and welcoming change, all home care personnel must know *why* these changes are taking place and affecting the way the agency does business and provides care.

OBQI Is Much More Than Medicare

Using outcomes to measure the effectiveness of care in a clinical setting is not unique to Medicare and the Conditions of Participation (COPs). Through outcome studies, payers can obtain information on the quality of care provided in various settings, especially home care. Many Medicaid programs have interest in OBQI as well as managed care companies and other payers. Performance Improvement (PI) and Quality Improvement (QI) programs have long been focused on the process of care, not the outcome. With the increasingly frequent question, "What difference does the care we render make?" all health care providers have been evaluating outcomes, rather than just structure and process.

Accrediting bodies, such as the Joint Commission on Healthcare Organizations (JCAHO), continue to be interested in PI initiatives to evaluate agencies as well as to have the agencies internally analyze their own performance. A new focus of JCAHO accreditation has been the agency's ability to evaluate the outcomes of care through the ORYX program, which will be discussed later in this chapter. Consumers who are increasingly encouraged to become empowered and make choices about their health care are also very interested in outcome-focused care. The American Association of Retired Persons (AARP), individual consumers, and other large consumer groups advocate that more information on the quality of health care be provided by organizations and segments of the health care industry to consumers.

With all this emphasis on outcomes and their relationship to cost and quality, home care professionals and agencies must change their operational focus in order to stay competitive. This chapter looks at the many ways OBQI and OASIS affect overall agency operations by pointing out how these two new activities interplay with:

1. The development of a core data set that can be used for many functions
2. Major revisions to the Medicare Conditions of Participation to be implemented in 1999
3. Current and future performance improvement and quality improvement activities
4. The JCAHO focus on outcomes of care through the ORYX process.
5. The use of benchmarks and benchmarking by consumer and payer groups to measure the quality of home health care, which affects consumer choices about choosing service providers.

Multiple Uses of OASIS Data Items—Building a Core Data Set

Although the home health industry has grown significantly in the 1980s and 1990s, little statistical information has been available to make sound analysis of the value and quality of the services provided. This has not only been true in the area of costs and allocation of resources, but also in the measurement of change in patients' treatments and health status. The information made available through the national collection of OASIS data and the OBQI and its subsequent analysis will be valuable for multiple uses. Medicare regulatory and reimbursement trends, prospective payment rates, managed care, and the development of a more integrated health service delivery system demand that home care provide the outcome and financial information necessary to justify its value in and to the system.

Developing a core data set of information that can be used for individual agency management and strategic planning as well as for comparing the agency with external benchmarks is critically important. The center of the core data set (Figure 2–1) is composed of:

♦ OASIS assessment items
♦ Additional assessment items (based on what the agency wants/needs to collect?)

Figure 2–1 *Core Data Set. Multiple agency uses of OASIS data when combined with other information.*

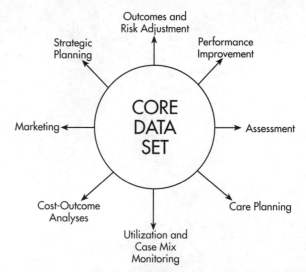

From: Shaughnessy, P. W., Crisler, K. S. and Schlenker, R. E. (1998). Outcome-based quality improvement in the information age. *Home Health Care Management and Practices* 10(2), 17.

♦ Visit data
♦ Cost-per-visit information

The information in the core data set can then be used for a variety of purposes, such as:

Determining Outcomes and Risk Adjustment

From this data emerge the agency's specific outcomes based on the health status attributes chosen for evaluation. For example, if the agency determines that dyspnea is an important health status attribute and looks at the focused outcome from the subgroup of patients with the primary diagnosis of congestive heart failure, then the data produced from the core data set can be analyzed to produce these outcomes. Additionally, this data can be analyzed and risk adjusted so that one agency's outcomes can be compared with those of a similar agency for external benchmarking purposes. For example, the outcomes produced previously for Agency A in a rural part of Texas can be risk adjusted and compared with those of Agency B, a home health agency in an urban area of New York.

Performance Improvement

The data from the core data set and subsequent OBQI activities can then be used in the agency's performance improvement activities. Using the same data set means that the agency is truly comparing "apples to apples" within the agency and makes the OBQI activities and the PI activities more interconnected and reliable.

Assessment

The home health agency can add whatever assessment items it feels are necessary to give appropriate information for patient care. Adding vital signs, for example, is an important aspect of basic assessment that is not found in the OASIS data set. Additionally, for specific patients, or subgroups of patients with certain diagnoses, additional assessment data can be added to the OASIS data set. For example, including baseline electrocardiogram (ECG) monitoring on the assessment, recertification and discharge assessment may be added to all assessment forms for a patient receiving care through a cardiac specialty home care program. Since this information is not a part of the OASIS data, it would be added to the core data set for this subgroup of patients and analyzed as part of the *global outcomes* of that patient subgroup.

Care Planning

The assessment information, both results of the OASIS and any additional assessment data, can then be used for comprehensive care planning by the home care team in conjunction with the patient. As home care nurses know from experience and research, if significant data are missed during initial assessment, not only the process of care is affected, but the outcomes as well. If the assessors are gathering the most reliable and valid information possible when OASIS data are collected, the potential for positive outcomes is more assured.

Monitoring Utilization and Case Mix

Information from the core data set can provide case mix data (the mix of cases, defined by age, sex, diagnoses, treatments, severity of illness, as well as other variables an agency may want to analyze). In this age of managed care contracts, reimbursement through prospective payment, and capitation contracting, monitoring this data on a daily basis is critical to the financial stability and viability of home care agencies. Additionally, completely understanding an agency's utilization and cost-per-visit information can be combined with outcome data to create a valuable tool for internal management decisions.

Analyzing Costs and Outcomes

When an agency is able to link the costs of providing visits to outcomes, analysis can occur that examines the ratio of outcomes to cost for various patient groups or subgroups as well as examining outcomes for patients with various payers. Management can then use this information to:

1. Address various management issues such as staffing, staffing ratios, and productivity
2. Develop successful contract negotiation strategies (to negotiate with some groups for more visits that have been found to directly result in better outcomes)
3. Structure an effective marketing plan that shows potential purchasers of service the cost-beneficial and cost-effective results of care experienced by patients already seen by the agency
4. Develop a reference group using the visit and cost-per-visit data submitted to a central data source, such as a state association or a national firm that specializes in collecting and analyzing that information. This reference group information can then be used and compared internally to develop and sell special programs or externally to compare like services with local, regional, state, and national providers when

considering organizational issues such as joint ventures and seamless delivery systems.

Marketing and Strategic Planning

When analyzing the larger picture of overall agency administration and management, two essential components of remaining successful in the home care marketplace emerge: marketing efforts and strategic planning. A core data set can provide the necessary information to support these two critical functions. As staff and managers get caught up in day-to-day operations, it becomes increasingly important to understand that every piece of data collected for the core data set, including OASIS data, can be used to assure the agency's long-term success and survival.

Using the Core Data Set for Other Matters

The uses of this data set are potentially endless. Overall agency outcome performance is becoming increasingly important for Medicare certification and accreditation. Payment determination and requirements placed on an agency by managed care contracts, Medicaid service contracts, and other quality management activities can be addressed by returning to the core data set to gather valid and reliable information. Shaughnessy, Crisler, and Schlenker (1998) state, "Systematic, uniformly defined, and rigorous data from home health agencies are essential to achieving objectivity and fairness in payment and quality assurance policies." It is clear that assuring the best data is collected, processed, and reported in an understandable and meaningful way is the only way home health agencies can ensure their long-term viability.

OBQI and OASIS Relative to the Conditions of Participation

To fully understand the impact that changes in the Conditions of Participation (COPs) have on the home health industry, it is first necessary to understand their history and purpose. Home health care benefits for elderly and disabled citizens are covered under the Hospital Insurance (Part A) and Supplemental Medical Insurance (Part B) benefits of the Medicare program. These benefits are described in the Social Security Act. In order to be reimbursable, the health care services must be provided by, or under an arrangement with, a home health agency that participates in the Medicare program. Section 1861(o) of the Act specifies certain requirements that a home health agency must meet in order to participate in

and receive reimbursement from the Medicare program. The intent of the conditions of participation is to protect elderly and disabled participants from receiving substandard or unsafe care by unsupervised or unscrupulous agencies. The conditions provide a framework and an outline of the requirements necessary to be a Medicare-certified home health agency.

The Conditions of Participation for home health agencies were established in 1973 and have been revised on several occasions; however, many of the current conditions have remained unchanged. Since home health care has grown so rapidly over recent years, it was deemed necessary to revise the conditions of participation to assure quality care for federal beneficiaries. The first total rewrite of the regulations was proposed in 1997, and a probable adoption of the revised COPs is to occur during 1999 with collection of the OASIS in 1998. Collaboration among representatives of the HCFA, consumer groups, the home health care industry, professional associations, regional home health intermediaries, and states, including state Medicaid agencies, are affecting the changes in the COPs. A primary recommendation was the inclusion of the core standard assessment data set and patient-centered, outcome-oriented performance standards that would encourage quality care. In addition, continuous quality improvement in home health care was to be encouraged. The fundamental principles followed in revising the conditions of participation included the following:

- Facilitate flexibility in how an agency meets the performance expectations and eliminate outdated process requirements that few believe are predictive of good outcomes for patients or necessary for preventing harmful outcomes
- Improve care and service outcomes
- Require that patient rights are assured
- Improve patient satisfaction
- Develop ongoing performance improvement expectations
- Focus on the continuous, integrated care process that a patient experiences across all aspects of home health services, centered around patient assessment, care planning, service delivery, and quality assessment and performance improvement
- Adopt a patient-centered, interdisciplinary, and multidimensional approach that recognizes the contributions of various skilled professionals and how they interact with each other to meet the patient's needs
- Stress quality improvements, incorporating to the greatest possible extent an outcome-oriented,

data-driven quality assessment and performance improvement program. Principal expectations for performance are incorporated into the powerful requirement that each home health agency participate in its own quality assessment and performance improvement program

♦ Collect data and add a core standard assessment data set in order to provide consumers with valuable information during their provider selection process (i.e., OASIS)

♦ Identify, develop, and validate outcomes (i.e., OBQI)

♦ Provide data to providers, consumers, and regulators that can be used to improve quality

The patient care section of the new COPs are to outline the following areas:

1. Patient rights
2. Comprehensive patient assessment
3. Patient care planning
4. Coordination of patient care services
5. Quality assessment and performance improvement of patient care
6. The standards on skilled professional services and home health aide services

The revisions to the entire COPs are to be extensive, and they do not all fall within the scope of this book. The following discussion focuses on how the COPs affect patient care assessment, planning, and care coordination that interact with OASIS and OBQI.

Review of Specific COPs Relative to OBQI and OASIS

The following citations are based on the Proposed Rules, Part 484 Conditions of Participation: Home Health Agencies, found in the *Federal Register*, Vol. 62, No. 46, Monday, March 10, 1997, pp. 11029–11044.

484.55 Comprehensive Assessment of Patients

The COPs describe a comprehensive assessment as one that focuses on the patient, is systematic in approach (i.e., a head-to-toe physical assessment), and includes an assessment by all disciplines involved in care. All assessments must focus on positive patient outcomes and quality of care. The assessment must be planned to meet the medical, nursing, rehabilitation, social, and discharge planning needs of the patient. The COPs also specify the inclusion of a patient medication assessment that incorporates drug–drug interactions, duplicative drug therapy,

and noncompliance with the specific drug regime. The proposed COPs indicate that the home care staff can delete the identification of adverse actions and contraindicated medications since this is considered a pharmacy responsibility.

The basis for satisfying the COPs relative to the comprehensive assessment of the patient is the inclusion of the OASIS into the agency's assessment forms. Interwoven throughout the proposed conditions is the term "outcomes"; patients must be informed about "expected outcomes" of treatment and "barriers" to treatment. By encouraging the patient to be involved in his/her own care, open communication between all team members is expected if the positive outcomes are to be reached as efficiently as possible. Each home health agency is given the flexibility to develop its own patient assessment form. The assessment can be as complex or as uncomplicated as an agency desires, but the assessment must include the OASIS in its entirety.

The proposed conditions mandate that a registered nurse must perform an initial assessment visit, based on the physician's orders, to determine the immediate care and support needs of the patient and the patient's homebound status at one of the following times:

1. Within 48 hours of referral
2. Within 48 hours after the patient's return home
3. Within 48 hours of the physician-ordered start-of-care date, if that is later

REMEMBER!

If rehabilitation therapy is the only service ordered, the appropriate therapist may do the assessment. (Individual agency policy may dictate who may perform initial assessments.)

If the timing of the visit is a problem, the COPs state that the initial visit does *not* have to include the patient's comprehensive assessment. The COPs allow that the assessment should be completed in a "timely manner based on the patient's immediate needs," but should be completed *no later than* five working days following the start of care (the date of the first home visit by a skilled professional). The comprehensive assessment must be revised as often as the patient requires, but *no less frequently* than every 62 days from the start-of-care date. Assessment is an important part of the newly proposed COPs, and using the OASIS data set is specified at time of discharge from the program and at other key times during the home care treatment course, such as an admission to the hospital.

In addition, the home health agency must notify the physician *promptly* if measurable outcomes are not being achieved. This notification of the physician should be nothing new for home health agencies. Prudent nursing care dictates notification of the physician when the patient is not progressing toward goals. Failure to notify the physician could be interpreted as a fraudulent attempt to continue a procedure that obviously isn't working in order to maintain the current level of visits, number of patients, or amount of revenue.

Care Planning

The COPs define care planning as a multidisciplinary team process in which members of the team share information. The patient's individualized care plan is to be completed within 5 to 10 days from the performance of the comprehensive assessment. Important aspects of the care planning standards include the need to compare progress to desired care outcomes and to ensure that as changes occur, revisions in the care plan are made and implemented in care delivery.

The COPs do not specify what a patient plan of care is, but they *do* continue to list information gathered on the HCFA-485 (mental status, functional limitations, etc.) as well as patient outcomes, services, care, and changes and revisions in care. As with the previous regulation, the signature of a doctor of medicine, osteopathy, or podiatry is needed on all patient orders, and periodic review of the plan of care by the physician ordering care is required.

Further discussion and examples of care planning can be found in Chapter 6, Using OASIS Data with the HCFA-485 and Patient Care Plan.

Review and Revision of the Plan of Care

The requirement that the patient's information be kept current and that the revised care plans show progress toward outcomes remains the same in the suggested revised COPs. Revisions need to be made every 62 days, beginning with the start-of-care date. Should the patient's medical condition or functional capacity change, the home health agency is responsible for promptly alerting the physician. This revised standard includes the 1994 written verbal order change stating that the order must be written, dated, and signed with a date of receipt by the registered nurse or qualified therapist responsible for furnishing or supervising the specified ordered services.

Proposed rule 42CFR Part 484 would require that the agencies use a standard core assessment data set (OASIS) when evaluating adult, nonmaternity patients. The purpose of this proposed regulation is to make the conditions of participation more patient-centered and outcome-oriented and to provide the home health agencies with more flexibility to operate their programs. All agencies will be required to develop, implement, and manage an outcome-based quality improvement program based on data collected by using the OASIS.

484.60 Care Planning and Coordination of Services

This aspect of the COPs relates to coordination of care, especially as it affects patient care planning. Inherent in coordination of care is the maintenance of a communication system among caregivers that leads to integration of services. At a minimum, the COPs require that communication and coordination be demonstrated by meeting and identifying the patient's needs, barriers to care, physician contact, and caregiver liaison. The COPs charge all disciplines that are providing care with the responsibility of contacting the physician when necessary. It is important, from HCFA's perspective, that the coordination of care demonstrates services that are timely, nonduplicative, and based on the current needs of the patient.

484.65 Quality Assurance and Performance Improvement

The COPs focus on quality assessment (QA) and performance improvement (PI) of the home health organization in a much different way than ever before. The standards as proposed, actually give organizations permission to delete several currently required components of home care. These are:

> Annual agency evaluations
> Quarterly utilization review
> Professional advisory group oversight

However, agencies should not immediately eliminate these processes, since many of these perform an important function in QA and PI activities. Additionally, when a home health organization is accredited by the Joint Commission on Accreditation of Healthcare Organizations (JCAHO), many of the PI activities are in place and provide a rich database for current and future programs and analysis. Specifics are spelled out by the proposed standards for QA and PI in the proposed COPs. These standards identify clearly what organizations must do to remain in compliance with this section. A further discussion of PI follows so that the concept can be thoroughly understood in the broader context as well as specifically applied to OBQI, OASIS, and the COPs intent.

OBQI Relative to Quality Improvement and Performance Improvement

Since the basis of OBQI involves examining the effects of patient care, outcomes are central to any continuous QI and PI program. Quality assurance has its roots in the context of manufacturing, where it may be based on decreasing the number of imperfect products produced in an assembly line. Historically, health care has used a similar method in attempting to improve the care provided by staff and, ultimately, the patient outcomes. But while this method works well in manufacturing, it has little benefit in health care and often causes the opposite effect from that desired.

Quality assurance generally employs an inspection style of investigation that often leans toward finger pointing and assigning blame. The focus tends to be on a randomly, chosen unscientific sample set rather than on the whole. Often only one or two persons are involved in this process and there may be no defined approach. Attempts to remedy identified problems often appear to be knee-jerk, reflexive behaviors and frequently cause staff to feel defensive and oppressed.

Quality improvement moves away from the negativism of finger pointing and blame assessing. The focus tends to be on improving the norm rather than the sample selected. All staff are involved; a scientific approach and statistical methods are used. Problems identified are systematically thought through and proactively approached. Staff members tend to feel positive about this process and offer less resistance since blame is not assigned to any one person or section of the organization.

The future of health care is in the transition to performance improvement. Performance improvement tends to follow these principles:

1. *Client-focused quality and value.* Quality and value are key strategic components that demand constant sensitivity to emerging client desires and health care marketplace requirements. Client-focused quality and value also demand ongoing awareness of new technology and new modalities for the delivery of home care services. Complacency in home care nursing is no more.
2. *Leadership.* Organizational leaders work together to set the direction and provide a clear mission, expectations, and values. Leaders take part in creating strategies, systems, and methods for achieving excellence in client care services. Leaders serve as role models in participating and improving the home care organization and its services.
3. *Management by fact.* Facts and data needed for organizational improvement can be of many types, including client, staff, administrative and business, and payer and customer satisfaction. The data collected from measurement activities are used to make operational and clinical decisions.
4. *Staff participation and development.* Improvement activities are conducted by all staff and may include participating on a performance improvement team or contributing to the development of new home care services.

Continuous quality improvement is a well-executed, continuous improvement process that has clear goals about what to improve, is fact-based and incorporates measures and/or indicators; includes cycles of planning, execution, and evaluation. CQI is nonjudgmental, focusing on key processes. CQI should be part of the daily work life of the entire staff and not just something to do to meet external requirements, such as accreditation or licensure. (Humphrey & Milone-Nuzzo, 1998)

Outcome-Based Quality Improvement and Performance Improvement

Outcome-based quality improvement uses a continuous quality improvement approach that focuses on patient outcomes. Under OBQI, reports based on systematic, uniform outcome measures are periodically provided to agencies. The outcome measures, then, are derived from the OASIS data items (Shaughnessy, Crisler, & Schlenker, 1998). Patient outcomes need to be the focus of quality evaluation, and there must be a systematic approach to the whole quality process if it is going to be valid and reliable. An agency outcome is the examination of patient outcomes averaged or benchmarked across some or all of an agency's patients.

OBQI involves a two-stage process for continuous quality improvement:

1. The *first-stage screen* involves an outcome analysis by patient group, risk factor, or case mix adjustment, if needed. Then outcome reports that trigger the examination of specific outcomes are generated.

2. The *second-stage screen* involves an analysis of care provided for the specific groups and the outcomes generated. This must include an assessment of the processes of care by the specific discipline involved. A final phase of the second-stage screen involves the identification of actions to change or care behaviors to reinforce before beginning the first-stage screen again (Shaughnessy & Crisler, 1995).

The concept of risk adjustment will be discussed in depth in the analysis section of this book; however, a brief discussion of the concept is needed to clarify the entire OBQI process. Shaughnessy and Crisler (1995) define a risk factor for a particular outcome as "a patient condition or circumstance that positively or negatively influences the likelihood of a patient attaining the outcome" (p. 9-2). Risk or case mix adjustment is necessary when two or more patient samples whose outcomes are being compared differ significantly. These differences concern factors or patient characteristics that can affect the patient's ultimate outcome. "The process of risk adjusting an outcome measure refers to any of several methods that can be used to eliminate or minimize the effects of risk-factor differences when comparing outcome findings between two samples of patients" (p. 9-4).

In the work done thus far on OBQI and OASIS through the MEQA project, the researchers admit that risk adjustment has its limitations since all conceivable factors that influence the patient's outcome are difficult to consider. Case mix is the analysis of the various types of patients (or cases) an agency has in its caseload. This analysis can look at patients from various perspectives, including their economic status, diagnosis and severity, type of reimbursement, level of social support, functional limitations, and so on. Case mix reports provide a summary of these significant variables or differences in an agencies "mix" of patients so that outcomes can be more clearly evaluated in light of another agency's data and/or as compared with national, regional, and state outcome statistics.

For example, if a majority of a home health agency's patients with a primary diagnosis of congestive heart failure (CHF) were found to be of extremely low economic status and their outcomes poor when compared to agencies throughout the region, a significant factor in these patients' not reaching their expected outcomes could be their inability to purchase the required medications. The factor of lower socioeconomic status could then be risk-adjusted so the agency's data would be more comparable to those agencies whose CHF patients were of a higher socioeconomic level.

JCAHO Accreditation and OBQI

What Is ORYX?

Home health organizations that are currently accredited by the Joint Commission on Healthcare Organizations (JCAHO) have long included performance improvement activities as a significant part of their ongoing daily operations. Since the majority of home health organizations are JCAHO accredited, this section will discuss the new initiatives and how they relate to OBQI and OASIS.

In 1997, the JCAHO Board of Commissioners approved a plan for integrating outcomes and other *performance measures* into the home care accreditation process. This new initiative is called ORYX, which is not a new acronym, but the name of a gazelle-like animal. For the first time, each JCAHO-accredited home care organization is now required to collect performance data related to the outcomes of its patient care and submit this data back to the Joint Commission on a continuing basis as part of the accreditation cycle. Through this ongoing data collection, it is expected that home care organizations will examine their care processes and take action to improve the results of care. Participation in the ORYX will be mandatory for all JCAHO-accredited home care organizations.

Table 2–1 provides the time frames required for participation in the ORYX initiative.

Performance Measurement Systems

The home care organization must select a performance measurement system from a vendor to which the home care organization agrees to submit performance data and from which it will receive comparative data. A listing of performance measurement systems that have contracted with the Joint Commission and those that are candidates for contracts can be obtained by contacting the commission's ORYX information line at (630) 792-5085. Many state home care associations have also become participants in ORYX and OBQI/OASIS data collection and feedback as well as benchmarking systems. A home care organization doesn't have to contract with only one measurement system. It may contract with multiple systems to meet the minimum number of clinical or perception-of-care measures that, combined, address the minimum required percentage of the organization's patient population.

Most of the performance measurement systems have four categories:

1. Clinical performance
2. Satisfaction

TABLE 2-1 *ORYX Participation Time Frames*

Time Frame	Activity Required
By 12/31/98	Select a performance measurement system
By 12/31/98	Select 2 clinical or perception-of-care performance measures that relate to at least 20% of the home care population served or 5 measures
By 12/31/98	Inform the Joint Commission of the performance measurement system(s) and performance measures selected
By 3rd quarter 1999	Collect data and submit to performance measurement system(s) selected
By 3/31/00	System begins submission of quarterly data to the Joint Commission
Ongoing on a quarterly basis	Joint Commission reviews data submitted and takes actions as indicated
Every three years	Joint Commission provides data to home care surveyor(s) to conduct survey and document observations

Friedman, M. M. (1998). Accreditation and the nurse column: ORYX: The next evolution in accreditation. *Home Healthcare Nurse, 16*(4), p. 238.

3. Health status
4. Administrative/financial

In selecting a performance measurement system, it is recommended that the system have a minimum number of 10 other home care organizations submitting data for comparison purposes. Otherwise, the data may be diluted, and valid comparative data may not be obtained. The selected measures must include five clinical or perception-of-care measures, or enough measures to address at least 20% of the home care organization's patient population admitted in the last 12 months, whichever is less (although the minimum number of clinical care measures required is two). The percentage of the population refers to the whole organization, not each individual home care service provided. The minimum number of performance measures in which the home health organization will submit data will increase over the next years, and the proportion of the patient population addressed by the measures will increase up to the year 2001.

What Are Performance Measures?

Performance measures are divided into two kinds: clinical measures and perception-of-care measures.

Clinical Measures

The Joint Commission defines a clinical measure as a quantitative tool designed to evaluate a process or outcome of care associated with the delivery of clinical services. The clinical measures may:

1. Focus on the appropriateness of clinical decision-making and implementation of the decisions (e.g., patient assessment) and be condition- or procedure-specific
2. Address an important function of patient care (e.g., infection control)

For home care organizations that provide durable medical equipment services, a clinical measure may assess the selection, delivery, setup, and maintenance of equipment. Because the definition of a clinical measure is so broad, it may be classified in more than one category. These measures are to be used to continuously improve patient outcomes.

Perception-of-Care Measures

A perception-of-care measure focuses on the delivery of clinical care from the perspective of the patient and/or the patient's family or caregiver. Examples of perception-of-care measures include, but are not limited to, patient education, medication use, pain management, communication plans and outcomes of care, prevention and illness, and improvement in health status.

Once measures are selected and the data are reported to the Joint Commission, the home care organization must continue collecting data on the measure(s) for at least one year. The organization *cannot* change midyear and select different measures. The Joint Commission also reserves the right to require a home care organization to continue using a measure longer than a year if the data submitted identify adverse patterns or trends. Likewise, if the data submitted identify a stable, in-control process, the Joint Commission can request that the home care organization change its measure(s) after one year.

If the home care organization doesn't meet the time frames established for participating in the ORYX initiative, a special type I recommendation will result, and a plan of correction will need to follow in order to stay accredited. The data transmitted to the Joint Commission will be used to make the home care survey process more continuous rather that performed episodically every three years. Although the accreditation decision will continue to be based primarily on the on-site review of compliance with standards, the data submitted quarterly may signal non-compliance with one or more of the home care standards. A home care organization's data will be reviewed by the Joint Commission and compared against data submitted by other home care organizations using the same measurement system, not different systems (benchmarking).

If significant variances in the data from other home care organizations using the same system are identified, a Joint Commission staff member may call or write the home care organization to determine what actions, if any, have been taken to respond to the variance. If the data show what is thought to be a compliance-with-standards problem, a written progress report or on-site survey may be required. The ORYX initiative is a new, dynamic process with ever-changing information. More ORYX information through the Joint Commission can be attained by calling (630) 792-5085. Additional information can be obtained through the Joint Commission's web site at *http:// www.jcaho.org.*

The Relationship Between ORYX and OASIS

With the Joint Commission's emphasis on outcomes and other performance measures and the importance Medicare has placed on OBQI and outcomes in the revised COPs, agencies are asking how these two systems will interface. Since managed care companies, payers, and consumers are also looking at outcomes and comparing agencies, a home care organization surely wants to provide the necessary performance improvement and outcome information in the most efficient and cost-effective way. Since the entire process of collecting information based on outcomes of care is just beginning, ways must be identified to assist agencies in complying with the demands of external sources with the least amount of resources. Currently, many of the performance measurement systems contracting with the Joint Commission are also OASIS-ready once the final regulations are published.

As the deadlines for the ORYX project and the OBQI/OASIS requirements come closer, the coordination of the systems will become more apparent. Additionally, the impact of both these projects on a home health organization's computer system and operations is tremendous. It is suggested that health care professionals follow the progress of the ORYX initiative closely if their agencies are JCAHO accredited. Additionally, when the final COPs are released, it is hoped that computer vendors, forms providers, state and national home care associations, and others will be active in the dialogue to make these systems work as seamlessly as possible.

OBQI and Patient Satisfaction

And what about patient satisfaction? Satisfaction surveys are currently being done in various ways, depending on the home care organization's preference, regulatory and accrediting requirements, and history of patient satisfaction information. The 50 demonstration agencies involved in the MEQA study used a patient satisfaction study called a Telephone Inquiry Questionnaire (TIQ; Figure 2–2). It is unclear whether Medicare through the COPs will require agencies to use this format, use their own format, or include a patient satisfaction report in the final regulations. However, PI and QI programs require that agencies solicit feedback from their patients and/or caregivers if the patient is unable to respond to the questionnaire or survey. With the movement toward more consumer and payer involvement in the choice of provider and with agency marketing efforts directed toward measuring levels of customer satisfaction, the use of patient satisfaction studies will likely become more important.

In the MEQA study, the TIQ was designed to assess patients' satisfaction with the home health care services they received when questioned within 14 days after they were discharged from the home health agency. Specific information was given on the number of patients to be called based on the number of agency admissions and type of discharge. There was great emphasis on using this questionnaire to interview patients and caregivers with a script that allowed for the uniformity of the questions in each telephone inquiry. Additionally, a caregiver, family member, or close friend familiar with the patient's home health care was asked to answer if the patient was unable. Never did the telephone interviewer ask the care providers (the person[s]) provided by the agency, such as a home health aide) to answer the questions on the survey. To be eligible to answer the TIQ, patients met the same eligibility criteria that applied to OASIS data collection and must have been discharged from home care for any reason except death. Also, patients who had been discharged from Medicare services, but might still be receiving some type of supportive services from the agency were also eligible *as long as the interview could still be conducted with the patient or caregiver.*

Benchmarking As Used By Consumers and Payers

The current climate in health care finds consumers who are informed about their health and illness, have access to an increasing amount of information, and are being forced to assume more responsibility about how their health care dollars are spent. This more knowledgeable client population, often unaware of the availability and scope of home health services, is asking more questions about the value and worth of all health care services. As people live longer and the cost of health care increases, it is not surprising that consumers of care as well as payers (also consumers of health care) are increasingly asking questions about cost and outcomes to determine the types of services they should purchase and from what organizations. To provide information for these groups, as well as acquire meaningful information for internal purposes, setting benchmarks and the process of benchmarking have increased in all health care organizations.

To continue to be seen as a viable alternative to institutionalization and to prove their worth, home care agencies should have a great interest in measuring their own performance. This can be accomplished in several ways:

1. By comparing a home health care organization's performance against its own past performance, called *internal benchmarking*
2. By comparing the organization's performance with other providers, called *external benchmarking*
3. By comparing the organization's performance against standards, called *standard benchmarking.*

In the 1970s, the concept of a benchmark evolved beyond a simple technical term to be used as a reference point. The word migrated into the business realm, where it came to signify a measurement process for conducting comparisons. Benchmarking can be used for strategic planning, restructuring, and financial management. Benchmarking is being increasingly used in health care to develop a higher level of quality comparison in many areas.

Benchmarks of care can only be developed when there is adequate and accurate data from which to develop meaningful analysis—i.e., the role of OASIS data in home care. The goal of using comparative data, or "benchmarks," is to provide essential information to health care agencies, patients, referral sources, and payers about the outcomes of home health care provided and the costs required to achieve these outcomes

(Wilson, 1997). With the intense competition in health care, constant improvement is increasingly important in order for an organization to remain viable and competitive. Using benchmarks allows a home health agency to analyze its market position based on quality indicators and to determine an action plan that allows it to remain competitive and grow.

Benchmarking is a continuous process of comparison, projection, and implementation. It involves comparing an organization with others of like kind, discovering best practices and trends, and meeting and exceeding the expectations set. Learning from others and looking closely at an organization's strengths and weaknesses through benchmarking activities will help set overall goals and define the focus of performance improvement activities. When an agency uses benchmarking, reference points are set ahead of time so performance can be better measured, evaluated, and improved upon.

For health care, one of the best ways of benchmarking is to use outcome data. Outcomes are useful benchmarks because they can:

1. Compare the effectiveness of services and care procedures
2. Determine trends by specific patient population groups, diagnoses, or demographic characteristics

Although several factors impact a patient's outcomes, especially in home health, outcomes are still seen as important measures in evaluation. Since databases and outcome measures on a regional and national basis are currently not available, the collection of OASIS data as a national mandate should provide rich data over time to look at both costs and outcomes, which will allow the creation of true benchmarks in the home health industry.

Since benchmarking is first measuring, then comparing, appropriate benchmarks cannot be developed without quality data, consistently collected. Wilson (1997) gives some examples of benchmarking measures that show how the process can be used in home care. Benchmarking can show an organization such information as:

♦ How much better are patients who received services from your agency? From your competitors? From others in the industry?
♦ How much did those services cost your organization and the patient? Your competitor's patients?
♦ How happy were your customers with the services they received from you? From your competitors?
♦ How long did it take to provide the services, and who provided them?

Hospitals and other health care providers are currently debating the use of "report cards" that can compare (benchmark) facilities in a certain area with others in regard to many factors such as number of procedures completed in a year, death rates from certain operations, etc. In other situations, payers such as Health Maintenance Associations (HMOs) and Managed Care Organizations (MCOs) evaluate costs and outcomes between providers to choose contract partners. These actions by consumers and payers force health care providers to become more competitive and able to justify their services and costs. The outcomes of the data collections used for benchmarking will be discussed in Section III of this book. From this discussion, it is hoped that home care professionals will understand the importance of collecting accurate and reliable data that can be used for internal, external, and standard benchmarking activities.

Summary

The material presented in this chapter was meant to assist the reader in seeing the OBQI and OASIS project in a larger context. The emphasis on outcomes and performance measures that indicate quality care at cost-effective levels is paramount in this discussion. These changes in evaluating health services based on outcomes cut across providers on all levels. Hospitals and long-term care facilities have been dealing with these issues for some time. It is hoped that the home care system will embrace this change and make these activities work externally as well as internally. The challenge will be to assure that everyone involved understands the importance and rationale behind this focus on outcomes and makes every effort to collect the best data possible so the analysis will be meaningful and helpful to all parties.

Incorporating OASIS into the Daily Operations of a Home Health Agency

Introduction

This chapter will discuss many of the main issues a home health organization must consider when determining how to integrate OASIS into daily operations. Specifically, it will explore the steps for incorporating the OASIS database into the agency's existing assessment form and process, the relationship of OASIS with critical pathways, or care pathways and the issues surrounding computerization of the OASIS data for OBQI activities. The authors have surveyed many of the 50 home health organizations participating in the Medicare Quality Assurance Project through the Center for Health Policy in Denver, asking them to share suggestions and ideas they have found helpful in integrating OASIS into their agencies. Their comments are interspersed throughout this chapter.

Steps for Incorporating OASIS into an Agency's Assessment Form

Many home health agencies view incorporation of the OASIS into their assessment form as an incredible expense of time and effort. But while the initial process is time consuming, the benefit achieved by reviewing outcomes and revising processes of care will be ample reward. The following tips will assist in implementing the OASIS in your agency's daily operations:

1. Educate the administrator, performance improvement or quality improvement manager, controller (if indicated), and other management personnel by:
   - Sharing the results of your research (readings, attendance at seminars, books, and journal articles), explaining operational and clinical aspects to those unfamiliar with those areas
   - Clarifying the purpose of reengineering the current forms and discussing the data to be collected and the anticipated benefit to the agency
   - Assuring administration that the professional staff time required to complete the forms will decrease once everyone is fully oriented; explaining the "learning curve" to be expected during the staff adjustment period
   - Responding confidently to questions as they arise from professional and business staff, being sure, when necessary, to say you do not know the answer and need to get more information before responding

2. Designate an OASIS coordinator to oversee the implementation process. The OASIS coordinator will assume the ultimate challenge of successfully integrating the data collection, documentation, and reporting systems into day-to-day operations. The coordinator will need a strong working knowledge of clinical operations, the OASIS assessment items, and pending regulatory requirements. The coordinator also needs sufficient authority to acquire and manage the financial and human resources necessary to make the project a success.

3. Establish a task force to design and coordinate OASIS efforts and create commitment and a sense of ownership among members. The task force should consist mainly of clinical field staff (nurses, therapists, and social workers) since they will be responsible for collecting the data and will be critical to success through their mentorship of other staff during the process. Since the coordinator will not be able to oversee every detail of the process, it is vital that these task force members provide support and encouragement for staff during the integration and implementation of the OASIS and OBQI.

4. Integrate the data items into your current assessment forms. Keep the forms as familiar as possible to decrease staff anxiety. Integration of the OASIS items can decrease the documentation burden for clinicians as well as the redundancy often found in current home care documentation systems. Items in the revised clinical documentation must be *exact duplicates* of the OASIS items. Inter-rater reliability has been tested and achieved on the items as written; uniformity of data cannot be assured if modifications are made.

REMEMBER!

The skip patterns must be maintained *exactly* as they are found in the OASIS document. Utmost care must be taken to assure that the form is as user friendly as possible and that the skip patterns do *not* result in missing essential assessment categories (MOO numbers).

5. Plan for printing and reproduction costs and/or the cost of a computerized program. The cost benefit for printing and reproduction should be projected far enough to determine if paper assessment forms will best serve the agency or if the purchase of a computerized system should be considered. The length of time from completion of the forms to agency implementation should be discussed and established with all entities involved (such as printers).

6. Plan for ICD-9 coding. Identify the person(s) doing this coding in the agency at the present time. If someone is to be assigned this task who has not been working with this system, he/she must be properly trained in order to correctly code diagnoses.

REMEMBER!

The OASIS data set requires only the global, three-digit ICD-9 codes, while more precise codes are necessary for accurate completion of the HCFA 485.

7. Plan for data entry. Who will do it? Will current data entry staff be responsible, or will someone from outside the agency be hired for this purpose? Are you collecting this data on a separate computer? This process must be thought through prior to implementation of data collection to avoid backlogging of OASIS data.

8. Review the process of patient satisfaction survey administration. Will all patients be asked to respond to the survey? Will a certain percentage of discharged patients be sampled? Will this survey be performed by telephone, or will a preprinted form be mailed to the patient or significant other? It is possible that a specific form for collecting patient satisfaction information developed by the Center (referred to as the TIQ, or telephone interview questionnaire; see chapter 2) will be required at some point to standardize the methods by which data are collected.

9. Modify forms or processes and procedures as needed. Revising or modifying the time frame within which initial, complete OASIS assessment information is collected may be in conflict with current agency policy. This may require rewriting the agency policy regarding admissions. It is advisable to review applicable admission and discharge policies and procedures at the same time the initial form changes are made.

10. Train agency staff as to the purpose of the project, uniform definitions of time points, follow-ups including discharge, any new forms, and all processes and procedures. Establish "buy-in" at all levels of the organization through continual instruction, communication, feedback, support, and supervision.

11. Before distributing the OASIS assessment forms to clinicians in the field, spend time educating your staff about the value of outcome measurement in home health care. This is a good time to begin positively reinforcing the value and utility the OASIS data set brings to an organization in the form of solid, reliable outcomes. It will be important to stress from the very beginning the differences between objective versus subjective data and how important accurate data will be for this process. If possible, provide staff with sample reports during these first educational sessions to emphasize and visually demonstrate to clinicians the possibilities and the power of this information. This can be a very effective way to redirect clinicians' attention away from the length of the forms and toward collecting the best information possible for improving care processes.

12. Regular meetings and/or other forms of communication to update staff and maintain their commitment and sense of involvement should follow these initial sessions. Staff will appreciate reminders of the critical role they play in the success of the organization's efforts in outcome measurement. They must also understand the implications of outcome measurement on their jobs. Quite simply, in today's competitive market, if staff does not do it right, the agency is not likely to survive over the long term nor are the staff members likely to keep their positions. Discussing the consequences for the agency from a regulatory and financial perspective becomes the "stick," while demonstrating the value of the information and how it is used becomes the "carrot."

13. Wilson and Associates (1998) stress that staff training must be approached with careful planning and accommodation of the clinicians' needs and schedule to the greatest extent possible. We already know that staff can often feel "put upon" by the volume of paperwork, so it is especially important to continually approach OASIS training in a positive fashion. A good starting point is to focus on the benefits of outcome measurement first because regulatory and compliance issues become self evident. Recommendations for the training session include:

    ♦ Review the purpose and intent of the OASIS items. Especially emphasize the amount of research necessary to develop questions that have inter-rater reliability and statistical significance. Allow staff ample time to question and discuss the timing of the assessments as well as the meaning of the individual outcome indicators. Depending on your staff's educational background, you may need to simplify the presentation to include those who have no research experience.

    ♦ Explain the need to follow the MOO numbers (acronym for the coding numbers listed on the form-MO140, for example) in their listed order and to answer as precisely as possible. Reinforce the significance of choosing the answer that fits the patient the majority (more than 50%) of the time.

    ♦ Do not read into the questions, and do not add extra options! Only mark one answer unless instructed to do so; do not fail to answer all questions unless a skip pattern is indicated.

- Stress the necessity of a thorough patient assessment before completing the form; do not guess or answer questions with indifference. These behaviors contribute to the "GIGO Principle" of data collection and eventual interpretation: Garbage In, Garbage Out.

- Be sure to point out the skip patterns, which save staff members some time. Skip patterns were designed into the OASIS to avoid unnecessary work during the patient assessment. For example, if the clinician determines that the patient does not have a surgical wound and answers "no" to OASIS question MO482, she does not need to respond to the next three questions that pertain to the number and status of surgical wounds.

- Make training sessions mandatory if possible.

- Be creative about ways to make the training sessions fun. For example, you may wish to use brief quizzes at the beginning or end of each session and offer a prize to the participant who comes up with the first correct or most unique response.

- Create or purchase an instruction manual like this one, that describes the purpose and guidelines for completion of the OASIS data set. Make it readily available to all providers. This manual should also clearly outline your agency's policies and procedures related to OASIS.

- Stress that OASIS is intended to become an assessment/care planning tool, rather than solely a data collection instrument.

- Emphasize the benefits to your organization of using OASIS, which include consistency of outcome measurement across units/organizations, facilitation of multidisciplinary team communication, and demonstration of the value of home health services.

- Consider providing some sort of food at the initial staff meeting. Food seems to be a great calmative—especially gooey, fattening, *chocolate* desserts! (Content stomachs make for more complacent minds.)

- Remember that in a group setting, some people are primarily visual learners, whereas others are auditory learners. It is a good idea to use visual aids such as overheads or flip charts and to provide a completed form for review while you are presenting the in-service. Regardless of your proficiency as an educator, some learners will simply forget or miss

certain key points. Display these critical elements in a prominent place where the staff tend to gather, such as the documentation area, snack room, and even the backs of bathroom doors. Be creative! We tend to remember information that attracts our attention and pleases or amuses us.

- Implement a trial period of data collection and utilization of the new tool. Usually one month of data collection experience will be adequate, provided staff members have been well prepared for the field work and have sufficient managerial support. Anticipate that many questions will occur initially, and ensure that a knowledgeable member of the team is available to respond on a 24-hour basis.

- If some agency staff have internalized the information and are performing the assessments completely and accurately, establish them as preceptors who can assist in field staff education and support. Preceptors can then be responsible for educating newly hired staff to accurately utilize the assessment forms through roles as preceptors and orientation speakers.

- Once everyone is collecting data correctly and the excitement has decreased, interest in the project may wane. Because data must be collected over a period of time and between at least two time points, a letdown between initiation of actual data collection and the generation of the outcome report is normal and to be expected. It is essential that managers not allow staff to lose momentum because it will be more difficult to obtain that same level of interest again. Continue to support and encourage staff members and keep upper-level managers informed of the overall progress. To accomplish this outcome, be accessible and supportive of staff and keep in mind that the ultimate goal of this project is to provide optimal care practices and improved outcomes for all patients through an impressive, razor-sharp, and motivated agency and staff.

REMEMBER!

What was done yesterday in home care is no longer applicable or a formula for success.

Establish a vision for the agency, detail steps for implementation, encourage a team approach, and act to implement and improve agency processes through the use of the OASIS and OBQI.

OASIS and Clinical Pathways

Many agencies have begun to use clinical pathways, to guide and focus care, intending to accomplish much with the limited time and resources allowed. The format for a clinical pathway is usually the same throughout the agency, and the content is developed by examining the specific clinical activities needed for a client with a specific diagnosis or procedure. A clinical pathway is similar to a standardized care plan; however, it has an added timeline that in home care is usually visits or weeks of care.

Managed care has forced all providers to evaluate the way they do things in search of the most effective, least expensive method. The need for standardized care and the inclusion of "golden standards" that are linked to proven positive outcomes is obvious. By reviewing outcomes of the care provided using data collected by the use of the OASIS, agencies will be able to tailor care to consistently produce the best outcomes possible. Clinical pathways may provide support in this endeavor.

Clinical pathways seek to standardize interventions, tools, information, and processes for achieving positive outcomes. While it is inevitable that some outcomes will not be positive, the standardization of care may make it easier to identify variances and sentinel events.

Some patients may be better served by being case managed according to protocol rather than by clinical pathways. A patient with a Foley catheter that has been in place for some time and is not anticipated to be discontinued would not fare well on an acute clinical pathway. However, the use of clinical pathways for patients with more defined and accessible discharge goals may be very realistic.

The benefits of clinical pathways may include the following:

♦ Clarification of the clinician's expectations and responsibilities by creating baseline standards for staff competencies through the detail of the interventions noted on the pathway, thereby matching patients with appropriately trained and certified staff
♦ Improvement in documentation
♦ Maintenance of continuity of care

♦ Early identification of variances or sentinel events that may affect the outcome of care
♦ Provide a helpful guide for new home care nurses or staff
♦ Better patient understanding of what is to be expected and when
♦ Patient involvement in developing and following the plan of care

In the 1980s, hospitals came under the control of diagnostic-related groupings (DRGs) and moved from cost-based care to a prospective payment system. Prospective payment is basically payment by diagnosis. However, all patients with similar diagnoses are not the same. For example, suppose that two patients enter the emergency room with chest pain. Both are admitted to the intensive care unit. One is discharged 24 hours later; the other remains for further testing and follow-up. In the first instance the hospital actually provided the care for less than the amount paid by the insurance, thus "making money" on this patient. In the second situation, the insurance company paid exactly the same amount as it did for the first patient who was discharged in 24 hours (as opposed to 72 hours for the second patient). After adding in the costs of the extra days of hospitalization plus the extensive testing that was necessary, the hospital actually "lost money" in caring for this patient. The same will be true of home care patients under prospective payment. As a result, many chronic, long-term patients may have difficulty finding an agency that will continue to care for them. These are the patients who may be discharged upon hospitalization and not readmitted to the agency.

At this same time, consumers are becoming more cognizant of their health care needs and how their health care dollars are spent. They are much more critical of the quality of care provided in comparison with the cost of services. Agencies that consistently exhibit positive outcomes are more likely to provide satisfied customers as well as secure managed care contracts. As consumers of health care services, managed care organizations will search for the most cost-containing, productive agencies that produce the best outcomes.

Clinical pathways should not be developed indiscriminately. Each agency should organize a committee to review the past year's admissions and determine the most frequent diagnoses. Most likely, problems such as congestive heart failure, total hip replacement, cancer, chronic obstructive pulmonary disease, and diabetes will be high on the list. Other contributory factors such as infections and pressure ulcers should be considered for pathways as well.

Standards of practice can be developed for all disciplines involved in patient care. Every discipline should be represented on the clinical pathway committee along with administrative and quality improvement staff. Primary goals or outcomes should be developed as well as interventions tailored to meet the goal. Interventions, which will provide the most efficient patient care without compromising quality, are desirable. The number of visits necessary to reach the goal at least 75% of the time (or whatever percentage figure the agency chooses) can be determined by averaging the number of visits required to reach the outcome in previous patients. This figure should be reevaluated at set intervals to ascertain the provision of safe and effective care. Clinical pathways should be flexible enough to allow variances; if more visits are required, the agency must notify the insurance company's utilization reviewer to extend visits until goals are met.

Clinical pathways developed using the data collected through the OASIS will be more global than specific. The Center for Health Policy and Services Research grouped patients according to quality indicator groups, or QUIGs. QUIGs were developed for both acute and chronic conditions. Acute conditions included the following:

◆ Acute orthopedic conditions (fracture, amputation, others)
◆ Acute neurologic conditions (stroke, head injury, others)
◆ Open wounds and lesions (pressure ulcers, surgical wounds, stasis ulcers)
◆ Terminal conditions (palliative care, end-stage AIDS)
◆ Acute cardiac/peripheral vascular conditions (e.g., congestive heart failure, peripheral vascular disease, hypertension)
◆ Acute pulmonary conditions (COPD, pneumonia, others)
◆ Acute diabetes mellitus
◆ Acute gastrointestinal disorders (ulcer, ostomies, liver disease, others)
◆ Contagious/communicable conditions (hepatitis, tuberculosis, others)
◆ Acute urinary incontinence/catheter
◆ Acute mental/emotional conditions
◆ Oxygen therapy
◆ IV/infusion therapy
◆ Enteral/parenteral nutrition
◆ Ventilator therapy

Agencies can use the QUIGs to group patients with various disorders. Initial outcomes should be reviewed and areas for remediation or reward identified. Those areas requiring remediation may indicate the need to revamp or revise the clinical pathway for those diseases included within this grouping. We will cover this in more detail in Chapter 7. If an agency demonstrates consistently exemplary outcomes within one or more groupings, exemplary practices used in reaching this status should be identified and included in the clinical pathway to improve and standardize the care provided. It may be necessary only to fine-tune the clinical pathway rather than revising it totally.

Computerization Issues

In Chapter 2, the importance of developing a core data set was discussed. With the increasing emphasis and importance placed on the many ways to use the data from that core data set, it is becoming more critical for agencies to have computer capabilities. Additional emphasis from many forces, including payers, consumers, and managed care, have combined to stimulate the collection and analysis of a great deal of information that can often only be compiled through the use of computers.

Several commercial options are now available for acquiring OASIS paper forms, not necessarily linked with computer data entry capacity. These include additional common assessment information and care planning mechanisms. Medicare surveyors will expect an agency to incorporate the OASIS data set into all aspects of the operation, including care planning systems and paperwork. With the newness of OASIS and the rush to market for many vendors, many forms were developed prior to the final HCFA regulations. It is important that, before making a final decision about whether to revise the forms you currently use or to purchase commercial versions, you give the decision a great deal of thought. However, it is important not to let the decision to purchase or what forms to purchase become a block to beginning the process. As the staff and managers work with the format, revisions and suggestions will make this transition a work in progress.

State and national home care associations, as well as regional and local groups, are in the process of developing not only the forms but also a way of collecting the data from the form via computerization. It is important to remember that just completing the paperwork is not enough. There must be a way to collect all the OASIS data, both on individual patients and on all agency patients, and to retrieve it in a format that is easily analyzed for OBQI purposes.

The HCFA has developed a computer program for the OASIS and OBQI project called HAVEN (Home Assessment Validation and Entry). The following information is an outline of the many aspects of HAVEN and how it is used in a home health organization.

What HAVEN *is*

♦ Software available at no cost
♦ Resides on the HHA's computer
♦ A tool for entering data, maintaining the database and submitting the assessment file
♦ Software that ensures data integrity
♦ A program that includes on-line help

What HAVEN is *not:*

♦ The only option
♦ A comprehensive tool for all HHA information processing requirements

Some other features of HAVEN

♦ It is a windows-based product
♦ Enforces all HCFA standard edits
♦ Imports and exports data
♦ Specific system requirements and recommended configurations avialable through HCFA
♦ Available on the Internet

COP ALERT!

Since this is a computer program that will continue to be supported by HCFA, there will be constant updates and upgrades provided through HCFA and the HCFA OASIS website at http://www.hcfa.gov/medicare/hsqb/oasis/oasishmp.htm

Even with paper forms for data collection, all agencies must plan to use a computerized tracking system to manage the information flow and identify patients due for follow-up assessments according to the OASIS timelines. Several software vendors either have available or are developing various levels of software that incorporate OASIS into their electronic clinical record systems. Whether you are using a comprehensive electronic clinical record system that integrates all clinical, billing, and statistical information, or a stand-alone software or paperwork system, it is important that the *exact* OASIS items are directly incorporated into the clinical record. Displays 3–1 and 3–2 on pages 30 and 31 provide guidelines for choosing a vendor and tips for working with the vendor on an ongoing basis.

Suggestions from Agencies Who Have Made It Work

We asked some demonstration agencies various questions we felt all home health organizations would ask if they had the opportunity. Following are the questions along with several answers for each.

How did you go about educating your staff regarding the initial implementation of OASIS data? How do you keep this going?

Answer: Basic OASIS information was presented formally at staff meetings initially to introduce the terms and concepts. A formal training program was conducted for all staff members who would be collecting the OASIS data eight days prior to the actual implementation of the new assessment forms so the information would be fresh in their minds. We continue to update OASIS information on a continual basis through memos, staff meetings, nursing team meetings, and orientation of new staff.

Answer: We have been collecting OASIS information since March of 1996. We initially had extensive training on OASIS through mandatory in-services. In these in-services, we used numerous handouts and overheads to clarify the main points of the process and intent of OBQI. We also gave each nurse a copy of our new assessment form that integrated OASIS and asked them to complete one on a recent patient they had admitted. We had another structured mandatory in-service when we modified the form based on OASIS-B.

Answer: All staff were initially required to attend training and informational meetings about OASIS and OBQI. At monthly staff meetings the agenda always includes an item for OASIS and OBQI questions and concerns. At this time in the agenda, problems are identified and addressed. Staff are instructed to come to all of these meetings prepared, with their questions and concerns *written down*, knowing they will be collected and answered either during the meeting or afterward via memo by management and administration.

Answer: After training of all current staff took place, information about OASIS and OBQI was made a part of orientation. We have an agency newsletter called *MOO's News* that addresses commonly asked questions and problems with the agency's unique situation and gives answers, including policy and procedures that are applicable.

Display 3-1 *Guidelines for Choosing a Computer Vendor*

1. Be certain that OASIS items are incorporated *verbatim* or in some form equivalent to how they appear in the OASIS.

2. The text of the computerized program must be an *exact duplicate* of the OASIS questions as published, since changing the question in any way would affect its reliability. The ability to produce exact duplicates of the OASIS questions in both the question and the multiple-choice responses has been a problem for some software vendors due to a limit on the number of characters allowed in each field.

3. OASIS items must be integrated into the total assessment. The OASIS items should be integrated *into,* not added *onto,* the end of the assessment. OASIS items may replace some of the original assessment questions, but the OASIS data set was not developed for universal patient assessment.

4. Care providers should *not* have the option to carry the same OASIS data item values from start-of-care to follow-up in describing or assessing patient health status. This often results in inaccurate follow-up data because providers are tempted to minimize their time by carrying forward the data from the initial time point instead of properly reassessing and recording the information at follow-up. The assessment must be completed in its entirety every 60 days and at discharge.

5. Abbreviations should not be allowed in either the paper or software versions of the OASIS.

6. The system must allow for skip patterns that must be followed. The skip patterns should be incorporated into the software. Without built-in skip patterns, the nurse must follow the directions on screen to get to the next appropriate question. For example, the directions may state, "Skip the next two questions." If the nurse forgets to skip as directed, an error should appear on the edit report and will need to be corrected before the data can be sent for analysis.

7. Data edit checks should be performed to ensure that *all* required items are completed. Failure to complete the assessment and other problems should be identified as the assessment is being completed. If the program does not do data editing, skipped questions may not be noticed until the agency runs the edit check prior to sending data out for analysis. When this occurs at this late point in data collection, the nurse/therapist must complete the skipped items in the assessment and reenter the data. This can be a very time-consuming process and can contribute to inaccuracies due to completing items long after the patient was assessed.

8. Since revisions to the OASIS will be published periodically, vendors must be able to efficiently and inexpensively update their software with OASIS changes in a timely manner.

9. Vendors must provide the capability to extract OASIS items for purposes of transmission to a central source for outcome comparisons and benchmarking, as well as for other agency internal applications that will naturally be of interest once OASIS data are computerized.

10. When selecting a vendor, meet with management and staff prior to meeting with the vendor representatives so that you can identify the data and reports that are required by regulation and the ones your organization can use as part of your ongoing PI and QI efforts. It is often easy to be "wowed" by the vendor's salesperson, who has an extensive list of available reports and data but may *not* have or thoroughly understand the information your agency needs. For example, hospital-based home health agencies often need data that coordinates with hospital information produced through another database and computer system. If this is the case, you should be sure your needs are first clear to your own staff and then appropriately communicated to the vendor representative. Once a vendor is chosen or if an organization's existing vendor has integrated OASIS into the system, an agency must be concerned about successfully working with the vendor as changes occur in the organization and in the OASIS instrument. The following suggestions can be helpful when working with a vendor on an ongoing basis.

Display 3-2 *Working with a Computer Vendor on an Ongoing Basis*

1. Develop a close working relationship with the vendor(s). There should be at least one person in the agency who is identified as the major coordinator and contact with the vendor. In larger agencies, a clinical liaison and an office liaison may be needed to coordinate all OASIS and OBQI issues with the vendor. This is not to say that other staff cannot talk directly with the vendor representative, but they should always coordinate their questions and contacts with the major coordinator. Additionally, there should be a major contact(s) at the vendor who is responsible for coordinating information with the organization.

2. Assure that your vendor is receiving all updated guidelines from the center and/or from HCFA. You may want to start a system of copying the vendor representative on printed or e-mail transmissions or discuss how they plan to keep their clients informed of changes and updates.

3. Educate your vendor about your individual and unique needs; this is essential to success. Both your agency and your vendor will benefit when you share current and accurate information that is unique to your market, organization, staff, or special program.

4. Keep up-to-date on the status of the current system as well as upgrades and updates. Agencies should also be prepared to do extensive testing if new or existing software has not yet been beta-tested or piloted sufficiently by other home health providers. The time spent testing the software may prevent serious or time-consuming problems from developing.

5. Implementing OASIS data, OBQI information, and other agency data may involve using both a paper and computer system. This requires a high level of coordination and sharing between the organization and the vendor.

6. Be clear on what reports you need and can use to reach your goals—too much is not always better. Most computer systems will generate many more reports than an organization can work with or needs. Be sure the ones generated are useful *and* are being used. Be prepared to make changes in the configurations of data that are necessary to reach performance and quality-improvement goals and outcomes. Always remember, there are reports that you need to know and ones that are *nice* to know but not a priority.

Answer: We started working with OASIS by developing a small work team, primarily made up of clinical field staff (nurses and therapists) who participated in a pilot project to test and refine our assessment form. After this was completed, the entire agency staff (including clerical, business office, management, specialty programs, and clinical departments) were required to attend formal in-services on OASIS forms, documentation, and procedure, led by the OASIS work team. The pilot test group was also used to develop and reevaluate the procedures, work flow, and paper trail developed for the agency. When specific problems were identified that seemed to be experienced by many, we followed up with remedial in-services. When OASIS-B came out, a committee of representatives from all disciplines was identified to revise the forms and procedures and to help in-service all staff.

Answer: One important in-service presented to all staff, both as groups and individually, used case studies, such as Medicare's denial of two out of five home health aide visits a week because of problems in the way the agency staff had documented coverage issues, especially homebound status. We showed the staff how the OASIS data provide information to support patients' need for assistance by examining their functional assessment as well as their physical assessment. For example, OASIS data might give us the information that a patient lives with an elderly spouse and has a daughter who works, and then tie this in with other aspects in the plan of care, such as receiving a physical therapy exercise program to reach the outcome of ambulating with the assistance of a cane. By clarifying and tracking this information, the payer, in this case Medicare, sees more clearly why this patient needs assistance from the therapist and the aide. We also repeat in-services to focus on various documentation issues. In-services should include the necessary documentation needed relative to every MOO number that is scored as a problem needing agency involvement.

Answer: We made a resource "Oasis Island" in the middle of the office. The setting had a large, cardboard palm tree, and under it the staff could find examples of patient OASIS assessment forms, outcome reports bound in a small binder, and books and journals containing articles relative to OASIS and OBQI. We provided two comfortable chairs and good lighting to encourage the staff to take a bit of time to read and become more independent in their own learning.

Answer: We used our employees who were on the OASIS experimental group as preceptors for our new orientees. They were not only excellent at teaching and reinforcing all agency policies and procedures with new staff, but they were very helpful in teaching the new orientees how to maximize their assessment visits and learn it the right way from the beginning.

Please share the paper trail your agency uses, from the completion of the form through the data entry process.

Answer: The forms go from field nurse to case manager to data entry to medical records through the following steps:

1. Assessment forms including OASIS data are placed in each admission chart.
2. The nurse places the completed forms in the designated area.
3. Medical review collects and reviews forms for completeness; if they are not complete, they go back to the staff nurse for completion.
4. Forms are given to the data entry designee by the medical reviewer, and information is entered into the computer tracking system.
5. Forms go to the filing clerks to be placed in the patient's clinical record.

Answer: The admission and discharge OASIS items are a part of the nurse and therapist's notes for these visits. On admission and follow-up, the nurse manager checks for completeness, and the office manager copies the form(s). The original completed form goes to the patient's clinical record, and a copy goes to our OASIS data entry coordinator to be put into the system.

Answer: Our agency has admission nurses who admit the patient and then turn the case over to a primary care nurse. The following procedure is our paper trail:

1. The intake coordinator completes the intake record with the demographic information, patient diagnoses, and initial physician orders and sends

this information to the admissions nurse. Our assessment form with the OASIS questions included is printed in triplicate.
2. The admissions nurse completes the assessment form, gives a copy to the primary nurse, and submits the other two copies to the coordinator or supervisor for review.
3. The coordinator or supervisor reviews the document for accuracy and then completes the OASIS routing slip. An original copy of the routing slip goes to the chart.
4. One copy of the assessment form is filed; the second goes to the input manager, who inputs the data into the computer and submits a list of all patients entered for that day. The list becomes a permanent part of the office records.
5. The input manager generates a computer report that is given to the supervisor so she knows who the primary nurse is for each patient. Our computer automatically queries if an assessment form hasn't been completed upon admission, discharge, or re-certification.

Answer: Our paper trail is as follows:

1. The field nurse completes the assessment with OASIS information.
2. The form goes to the quality assurance nurse for review, and the field nurse makes corrections as needed.
3. The form is sent to data entry to be entered into the computer.
4. After data entry, the original form is filed in the patient's clinical record.

Additional examples of paper trails that agencies have used when integrating OASIS data are found in Figures 3–1 and 3–2.

What suggestions would you give to other agencies that are making the transition to collecting this additional information through their computer system? Through their manual system?

Answer: Concentrate on OASIS *only* for a few weeks—don't introduce anything else new for a while.

Answer: If at all possible, use a computer system to collect the assessment data in the field as well as to collect it for analysis. A manual, paper system is expensive in printing and labor costs, especially when analyzing the data for the OBQI reports.

Figure 3-1 *Agency A's OASIS Paper Trail.*

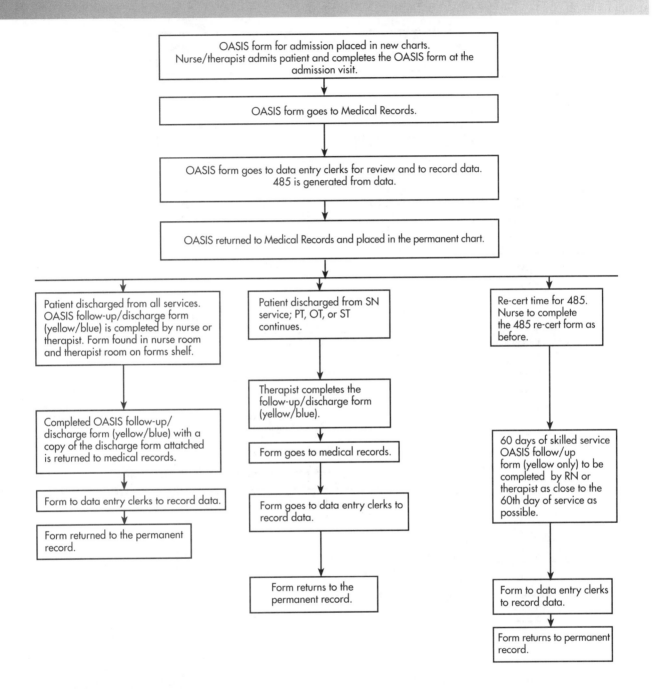

Answer: If using a manual system, we would suggest the following:

1. Professional staff who are collecting the information, as well as management and data entry personnel, should establish and use a calendar and/or tickler system on paper or on a computer to ensure that follow-ups are completed on time and accurately.

2. When you are just beginning to have staff collect OASIS data, designate a nurse to check all forms for completeness and accuracy for at least two to three months. Additionally, this nurse can identify specific problem areas and/or staff that are having difficulty so that in-services and individual remedial assistance can be provided.

Figure 3-2   *Agency B's OASIS Paper Trail.*

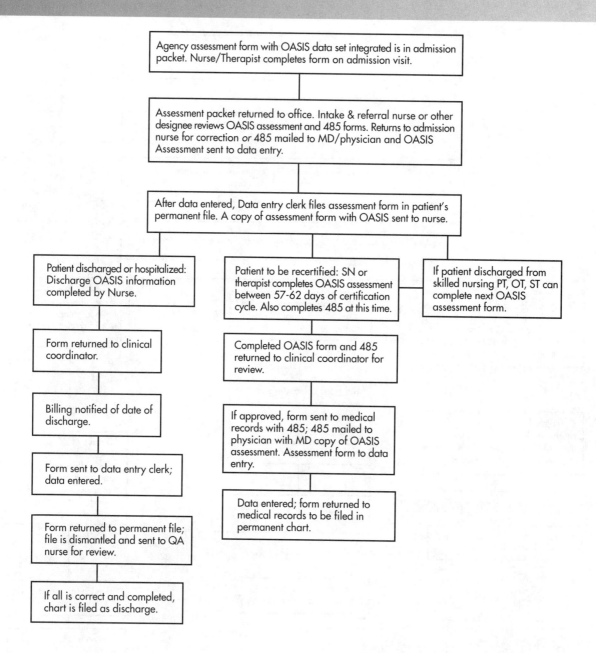

Agency assessment form with OASIS data set integrated is in admission packet. Nurse/Therapist completes form on admission visit.

Assessment packet returned to office. Intake & referral nurse or other designee reviews OASIS assessment and 485 forms. Returns to admission nurse for correction *or* 485 mailed to MD/physician and OASIS Assessment sent to data entry.

After data entered, Data entry clerk files assessment form in patient's permanent file. A copy of assessment form with OASIS sent to nurse.

Patient discharged or hospitalized: Discharge OASIS information completed by Nurse.

Patient to be recertified: SN or therapist completes OASIS assessment between 57-62 days of certification cycle. Also completes 485 at this time.

If patient discharged from skilled nursing PT, OT, ST can complete next OASIS assessment form.

Form returned to clinical coordinator.

Completed OASIS form and 485 returned to clinical coordinator for review.

Billing notified of date of discharge.

If approved, form sent to medical records with 485; 485 mailed to physician with MD copy of OASIS assessment. Assessment form to data entry.

Form sent to data entry clerk; data entered.

Data entered; form returned to medical records to be filed in permanent chart.

Form returned to permanent file; file is dismantled and sent to QA nurse for review.

If all is correct and completed, chart is filed as discharge.

---

3. Periodically, clinical managers should visit patients to check the accuracy (inter-rater reliability) of the OASIS data. It is not enough to just check that all the boxes are checked—the accuracy of the data is also important. This can be done on supervisory visits and as part of the performance appraisal process.

Answer: We do not have computerized patient records; we use the OBQI and OASIS forms as the

nursing assessment and have revised the areas of our current assessment form to contain the additional items we wanted to include. So, instead of taking our current assessment form and integrating the OASIS data into it, we took the OASIS form and integrated our current assessment form wherever necessary.

Answer: Set up some kind of up-front review to make sure the form is completed correctly so you can have confidence in the data for evaluating outcomes. Also, keep track of the nurses' timeliness in turning in forms based on the agency policy. For example, if you require staff to submit completed assessment forms within 48 hours of the admission visit, this should be true of the OASIS information also.

Answer: If you currently have a computer system, keep up with your vendor's knowledge and ability to collect OASIS data and produce OBQI reports. Although we are on computer, we manually track on each patient's record the actual OASIS M00 items at start of care, follow-ups, and discharge.

What kind of strategies did you develop to address patient and staff concerns regarding the depth of information needed and the length of time it takes to complete the form?

Answer: Keep focused on the positive aspects of the form. It is a comprehensive tool that provides the information necessary to justify care and payment as well as to make your documentation easier and more accurate. We stressed that staff were already assessing most of the items on the form. It is important to have everyone thoroughly understand the skip patterns and use them correctly *every* time. Our nurses who used the form during the pilot period were great advocates for OASIS.

Answer: Nurses who are paid per visit get an increased rate to do initial assessments. We found it takes an average of about 1½ to 2 hours to do the total admission. Research has shown that, after the longer time involved in learning OASIS and how to implement it, the additional time added to a visit to complete the information after that initial orientation was minimal. Most staff did not find the time element to be a problem.

Answer: Our agency's current forms were incorporated into OASIS and grouped by a system-by-system, head-to-toe approach when performing an assessment. Since staff is expected to do a thorough assessment anyway, they learned that OASIS did not take as long as they had anticipated. It was also stressed that documentation on the follow-ups could be used to supplement their documentation on re-certifications.

Answer: After the initial learning curve experienced by staff, we found it only takes five minutes longer to complete the assessment form using the OASIS data set.

How have you used the outcome data in your PI program?

Answer: To decrease the number of rehospitalizations and emergent care visits.

Answer: We implemented education programs on pain management and compensating for sensory loss.

Answer: We developed a congestive heart failure pathway that could be used by a care team of therapists, nurses, and aides.

Answer: We had a problem with an increase in emergent care, and we learned from our OBQI data that we can't bring the rate down because many patients use the emergency room as their physician. They prefer to seek emergency room help rather than wait until they can see their primary physician. It was good to have the concrete information to justify this phenomenon so we didn't see it as something we could control that affected patient outcomes.

Answer: We use OASIS data in our quality improvement program for an annual outcome report to the state as well as for our process-of-care investigation.

Please share the main things you would recommend that all agencies do when implementing OASIS?

- We are small, but I recommend implementing OASIS agency-wide, not just for Medicare patients. It decreases confusion, and you really need the data on all patients to conduct process-of-care investigation.
- Involve therapists from the beginning.
- Integrate as much as possible from day one. Don't forget to integrate the information with the 485.
- Integrate, integrate, integrate!!!
- Make sure the agency has sufficient staff. No one should have two admissions in one day.
- Get extra staff to do telephone interview questionnaires (TIQs). Volunteers can be used for this purpose.
- Look at how implementing OASIS and OBQI affects your entire agency, and support and add to staff as needed.
- Communicate information to all staff repeatedly to reinforce the changes.
- Check your systems and processes repeatedly.
- Reinforce the learning at regular intervals.

- Educate—educate—educate.
- Emphasize the benefits of OASIS, especially the fact that we will be able to benchmark with other home health agencies on a local, regional, state, and national basis.
- Designate a nurse or therapist to check all OASIS forms initially so problems can be identified and actions taken to resolve problems quickly.
- Develop a tracking system and an OASIS calendar to identify when follow-ups are due.
- Educate staff.
- Get input from staff when developing modifications.

List the main things you feel agencies should do and *not* do when implementing OASIS and OBQI.

- **Don't** develop modifications in isolation.
- **Don't** rush the process, allow for a learning curve.
- **Do** understand that productivity will go down overall the first three months of implementation.
- **Don't** leave it up to staff to remember when follow-ups are due.
- **Don't** assume that one in-service is enough.

- **Don't** minimize the importance of answering the OASIS items accurately or think that the process is foolproof.
- **Don't** assume everything is working as originally discussed.
- **Don't** take on too many things at once. If integrating OASIS, do only that!
- **Don't** become complacent with record reviews, and documentation.
- **Don't** contradict yourself; read the OASIS questions *carefully*. If OASIS is not done correctly and documentation does not support the need for home health services, denials may result.
- **Don't** present OASIS as a "government mandate" form. Stress the importance to QI, patient outcomes, etc.
- **Don't** do it alone. Be sure to have a leadership team in place comprised of all agency personnel (QI, nursing staff, administrator, etc.).
- **Don't** read into questions. This may cause the patient to be scored at an incorrect level.
- **Do** keep up with the literature on OASIS and OBQI through books, journal articles, seminars, and meetings that will help you anticipate problems and make the best decisions.

Part II

Training Staff to Use OASIS

Introduction

Home care nurses and therapists can collect the OASIS data. Since the home care nurse is most involved, simply based on the volume of patients admitted to home health for nursing, Part II will discuss the nurse's role in collecting the OASIS data. The material presented can be used to teach and train all home care professionals. This chapter is written in a conversational tone from the perspective of a staff nurse. Written this way, it will help the reader clearly understand the content as well as review the current Medicare regulations as they relate to the collection of OASIS data.

What Is Outcome Research and Why Do I Have to Do It?

Perspectives of a Staff Nurse

Home care nurses provide care for multiple patients with various problems in the privacy of each patient's home. By combining professional excellence with compassion and clinical competency with caring, these nurses take the profession of nursing to another level of responsibility. Home care nurses are often called upon to make clinical judgments in the field without the benefit of sophisticated equipment or even the support of another professional nurse's opinion regarding the clinical findings. Due in part to the necessity for independent decision-making and the ability to make do with what is available, home care nurses often develop individualized methods of performing procedures and providing care.

The home care nurse must have a general understanding of the basic provisions of the Medicare home care benefit. Without this understanding, the reasoning behind agency policies and procedures may seem extravagant or foolish. Medicare uses the same general terms and concepts that most home health care insurance providers use in their policies, so if the nurse understands Medicare, it will be easier to understand the various coverage guidelines that are used by other national payers. In addition, failure to understand the concept of "homebound" status and the requirement for skilled nursing interventions at each visit may result in lost revenue for the agency and a reprimand for the nurse.

Medicare coverage criteria for home care include the following:

♦ The patient must be homebound.
♦ The services provided are ordered by a physician and included in a plan of care.
♦ The services provided are reasonable and necessary.
♦ The patient must have a need for a skilled service—that is, skilled nursing, physical therapy, or speech therapy.
♦ The care provided must be considered part-time and intermittent.

The nurse is responsible for understanding what types of services are considered skilled by Medicare. These services will fall into one of four categories:

♦ Observation and assessment of the patient
♦ Teaching and training activities
♦ Performance of skilled procedures and treatments
♦ Management and evaluation of the care plan

The nurse must coordinate care provided by other disciplines and assure that interdisciplinary communication not only occurs at reasonable intervals but also is documented. Several disciplines may provide home care to the patient within the same certification period. If these disciplines are contracted services, not employed by the home health agency, interdisciplinary communication may be neglected.

Why Should I Be Concerned with Outcomes?

Until recently, evaluation of outcomes in home care focused primarily on documentation for reimbursement and inclusion of all the Medicare and state requirements to avoid reprimands and lost income. Individual nurses became adept at documenting, using the appropriate Medicare terminology. Those who did not were frequently subject to finger pointing, 100% documentation review, and other evaluation methods that were often intimidating and embarrassing. Nurses who may have been providing exemplary care while not documenting as such often left the home health arena for the checklists and problem-oriented charting of acute care.

Outcome measures examine the end results of nursing care and measure behavioral changes in the client rather than examining the process used by the nurse to effect that client change. While documentation of teaching and patient responses is still important, the concern is not about *how* the client learned the appropriate technique, etc., but rather how well the client is able to perform the designated procedure. The use of outcomes to measure patient progress is less rigid and more patient-oriented than previous processes and is more concerned with where the patient ends up than with what route the patient or nurse used to get there.

In order to measure outcomes, basic criteria must be defined. These criteria are developed from the standards of care and identify behaviors that the client should achieve as a result of nursing interventions. General disease categories such as congestive heart failure may have as a standard the statement, "The patient will remain free from exacerbation of CHF." But how is this defined? A set of measurable criteria must be established so that all involved caregivers will be able to identify when the patient has met this standard. Such identifiers may include the following:

♦ Cardiac status stable as evidenced by _____ (parameters).
♦ Patient reports decrease or absence of shortness of breath (SOB), chest pain by _____.

♦ Patient verbalizes understanding of and adheres to medication regimens.

♦ Patient /caregiver verbalizes side effects and actions of anticoagulant therapy.

Agencies may choose to evaluate either global or focused outcome measures. Global outcome measures are those that pertain to all patients, such as their ability to perform ADLs, etc. Focused outcome measures pertain to a certain group of patients, such as those with cardiac conditions, pulmonary conditions, etc. These measures are based somewhat on the same conceptual approach as was used to develop Diagnostic Related Groups (DRGs) for hospitals and Resource Utilization Groups (RUGs) for nursing homes. Both DRGs and RUGs were developed to take into consideration patient characteristics that influence patient-level resource consumption or cost. DRGs have been somewhat effective in controlling hospital costs but have been less than perfect in cases in which the patient for some reason exceeded the baseline DRG reimbursement.

The Center for Health Policy Research developed a similar method of grouping patients, called quality indicator groups (QUIGs). QUIGs were developed for both acute and chronic conditions. Acute topics include orthopedic conditions (fractures, amputations, etc.), neurologic conditions (CVAs, head injuries, etc.), cardiac/peripheral vascular disease (CHF, angina, MI, others), and several other acute conditions. Included in this grouping are patients with oxygen therapy, IV/infusion therapy, parenteral/enteral nutrition, and ventilator therapy. Chronic QUIGs include such conditions as dependence in living skills, personal care, ambulation and mobility, pain, medication administration, and others. Patients may belong to more than one QUIG at a time and may have both acute and chronic conditions.

It is inevitable that patient outcomes will become tied in with the prospective payment system proposed by Medicare. Since reimbursement will be driven by the effectiveness with which nursing care improves patient outcomes, both management and staff will be concerned with providing the best outcomes possible. The increased involvement of managed care will make it necessary for clinical pathways to be developed and closely adhered to.

It is also important to understand and measure outcomes, as this is a requirement for certification by entities such as the Joint Commission on Accreditation of Healthcare Organizations (JCAHO). Since managed care is increasingly involved with not only payment, but measuring the effect of today's health care services, agencies that hope to obtain contracts must be accredited, certified, and show more cost-effective, positive outcomes than their competitors. Agencies that can demonstrate positive outcomes on a regular basis are more likely to obtain and retain managed care contracts, thereby prolonging their existence. Since the bulk of responsibility for determining and evaluating patient outcomes falls directly on the shoulders of the staff nurses and therapists, the style and content of all of Part II and this chapter on training are meant to be easily understandable and therefore easy to learn. Just as the introduction in Chapter 1 answered questions frequently asked by those who need to collect OASIS data, this chapter also answers some common questions. Examples have been provided to clarify content and help the reader apply the material to practice.

What Happens If I Mess Up?

Generally speaking, the OASIS questions are fairly self-explanatory and straight-forward in the information they are seeking. Each question specifically asks the assessor to answer with the way the patient responds 50% or more of the time. Specific qualifiers, such as discharge from a hospital or other facility within the past 14 days, have been underlined in order to catch the attention of the assessor and to attempt to prevent incorrect responses. A combination of assessment and interview will be necessary to accurately answer the questions, since some things can only be related to the assessor by the patient or caregiver. Each question gradually builds the knowledge base regarding the patient; by the time question *MO780—Management of Oral Medications* is reached by the assessor, many other questions have been asked that help determine the patient's ability to manage his/her medications. For instance, questions regarding cognitive abilities, anxiety level, and ability to perform ADLs and IADLs have already been responded to; more than likely a patient with altered cognitive abilities, high anxiety, and limited ability to perform ADLs will need some sort of assistance with medications. The entire process is a bio-psycho-social assessment of the client. Nothing is asked during this assessment that the nurse should not have been investigating prior to using the OASIS. In fact, at several agencies, staff nurses said the OASIS made their assessments easier by prompting appropriate questions and providing a place to document findings such as lack of caregiver, equipment management, and the ability to prepare meals.

It is, however, necessary for the assessor to thoroughly understand what each question is seeking to answer. If the assessor moves too quickly through the assessment before being completely comfortable with the MOO items, incorrect responses may be chosen that may affect the outcomes of care provided. For instance, evaluating a patient too high on the scale may result in little or no change in outcomes at the end of the assessment cycle when in fact the patient did improve from his previous status but the nurse had evaluated him at a higher status initially. Thus, a patient who was short of breath with moderate exertion (e.g., while dressing, using commode or bedpan, walking distances less than 20 feet) may have improved from SOB with minimal exertion, but since the evaluator marked the moderate exertion response at the initial visit, it appears the patient is worse, not better.

If speech therapy, occupational therapy, or physical therapy is required to assist in care of a patient, the OASIS assessment should demonstrate why the therapist is needed. A patient who has no difficulty chewing or swallowing and expresses him/herself with minimal difficulty may not justify a speech therapist visiting two or three times per week. Rest assured that these inconsistencies will not be missed by surveyors. All documentation, including the OASIS, must be consistent across the board.

In addition, trying to make an agency "look good" by having consistently positive outcomes may be problematic as well. Any agency that starts out with very ill patients who always improve consistently while on service may well be scrutinized. All patients do not get better—that is a fact everyone who works in health care and home care knows. Some improve and are discharged from services, some become worse and are discharged to nursing homes or die, and some simply continue on much the same with little or no improvement or worsening of condition (i.e. chronic illnesses). Agencies who have consistently better-than-average or lower-than-average patient outcomes will most likely be subject to review.

What Exactly Am I Looking For?

Understanding Each of the OASIS Items

What do these questions mean? OASIS items are identified by the use of numbers preceded by MO or MOO (i.e., MOO10, MO190). You may hear these referred to as "moo numbers," as in the sound a cow makes. Each of these identifiers is unique, and *the numbering must not be changed in any manner*, as all Medicare-certified agencies will be using the same numbers to collect data.

The entire set of MOO numbers may appear overwhelming when first reviewed. Because the structure of each question is in multiple-choice format, more space is taken up than if fill-in-the-blank or true-false queries had been used. Each item is specifically designed to elicit particular responses and has been extensively tested for reliability. It is imperative that nurses are familiarized

with each item on the assessment in order to feel comfortable using the tool and to gather meaningful data. Observe items where "Mark all that apply" or skip patterns are indicated. Select the response that indicates the patient's usual condition, one that he or she exhibits more than half the time. Be precise and judicious in the use of the "not applicable" (NA) and "unknown" (UK) responses.

The following paragraphs will dissect the OASIS question-by-question, with detailed information regarding what each response is seeking. Each nurse should carefully review this section prior to actually using the OASIS to gather patient data.

MOO10—Agency ID MOO10 seeks *only* the agency identifier. During the MEQA study, each participating agency was assigned an eight-digit identifying number for reporting data. This number was then used when the data was published, allowing benchmarking among agencies without actually knowing who the agencies were.

Currently it is not known whether a number will be assigned to the agency by Medicare, if the Medicare provider number will be used, or if some other form of identifier will be developed. Whatever is the case, the number must be used consistently; it may be wise to have the number preprinted on pen and paper forms or designed to permanently appear electronically as the response to this question if using a computer program.

MOO20—Patient ID (Identifying) Number This number can be totally numerical or a combination of alphanumerical identifiers. When the OASIS study began, the 50 pilot agencies were instructed to only include new admits into the study and not to go back to fill out retrospective admissions, 60 days, etc., on patients admitted prior to the study start date. In order to keep OASIS patients separate from other patients, many agencies chose to continue their original method of patient identification but to add an "O" to the number (i.e., 360-O), which separated the OASIS from the non-OASIS patients. At present, Medicare has issued no specifics as to how the patient identification must work, and probably they will not do so. Whatever method is chosen must be used consistently.

MOO30—Start-of-Care Date (SOC) The start-of-care (SOC) date is the six-digit number that reflects the date of the first Medicare billable service. This date remains unchanged on subsequent plans of treatment (POC) or re-certs (re-certifications) until the patient is discharged. Since there is space for two-digit numbers (e.g., 12/21/97), any single-digit entries should be preceded by a zero (e.g., 01/03/98). The start-of-care date should be the same on the 485 as it is on the OASIS form. The recertification date (60-day reassessment) could vary, but ideally the OASIS reassessment and the 485 should be completed at the same time.

The time frame used by the Center and the demonstration agencies and anticipated to be used by HCFA in the new COPs for agencies to complete the OASIS data set is from the 57–62 day of the certification cycle. This creates a significant problem with "turning around" the 485, since the physician's signature is required on the 485 *prior* to the beginning of the new re-certification period and prior to billing for services for that particular patient.

REMEMBER!

Whatever the final ruling for time of completion of the OASIS data set, keep in mind that if there are several policies to choose from, the strictest policy is binding. If your agency has a policy that states the signed 485 must be back in the office by seven days from the date it was sent for the signature, that policy *will* be upheld, and late 485s will be considered out of compliance by state surveyors. A thorough review of all agency policies should be undertaken to determine the feasibility of these dates relative to agency operations and state licensure as well as Medicare regulations.

MOO40—·Patient's Full Name Be sure you have spelled the patient's first and last name correctly with the middle initial and suffix, if available, exactly as you did on the HCFA Form 485.

MOO50—Patient State of Residence MOO50 requests the patient's state of residence *during the home care episode.* Where does the patient *actually* live? The majority of home health patients will live within the state where the services are provided, but if they do not, indicate the state of their primary residence.

MOO60—Patient Zip Code Use five-digit zip codes only. It may be necessary to find the zip code in the phone book white pages or call the postal service.

MOO63—Medicare Number Be sure to include any prefix or suffix and all letters attached to the number. Be sure the number is the same on the OASIS assessment and the 485 to prevent confusion. It is always necessary for the nurse or therapist to actually see the patient's Medicare card to obtain this information. Additionally, the card should be rechecked every time OASIS data is collected.

MOO64—Social Security Number

MOO65—Medicaid Number

MOO66—Birth Date (Patient's) Adequate space is allowed for the entire year of birth. Precede all single-digit numbers with a zero, thus 02/05/45. Again, check the date of birth carefully, as it is important for coverage/benefits as well as accuracy of demographic data.

MO69—Gender MO69 simply asks whether the patient's gender is male or female. Be sure to consistently check the correct box; it is a bit disconcerting when patients change sex in the middle of a certification period!

MOO72—Primary Referring Physician ID This number should correspond with the physician identifyer on the HCFA 485.

MOO80—Discipline of Person Completing Assessment What is the discipline of the person who is completing the assessment? Is it a registered nurse (RN), physical therapist (PT) or speech language pathologist/speech therapist (SLP/ST)? The assessment may be completed by any of the aforementioned disciplines, but should compliment the agency policy. Thus, if only registered nurses are allowed to admit patients and complete the 485s by agency policy, only registered nurses should complete the OASIS. If a patient is admitted as a "PT only" case, the physical therapist can fill out the assessment. Rather than using a nursing assessment, it may be simpler to integrate the OASIS questions into the physical therapy assessment and instruct all physical therapists who may be responsible for completing the form in its proper use.

MOO90—Date Assessment Information Recorded MOO90 simply asks the date the assessment information *is being recorded.* This may or may not duplicate the SOC date listed earlier. Again, add a zero to single-digit numbers.

MO100—This Assessment Is Currently Being Completed for the Following Reason: For what reason is the assessment currently being completed? Indicate only one response here. Is this the start-of-care or resumption of care after an inpatient stay? Resumption of care after an inpatient stay is used if the patient is in the hospital for 48 hours or more and is *not* discharged formally from the agency.

Originally, OASIS guidelines for the MEQA study required that patients be formally discharged from the agency if they were hospitalized for 48 hours or more and readmitted to the agency after discharge from the hospital. This indicated the start of a new episode of care, since the patient's condition undoubtedly had changed based on the reason for hospitalization. Some agencies disliked the 48-hour mandatory discharge and requested it be changed. The intent was to increase the number of hours the patient could be placed on "hold" to 72; what resulted was the option to discharge the patient as before or keep the patient on services. The catch: When a patient resumed care by the home health agency, he/she was re-certified with the completion of a new 485. The original SOC date could be retained, but the new data collection requirements at time of resumption of care were identical to the SOC. The 62-day data collection cycle began anew with the resumption and re-certification. Confused? But wait—if you're not careful, it can get even more confusing.

In the *proposed* Conditions of Participation (COPs), HCFA is requiring that the OASIS be administered within 48 hours of the patient's return from a hospital admission except when the hospital admission was for diagnostic tests "because we believe hospital admissions are predictive of likely changes in patient status and, therefore, important to capture for care planning and quality assessment and performance purposes."

Therefore, it may be easier to simply discharge the patient upon hospitalizations of 48 hours or more to prevent confusion about which form to use, how to determine re-certification dates, etc. Some agencies may develop a policy that discharges all patients upon admission to the hospital, regardless of the length of their stay. This is an important policy agencies must thoughtfully develop and one that must be consistently carried out by the staff.

COP ALERT!

This information is based on the CHPR study with the 50 agencies. The COPs will outline specifically how this is to be handled. Please refer to the most current COPs for detailed information.

Other reasons for completion of the form that can be listed in MO100 include:

♦ *Discharged from the agency—not to an inpatient facility*
♦ *Transferred to an inpatient facility—discharged from the agency*

♦ *Transferred to an inpatient facility—not discharged from the agency*
♦ *Died at home*
♦ *Re-certification reassessment (follow-up)*
♦ *Other follow-up*

In order to simplify the collection of this information, some agencies chose to identify SOC, reassessment, and discharge forms with different colors—e.g., green for admission (SOC), yellow or pink for reassessment (60-day follow-up), and blue for discharge. Whatever method is chosen, remember to observe the skip patterns closely.

MO140—Race/Ethnicity (as identified by patient)
Choices include White; Black or African-American; Hispanic or Latino; Asian, Native Hawaiian or Pacific Islander; American Indian or Alaskan Native and unknown. Please ask the patient to identify his race or ethnicity rather than guessing; this is important demographic information and could be used to specifically study a subset of patients by race/ethnicity.

MO150—Current Payment Sources for Home Care (mark all that apply) This is one question where the assessor is asked to *mark all that apply.* It is necessary for the assessor to specifically inquire regarding payment sources, and 11 choices plus "unknown" are listed. It is important that the appropriate sources be indicated, as this could be the first indication of the need for a social services referral or other assistance with finances.

MO160—Financial Factors (mark all that apply)
MO160 surveys the ability of the patient/family to meet basic health needs. Again, the assessor is asked to *mark all that apply.* This question is very important in providing care and ensuring positive outcomes, as patients who may seem noncompliant may simply be so because they can't afford the basic health care they require. Again, this is an area where social services can intervene. Drug companies often provide assistance for needy patients, and food pantries may provide necessary nourishment; what is needed is for someone to take actual steps to enroll the patient, assist with filling out forms, etc. Since this topic is often a sensitive area that patients may choose to avoid discussing, it may be necessary to use a combination of interview and assessment to accurately respond to this question.

MO170—From Which of the Following Inpatient Facilities Was the Patient Discharged During the Past 14 Days? (mark all that apply) MO170 asks *if* the patient has been discharged as an inpatient within the past 14 days, and it is possible that the patient may have been in more than one during this time period. Inpatient facilities can be acute, skilled, or custodial care. The assessor is requested to mark all that apply, since it is possible for a patient to have been discharged from an acute hospital to a skilled facility for a short stay within the past 14 days. This question also includes a "skip pattern," telling the assessor to *skip to MO200 if the NA box is checked.*

MO180—Inpatient Discharge Date (most recent) Even though the patient may have been in more than one facility in the past 14 days, *the discharge date requested is the last, or most recent.* Again, for single-digit dates, precede the number by a zero (i.e., 07). If the patient has *not been discharged* from an inpatient facility in the past 14 days, the assessor should *skip this item.*

MO190—Inpatient Diagnoses and Three-digit ICD-9 Code Categories for Only Those Conditions Treated During an Inpatient Facility Stay Within the Last 14 Days (no surgical or V-codes) The only diagnoses that should be considered here are those that required intervention. Thus, if a patient was admitted for pneumonia, which required hospitalization and treatment, but also has congestive heart failure, which did not require any treatment change during the hospitalization, only the pneumonia should be listed. If a diagnosis was not treated during an inpatient admission, do not list it. *If the patient was not discharged from an inpatient facility, this item should be skipped.*

All codes entered here must be medical— *no surgical or V-codes are allowed.* This is because the data set was devised to group patients into general categories (i.e., cardiac, pulmonary, integumentary, etc.) rather than specific diseases or conditions. This will become much clearer when your agency actually begins reviewing patient outcomes at the end of the data collection cycle. Again, if the patient was *not* discharged from an inpatient facility, this item should be *skipped.*

MO200—Medical or Treatment Regimen Change Within Past 14 Days Has the patient experienced a change in medical or treatment regimen (e.g., medication, treatment, or service change due to new or additional diagnosis, etc.) within the last 14 days? Has the physician ordered a new treatment, new medication, or new service within the past 14 days? This could be a new diagnosis or an exacerbation of an old one that resulted in a new treatment modality or service needed. This question is essentially asking why you are now in the home. In other words, *has something changed with the patient that would necessitate home health services?*

NURSING ALERT!

Watch this question; if answered incorrectly or in haste, it can cause many problems later. If there has been no change as just described, mark "no" and skip to MO220.

MO210—List the Patient's Medical Diagnoses and Three-digit ICD-9 Code Categories for Those Conditions Requiring Changed Medical or Treatment Regimen (no surgical or V-codes) MO210 asks the assessor to list the patient's medical diagnoses and three-digit ICD-9 code categories for those conditions requiring *changed* medical or treatment regimen. Again, no surgical or V-codes may be used. For example, perhaps Mrs. Jones has had an exacerbation of her current condition, congestive heart failure (CHF), and now requires an additional medication or an increased dose. Or perhaps she requires physical therapy for gait training as well as teaching regarding medication changes, thorough assessment for effectiveness of medication, etc. In this case the diagnosis would be CHF, and the ICD-9 code would be 428.0. (The data input program developed by the Center was only designed to hold three digits of the ICD-9 code. This supports the global view of the disease, disorder, etc., rather than the specific.) It is still appropriate to enter more than three digits *on the 485* to specify the disease process more precisely.

COP ALERT!

It is not known at this time what the COPs will specify regarding entering of the ICD-9 code. Please refer to the COPs for specific information regarding this category.

MO220—Conditions Prior to Medical or Treatment Regimen Change or Inpatient Stay Within Past 14 Days MO220 asks what conditions were present *prior* to medical or treatment regimen change or inpatient stay within the past 14 days. For example, the patient may have been admitted with one of the following preexisting conditions: urinary incontinence, indwelling/suprapubic catheter, intractable pain, impaired decision-making, disruptive or socially inappropriate behavior, or memory loss to the extent that supervision is required.

That information is to be indicated here. Further responses include:

- ◆ None of the above
- ◆ Not applicable
- ◆ Unknown

REMEMBER!

Be very careful with this question. It may be grounds for denial of payment for visits if you indicate that you are teaching to or providing care for a condition that *preceded* the hospital stay. After all, if the patient could contend with the problem prior to hospitalization, why can't they now? And if not, what has changed? Careful documentation here can potentially prevent denials.

In addition, if you indicate the patient has memory loss to the extent that supervision is required, you must be sure that all teaching is being done with the caregiver and not only to the patient! You *must* include teaching of the caregiver in your documentation, or the visits may be denied as a waste of time. Always think defensively and document as such.

MO230/MO240—Diagnoses and Severity Index These

two MOO numbers are frequently bundled together in assessment forms. Specifically, they are asking for diagnoses and severity index of *each problem* for which the patient is receiving home care and the ICD-9 code category. The assessor is also to rate the diagnoses using the severity index provided. The severity index follows:

- **0** Asymptomatic, no treatment needed at this time
- **1** Symptoms well controlled with current therapy
- **2** Symptoms controlled with difficulty, affecting daily functioning; patient needs ongoing monitoring
- **3** Symptoms poorly controlled; patient needs frequent adjustment in treatment and dose monitoring
- **4** Symptoms poorly controlled; history of rehospitalizations

MO230 asks for the primary diagnosis and ICD-9 code for this episode of care. **MO240** asks for other diagnoses for which care may be provided or which may be co-morbidities. Again, no surgical or V-codes can be used.

This particular category can be a minefield for agencies. It must be stressed to the assessors that if a patient

is actually a "0" or a "1," he/she probably doesn't require skilled care for that diagnosis, and provided care may well be denied. A rating of "2" will not support frequent home care visits for extensive periods of time. Assessing a patient as "3" or "4" will require more frequent home health visits and greater amounts of teaching. In fact, the patient may only need visits for the primary diagnosis; the other diagnoses may be currently under control.

NURSING ALERT!

Thorough, complete, thoughtful documentation is absolutely essential, with the assessor continuously painting a picture of all teaching, treatments, and other services in a way that assures reviewers of the need for acute care and the appropriateness of the care being provided. This area requires careful review by the quality assurance department prior to being placed on the chart.

MO250—Therapies the Patient Receives at Home (mark

all that apply) MO250 asks for information regarding therapies the patient receives *at home*. This includes only the therapies actually administered at home and *not* in outpatient facilities. Therapies included are:

- **1** IV or infusion therapy (excludes TPN)
- **2** Parenteral nutrition (TPN or lipids)
- **3** Enteral nutrition (nasogastric, gastrostomy, jejunostomy, or any other artificial entry into the alimentary canal)
- **4** None of the above

The assessor is asked to mark all that apply.

MO260—Overall Prognosis You must read this ques-

tion carefully and select the correct response. You are *not* expected to know *exactly* how well this patient will do, but in your opinion and based on your professional assessment and clinical experience and decision-making, how well do you *expect* him to recover?

MO270—Rehabilitative Prognosis MO270 relates to

your description of the patient's prognosis for *functional status:*

- **0** Guarded; minimal improvement expected
- **1** Good; marked improvement expected
- **UK** Unknown

Answer this question to the best of your ability; avoid using "unknown" unless you really have no idea if the patient can improve his functional status. Answering with a "0" or "1" is best.

MO280—Life Expectancy (physician documentation is not required)

This question simply asks if, in your opinion, the patient's life expectancy is greater than or less than 6 months. It isn't necessary to have this documented by the physician or have a Do Not Resuscitate (DNR) order in place. Simply speaking, do you think this patient will live for 6 more months or not? Is he/she extremely debilitated, very ill? Do you expect a good recovery from this episode of illness? Don't dwell on this question too much—just answer it with your best clinical judgment.

MO290—High-Risk Factors Characterizing This Patient (mark all that apply)

MO290 asks whether this patient has any high-risk factors such as heavy smoking, obesity, or alcohol or drug dependency. Again, a combination of interview and assessment approaches is necessary. In fact, you may not either assess or elicit this information at the initial assessment visit (SOC) but may be aware of it at reassessment (re-cert). If you believe the patient exhibits none of these factors, mark "none of the above"; if you are unsure, but believe there is a distinct possibility, indicate "UK" (unknown).

MO300—Current Residence

MO300 refers to the patient's *current* living arrangements. Does he currently live in:

1 Patient's owned or rented residence (house, apartment, or mobile home owned or rented by patient/couple/significant other)
2 Family member's residence
3 Boarding home or rented room
4 Board and care or assisted-living facility
5 Other (specify)

This question has no hidden meaning; it simply asks, *where does the patient live?*

MO310—Structural Barriers in the Patient's Environment Limiting Independent Mobility (mark all that apply)

What structural barriers in the patient's environment *do* or *potentially could* limit independent mobility? Keep the patient's endurance in mind. This also could indicate the need for a social service consult, since some community assistance may be available to build wheelchair ramps, widen doorways, etc. What is the severity of the barrier? Are there stairs inside the home that the patient *must* climb on a regular basis? On an optional basis? Stairs leading from inside the house to outside? How much will these barriers affect your patient's mobility?

MO320—Safety Hazards Found in the Patient's Current Place of Residence (mark all that apply)

The presence of safety hazards also could trigger a social service consult. Numerous uncorrected safety hazards may jeopardize the ability of the agency to provide safe care at home. Such findings must be documented in the clinical notes on the patient's agency record. Remember, a thorough safety assessment is necessary at the time of the initial visit anyway, you just are reminded to document it here.

MO330—Sanitation Hazards Found in the Patient's Current Place of Residence (mark all that apply)

This section could identify unsafe conditions that must be corrected before home care can be provided. For instance, if a patient is to receive intravenous therapy at home and a caregiver (or the patient) is to be taught, it is necessary to have adequate facilities to maintain cleanliness of the equipment, refrigerate medication until time to administer it, and prevent infection of the line and of other household members. A social service referral may address some of the problems; others may be solved by ingenious, creative staff; or the patients condition may simply be inappropriate for home care. Problems in this area should be reported to the case manager or supervisor.

MO340—Patient Lives With (mark all that apply)

MO340 seeks to determine if there is someone else inside the home besides the patient. Does the patient:

1 Live alone
2 Live with a spouse or significant other
3 Live with another family member
4 Live with a friend
5 Live with paid help (other than the home care agency staff)
6 Live with other than the above

REMEMBER!

Be sure to document thoroughly if the patient lives with someone who is able to provide or assist with his care. Keep in mind that the surveyors won't be able to determine this by the question alone and will investigate the situation further by reviewing your notes.

MO350—Assisting Person(s) Other Than Home Care Agency Staff (mark all that apply) Does anyone assist the patient other than home care agency staff? MO350 seeks to find out *who* if anyone may be providing the patient with assistance. *If* the response is "4" (none of the above) or "UK" (unknown), the assessor is directed to skip to another point in the assessment form. If there are assisting persons such as relatives, friends, neighbors, a person residing in the home (excluding paid help), or paid help, indicate the correct response.

MO360—Primary Caregiver Taking Lead Responsibility for Providing or Managing the Patient's Care, Providing the Most Frequent Assistance, etc. (other than home care agency staff) If the correct response is "0" (no one person) or "UK," the form skips to another section of the assessment.

NURSING ALERT!

If any of the *other* choices are made, document accurately *exactly* what these caregivers do for the patient. Just because an individual states they have taken the lead responsibility for providing or managing the patient's care doesn't mean that the care being provided is appropriate or adequate. For example, a patient can live with a spouse who takes lead responsibility for providing or managing the patient's care. This spouse may be elderly and infirm and unable to provide the personal care required for maintaining skin integrity or lacking the strength to safely ambulate a debilitated patient. Careful assessment and thorough documentation in this area can prevent the denial of payment for visits due to overuse of services.

MO370—How Often Does the Patient Receive Assistance from the Primary Caregiver? This question should be answered to the best of the assessor's ability since using the option "unknown" leaves a significant opening for denial of services. In addition to indicating how often the patient receives assistance from the primary caregiver, document exactly what the caregiver does and how successfully he/she does it. Read the responses carefully and give careful thought to your choice.

MO380—Type of Primary Caregiver Assistance (mark all that apply) This question is also very important, as

primary caregiver assistance can range from total personal care to providing housing or being the power of attorney for the patient without being involved in personal care. Document what the caregiver *actually does* for the patient. Avoid using "UK" if possible.

MO390—Vision with Corrective Lenses If the Patient Usually Wears Them MO390 seeks to determine the amount of visual impairment the patient currently exhibits and, ultimately, the effect this will have on safety in the home, patient teaching, and the ability of the patient to improve his/her level of function. Document limited vision in the clinical notes to justify the frequency and amount of care provided.

MO400—Hearing and Ability to Understand Spoken Language in Patient's Own Language (with hearing aids if the patient usually uses them) Responses here range from "0" (no observable impairment) to "4," which indicates the patient is unable to hear and understand familiar words or common expressions consistently, *or* the patient is nonresponsive. Again, please read the responses carefully to match the patient's situation closely. Document any hearing impairment in the clinical notes, particularly if there is the potential for this hearing loss to affect the outcomes of care.

MO410—Speech and Oral (Verbal) Expression of Language (in patient's own language) Is the patient able to express his needs clearly, completely, and easily in all situations with no observable impairment, or does he have some degree of impairment? How severe is it? Will it affect the outcomes of care? Document hearing impairment well.

MO420—Frequency of Pain Interfering with Patient's Activity or Movement MO420 requires pain to be measured on a 0–3 scale:

    0 No pain, or pain does not interfere with activity or movement
    1 Pain less often than daily
    2 Pain daily, but not constantly
    3 Pain all of the time

Once the level of pain has been determined, document any comments on pain management, such as:

◆ What is being used, how frequently, any improvement or regression?
◆ How is pain affecting the patient's ability to provide self-care?
◆ Can the pain be adequately managed?

This information may indicate a patient-related variance that can greatly affect expected outcomes.

MO430—Intractable Pain A definition of intractable pain is contained within the question,

> *Is the patient experiencing pain that is not easily relieved, occurs at least daily, and affects the patient's sleep, appetite, physical or emotional energy, concentration, personal relationships, emotions, or ability or desire to perform physical activity?*

REMEMBER!

Assess the patient carefully, discuss the type and frequency of pain, relief measures, and ability to perform ADLs. Answer the question with a "yes" or "no." Again, document intractable pain in the clinical notes.

MO440—Does This Patient Have a Skin Lesion or an Open Wound? (This excludes "Ostomies.") Specifically, *does the patient have a perfectly intact integument?* If not, respond "1" (yes) to the question.

If there is *no* break, skin tear, rash, irritation, stasis ulcer, pressure ulcer, surgical wound, or other break in the integumentary system, the correct response is "0" or (no). If this question is answered "no," the assessor is directed to *skip* to MO490, which discusses dyspnea or shortness of breath. This is another area where a rather large problem (skin condition) is broken down into three separate sections for which data are to be obtained—pressure ulcers, stasis ulcers, and surgical wounds.

NURSING ALERT!

All other breaks in the integument are considered a skin lesion or an open wound, but detailed information is not being collected for all the other possible injuries, such as skin tears, rashes, IV sites, etc. Anything other than a perfectly intact integument requires a "yes" response.

Some of the following MOO items will not refer to all types of wounds/lesions, but only to selected types as just discussed.

MO445—Does This Patient Have a Pressure Ulcer? If a pressure ulcer is present, mark "1" (yes); if not, mark "0" (no). If the response is "no," *skip* to MO468.

MO450—Current Number of Pressure Ulcers at Each Stage (circle one response for each stage) MO450 asks the assessor to circle the number of pressure ulcers present in each of the five categories developed by the Agency for Health Care Policy and Research (AHCPR) and listed in the AHCPR Guideline for Care of Pressure Ulcers (1994).

Read the responses carefully and mark the appropriate number in the appropriate stage. Response e asks if there is a least *one pressure ulcer* (in addition to those previously mentioned) that cannot be observed due to the presence of eschar or a nonremovable dressing, including casts. Respond to this question with "yes" or "no."

MO460—Stage of Most Problematic (Observable) Pressure Ulcer Again, use the AHCPR Pressure Ulcer Stages from MO450.

MO464—Status of Most Problematic (Observable) Pressure Ulcer Pressure ulcer status options include fully granulating, early/partial granulation, not healing, or NA (no observable pressure ulcer).

REMEMBER!

Answer MO450, MO460, and MO464 *only* if the patient actually has a pressure ulcer; if none has been observed, *skip* to MO468.

MO468—Does This Patient Have a Stasis Ulcer? MO468 simply asks if the patient has a stasis ulcer. If one is present, mark "1" (yes). If none is observed, mark "0" (no). Be certain to assess the patient carefully to avoid overlooking a stasis ulcer that may be present upon admission, or when assessing at a later date, one that was *not* observed at an earlier time.

Again, if the answer to MO468 is "no," the assessor is directed to go to MO482, the section asking, "Does the patient have a Surgical Wound?"

An agency may desire to make this section more comprehensive and improve the specificity of the documentation regarding pressure sores and stasis ulcers by using various assessment tools for documenting the status of wounds. Using the AHCPR guidelines for wounds and checking with companies that provide wound care products is often an efficient way to proceed.

COP ALERT!

The information provided here in MO468 can be carried over to the clinical documentation, an area that requires comprehensive, clear documentation to receive reimbursement. Often in audits this area is notoriously lacking in adequate documentation.

MO470—Current Number of Observable Stasis Ulcer(s)
MO470 asks for the current number of observable stasis ulcers (e.g., how many can you see during your assessment?). Responses vary from "0" (a stasis ulcer may be covered with a dressing that is not to be removed) to "4" or more.

MO474—Does This Patient Have at Least One Stasis Ulcer That Cannot be Observed Due to the Presence of a Nonremovable Dressing? This is to be answered "yes" or "no."

MO476—Status of Most Problematic (Observable) Stasis Ulcer Choose the best response that most closely describes the condition of the most problematic ulcer.

REMEMBER!

You will be comparing the ulcer 60 days from admission for improvement or deterioration.

MO482—Does This Patient Have a Surgical Wound?
MO482 asks if the patient has a wound that was caused during a surgical procedure such as a laparotomy. If the response is "no," the assessor is directed to *skip* to MO490, which relates to the patient's pulmonary status. If the answer is "yes," proceed to MO484.

MO484—Current Number of (Observable) Surgical Wounds What is the current number of *observable* surgical wounds? If a wound is partially closed *but has more than one opening*, consider each opening an individual wound. Again, assess the wound carefully to assure accurate documentation regarding the presence of wounds.

MO486—Does This Patient Have at Least One Surgical Wound That Cannot Be Observed Due to the Presence of a Nonremovable Dressing? The response is "yes" or "no."

MO488—Status of Most Problematic (Observable) Surgical Wound Responses for MO488 range from "1" (fully granulating) to "3" (not healing). There is also "NA," which can be indicated if the assessor is unable to observe the surgical wound. This fact should be well documented in the clinical notes and include:

♦ The reason the wound was not observed
♦ Any drainage or odor noted
♦ The presence or absence of redness at the site

COP ALERT!

According to the Medicare Guidelines for Coverage of Services,

Care of wounds (including but not limited to ulcers, burns, pressure sores, open surgical sites, fistulas, tube sites and tumor erosion site(s) when the skills of a licensed nurse are needed to provide safely and effectively the services necessary to treat the illness or injury is considered to be a skilled nursing service. For skilled nursing care to be reasonable and necessary to treat a wound, the size, depth, nature of drainage (color, odor, consistency and quantity), condition and appearance of the skin surrounding the wound must be documented in the clinical findings so that an assessment of the need for skilled nursing care can be made.

Coverage or denial of skilled nursing visits for wound care may not be based solely on the stage classification of the wound but rather must be based on all of the documented clinical findings. Moreover, the plan of care must contain the specific instructions for the treatment of the wound. Where the physician has ordered appropriate active treatment (e.g., sterile or complex dressings, administration of prescription medications, etc.) of wounds with the following characteristics, the skills of a nurse are usually reasonable and necessary:

A. Open wounds that are draining purulent or colored exudate or have a foul odor or for which the patient is receiving antibiotic therapy
B. Wounds with a drain or T–tube
C. Wounds that require irrigation or instillation of a sterile cleansing or medicated solution into several layers of tissue and skin and/or packing with sterile gauze
D. Recently debrided ulcers
E. Pressure sores (decubitus ulcers) with the following characteristics:

1. Partial tissue loss with signs of infection such as foul odor or purulent drainage
2. Full-thickness tissue loss that involves exposure of fat or invasion of other tissue such as muscle or bone

Also remember that orders for daily wound care must have a finite and predictable end listed. Please refer to the Medicare coverage of services for other types of wounds that may be covered for skilled care.

MO490—When Is the Patient Dyspneic or Noticeably Short of Breath?

Again, a combination of assessment and interview may be necessary here. Every response listed can be assessed during the initial patient visit. If the options are not visually assessed, ask the caregiver or patient when he/she is short of breath. It isn't necessary to actually pull out a tape measure and mark off 20 feet, but as closely as possible, estimate whether the patient can walk more or less than 20 feet without becoming dyspneic. You can use your own foot to simulate 1 foot of distance to be more accurate in your documentation. Other measures include asking the patient, "Do you become short of breath when:

♦ Walking
♦ Climbing stairs
♦ Eating, talking
♦ Performing ADLs
♦ Agitated
♦ At rest

MO500—Respiratory Treatments Utilized at Home (mark all that apply)

Does the patient require intermittent or continuous oxygen? Is he ventilator-dependent, continually or at night? Does he require continuous positive airway pressure (CPAP)? (Individuals with sleep apnea may use nasal CPAP when sleeping. Inquire about the possibility of previously diagnosed sleep apnea). Since respiratory treatments frequently become a way of life for many individuals, they may not think to mention it unless prompted. If none of the treatments are used, mark "none of the above."

MO510—Has This Patient Been Treated for a Urinary Tract Infection in the Past 14 Days?

Responses for MO510 range from "no" to "unknown," with "NA" indicating the patient is on prophylactic treatment for recurrent urinary track infections (UTI). Be sure to integrate this question *prior to MO520* because this question *skips* you to another section. Caution must be taken to keep the sequencing of forms correct so the assessor can collect the required data.

REMEMBER!

This question in MO510 is simple. Has the patient been treated for a UTI or not? If the patient is unsure, ask the caregiver. Examine his/her medications carefully. Phone the physician's office if the patient is unsure. Remember, the item asks *only* about *treatment*.

MO520—Urinary Incontinence or Urinary Catheter Presence

Response "0" of MO520 states, "No incontinence or catheter (includes anuria or ostomy for urinary drainage). Therefore, if the patient has no incontinence, no catheter, no anuria, or has an ostomy for urinary drainage, "0" is the correct response. If this response is chosen, you are asked to *skip MO530 and move on to MO540*, which discusses the gastrointestinal system.

Response "1" indicates the patient is incontinent. The patient is incontinent if he/she experiences total incontinence (involuntary voiding), occasionally dribbles, leaks, drips, or whatever. A large percentage of elderly individuals will fall into this category, even if they haven't totally lost control of their bladders. Response "2" indicates that the patient requires a urinary catheter (i.e., external, indwelling, intermittent, suprapubic). If that is the case, you are again asked to *skip to MO540*.

NURSING ALERT!

Question MO520 causes problems for many nurses; in fact, some have attempted to include another box that says "occasionally dribbles," since they don't think this indicates incontinence. For the purpose of the OASIS, it does. And remember, you can't add anything to the questions, so don't try to read into the question or try to write new ones—you *must* adhere to them as they are written.

MO530—When Does Urinary Incontinence Occur?

MO530 asks *specifically*, "When does urinary incontinence occur?" If the patient is "occasionally" incontinent, does the incontinence occur:

♦ With exertion, sneezing, coughing
♦ Only at night
♦ During the day and night

♦ The patient can prevent incontinence by following a timed-voiding program.

MO540—Bowel Incontinence Frequency The responses to MO540 are self-explanatory, and only one should be marked. Avoid using the "UK" (unknown) option unless absolutely necessary since no useful data can be obtained from it. If the patient has an ostomy for bowel elimination, mark "NA."

MO550—Ostomy for Bowel Elimination: Does This Patient Have an Ostomy for Bowel Elimination That (Within the Last 14 Days) (a) Was Related to an Inpatient Facility Stay, or (b) Necessitated a Change in Medical or Treatment Regimen? Responses to MO550 include:

  0 Patient does *not* have an ostomy for bowel elimination.
  1 Patient's ostomy was not related to an inpatient stay and did not necessitate change in medical or treatment regimen.
  2 The ostomy was related to an inpatient stay or did necessitate change in medical or treatment regimen.

In other words, has the patient had *any problems* with his/her ostomy? Perhaps it's relatively new, has developed problems, etc. The skilled nurse will most likely need to make increased visits to teach the patient regarding the change in medical or treatment regimen.

REMEMBER!

Document carefully in the clinical notes:

♦ The treatment plan
♦ Why you need to visit the patient
♦ Visit frequency and duration
♦ What you are teaching
♦ The patient's response

MO560—Cognitive Functioning (Patient's Current Level of Alertness, Orientation, Comprehension, Concentration, and Immediate Memory for Simple Commands) MO560 refers to the patient's level of functioning the *majority of the time.* This asks the assessor to determine the patient's current level of alertness, orientation, comprehension, concentration, and immediate memory for simple commands. Review all the possible responses and answer to the best of your ability.

NURSING ALERT!

This entire section can be problematic if the assessor answers the questions without carefully reading and digesting the options. While the response should indicate how the patient functions *the majority of the time,* if you indicate that the patient has *significant cognitive problems, be sure to direct teaching to the caregiver as well and document this in the clinical notes.* Nonreimbursement for the care can result if it appears the patient is unteachable and it has not been documented that the family or caregiver is involved in patient education.

MO570—When Confused (Reported or Observed) This can be observed by the assessor or reported by the patient or caregiver. If the patient is "occasionally confused," indicate the situation during which the confusion occurs. Mark only *one response* for this question.

MO580—When Anxious (Reported or Observed) Anxiety can be observed, self-reported, or reported by the caregiver or another individual. Please read the responses carefully and indicate as precisely as possible *when* the anxiety occurs. Again, try to avoid using "NA," since this doesn't mean that the patient *isn't anxious;* it means that the patient is actually *nonresponsive.*

MO590—Depressive Feelings Reported or Observed in Patient (mark all that apply) The responses to MO590 are actually arranged in increasing severity except that option 6 indicates *none of the feelings* reported or observed. Keep in mind that hopelessness and/or recurrent thoughts of death may be noted in the elderly population at varying times, particularly after a change in residence or the loss of a loved one. If the assessor receives any indication of such severe depression that suicide may be considered, he/she should notify the appropriate physician, family members, etc. If the patient isn't severely depressed but has mentioned death, this may be a good time to discuss living wills and advance directives with a patient who has indicated at admission that he/she doesn't have one yet.

MO600—Patient Behaviors (Reported or Observed) (mark all that apply) These behaviors can be observed by the assessor, self-reported by the patient, or reported by another individual. Again, mark all that apply. These behaviors indicate possible safety hazards, as the patient may have memory loss, show impaired decision-making ability, be verbally or physically abusive, exhibit disruptive, infantile, or socially inappropriate behavior, be delusional, hallucinatory, or exhibit paranoid behavior.

If "occasional" is marked, does the behavior occur at least once a week? If the condition is severe enough, the home health agency may be unable to provide safe care in the home. Or perhaps the patient can be safely cared for at home, but a qualified psychiatric nurse should be making the visits. If the agency does not provide this service, perhaps referral to another agency that does would be most appropriate for this patient.

MO620—Frequency of Behavior Problems (Reported or Observed)

MO620 asks for the *frequency* of behavior problems (reported or observed) such as wandering episodes, self-abuse, verbal disruption, physical aggression, etc. Since these behavior problems can also affect patient safety (as well as staff and family), determination of the frequency of occurrence of these behaviors is vital. Do they never occur or occur less than once a month, once a month, several times each month, several times a week, or at least daily? Remember that it is not necessary for the assessor to observe these behaviors; the family or caregiver may report them.

MO630—Is This Patient Receiving Psychiatric Nursing Services at Home Provided by a Qualified Psychiatric Nurse?

According to the description in the Medicare coverage of services, section 205.1,

> *Psychiatrically trained nurses are nurses who have special training and/or experience beyond the standard curriculum required for a registered nurse. The services of the psychiatric nurse are to be provided under a plan of care established and reviewed by a physician.*

Does the patient currently receive visits by a psychiatric nurse who fits this description? Respond by indicating "yes" or "no." If the patient does receive home care but exhibits these problems, it may be prudent to "share" the patient with a psychiatric nurse by alternating visits.

ADL/IADLs Section

Items MO640 through MO800 deal with the patient's ability to perform activities contributing to independent living, including both activities of daily living (ADLs) and instrumental activities of daily living (IADLs). What the patient actually does from day to day or could do in the future is not the issue. The assessor must measure only what the patient is able to do the day when the OASIS data is completed. To assist you in completing this section, remember:

- ♦ If the patient's ability to perform these activities varies somewhat, choose the response describing the ability more than 50% of the time.
- ♦ The "current" column should be completed for all patients; the "prior" column should be marked at start of care (or resumption of care) to describe the patient's ability 14 days prior to start of care.
- ♦ All items present the most independent level first, then proceed to the most dependent.
- ♦ The word "unable" is underlined the first time it describes a change from "able" to "unable" in the responses.
- ♦ Avoid the "UK" response if at all possible.
- ♦ Keep in mind that negative responses (decreased level of functioning) may indicate the need for a home health aide, physical therapy, occupational therapy, SLP/speech therapist, or registered dietician.

MO640—Grooming

Read these responses carefully before choosing one. Responses range from "0" (able to groom self unaided, with or without assistive devices or adapted methods) to "3" (patient depends entirely upon someone else for grooming needs).

For the admission assessment, a combination of assessment and interview techniques may be necessary; for re-certification information, it may be beneficial to have the assistance of the home health aide, physical therapist, and/or occupational therapist when completing this section. This question addresses the ability to manage personal care needs, *excluding bathing*.

MO650 and MO660—Ability to Dress Upper and Lower Body

Review the choices carefully. They are divided into four levels of ability:

0 The patient is able to get clothes out of closets and drawers, put them on, and remove them from the upper or lower body without assistance.

1 The patient is able to dress upper and lower body without assistance *if* clothing and shoes are laid out or handed to the patient.

2 Someone must help the patient put on upper body clothing or must help the patient put on undergarments, slacks, socks or nylons, and shoes.

3 Patient depends entirely upon another person to dress the upper or lower body.

MO670—Bathing

The response to this section *does not include grooming*, which was covered in MO640. As in the previous questions, the ability to wash the entire body ranges from the ability to do so independently to the inability to effectively participate in bathing and the need to be totally bathed by another person. Read each response carefully; each is designed to indicate a specific level of dependence. The response to these questions, combined with responses to previous questions related to self-care, either directly or indirectly will help justify the amount and frequency of assistance the patient requires.

REMEMBER!

Your ultimate goal is to improve the patient's outcomes based on the care you provide. Do not encourage dependence to maintain services in the home.

MO680—Toileting   MO680 refers to the ability of the patient to get to and from the toilet or bedside commode. Once again, the ability ranges from independence to total dependence upon another person.

MO690—Transferring   MO690 pertains to the patient's ability to transfer self:

- ◆ To move from bed to chair
- ◆ To move on and off toilet or commode
- ◆ To get into and out of the tub or shower
- ◆ To turn and position self in bed if the patient is bedfast
- ◆ The amount of assistance the patient needs to get up in a chair, to transfer in the bathroom, or to turn self in bed.

Choices range from independent transfer to total inability to transfer or turn self in bed. Read the responses carefully and choose the one that most closely fits your patient 50% or more of the time.

MO700—Ambulation/Locomotion   MO700 describes the patient's ability to *safely* walk or use a wheelchair on a variety of surfaces. Keep in mind that some patients who *can* ambulate often do so in an unsafe manner. Read the responses carefully. How does the patient move about 50% or more of the time? Does he/she do so independently on all types of surfaces, either walking or in a wheelchair? Is the patient able to do so with the use of a walker or cane? Is he/she bedfast, unable to ambulate or be up in a chair?

MO710—Feeding or Eating   MO710 discusses the patient's ability to feed him/herself meals and snacks. *This section does not pertain to preparing the food to be eaten, but to the actual process of eating, chewing, and swallowing.* Based on your assessment, is the patient able

to independently feed him/herself, or are various levels of assistance needed?

NURSING ALERT!

If the patient has difficulty chewing and swallowing, consider the services of a speech/language pathologist or dietician. Also keep in mind the potential for Master's in Social Work (MSW) intervention for referral assistance re: meal preparation and other tasks such as housekeeping, laundry, shopping, etc.

MO720—Planning and Preparing Light Meals   If the patient does not routinely plan and prepare meals, could he/she physically, cognitively, and mentally complete the task if required? This doesn't ask if the patient wants to or likes to, but if he/she *can* fix a sandwich or cereal or reheat delivered meals. Don't be encouraged to provide services the patients are capable of performing for themselves. The intent of home care services is to return the patient to a level at which he/she can perform as much self-care as possible, not to foster or otherwise encourage dependency.

MO730—Transportation   MO730 concerns transportation, the physical and mental ability to *safely* use a car, taxi, or public transportation (bus, train, subway). Bear in mind that this question may negate homebound status. This question could be answered positively in that the patient *can* independently drive a regular or adapted car or use a regular or handicap-accessible bus; homebound status is built around the fact that he/she actually *does* leave the home frequently. *Answer the question honestly and to the best of your knowledge.*

If the patient is able to leave home by his/her own transportation, or even with the assistance of a caregiver, carefully document the reason the patient is confined to the home and indicate that it is a "considerable and taxing effort" for the patient to leave the home.

COP ALERT!

Never forget to document homebound status accurately and thoroughly. Always refer to the current Medicare guidelines for coverage for specific homebound situations.

MO740—Laundry MO740 refers to the patient's ability to do his/her own laundry—to carry laundry to and from the washing machine, to use the washer and dryer, and to wash small items by hand. Once again, this does not refer to the patient's *desire* to do laundry, *just his/her ability to do so.*

The "0" response means the patient has the ability to independently take care of all laundry tasks *or* is physically, cognitively, and mentally able to do laundry and access facilities, but has not routinely performed laundry tasks in the past (i.e., prior to this home care admission). Could he/she physically, cognitively, and mentally do the laundry if necessary? Please review the options carefully and choose the one that best describes your patient.

MO750—Housekeeping MO750 describes the patient's ability to safely and effectively perform both light housekeeping and heavier cleaning tasks. If an individual does not routinely perform a particular task, could he/she do so if required? Is he/she physically, cognitively, and mentally able to do housekeeping? And remember, this doesn't mean housekeeping based on *your* standards but on those of the patient; what seems cluttered to you may be just the way the patient wants it. However, be sure the patient isn't in danger from the clutter in the house.

MO760—Shopping MO760 discusses the patient's ability to plan for, select, and purchase items in a store and to carry them home or arrange delivery. Again, be careful with the answer you choose for this question; if the patient is able to leave the home frequently for shopping excursions, he/she probably negates the homebound requirement. Choose the answer that best describes your patient. If he/she does not routinely perform this task, could he/she physically, cognitively, and mentally do so if necessary?

MO770—Ability to Use Telephone MO770 relates to the patient's ability to use the telephone and to answer, dial numbers, and effectively communicate using this instrument. This question is fairly clear, and the responses should not cause confusion. Keep in mind your patient's safety; if he/she can't use the telephone effectively to communicate, what will he/she do in an emergency? How will you ensure safety for your patient? Carefully document all interventions related to patient safety.

MO780—Management of Oral Medications MO780 examines the patient's ability to prepare and take all prescribed oral medications reliably and safely, including the correct dosage at the appropriate times/intervals. This excludes injectable and IV medications. *Again, this refers to ability, not compliance or willingness.* The following questions help clarify this section:

♦ Is the patient able to manage his/her own medications?
♦ Does he/she take them appropriately?
♦ Could the patient do so if he/she so desired? (This could be the patient who knows he/she is to take one blood pressure pill daily but chooses to only take half a pill to save money or the patient who takes more medication than has been prescribed because he/she believes "more is better.") What about the elderly individual who chooses not to take her diuretic as ordered because it leads to visiting the restroom too often and it's too hard to do so?
♦ Is the patient able to take medications correctly if someone else sets them up or if he/she is reminded daily to take the medications?
♦ Is the patient unable to take the medication unless someone else administers it?
♦ Is there a willing and able caregiver?
♦ Could a neighbor be enlisted to remind the patient to take his/her medications?
♦ How much and what type of interventions will you need to develop to help this patient successfully take his/her medications?

Respond to the question to the best of your knowledge by using your assessment skills and interview of the patient/caregiver. Be careful not to spend a lot of time dissecting this question.

MO790—Management of Inhalant/Mist Medications Does the patient require inhalant/mist medications? MO790 refers to this type of patient. Remember this refers to inhalant/mist medications *only.* Some questions to help in your assessment are:

♦ Can he/she use nebulizers and metered dose inhalers (MDIs) reliably and safely?
♦ How much assistance is required?
♦ How much teaching?
♦ Should a registered respiratory therapist be consulted for the appropriate teaching?
♦ Would the use of a "spacer" help this patient be compliant?
♦ Would the assistance of an occupational therapist help the patient develop the ability to maneuver the MDI?

Answer the question, then plan your interventions. This shows how your care plan and 485 can be developed with the use of the OASIS.

MO800—Management of Injectable Medications MO800 refers to the patient's *ability* to prepare and take all prescribed injectable medications reliably and safely, including the correct dosage at the appropriate times/intervals. *This excludes IV medications.* Remember, you're looking for the *ability, not willingness* of the patient to self-administer injectables. Some helpful questions for this section are:

♦ Can the patient independently prepare and administer the medication?
♦ Can he/she do so if individual syringes are prepared in advance by someone else *or* if he/she is given daily reminders?
♦ Is he/she unable to take injectable medications unless they are administered by someone else?

Other responses include "NA" (no injectable medications ordered) and "UK." Avoid using "UK" if at all possible.

COP ALERT!

Medicare isn't going to pay indefinitely for nursing visits to administer injectables if there is any possibility of someone else (caregiver, spouse, etc.) learning to do so. Explore all the options. Document findings carefully and completely.

MO810—Patient Management of Equipment (Includes Only Oxygen, IV/Infusion Therapy, Enteral/Parenteral Nutrition Equipment or Supplies)

MO810 is seeking to determine how the patient manages his/her medical equipment. This relates *only* to oxygen, IV/infusion therapy, and enteral/parenteral nutrition equipment or supplies. If more than one type of equipment is being used, determine which one requires *the most assistance.* For instance, the patient may be able to manage his/her oxygen without extreme hardship but has considerably more problems managing IV therapy or the pump for enteral nutrition. If the patient requires *none* of the listed equipment, "NA" should be marked and the assessor directed to skip the next question.

REMEMBER!

Read all the options carefully and remember that this question *does not address compliance or willingness, but only ability.*

MO820—Caregiver Management of Equipment (Includes Only Oxygen, IV/Infusion Therapy, Enteral/Parenteral Nutrition Equipment or Supplies)

MO820 asks how well the caregiver can manage equipment required for the patient's care. Included are oxygen, IV/infusion equipment, enteral/parenteral nutrition, and ventilator therapy equipment or supplies. If the patient uses no equipment of this type, this question should be skipped. If more than one type of equipment is being used, answer the question based on the equipment for which the most assistance is required.

Again, *only ability is addressed, not compliance or willingness.* If this question identifies the presence of a caregiver who can successfully manage the patient's equipment, visits for teaching the management of this equipment will be very limited.

This is the final question to be used at start of care. The following two questions are included in the reassessment that is done at re-certification (57–62 day of care).

Additional Questions for Re-certification

MO830—Emergent Care   MO830 refers to *emergent care.* Emergent care means an *unscheduled visit* to the hospital or emergency facility. For example, if the patient went to the emergency room and then was hospitalized, the patient *did* receive emergent care. If the patient was "held" at the hospital for observation and then released, the patient *did* receive emergent care. Please respond to this question to the best of your ability. Occasionally patients "disappear" and can't be found when the scheduled visit is supposed to be made. It is very important that all effort be made to locate the patient by contacting friends, family, caregivers, the physician's office, or others.

MO840—Emergent Care Reason   MO840 asks the reason the patient/family sought emergent care. This question directs the assessor to mark all reasons that apply. If the reason is unknown, indicate "UK." Some of these problems indicate sentinel events that may have a negative effect on the outcomes of that patient's care.

Additional Questions When the Patient Is Admitted to an Inpatient Facility or Discharged from the Agency

The remaining options include data items collected at inpatient facility admission or discharge *only.*

MO855—To Which Inpatient Facility Has the Patient Been Admitted? Indicate if the patient was admitted to a hospital, rehabilitation facility, nursing home, or hospice. If there was no inpatient facility admission but the patient was discharged, mark "NA."

NURSING ALERT!

Skip patterns appear here as well:

♦ If the response is "hospital," the assessor is instructed to skip to MO890.
♦ If to rehabilitation facility, skip to MO903.
♦ If to nursing home, skip to MO900.
♦ If to hospice, skip to MO903.

Be aware of and follow the skip patterns.

MO870—Discharge Disposition MO870: Where is the patient after discharge from your agency? Choose only *one* response here. Options include the following:

1 Patient remained in the community (not in hospital, nursing home, or rehab facility).
2 Patient transferred to a noninstitutional hospice (skip to MO903).
3 Unknown because patient moved to a geographic location not served by this agency (skip to MO903).
UK Other unknown (skip to MO903).

MO880—After Discharge, Does the Patient Receive Health, Personal, or Support Services or Assistance? (mark all that apply) This question is seeking information regarding assistance or services provided by family and friends and other community resources such as meals-on-wheels, homemaker assistance, transportation assistance, assisted living, board and care, etc.

REMEMBER!

If the patient is admitted to a facility, this question should be skipped. Once this question has been answered, skip to MO903.

MO890—If the Patient Was Admitted to an Acute Care Hospital, for What Reason Was He/She Admitted? Options include emergent, urgent, and elective care.

Emergent care is unscheduled, such as what may occur after a fall resulting in fractures or lacerations.
Urgent care is care scheduled within 24 hours of admission.
Elective hospitalization is scheduled more than 24 hours before admission (as for surgery).

Answer these questions to the best of your ability. Again, the "UK" option exists.

MO895—Reason for Hospitalization (mark all that apply) More than one of the options may apply; mark all that do. The categories are classified much the same way as the OASIS admission assessment. A patient can be admitted for a medication problem, injury from a fall, respiratory problem, wound, endocrine problem, GI bleeding or obstruction, CHF or heart failure, myocardial infarction, chemotherapy, scheduled surgical procedure, urinary tract infection, IV catheter-related infection, deep vein thrombosis, pulmonary embolism, uncontrolled pain, psychotic episode, and of course, other reasons as well. If "other than the above" is chosen, the OASIS directs you to skip to MO903.

MO900—For What Reason(s) Was the Patient Admitted to a Nursing Home (mark all that apply) Was the patient admitted for therapy services, respite care, hospice care, permanent placement, because he/she was unsafe for care at home, for another unspecified reason, or is the reason simply unknown (UK)? (If "UK," go to MO903.)

MO903—Date of Last (Most Recent) Home Visit This may or may not be the date of discharge. For example, the last skilled nursing visit may have occurred on Tuesday; then the patient entered the hospital unexpectedly and was discharged on Thursday before the next scheduled visit. Complete the OASIS using the date (and assessment) from the *last visit* (here, the one on Tuesday).

MO906—Discharge/Transfer/Death Date Enter the appropriate date in the indicated spaces; if the date is a single digit, precede this digit with a "0." The date of death should only be used if the patient died *at home*. If for some reason this date is unknown, mark "UK."

Using OASIS Data as Triggers for Referrals for Other Services

The OASIS data set was designed to be used by the professional services of nurses and therapists). Some agencies will limit the use of the assessment form to registered nurses or to only the skilled service that is admitting or discharging the case. As in all situations, agency policy should be followed because Medicare regulations do not specifically govern these policies. At times, it is difficult to determine when to share care with other disciplines or specialty programs for assistance with certain aspects of patient care. Several of the OASIS questions are designed to help the nurse see and document more clearly when referral to another service is indicated.

The staff nurse or appropriate agency designee who determines that a referral is needed can use the information in Figures 4–1 and 4–2 on pages 59–64, OASIS Triggers for Referral, to assist in identifying a potential need for service. Covered in these figures are referrals to the services of medical social worker (MSW), physical therapist (PT), occupational therapist (OT), speech/language pathologist (S/LP), dietician, Hospice, and other specialty services such as diabetes educator (CDE), enterostomal therapist (ET), or other specialty programs that may be available in the agency.

To use Figure 4–1, the OASIS items are listed in the left-hand column of the form by MOO numbers, with the disciplines identified across the top portion. An asterisk in the column beneath each discipline identifies whether a referral to this particular discipline would be beneficial if the patient is scored by a certain number in the specific MOO section. For example, for MO160, financial factors limiting the ability of the patient/family to meet basic needs, referral to an MSW is recommended if any of the options (i.e., 1,2,3, or 4) are chosen. Figure 4–2 is a quick reference guide to 4–1.

NURSING ALERT!

To help learn the MOO numbers and the Trigger for Referral Table in your practice, try the following exercise: Choose a patient from your caseload, and using one of the two sample assessment forms that include OASIS information found in Appendix B and C, complete the assessment of the patient using the form. By doing this exercise alone, in a small group, or as an in-service, the assessor can become familiar with the data set before using it directly on a home visit.

Figure 4–1 *OASIS Triggers for Referral to Other Services.*

MO #s	MSW	PT	OT	ST	Dietician	Hospice	Other Specialty Services
MO 150							
3	*						
5	*						
6	*						
10–11	*						
MO 160							
1 thru 4	*						
MO 170							
2	*	*	*	*			
3	*	*	*	*			
MO 220							
1							
2							*
3						*	
4	*						
5	*						
6	*						
MO 250							
1	*				*		*
2	*				*		*
3	*				*		*
MO 260							
0						*	
1							
MO 280							
0							
1						*	
MO 290							
1	*						
2					*		
3	*						
4	*						

Figure 4-1   *Continued*

MO #s	MSW	PT	OT	ST	Dietician	Hospice	Other Specialty Services
MO 310							
1	*	*					
2	*	*					
3	*	*					
4	*	*					
MO 320							
1 thru 10	*						
MO 330							
1 thru 12	*						
MO 340							
1	*						
MO 350							
3	*						*
4	*						*
MO 360							
0	*						*
UK	*						*
MO 370							
1	*						*
2	*						*
MO 380							
1 thru 7	*						*
MO 390							
1	*						*
2	*						*
MO 400							
2	*						
3	*						*
4	*						*
MO 410							
2				*			
3	*			*			
4	*			*			
5	*			*			

Figure 4-1 *Continued*

MO #s	MSW	PT	OT	ST	Dietician	Hospice	Other Specialty Services
MO 420							
2	*	*	*				*
3	*	*	*			*	*
MO 430							
1	*					*	*
MO 440							
1					*		*
MO 445							
1					*		*
MO 468							
1		*					*
MO 476							
3					*		*
MO 482							
1							*
MO 490							
1		*	*				
2		*	*				
3	*	*	*				
4	*	*	*			*	*
MO 500							
1 thru 3							*
MO 520							
1							*
2							*
MO 530							
1							*
2							*
MO 540							
2							*
3							*
4							*
5							*

Figure 4-1   *Continued*

MO #s	MSW	PT	OT	ST	Dietician	Hospice	Other Specialty Services
MO 550							
1							*
2							*
MO 560							
2	*						
3	*						
4	*						*
MO 570							
3	*						
4	*						
NA						*	
MO 580							
3	*						
NA						*	
MO 590							
1 thru 5	*						*
MO 600							
1 thru 7	*						*
MO 610							
1 thru 6	*						*
MO 620							
1 thru 5	*						
MO 640							
1 thru 3	*	*	*				*
MO 650							
1 thru 3	*	*	*				*
MO 660							
1 thru 3	*	*	*				*
MO 670							
2 thru 5	*	*	*				*
MO 680							
1 thru 4	*	*	*				*
MO 690							
1 thru 5	*	*	*			*	

Figure 4-1 *Continued*

MO #s	MSW	PT	OT	ST	Dietician	Hospice	Other Specialty Services
MO 700							
1 thru 5		*	*				*
MO 710							
1 thru 5				*	*		*
MO 720							
1 thru 2	*		*		*		*
MO 730							
1 thru 2	*	*	*				*
MO 740							
1 thru 2	*		*				*
MO 750							
1 thru 4	*		*				*
MO 760							
1 thru 3	*		*		*		*
MO 770							
1 thru 5	*		*	*			*
MO 780							
1 thru 2	*		*	*			*
MO 790							
1 thru 2		*	*				*
MO 800							
1 thru 2	*						*
MO 810							
1 thru 4	*	*	*				*
MO 820							
1 thru 4	*						*
MO 840							
1 thru 9	*						*

Figure 4-2 *Summary of Possible Referral Related to MOO Numbers.*

MSW	PT	OT	ST	Dietician	Hospice	Specialty Services
MO150	MO170	MO170	MO170	MO250	MO220 (3)	MO220 (2)
MO160	MO270	MO420	MO410	MO290	MO260	MO250
MO170	MO310	MO490	MO710	MO440	MO280	MO350 (3, 4)
MO220	MO420	MO640	MO770	MO445	MO420	MO360 (3,4)
MO250	MO468	MO650	MO780	MO476	MO430	MO370 (1, 2)
MO290	MO490	MO660		MO710	MO490 (4)	MO380 (1–7)
MO310	MO640	MO670		MO720	MO570 (NA)	MO390 (1, 2)
MO320	MO650	MO680		MO760	MO580 (NA)	MO400 (3, 4)
MO390	MO660	MO690			MO690	MO429 (2, 3)
MO400	MO670	MO700				MO430 (1)
MO410	MO680	MO720				MO440 (1)
MO420	MO690	MO730				MO445 (1)
MO430	MO700	MO740				MO468 (1)
MO490	MO730	MO750				MO473 (3)
MO560	MO790	MO760				MO482 (1)
MO570	MO810	MO770				MO490 (4)
MO580		MO780				MO500 (1–3)
MO590		MO790				MO520 (1, 2)
MO600		MO800				MO530 (1, 2)
MO610		MO810				MO540 (2–5)
MO620						MO550 (1, 2)
MO640						MO560 (4)
MO650						MO590 (5)
MO660						MO600 (7)
MO670						M610 (6)
MO680						MO640 (1–3)
MO690						MO650 (1–3)
MO720						MO660 (1–3)
MO730						MO670 (2–5)
MO740						MO680 (1–4)
MO750						MO680 (1–4)
MO780						
MO800						
MO810						
MO820						
MO840						

Learning OASIS by the Functional Assessment Approach

5

Leslie Jean Neal, PhD, RN, CRRN

Introduction

The OASIS information gathered by the professional on admission, follow-up, and discharge is based on the assessor's ability not only to understand the question, but also to clinically determine if improvement, decline, or stability is present as compared to previous data collections; thus mastering and refining functional assessment skills is critical. This chapter discusses several items in the data set that are easier to learn and better understood when using a functional assessment strategy as the base. It is suggested that assessors study this section in addition to Chapter 4 to improve their ability to judge *to the best of their ability* how to score patients using the OASIS data set.

Why Functional Assessment and Outcomes?

As stated throughout this book, it is essential that the assessors responsible for collecting OASIS information thoroughly understand the questions and ask them consistently just as they are worded. Chapter 4 provided an overview of the OASIS data set in the section, "What Exactly Am I Looking For? Understanding each of the OASIS items." That section is helpful in assuring that assessors understand the meanings of the various M00 number categories so that they can implement the assessment consistently.

Several of the outcomes measured by the OASIS data set are functional outcomes that pertain to either activities of daily living (ADL) or instrumental activities of daily living (IADL). Throughout the research, changes in functional status have emerged as extremely important when developing an outcome measure system for home care. (Shaughnessy & Crisler, 1995, pp. 2–10). The four major reasons for this focus on functional ability when looking at OBQI and OASIS are:

1. A given amount of independence in functioning (both ADL and IADL) is necessary to remain at home. (This amount depends on the patient's home support system and physical environment.)
2. Even when care is specifically targeted at changing a physiologic, cognitive, or emotional problem, the end result of care is often to permit the patient to function better.
3. After considerable review, discussion, and debate, the many clinical panels convened through the demonstration project converged on functional outcomes as essential.
4. Empirical analyses show that functional outcomes tend to be a good barometer of an agency's performance in other areas (Shaughnessy & Crisler, 1995, pp. 2–11).

This focus on a client's ability to function is included among several questions in the OASIS data set. While many people consider "function" to be related mostly to ADL and mobility, it actually encompasses much more. This chapter includes:

1. A description of the most common instruments used to perform a functional assessment.
2. A discussion of each of the OASIS questions (listed by M00 number as in Chapter 4) *that are relevant to functional assessment.* Some of the

OASIS questions that relate to the assessment of the environment and the client's safety in the home are also included because it is important for the home care professional to be able to determine whether the client has the functional ability to navigate his/her environment safely. Note that not *all* OASIS data items are discussed in this section of the chapter, only the ones that need clarification relative to functional assessment. Many are obvious and need no clarification, and those will *not* be discussed.

3. Tips about collecting this information quickly and efficiently. These are included throughout the chapter to assist the assessor in obtaining the most accurate and consistent data in the most efficient way.

Common Functional Assessment Instruments

OASIS items are to be integrated into an agency's current forms *exactly as they are worded.* As OASIS is integrated within an agency's existing paperwork system, if there are items in OASIS that are duplicated on existing forms, the guidelines require that you replace the similar question with the OASIS question(s). For agencies that have been assessing activities of daily living, any existing ADL measurement scales and definitions must be replaced with OASIS ones. In this chapter, various OASIS items that measure functional ability are discussed in relation to several functional assessment tools extensively used in health care. This approach is taken to help the assessor learn what the OASIS questions mean and how to score the patient using the OASIS data set. It is not recommended that any of these forms be used by an agency to collect additional information or to add to the already overwhelming amount of paperwork.

Many different instruments are used to measure functional ability (Mosqueda, 1994). Three common tools that have been used extensively will be presented here: the Barthel Index, the Functional Independence Measure (FIM), and the PULSES Profile. All three have been tested for reliability and validity and are presented to give the assessor a broader understanding of the ways to measure a person's function while learning how to use the OASIS data set. The home care professional typically does not have the time to assess functional ability using several tools, but familiarity with these tools can help in understanding the kind of information being requested when the OASIS asks about functional ability.

The Barthel Index

The Barthel Index (Display 5–1) (Mahoney & Barthel, 1965) is a simple-to-use tool for assessing whether the client is independent or requires assistance with basic ADL. Each activity is rated "0," "5," or "10," depending on the specific activity and whether or not the client needs assistance performing it. A total score of 100 means the client "is continent, feeds himself, dresses himself, gets up out of bed and chairs, bathes himself, walks at least a block, and can ascend and descend stairs" (Mahoney & Barthel, 1965, p. 62). This score does not mean the client can necessarily live alone, just that he should not require attendant care.

Since it was first published, the Barthel Index has been modified in various ways and tested with patients to see whether it remains valid for measuring functional ability. It is still used and is applicable to a variety of settings including home care. The Barthel Index can be helpful when attempting to assess functional ability for OASIS because it is very simple to use and can be performed quickly. As indicated, the authors of the tool have provided helpful guidelines for determining whether the client is independent or needs assistance. However, the Barthel Index measures *basic* ADL: feeding, moving, bathing, toileting, bowel and bladder management, and dressing. It does *not* measure instrumental ADL (IADL), which includes activities such as cooking and shopping. That is why a total score of 100 means the patient is independent with regard to these basic ADLs but does not necessarily mean the patient can live alone.

Functional Independence Measure (FIM)

The Uniform Data System for medical rehabilitation, called the Functional Independence Measure (FIM; Figure 5–1), also measures basic ADL and communication and social cognition. It is particularly useful for measuring "disability and outcomes of rehabilitation" (Pollack, Rheault, & Stoeker, 1996, p. 1056).

Social cognition and communication are important to measure because they impact whether or not the client

Figure 5–1 *Functional Independence Measure*

TABLE
FUNCTIONAL INDEPENDENCE MEASURE (FIM)

LEVELS		
	7 Complete Independence (Timely, Safely) 6 Modified Independence (Device)	NO HELPER
	Modified Dependence 5 Supervision 4 Minimal Assist (Subject = 75%+) 3 Moderate Assist (Subject = 50%+) **Complete Dependence** 2 Maximal Assist (Subject = 25%+) 1 Total Assist (Subject = 0%+)	HELPER

	ADMIT	DISCHG	FOL-UP
Self Care			
A. Feeding	___	___	___
B. Grooming	___	___	___
C. Bathing	___	___	___
D. Dressing - Upper Body	___	___	___
E. Dressing - Lower Body	___	___	___
F. Toileting	___	___	___
Sphincter Control			
G. Bladder Management	___	___	___
H. Bowel Management	___	___	___
Mobility			
Transfer:			
I. Bed, Chair, W/Chair	___	___	___
J. Toilet	___	___	___
K. Tub, Shower	___	___	___
Locomotion			
L. Walk / Wheelchair	w ___ c ___ ___	w ___ c ___ ___	w ___ c ___ ___
M. Stairs	___	___	___
Communication			
N. Comprehension	a ___ v ___ ___	a ___ v ___ ___	a ___ v ___ ___
O. Expression	v ___ n ___ ___	v ___ n ___ ___	v ___ n ___ ___
Social Cognition			
P. Social Interaction	___	___	___
Q. Problem Solving	___	___	___
R. Memory	___	___	___
TOTAL	☐	☐	☐

Source: Uniform Data System for Medical Rehbilitation (1993), UB Foundation Activities. SUNY at Bufalo, NY. Used with permission.

Display 5-1 *Barthel Index*

	With Help	**Independent**
1. Feeding (if food needs to be cut up = help)	5	10
2. Moving from wheelchair to bed and return (includes sitting up in bed)	5–10	15
3. Personal toilet (wash face, comb hair, shave, clean teeth)	0	5
4. Getting on and off toilet (handling clothes, wipe, flush)	5	10
5. Bathing self	0	5
6. Walking on level surface (or if unable to walk, propel wheelchair) *score only if unable to walk	*10	*15
7. Ascend and descend stairs	5	10
8. Dressing includes tying shoes, fastening fasteners)	5	10
9. Controlling bowels	5	10
10. Controlling bladders	5	5

A patient scoring 100 BI is continent, feeds himself, dresses himself, gets up out of bed and chairs, bathes himself, walks at least a block, and can ascend and descend stairs. This does not mean that he is able to live alone: he may not be able to cook, keep house, and meet the public, but he is able to get along without attendant care.

Definition and Discussion of Scoring

1. Feeding

10 = Independent. The patient can feed himself a meal from a tray or table when someone puts the food within his reach. He must put on an assistive device if this is needed, cut up the food, use salt and pepper, spread butter, etc. He must accomplish this in a reasonable time.

5 = Some help is necessary (with cutting up food, etc., as listed above).

2. Moving from wheelchair to bed and return

15 = Independent in all phases of this activity. Patient can safely approach the bed in his wheelchair, lock brakes, lift footrests, move safely to bed, lie down, come to a sitting position on the side of the bed, change the position of the wheelchair, if necessary, to transfer back into it safely, and return to the wheelchair.

10 = Either some minimal help is needed in some step of this activity or the patient needs to be reminded or supervised for safety of one of more parts of this activity.

5 = Patient can come to a sitting position without the help of a second person but needs to be lifted out of bed, or if he transfers with a great deal of help.

3. Doing personal toilet

5 = Patient can wash hands and face, comb hair, clean teeth, and shave. He may use any kind of razor but must put in blade or plug in razor without help as well as get it from drawer or cabinet. Female patients must put on own makeup, if used, but need not braid or style hair.

4. Getting on and off toilet

10 = Patient is able to get on and off toilet, fasten and unfasten clothes, prevent soiling of clothes, and use toilet paper without help. He may use a wall bar or other stable object for support if needed. If it is necessary to use a bed pan instead of a toilet, he must be able to place it on a chair, empty it, and clean it.

5 = Patient needs help because of imbalance or in handling clothes or in using toilet paper.

5. Bathing self

5 = Patient may use a bath tub, a shower, or take a complete sponge bath. He must be able to do all the steps involved in whichever method is employed without another person being present.

Mahoney, F & Barthel, D. (1965). Functional evaluation: The Barthel Index *Maryland State Medical Journal*, 14 (2), 61–65.

Display 5-1   *Barthel Index—Continued*

6. Walking on a level surface

15 = Patient can walk at least 50 yards without help or supervision. He may wear braces or prostheses and use crutches, canes, or a walkerette but not a rolling walker. He must be able to lock and unlock braces if used, assume the standing position and sit down, get the necessary mechanical aides into position for use, and dispose of them when he sits. (Putting on and taking off braces is scored under dressing.)

10 = Patient needs help or supervision in any of the above but can walk at least 50 yards with a little help.

6a. Propelling a wheelchair

5 = If a patient cannot ambulate but can propel a wheelchair independently. He must be able to go around corners, turn around, maneuver the chair to a table, bed, toilet, etc. He must be able to push a chair at least 50 yards. Do not score this item if the patient gets score for walking.

7. Ascending and descending stairs

10 = Patient is able to go up and down a flight of stairs safely without help or supervision. He may and should use handrails, canes, or crutches when needed. He must be able to carry canes or crutches as he ascends or descends stairs.

5 = Patient needs help with or supervision of any one of the above items.

8. Dressing and undressing

10 = Patient is able to put on and remove and fasten all clothing, and tie shoe laces (unless it is necessary to use adaptations for this). The activity includes putting on and removing and fastening corset or braces when these are prescribed. Such special clothing as suspenders, loafer shoes, dresses that open down the front may be used when necessary.

5 = Patient needs help in putting on and removing or fastening any clothing. He must do at least half the work himself. He must accomplish this in a reasonable time.

Women need not be scored on use of a brassiere or girdle unless these are prescribed garments.

9. Continence of bowels

10 = Patient is able to control his bowels and have no accidents. He can use a suppository or take an enema when necessary (as for spinal cord injury patients who have had bowel training).

5 = Patient needs help in using a suppository or taking an enema or has occasional accidents.

10. Controlling bladder

10 = Patient is able to control his bladder day and night. Spinal cord injury patients who wear an external device and leg bag must put them on independently, clean and empty bag, and stay dry day and night.

5 = Patient has occasional accidents or cannot wait for the bed pan or get to the toilet in time or needs help with an external device.

A score of 0 is given in all of the above activities when the patient cannot meet the criteria as defined above.

The advantage of the BI is its simplicity. It is useful in evaluating a patient's state of independence before treatment, his progress as he undergoes treatment, and his status when he reaches maximum benefit. It can easily be understood by all who work with a patient and can accurately and quickly be scored by anyone who adheres to the definitions of items listed above. The total score is not as significant or meaningful as the breakdown into individual items, since these indicate where the deficiencies are.

Any applicant to a chronic hospital who scores 100 BI should be evaluated carefully before admission to see whether such hospitalization is indicated. Discharged patients with 100 BI should not require further physical therapy but may benefit from a home visit to see whether any environmental adjustments are indicated. Encouragement by family and others may be necessary for a patient to maintain his degree of independence.

can function safely and communicate his needs to others. While the Barthel Index has been tested with a wide variety of subjects, the FIM has been used mostly with younger patients and has not undergone a lot of testing with community-based elderly (Pollack et al., 1996). Even so, it can be a useful tool for assisting the home care professional to gather sufficient and appropriate information for answering the OASIS questions accurately.

PULSES

The PULSES Profile (shown in Display 5–2) (Moskowitz & McCann, 1957) is similar to both the Barthel Index and the FIM. However, it expands functional assessment to include "support factors" or how much emotional, family, social, and financial support the client has. It also includes the client's physical condition and some sensory components to functional ability. PULSES is an acronym whose letters stand for the components of the assessment:

P: physical condition
U: upper limb functions
L: lower limb functions
S: sensory components
E: excretory functions
S: support factors

The client is given a score of "1" if he/she is independent in that area, a "4" if fully dependent in that area, and a "2" or "3" if his/her ability falls somewhere in between.

While the Barthel Index and the FIM measure discrete or basic functions, and the FIM includes social cognition and communication categories as well, the PULSES Profile measures the abilities necessary to perform ADL.

Assessing Function Using the OASIS Data Set

In this chapter each OASIS question that pertains to functional ability will be addressed. This section of the chapter is presented in a format like the section in Chapter 4 called, "What Exactly Am I Looking For?" with each of the MOO-numbered items listed, followed by an interpretation of that question from a functional assessment perspective.

As stated earlier, since environment and safety are important areas to assess for measuring functional ability, these factors will also be discussed. It is important that the home care professional understand how to mea-sure function and how to measure it *consistently* over the course of the client's stay on service. This information will be instrumental in determining whether or not the client should be discharged or re-certified. A few basic rules to keep in mind with all the questions that will be discussed include:

1. To simplify the discussion, in this section, the patient will always be referred to as "he."
2. Whether or not the patient needs the assistance of *another person* is key to determining which answer to mark.
3. The patient's *understanding of the concept* of an activity is just as important as the patient's physical ability to perform the activity when measuring function.
4. The answer "unknown" will not be addressed for most of the questions. Only if you have no idea or way of knowing how to rate the patient on a particular question, should you mark the box labeled "unknown."
5. Certain words have been italicized to help you focus on the key to locating the most accurate answer.

REMEMBER!

Read all possible answers before scoring.

MO270—Rehabilitative Prognosis: *Best* Description of Patient's Prognosis for Functional Status   This is not a question to be taken lightly. Its answer could make a big difference in how much and what kind of care the patient receives. To answer this question, the professional is asked to rate the patient's rehabilitative prognosis as "guarded," "poor," or "unknown." Since this question may appear vague and rating certain patients may be difficult, using one of the above-mentioned tools for functional assessment may be helpful. The professional need not use yet another form or make the form a part of the patient's clinical record. For instance, carrying a card version of the Barthel Index can help the professional quickly determine what this patient's status is. After determining what it *is*, it will be easier to predict what it *will be*. Knowing the patient's previous health history will also help answer this question.

Display 5-2 *PULSES Profile*

P. Physical condition, including diseases of the viscera (cardiovascular, pulmonary, gastrointestinal, urological, and endocrine) and cerebral disorders that are not enumerated in the lettered categories below
   1. No gross abnormalities considering age of individual
   2. Minor abnormalities not requiring frequent medical or nursing supervision
   3. Moderately severe abnormalities requiring frequent medical or nursing supervision yet still permitting ambulation
   4. Severe abnormalities requiring constant medical or nursing supervision or confining individual to bed or wheelchair
U. Upper extremities, including shoulder girdle, cervical, and upper dorsal spine
   1. No gross abnormalities considering age of individual
   2. Minor abnormalities with fairly good range of motion and function
   3. Moderately severe abnormalities but permitting performance of daily needs to a limited extent
   4. Severe abnormalities requiring constant nursing care
L. Lower extremities, including pelvis, lower dorsal, and lumbosacral spine
   1. No gross abnormalities considering age of individual
   2. Minor abnormalities with fairly good range of motion and function
   3. Moderately severe abnormalities permitting limited ambulation
   4. Severe abnormalities confining individual to bed or wheelchair
S. Sensory components relating to speech, vision, and hearing
   1. No gross abnormalities considering age of individual
   2. Minor deviations insufficient to cause any appreciable functional impairment
   3. Moderate deviations sufficient to cause appreciable functional impairment
   4. Severe deviations causing complete loss of hearing, vision, or speech
E. Excretory function, that is, bowel and bladder control
   1. Complete control
   2. Occasional stress incontinence or nocturia
   3. Periodic bowel and bladder incontinence or retention alternating with control
   4. Total incontinence, either bowel or bladder
S. Mental and emotional status
   1. No deviations considering age of individual
   2. Minor deviations in mood, temperament, and personality not impairing environmental adjustment
   3. Moderately severe variations requiring some supervision
   4. Severe variations requiring complete supervision

Profile

P	U	L	S	E	S

From Moskowitz E and McCann CB: J Chronic Dis 5:343, 1957, Vol 5, p 342.

For MO270, the patient can be scored according to the following:

♦ Mark "good" (box "1") for your OASIS answer if the patient has otherwise had independent function and is now dependent or unable to live alone because of surgery or an intervention that is supposed to give the patient only a *temporary impairment*. Also mark this answer if the patient has an illness that he/she should be able to recover from and eventually resume normal activities.

♦ Mark "guarded" (box "0") if the patient has had a stroke, has a chronic illness, or is not expected to fully recover from whatever condition(s) he has. Stroke patients often make significant recoveries of functional status, but this is very dependent on the patient and on the care he receives. The next time you answer this question about this same stroke patient, he may have recovered some function and be continuing to work hard at therapy so that he can be marked "good."

♦ Mark "unknown" (box "UK") if there is no way of determining whether this patient will improve or decline in function.

MO310—Structural Barriers in the Patient's Environment Limiting Independent Mobility You are asked to *mark all that apply*. To determine whether there are structural barriers that limit the patient's independent mobility, the assessor must first make a thorough assessment of the home. The patient can be scored according to the following:

♦ Answer "none" (box "0") means the patient can navigate hallways, ambulating unassisted or with an assistive device or wheelchair, get to all the areas in the home that he needs to in order to fully care for himself and get help (bathroom, kitchen, bedroom), and obtain whatever he/she needs, such as food, the toilet, the phone, or the fire extinguisher while in those areas.

♦ If the patient needs to use stairs to get to the toilet, bedroom, or kitchen, mark box "1." Even if the patient can manage the stairs with or without assistance or an assistive device, this answer should be marked if the patient must use the stairs to get to these areas.

♦ Answer "2" refers to stairs in the home that the patient does not have to use to get toileted, to eat or to sleep. If there are stairs that lead to other areas, mark this answer as well, whether or not the patient uses them.

♦ If there are stairs that go from the inside of the house to the outside, mark "3," whether or not the patient uses them.

♦ Narrow doorways, blocked doorways, or doorways that do not permit a wheelchair, walker, or an obese person (if applicable) to pass through require a check in box "4."

MO320—Safety Hazards Found in the Patient's Current Place of Residence You are to *mark all that apply*. The assessor cannot answer this question without a thorough inspection of the home. This question uses the words "inadequate," "unsafe," "lack," and "improperly." These are very subjective words, and it is up to the professional to determine as objectively as possible, whether or not they apply to the patient's home. The patient can be scored according to the following:

♦ "None" means there are *no safety hazards,* not just the safety hazards mentioned in the answers to the question.

♦ "Inadequate" refers to anything that doesn't meet the standard. Everyone's standards are different, but it is suggested that you compare the patient's home with regard to safety within your own home. An "inadequate" floor means that no one, especially the patient, can walk upon it without falling on it or through it, slipping, or sliding. Do not assume that the patient will always wear skid-proof shoes. Also, safety in the environment refers to safety for *everyone* who enters there. An "inadequate" roof is one that leaks or does not give protection from the weather. The same can be said of windows.

Lighting may be adequate for the patient's needs. You are assessing here whether the patient has enough lighting to use if he wants to, *not* whether there are enough lights on for *you* to do your work. Also, there should be a light switch that the patient can manipulate both at the bottom and at the top of the stairs for adequate safety.

♦ Gas and electrical appliances may be safe for others in the home to use if they do so correctly. However, if your patient cannot demonstrate proper use of these appliances to you, consider them unsafe. "Inadequate" heating or cooling is determined by the capability of the home to provide heat or cool air and also by the patient's ability to turn the heat or cool air on and off. Fire safety devices include a working smoke detector (check the batteries) and a fire extinguisher that the patient can get to, knows how to use properly and quickly, and is physically able to handle.

♦ *Unsafe* floor coverings can severely limit the patient's ability to function independently because if they prevent safe ambulation, the patient can't get to where he needs to toilet, eat, and sleep. Floor coverings are unsafe if they slide or have borders (fringe or rubber) that can catch someone's foot or the tip of a walker or cane. "Inadequate" stair railings means railings that are not very stable and cannot support the patient's weight if he must lean on them while using the stairs. Any wobbling of the railings means they are unsafe. The railings should be safe for *everyone* who uses them.

♦ *Lack* of anything is self explanatory; it simply means the person doesn't have something that would make the residence safer. For example, the lack of a working smoke detector is a safety hazard.

♦ *Improperly stored* hazardous material refers to paint and other chemicals that are fire hazards, have toxic fumes, or are not tightly sealed and placed out of the reach of children or cognitively impaired adults. The best places for storing these items are a garage or shed.

♦ Check "other" if you think there is *anything* in the patient's environment that might possibly be unsafe.

REMEMBER!

Sensory status is critical to functional ability.

Sensory status is very important in determining functional ability. This section is an example of how the PULSES Profile could be helpful to the professional using the OASIS. Consult the PULSES for questions regarding sensory ability. If the patient has visual, hearing, understanding, or speech impairments, be sure to consider these when assessing overall functional ability later in the OASIS assessment.

MO390—Vision with Corrective Lenses if the Patient Usually Wears Them This question requires that you *test* the patient's vision while he is wearing his contact lenses or eyeglasses *if* he customarily uses them. Ask the patient to read aloud from a section of newspaper or a paragraph from a book with regular type. Ask the patient to read his medicine bottles. The patient can be scored according to the following standards:

♦ If he can read the words to you, even if he must bring the writing close to his eyes, mark box "0." As or after you have the patient read, ask him to tell you what the writing means. His ability to understand what he has read will aid you in another OASIS question. Additionally, when you ask him to read for you, do not demonstrate what you are asking him to do unless he shows *clearly* that he does not understand your instructions. The ability to understand verbal language will also be important to your assessment.

♦ Mark box "1" if the patient cannot read the medication label or newspaper, but can count your fingers when held at arm's length from his eyes. Ask the patient to point out objects on the floor, in far corners of the room, and above his head. If he does not appear to understand your directions, watch his eyes as you move about the room and see whether they follow you. If the patient can point out the objects or follow you with his eyes, mark box "1."

♦ If the patient is not able to understand *and* his eyes do not follow you or another person in the home, he cannot read from newsprint, and he cannot point out objects, mark box "2" for severely impaired.

MO400—Hearing and Ability to Understand Spoken Language in Patient's Own Language (with hearing aids if the patient usually uses them) If the patient regularly wears a hearing aid, test his hearing while he is wearing it. This question depends upon the patient's ability to hear and understand. Test the patient in his own language. If he can hear but does not understand, this will be noted in the neurological/behavioral section. If he can't hear but can understand sign language, this will be noted in the neurological/behavioral section. The main objective of this question is sensory.

NURSING ALERT!

If you do not speak the patient's language, make sure that someone who does tests his vision and hearing ability.

The patient can be scored considering the following:

◆ To earn a mark in the "0" box, the patient must be able to hear *and* understand *complex* conversation. This is best tested by performing some patient teaching and then, after 10–15 minutes, asking the patient to explain what you have taught him. The teaching should include several steps of a procedure or several items to remember. It is important to perform the teaching for approximately 10 minutes, move on to another activity, and then ask the patient 10–15 minutes later to tell you what he learned during the teaching. Within 24 hours, ask the patient in person or over the phone if he remembers the basic content taught. In this way you can test several things that are important in OASIS:

- ◆ That the patient understands complex instructions, *MO400*
- ◆ That the patient has immediate recall (can remember something after 15 minutes have elapsed), *MO560*
- ◆ That the patient can remember something that occurred in the last 24 hours, *MO610*

NURSING ALERT!

Consider all the items listed below when scoring:

❑ If the patient hears *and* understands your *complex* instructions but needs some prompting, needs you to speak louder, or needs repetition, mark box "1."

❑ If the patient can only hear and understand *simple* instructions, such as "open your mouth" or "stand up," and needs to be prompted frequently when he tries to explain what he understands, mark box "2."

❑ If the patient cannot hear and understand even simple commands and must have *continual repetition or demonstrations* to help him understand, mark box "3."

❑ If the patient does not respond to you *at all* or is unable to hear and understand *familiar* words or expressions, such as his name or the words to "Happy Birthday" (if he is an English-speaking American) or familiar expressions from his own language, mark box "4."

MO410—Speech and Oral (Verbal) Expression of Language (in patient's own language)   The patient can be scored according to the following:

◆ If the patient is able to have a conversation 10–15 minutes long using clear pronunciation and appropriate pauses between words, mark box "0." Judge the patient's ability to verbally communicate by comparing it to your own. If the patient speaks very quickly, uses words that do not make sense, speaks very slowly, or uses a tone of voice that is not appropriate to the topic of conversation, you cannot mark box "0." It is helpful to ask the patient why he thinks you are visiting him, what he thinks his health needs are, and how he feels about your visit. Or simply ask him how he feels today. These questions will require him to speak and express his feelings.

REMEMBER!

Test the patient in his own language.

If your patient can express himself clearly and intelligibly to someone who speaks his own language, including American sign language, do not mark any box but "0."

◆ Mark box "1" if the patient makes conversation that is possible to understand and makes sense, but needs more time to express himself or you must remind him of what he was saying, such as, "You were talking about the weather, Mr. Smith." If there are some errors in the words he picks or if his grammar or speech is *occasionally* hard to understand, also mark box "1."

◆ If the patient has difficulty expressing simple and direct ideas, such as "I am in pain" or "I am hungry" and needs your help to pick the correct words, mark box "2." This patient may only speak in very short phrases. Ask this patient to repeat a phrase such as "it is sunny" and listen to whether he can say it clearly *and* use the same tone of voice you used when you said it. If he cannot do either, mark box "2."

◆ If you must guess to understand what your patient is trying to say, mark box "3." Typically this patient will only speak using single words or short

---

Display 5-3 *Borg Category-Ratio Scale for Rating of Perceived Breathlessness*
(Self-rating scale comparing breathlessness at different points in time)

0	Nothing at all	**5**	Severe
0.5	Very, very slight	**6**	
1	Very slight	**7**	Very severe
2	Slight	**8**	
3	Moderate	**9**	
4	Somewhat severe	**10**	Very, very severe (almost maximal)

Adapted from "Recommended Respiratory Disease Questionnaires for Use with Adults and Children in Epidemiological Research (Part 2)" by B. G. Ferris, 1978, American Review of Respiratory Disease, 118, 7-53. In Hoeman, S. P. (1996) *Rehabilitation Nursing,* 2nd Ed, pg. 369. St. Louis: . C. V. Mosby.

---

phrases. If the patient cannot express himself in any way that can be understood by the average person (who speaks his language) because he speaks in nonsense words, mark box "4."

♦ If he cannot respond or will not respond, mark box "5."

MO420—Frequency of Pain Interfering with Patient's Activity or Movement MO420 has a choice: "Patient has *no pain* or *pain does not interfere with activity or movement*" (box "0"). It is unlikely that your patient in home care, especially an elderly patient, will meet this criterion. Most of our elderly patients have chronic pain, typically arthritis. Although they may carry on with their activities or movements despite the pain, *it is important to ask whether the pain exists.* If it does, do not mark this box.

Pain does not have to be severe to fit the answer "All of the time" (box "3"). As long as there is pain, regardless of the type or severity, it should be counted, and you must check the box that best fits its frequency. *Pain can seriously impair functional ability.* A patient in moderate to severe pain will score differently than a patient who has mild or no pain on most of the questions discussed in this chapter.

MO430—Intractable Pain Is the patient experiencing pain that is *not easily relieved,* occurs at least daily, and affects the patient's sleep, appetite, physical or emotional energy, concentration, personal relationships, emotions, or ability or desire to perform physical activity?

This is pain that is unbearable because it is chronic or unrelenting and affects ADL and IADL. If the patient is able to perform *any* ADL without needing pain medication, then it is unlikely that the patient has intractable pain.

Integumentary Status—MO440 to MO488 Specific questions related to integumentary status will not be dis-

cussed in this section. However, it is important for the professional to know that wounds can be disabling and therefore affect functional ability (Neal, 1995). If the patient cannot perform ADL or IADL because of the wound itself, the dressings, or the accompanying pain, then the wound impairs the patient's functional ability.

Respiratory Status Respiratory status also affects functional ability. The ability to breathe without effort determines whether the patient can perform ADL or IADL. Additionally, the need to drag oxygen tubing, not to mention the safety hazard the oxygen and the tubing present, and to perform nebulizer treatments periodically may severely limit where the patient can go and what the patient can do. The Borg Category-Ratio Scale for Rating of Perceived Breathlessness (Display 5–3) and the Breathlessness Scales from the ATS-DLD Questionnaire (Display 5–4) can be used when questioning patients to better determine the extent of their dyspnea.

For MO490 The patient can be scored according to the following:

♦ To mark box "0," the patient should *not* be short of breath while at rest (sitting or standing), talking, eating, or engaged in mild activity, such as toileting, walking, or demonstrating a procedure to you. The patient in this category is expected to be short of breath (SOB) when running (if he is able to run).

♦ Mark box "1" if the patient becomes short of breath after walking more than 20 feet (this must be measured; use your own foot to simulate 1 foot of distance) or during or after walking upstairs. To determine whether the patient is dyspneic or SOB, observe the patient for the following:

  ♦ Slowing down or stopping the activity before it is completed

> ### Display 5-4   *Breathlessness Scales from the ATS-DLD Questionnaire*
> *(Scale used by nurse to assess patient's breathlessness)*
>
> **1.** Are you troubled by shortness of breath when hurrying on the level or walking up a slight hill?
> **2.** (If yes) Do you have to walk slower than people of your age on the level because of breathlessness?
> **3.** (If yes) Do you ever have to stop for breath when walking at your own pace on the level?
> **4.** (If yes) Do you ever have to stop for breath after walking about 100 yards (or after a few minutes) on the level?
> **5.** (If yes) Are you too breathless to leave the house or breathless on dressing or undressing?
>
> Adapted from "Recommended Respiratory Disease Questionnaires for Use with Adults and Children in Epidemiologocal Research (Part 2)" by B. G. Ferris, 1978, American Review of Respiratory Disease, 118, 7-53. In Hoeman, S. P. (1996) Rehabilitation Nursing, 2nd Edition, p. 369. St. Louis, C.V. Mosby.

+ Sitting down midway through or immediately after finishing the activity

+ Breathing deeply or in quick, shallow breaths

♦ Ask the patient if he has chest tightness or pain. Each of these signs indicates dyspnea or SOB. If the patient is dyspneic or SOB while dressing, toileting, or walking less than 20 feet, mark box "2."

♦ If talking, eating, performing other *basic* ADL, or feeling anxious cause dyspnea or SOB, mark box "3."

♦ If the patient has dyspnea or SOB while sleeping, sitting, or lying still, mark box "4."

Neurological/Emotional Behavioral Status Cognitive ability is an important component of function. If the patient is unable to focus on a task, cannot remember the steps involved in the task, requires prompting, or is delirious or comatose, independent function is unlikely. Also, depressive feelings can impair function because, although the impairment is psychological, the patient is unable to perform functional activities. Observe the patient carefully at the start of your visit for the following:

♦ Does he make eye contact with you? He should.

♦ Does he greet you? He should.

♦ Does he say appropriate things to you? He should. In other words, does anything he says make you feel uncomfortable or unsafe around him? It shouldn't.

♦ Does he appear well groomed? He should.

♦ What is his tone of voice and mood? His mood should be appropriate to your conversation, and his tone of voice should match his meaning.

If, after having a *complex* conversation (as discussed earlier), you determine that the patient clearly understands you and there is *no doubt* about his being confused

or disoriented, then do not ask the following questions. If this is not the case, to determine how to score the patient, ask the following questions. Try not to ask them all at once. It is helpful if you can work them into the conversation.

♦ Where are you now? *Or,* What is your address?

♦ What is the date? (particularly the month and year)

♦ What is [caregiver's] name?

♦ Do you know why I am here? *Or,* How do you feel about my being here?

♦ How many hours of sleep (average) do you get each night? (Ask this of all patients; it will give you clues about patients' emotional status and the presence of pain.)

♦ Finally, ask the patient to perform a simple task, such as getting you a drink of water, showing you where the bathroom is so you can wash your hands, or handing you the telephone.

REMEMBER!

Again, try to incorporate gathering this information into the visit. Do not make it obvious that you are testing the patient. The information you collect based on these questions and your observations will help you answer all of the questions in this section.

MO560—Cognitive Functioning (patient's current level of alertness, orientation, comprehension, concentration, and immediate memory for simple commands) The patient can be scored according to the following:

- If the patient made eye contact with you, was able to answer all your questions accurately, and could complete the simple task, mark box "0."
- If he needed prompting or reminders because he is stressed by your visit or by his illness but can otherwise perform appropriately, mark box "1." If the patient is unable to tell you, ask caregivers whether the patient usually understands and can verbalize what is going on. Try to determine whether it is only the situation that is causing the need for prompting.
- If the patient *must have a quiet environment* to perform appropriately (as determined by the answers to your questions and your observations) or needs *some assistance or direction* in certain situations, mark box "2." This means the patient can do *most but not all* of the following without assistance:
  - Understand where he is, why you are there, what is happening, and the date, especially the month and year
  - Be able to concentrate on what you are saying or pay attention when you speak
  - Respond to simple commands and perform them correctly
- Mark box "3" if the patient shows *any* of the following behaviors during more than half the length of your visit:
  - Is not alert—that is, he is not awake or aware of his surroundings. (He does not have to know where he is, just that he is somewhere.)
  - Does not know where he is
  - Does not know who he is or who you are, assuming you have identified yourself as the nurse or therapist. (He does not need to know your name.)
  - Does not know what his situation is
  - Does not know the date, at least the month and year
  - Cannot shift attention from one person or thing to another appropriately
  - Cannot recall directions given 10–15 minutes ago
- If the patient is comatose, constantly disoriented (does not know where or who he is), or is delirious or confused *all of the time,* mark box "4."

MO570—When Confused (reported or observed) The patient can be scored according to the following:

- To answer "0" ("never") to this question, remember that it means *never,* under any circumstances.

- *New and Complex Situations* ("1") means confusion *only* when there is a change of environment such as returning home or becoming newly hospitalized.
- *On awakening or at night only* ("2") means that the patient is *temporarily* confused upon just waking up or when getting up in the middle of the night. This confusion should last only 5–10 minutes until the patient is once again aware of where he is.
- *During the day and evening, but not constantly* ("3") means that the patient has *occasional* confusion; he is not confused all of the time. When he is confused, it is unrelated to having been sleeping or to the darkness of night.
- *Constantly* ("4") means the patient is *always* confused. He does not have *any* moments when he understands what is going on around him. If the patient has moments here and there when he is lucid, but is mostly confused, mark box "3."

MO590—Depressive Feelings Reported or Observed in Patient (mark all that apply) The patient can be scored according to the following:

- If the patient appears sad or unhappy, mark box "1." This does not necessarily mean the patient is mentally ill. He might only be sad for a brief time.
- However, if the patient talks of blaming himself or speaks of his illness or injury as a failure, mark box "2."
- If the patient does not seem to cheer up or become less unhappy or reproachful after you have tried to comfort him, mark box "3."
- If the patient states that he thinks about dying or death (not suicide), mark box "4."

NURSING ALERT!

It is important to ask the unhappy patient whether he has thought of death or suicide. If he has thought of suicide, ask whether he has a plan to kill himself. If so, call his doctor or send him to the emergency room immediately.

- If the patient has thought of suicide, mark box "5."
- If none of these sad, hopeless, reproachful, suicidal feelings are expressed even after you ask about them, mark box "6."

MO610—Behaviors Demonstrated at Least Once a Week (reported or observed; mark all that apply) The patient can be scored according to the following:

♦ Mark box "1" for *any* of the following behaviors:
  ♦ Inability to recognize people the patient should know
  ♦ Inability to recognize his own home
  ♦ Inability to remember what has happened in the last 24 hours
  ♦ Memory loss such that the patient needs supervision in order to be safe in his home environment
♦ Mark box "2" if the patient displays *any* of the following:
  ♦ Inability to bathe, feed, toilet, dress, or groom himself with or without the assistance of others
  ♦ Inability to stop his activities when they should stop. For example, the patient continually brushes his hair or washes his hands.
  ♦ Inability to protect himself because he commits unsafe acts. For example, he lights matches for no reason or walks outside in freezing weather wearing only his underwear.
♦ Mark box "3" if the patient makes sexual comments, makes threats, or uses profanity excessively.
♦ Mark box "4" if he displays violent behavior.
♦ Mark box "5" if he acts like a child (using baby talk, whining, throwing a tantrum) and disrupts the visit unnecessarily.
♦ Mark box "6" if he talks of seeing things that do not exist or claims that people "are out to get" him.
♦ Mark box "7" if the patient *does not display any of the above behaviors*.

ADL/IADL

REMEMBER!

For MO640–MO800, complete the "current" column for all patients. For these same items, complete the "prior" column only at start of care; mark the level that corresponds to the patient's condition 14 days prior to start of care. In all cases, record *what the patient is able to do.*

MO640—Grooming: Ability to Tend to Personal Hygiene Needs (i.e., washing face and hands, hair care, shaving or makeup, teeth or denture care, fingernail care) Grooming refers to the patient's ability to wash his face and hands, brush his hair, brush his teeth, shave, apply makeup (females only), and present an overall neat, clean personal appearance.

The patient can be scored according to the following:

♦ If the patient is able to perform these grooming tasks *alone,* even if he must use assistive or adaptive devices such as a long-handled mirror, reacher, extender, or thickened handles, check box "0."
♦ If he needs the grooming equipment or assistive devices placed within reach, check box "1."
♦ If the patient must have the help of another person or must be groomed *entirely* by another person, check box "2" or "3," respectively. *Do not check both.*

MO650—Ability to Dress Upper Body, with or without Dressing Aids (including undergarments, pullovers, front-opening shirts and blouses, zippers, buttons, and snaps) The patient can be scored according to the following:

♦ To mark the "0" box, make sure the patient is able to perform *all* the activities required for dressing. Think carefully about what a person must do to dress. The patient must be able to retrieve the clothes from the closet or drawer and put them on and take them off the upper body *completely* and *without the help of another person.* If assistance is needed, it must only come from assistive or adaptive devices such as a button-holer or velcro.
♦ If the patient can dress and undress *completely* but cannot get the clothes out of the drawer or closet, mark box "1." Remember that to retrieve clothes independently requires being able to get into the room where the clothes are, get next to the bureau or into the closet, open the drawer or reach the hanger, and bring out the clothes.
♦ If the patient needs the assistance of *another person,* even if only to perform a task like putting on or taking off a brassiere, box "2" must be marked.
♦ If the patient must be dressed *completely by another person,* check box "3."

MO660—Ability to Dress Lower Body, with or without dressing Aids (including undergarments, slacks, socks or nylons, shoes)

REMEMBER!

This section is very similar to the dressing of the upper body.

The patient can be scored according to the following:

◆ To receive a mark in box "0" the patient must *not* need the assistance of *another person* to dress. Aids such as a shoe horn, velcro shoes, a sock aid, elasticized pants, or any other dressing aid may be used.

◆ Can the patient get to these aids? If not, the patient needs the assistance of *another person* to lay them out. If this is the case, or if the clothing or shoes must be *laid out* and then the patient can put them on by himself, mark box "1."

◆ If the patient needs only the *partial* assistance of *another person* to *apply* the clothing or shoes, mark box "2"

◆ If the patient must be *completely dressed by another person,* mark box "3."

◆ If the patient can dress himself completely independently but needs someone to tie his shoes, mark box "2."

MO670—Bathing: Ability to Wash Entire Body (excludes grooming [washing face and hands only])

The patient can be scored according to the following:

◆ If the patient is able to wash his entire body in the bathtub or shower (this does not necessarily include hands and face) *without the assistance of another person,* mark box "0." This means the patient does not need a tub or shower seat, non-skid mat, long-handled scrub brush, or other aid.

◆ If the patient must be watched or supervised while bathing or showering, he is not independent. If the use of devices such as those just mentioned is enough to make the patient independent in bathing or showering, mark box "1."

◆ If he needs someone to *occasionally* supervise him *for any reason,* to assist him in or out of the tub or shower, or to wash *at all,* mark box "2." This includes needing assistance at any time.

◆ If the patient must be supervised *or* assisted *at all times* while in the tub or shower, even if he can wash himself completely, mark box "3."

◆ If the patient must be bathed outside the tub or shower because he is unable to use them *for any reason,* mark box "4."

◆ The inability to participate in any way that might be considered washing so that the patient *must be bathed by another person entirely* is recorded in box "5."

MO680—Toileting: Ability to Get to and from the Toilet or Bedside Commode
The patient can be scored according to the following:

◆ If the patient can get to and from the bathroom toilet *without the assistance of another person,* even if he must use a walker, wheelchair, or other assistive device, and if he is able to perform his own perineal hygiene, mark box "0." If the patient needs supervision or needs someone to open the door for him, *do not* mark this box.

◆ If the patient needs to be supervised, assisted, or helped by *another person,* mark box "1." This includes the incontinent patient who does not go to the bathroom in time to control his urine or bowel movements unless he is told to do so.

◆ If the patient cannot make it to the bathroom because of incontinence, poor mobility, memory loss, or any other reason, but can make it to the *bedside commode* with or without the assistance of another person, mark box "2."

◆ If the patient cannot get to the toilet or bedside commode *under any circumstances,* but can use a *bedpan or urinal* without the assistance of another person, mark box "3."

◆ Mark box "4" if the patient cannot use the bedpan or urinal *without the assistance of another person.*

MO690—Transferring: Ability to Move from Bed to Chair, On and Off Toilet or Commode, into and out of Tub or Shower, and Ability to Turn and Position Self in Bed if Patient Is Bedfast
The patient can be scored according to the following:

◆ To "independently transfer" (box "0") means the patient is able to move from one place to another, including turning and repositioning in bed, *without the assistance of another person or of an assistive device* such as a trapeze or sliding board.

◆ Mark box "1" if a device must be used or if "minimal assistance" is needed. Minimal means that another person may provide guarding or supervision or may hold the patient's arm or arms during the transfer. This patient can do every part of the transfer himself or with an assistive device such as a trapeze or sliding board but just needs someone to guide or monitor him for safety purposes.

♦ If *the assistance of another person* is required for the transfer to occur, but the patient can bear weight on at least one limb and pivot, mark box "2."

♦ If the patient cannot bear any weight or pivot, mark box "3."

♦ If the patient is bedbound, meaning he cannot get out of bed without being carried, but he can turn himself in bed, mark box "4."

♦ If the patient cannot even turn himself in bed, mark box "5."

MO700—Ambulation/Locomotion: Ability to Safely Walk, Once in a Standing Position, on a Variety of Surfaces   The patient can be scored according to the following:

♦ To give a patient a score of "0" in this category, be sure the patient needs *no assistance whatsoever.* The patient must be able to walk safely and without assistance from another person or device.

♦ If the patient needs a device of *any kind* to be able to walk on his own, *or* needs to be supervised to be able to walk safely, *or* needs any assistance from a device or a person to walk in particular areas or on particular surfaces, mark box "1."

♦ If he *only* requires supervision or the assistance of another person to be able to walk, mark box "2." This score means the patient *always* needs supervision or assistance to walk, but that is all he needs.

♦ If the patient *must* have a wheelchair for mobility, mark box "3." This means the patient can use his wheelchair without any assistance.

♦ If the patient can *neither walk nor wheel himself in a wheelchair* but can sit in a chair, mark box "4." This means the patient may need to have his wheelchair pushed by someone else.

♦ If the patient cannot walk or use a wheelchair and must remain in bed, mark box "5."

MO710—Feeding or Eating: Ability to Feed Self Meals and Snacks (Note: This refers only to the process of eating, chewing, and swallowing, not preparing the food to be eaten)   The patient can be scored according to the following:

♦ To earn a mark in box "0," the patient must be able to bring the food to his mouth, chew it, and swallow it. If the patient uses assistive devices

such as utensil adapters or special plates/bowls, dicem to help stick the plate to the table surface, or other devices to feed himself independently, he still gets a "0."

♦ If the patient must have his meal arranged in front of him, be assisted or supervised *occasionally,* be coaxed or reminded to eat the meal, or needs food that has been altered in texture in order to feed himself, mark the "1" box. He may or may not need assistive devices.

♦ If he requires supervision or assistance *throughout* the meal or snack or else he cannot eat, mark box "2."

♦ If the patient can eat using his mouth *but must also* receive food through his nose or stomach, mark box "3."

♦ If he *only* receives food through his nose or stomach, mark box "4."

♦ Finally, if he *cannot take in any food* through his mouth, nose, or stomach, mark box "5."

MO720—Planning and Preparing Light Meals (e.g., Cereal, Sandwich) or Reheat Delivered Meals   "Light meals" refers to a small meal or one that does not include a hot meat, vegetable, and starch. For home care patients, it could also mean a delivered meal that is to be reheated by the patient later. A light meal could be a sandwich, bowl of cereal, bowl of soup, or small salad. The ability to plan and prepare meals is an important part of function because if the patient cannot do these things, he will need help from others.

The patient can be scored according to the following:

♦ If the patient *understands* how to plan and prepare the meal—that is, he knows what constitutes a sandwich or a salad, how to open a can of soup, how to heat food and use utensils safely—and *can actually do these things,* mark box "0." If he understands and can do these things but *has not done* them in the past or *does not plan* to do them, you can also mark box "0."

♦ However, if for any physical, mental, or cognitive reason, this patient *cannot plan or prepare meals on a regular basis,* mark box "1."

♦ Mark box "2" if he *cannot under any circumstances or at any time* prepare or reheat meals.

MO730—Transportation: Physical and Mental Ability to Safely Use a Car, Taxi, or Public Transportation (bus, train, subway)   To be able to travel independently, the patient must have the *physical ability,* whether or not he uses assistive devices, *and* the mental ability to use transportation safely. The patient can be scored according to the following:

- ◆ If the patient can drive his own car with or without adaptations or if he can use bus or van transportation *without* the assistance of *another person,* mark box "0."
- ◆ If he *must have assistance* or the company of *another person* to ride the bus or van *or* if he can only ride in a car as a passenger, mark box "1."
- ◆ If an ambulance is the *only* means of transportation the patient can use safely, mark box "2." In this case, this patient cannot be moved into a car, bus, or van because of his medical condition, functional limitations, or the limitations of his caregivers. If he can be moved into a car, bus, or van, but it is *less safe* for him than an ambulance would be, mark box "2."

MO740—Laundry: Ability to Do Own Laundry (to carry laundry to and from washing machine, use washer and dryer, wash small items by hand)

The ability to do laundry is an IADL. That is, it is not as necessary to basic function as are feeding, toileting, and bathing. To say that the patient can do his own laundry means that he must *understand* what he is doing, why he is doing it, and how to do it. He must also be physically, cognitively, and mentally able to move the dirty laundry from where it is kept to the washing machine or sink, apply soap, turn on the water, move the laundry into the dryer or hang the clothes in an appropriate place to dry (for instance, not out in the rain), and transport the laundry to where it belongs (i.e. drawers, closets, etc.).

The patient can be scored according to the following:

- ◆ If the patient can perform *all* of these functions *without* the assistance of another person, mark box "0."
- ◆ If the patient can only do light laundry (such as handwashing underwear), *but must have the help of another person for whatever reason* to do more than light laundry (a few loads of laundry), mark box "1."
- ◆ If the patient's limitations, whatever they may be, prevent him from doing any laundry by himself *without the help or supervision of another person,* mark box "2."

MO750—Housekeeping: Ability to Safely and Effectively Perform Light Housekeeping and Heavier Cleaning Tasks

Housekeeping is another IADL category. *Light housekeeping* refers to tasks such as dusting, wiping surfaces, changing bed linens, and tidying. *Heavy cleaning*

means tasks such as vacuuming, taking out the trash, mowing the yard, and moving furniture.

The patient can be scored according to the following:

- ◆ If the patient can physically, cognitively, and mentally perform all these tasks, mark box "0." The patient must *understand* what the task is, how it is performed, and *be able to perform it safely.* A patient who can do all of the above, but hasn't done these tasks in the past or does not intend to do these tasks, also gets a check in this box.
- ◆ If the patient can *only* perform the light tasks without the assistance of another person, mark box "1."
- ◆ If the patient can perform housekeeping tasks but must have *occasional assistance* or the *supervision of another person* to perform them safely, mark box "2."
- ◆ If the patient must *always* have supervision or assistance to perform tasks safely, mark box "3."
- ◆ If the patient *cannot under any circumstances* participate in *any* housekeeping tasks, mark box "4."

MO760—Shopping: Ability to Plan for, Select, and Purchase Items in a Store and to Carry Them Home or Arrange Delivery

Shopping is another IADL task. To shop independently, a person must *understand* the concept of shopping, why it is done, how and where it is done, and then be able to do it *without the assistance of another person.* An individual must be able to determine what food items are lacking in the home, what food items are needed, and where and how to go to the appropriate store and bring the items home. Independent shopping is determined by the patient's ability to get to the store, select the items, pay for them, bring them or have them delivered home, carry in the bags, unpack the bags, and put the items away.

The patient can be scored according to the following:

- ◆ If the patient performs these shopping tasks or has the capacity to do them *without the assistance of another person during any part of the process* (even if he has not or does not plan to do them), mark box "0."
- ◆ If the patient is able to get to the store and select and purchase the items, but needs help when shopping for *a lot of items* or needs *the assistance of another person at all* during shopping, mark box "1." (Most home care patients will not get a score of "0" or "1" because they are usually expected to be homebound in order to receive care.)

♦ If the patient cannot go to the store, but can identify what is needed, select the items, and arrange for home delivery, mark box "2." In this case, the patient *understands* the concept of shopping but is physically unable to get to the store.

♦ If the patient *always* needs another person to do the shopping, mark box "3." In this case, another person may be needed to do the shopping because the patient is unable to shop in person or from home because of physical, cognitive, or mental disabilities.

MO770—Ability to Use Telephone: Ability to Answer the Phone, Dial Numbers, and Effectively Use the Telephone to Communicate The ability to use the phone requires several steps: The patient must be able to *understand* the concept of making a call, know who he is calling, know why he is calling, locate the correct phone number, dial the numbers, and make appropriate (socially correct) conversation.

The patient can be scored according to the following:

♦ If he can do all the activities listed in MO770, mark box "0."

♦ If he can do all the activities listed in MO770 but must use a special phone or adaptive equipment on his phone, mark box "1."

♦ If the patient can answer the phone and speak appropriately *all the time* but cannot make the phone call himself, mark box "2."

♦ If the patient *cannot* answer the phone or carry on an appropriate conversation *all of the time*, mark box "3." In this case, the patient might not always be coherent enough to sustain a conversation or to answer the phone. If the patient is asleep or does not want to be bothered answering the phone, but is *capable* of doing so, do not mark this box.

♦ If the patient cannot answer the phone at any time but can listen if the receiver is held to his ear or if he is put on speaker phone, mark box "4."

♦ If the patient *cannot use the phone at any time for any reason,* mark box "5."

Conclusion

Many questions on the OASIS concern the functional abilities of home care patients. Function does not only mean mobility, but is also concerned with:

1. The patient's ability to perform ADL and IADL
2. The patient's ability to manage *safely* in, around, and outside the home
3. The patient's cognitive resources
4. The patient's use of devices or equipment that compensate for any deficit

Independent function depends on the patient's intact mental, physical, *and* cognitive resources. A patient may use an assistive or adaptive device and still be independent because he is independent from the *assistance of another person*. If the patient needs the *assistance of another person* for any reason to perform a particular function, then the patient is *not* performing that particular function independently. If the patient cannot think, see or hear clearly, speak and understand his own language, get and eat food, toilet, dress or groom himself, or move, he has a functional impairment. The health care professional must assess the extent of the functional impairments and then assist the patient to become as independent as possible despite those impairments.

The positive aspect of collecting all this information through the valid OASIS data set is that *finally* home care professionals can accurately document information that truly "paints a picture" of the complex situations we find our patients in. This complete assessment of the patient's functional limitations and strengths can help our patients, families, caregivers, team members, payers, and the general public understand how really important adequate home care services are to the communities we serve and to the nation as a whole.

Using OASIS Data with the HCFA-485 and Patient Care Plan

6

Introduction

The astute home health nurse is continuously looking forward from the task at hand. During admission of a patient, the nurse is developing the nursing care plan, setting nursing goals, estimating the length of time needed to reach those goals, and preparing the Plan Of Care (POC) to be sent to the physician for signature. This chapter will help the nurse develop familiarity with the OASIS assessment items and the way these items interlock with the HCFA-485 (Health Care Financing Administration) data fields so the POC can be completed with a minimum of error.

Medicare is currently the largest payment source for home care in the United States, so it is important that the home care nurse learn all the aspects of the Medicare home care benefit. Like a house, once the foundation is built, changes in the locations of rooms and entrances should not affect the integrity of the structure itself. Like the rooms in a house, changes occur periodically in Medicare coverage and benefits, but the purpose of the program (the foundation) remains the same.

The criteria for Medicare coverage are explained in detail in the Medicare Home Health Agency Insurance Manual (HIM-11) revised by HCFA. Some agencies have taken parts of the HIM-11 and written explanations to help the nurse understand specific language and coverage guidelines. The latest proposed revision was published in the March 10, 1997, issue of the *Federal Register.* The changed version focused on quality improvement to be implemented by incorporating an "outcome oriented, data supported quality assessment and performance improvement" approach. This change is to be supported by the OASIS core standard assessment data set. The fundamental principles that guided the development of the revised conditions of participation included the following:

♦ Stress quality improvement, incorporating to the greatest extent possible outcome-oriented, data-supported quality assessment and performance improvement
♦ Facilitate flexibility in how a home care organization meets the performance requirements
♦ Eliminate unnecessary administrative requirements
♦ Ensure patient rights
♦ Focus on continuous, integrated care centered around patient assessment, care planning, coordination of service delivery, and quality assessment and performance improvement
♦ Incorporate the program integrity approaches (*Federal Register,* Vol. 62, No. 46)

In 1999, HCFA is expected to issue the revised "Conditions of Participation," which will mandate that agencies track all clinical data in the official OASIS format. OASIS appears to be the beginning of nationwide data collection on the home health industry and will be a basis for prospective payment.

The mandate to incorporate the OASIS into all agency assessment forms used for Medicare patients is upon us. Rather than resisting the impending changes, home health agencies must utilize the OASIS to its fullest extent. This may include not only incorporation of OASIS into assessment forms, but also the development of clinical pathways, care plans, and documentation, and the completion of the Home Health Certification and Plan of Care (POC), also known as Form HCFA-485 (or just "the 485").

The HCFA-485 is a multicopy form containing 28 separate fields. This same form is also available in computer-generated programs. The skilled nurse must in some fashion complete the POC (the 485) at the start of care when the patient is admitted to services, at re-certification (60–62 days after admission), and at discharge from the agency. If circumstances permit, patients may receive more than one re-certification; however, this is becoming increasingly rare with the advent of managed care and the bundling of services.

The following section lists the 28 fields of the POC and shows the connection between these fields and items from the OASIS. Figure 6–1 can be used as a guide to understanding exactly where the various MOO numbers relate to the field numbers on the 485.

1. Patient's HI Claim Number This question is answered by MOO63. The patient's HI claim number is his/her Medicare number. Include any suffixes to this number.

2. Start-of-Care Date MOO3O answers this. What is the start-of-care date for this patient?

3. Certification Period (From: To:) Usually the certification period begins with the SOC date. Thus, if a patient's SOC was 04/04/98, the certification period would run from 04/04/98 to 06/04/98.

4. Medical Record Number MOO2O asks for the patient ID number. Whatever number your agency uses for a patient identifier should be entered here.

5. Provider Number What provider number has been issued to the agency by HCFA? This number should be entered here. MOO1O Agency ID *may* be the same number if HCFA chooses to have agency data transmitted in this manner since every agency will need an identifying number to transmit and receive data and remain anonymous to other agencies.

6. Patient's Name and Address MOO4O, MOO5O, and MOO6O ask for the patient's last name, state of residence, and zip code. Complete name and address must be entered on the POC, field 6.

7. Provider's Name, Address, and Telephone Number The OASIS does not request this specific information because it would reveal the agency and prevent anonymity.

Figure 6-1 *Example of how OASIS data corresponds with fields on the HCFA-485.*

HOME HEALTH CERTIFICATION AND PLAN OF CARE

| 1. Patient's HI Claim No. *M0063* | 2. Start Of Care Date *M0030* | 3. Certification Period From: | | 4. Medical Record No. *M0020* | 5. Provider No. |

6. Patient's Name and Address
M0040
M0050
M0060

7. Provider's Name, Address and Telephone Number
To:

| 8. Date of Birth *M0066* | 9. Sex ☐ M ☐ F |
| *M0069* | |

10. Medications: Dose/Frequency/Route (N)ew (C)hanged
M0160
M0500

Also consider the mo #'s which deal with pain, vision, cognitive functioning, and manual dexterity when completing this section.

11. ICD-9-CM | Principal Diagnosis
M0230 | Date

12. ICD-9-CM | Surgical Procedure | Date

13. ICD-9-CM | Other Pertinent Diagnoses | Date
M0240
Also consider M0200, M0210, and M0220

14. DME and Supplies *M0250 M0500 M0520*
M0810 M0820

15. Safety Measures: *M0680, M0690, M0700,*
M0770

16. Nutritional Req. *M0710, M0720*

17. Allergies:

18.A. Functional Limitations

1	☐	Amputation	5	☐	Paralysis	9	☐	Legally Blind
2	☐	Bowel/Bladder (Incontinence)	6	☐	Endurance	A	☐	Dyspnea With Minimal Exertion
3	☐	Contracture	7	☐	Ambulation	B	☐	Other (Specify)
4	☐	Hearing	8	☐	Speech			

M0390, M0400, M0410, M0490, M0520, M0540

18.B. Activities Permitted

1	☐	Complete Bedrest	6	☐	Partial Weight Bearing	A	☐	Wheelchair
2	☐	Bedrest BRP	7	☐	Independent At Home	B	☐	Walker
3	☐	Up As Tolerated	8	☐	Crutches	C	☐	No Restrictions
4	☐	Transfer Bed/Chair	9	☐	Cane	D	☐	Other (Specify)
5	☐	Exercises Prescribed						

M0640 → M0700, M0720

19. Mental Status:
| 1 | ☐ | Oriented | 3 | ☐ | Forgetful | 5 | ☐ | Disoriented | 7 | ☐ | Agitated |
| 2 | ☐ | Comatose | 4 | ☐ | Depressed | 6 | ☐ | Lethargic | 8 | ☐ | Other |

M0560 M0570 M0580 M0590 M0600

20. Prognosis:
| 1 | ☐ | Poor | 2 | ☐ | Guarded | 3 | ☐ | Fair | 4 | ☐ | Good | 5 | ☐ | Excellent |

M0260

Figure 6-1 *Continued*

21. Orders for Discipline and Treatments (Specify Amount/Frequency/Duration)

M0220
M0250

M0440 - Skin lesion or open wound
M0445 - Pressure ulcer
M0468 - Stasis ulcer
M0480 - Surgical wounds

M0500 - resp treatment
M0550 - ostomy

M0780
M0790
M0800
M0810
M0820

M0830
M0840 ⟩ *May precipitate change in orders.*

Consider "triggers for referral" (see chapter 4) in order to include referrals to other disciplines, orders, etc. here.

22. Goals/Rehabilitation Potential/Discharge Plans

M0270
M0640 → M0820

23. Nurse's Signature and Date of Verbal SOC Where Applicable:

25. Date HHA Received Signed POT

24. Physician's Name and Address

26. I certify/recertify that this patient is confined to his/her home and needs intermittent skilled nursing care, physical therapy and/or speech therapy or continues to need occupational therapy. The patient is under my care, and I have authorized the services on this plan of care and will periodically review the plan.

27. Attending Physician's Signature and Date Signed

28. Anyone who misrepresents, falsifies, or conceals essential information required for payment of Federal funds may be subject to fine, imprisonment, or civil penalty under applicable Federal laws.

Form HCFA-485 (C-4) (02-94) (Print Aligned)

1 - PROVIDER

8. Date of Birth MO066 answers this.

9. Sex MO69 answers this.

10. Medications: Dose/Frequency/Route (N)ew (C)hanged OASIS does not specifically ask for patient medications. However, this should be a part of the agency assessment form. Remember that the OASIS was not intended to be used as a complete assessment but to be integrated into the agency's assessment form to improve data collection. MO160 asks if the patient has adequate finances to meet his basic health needs. Inability to afford medicine or medical supplies should be considered here and may trigger a referral to social services. Don't forget to include medications used in respiratory treatments. Although MO500 doesn't specifically deal with respiratory medications, it does trigger the response. Also consider the MOO numbers that deal with pain, vision, cognitive functioning, and manual dexterity when completing this section. Any of these may interfere with appropriate medication usage.

11. ICD-9-CM: Principal Diagnosis and Date MO230 asks for the primary diagnosis and ICD code as well as a severity rating for this diagnosis. The *primary diagnosis* and the *principal diagnosis* should be the same.

12. ICD-9-CM: Surgical Procedure Since OASIS does not permit the use of surgical or V-codes, this information will not be found in an OASIS item. However, surgery should be documented at some point in the physical assessment.

13. ICD-9-CM: Other Pertinent Diagnoses This field corresponds with MO240, "Other Diagnoses." Please list other diagnoses here in order of their significance to or effect on the patient. Since MO240 requires a severity rating for each diagnosis, it should be relatively easy to transpose these in order of severity to the 485. Remember to review MO200, MO210, and MO220 for changed diagnoses or conditions as well.

14. DME and Supplies MO250, MO500, MO520, MO810, and MO820 will assist in completing this field. These items speak to specific conditions in which durable medical equipment or supplies may be used. Failing to complete this field on the 485 may result in noncoverage of supplies.

15. Safety Measures MO680, MO690, MO700, and MO770 relate to this field. These questions concern personal safety when toileting, transferring, and ambulating. MO770 asks if the patient can effectively use a phone. In truth, all the numbers from MO640 through MO800 can indicate if a patient has at least some degree of impairment that may lead to lack of safety. When integrating the OASIS into the agency assessment, leave room to document other safety issues such as throw rugs and electrical cords.

16. Nutritional Requirements MO710 and MO720 address the patient's ability to feed him/herself meals and snacks (actually eating, not preparing) and to the patient's ability to plan and prepare light meals. While this does not mention a specific diet, which is what is required in field 16, it does tend to cause the assessor to follow up on patient problems such as ill-fitting dentures, inability to prepare meals, etc.

17. Allergies This field is not addressed by the OASIS. However, it must be a part of the patient assessment because allergies must be listed on the medication sheet.

18A. Functional Limitations MO390, MO400, MO410, MO490, MO520, and MO540 all address functional limitations specific to this field. If these limitations are indicated on either the assessment form or the 485, be sure that they support each other. Failure to document functional limitations on the assessment may result in failure of Medicare to pay for the service provided.

18B. Activities Permitted MO640 through MO700 address the patient's activity level and potential for activity. While MO720 relates to the ability to plan and prepare meals, it may be assumed that some level of activity is necessary for this to occur. Again, be sure that the assessment and the 485 are in agreement with each other. Keep in mind that a decreased activity level may indicate the need to refer the patient to physical or occupational therapy.

19. Mental Status Mental status is discussed by the OASIS under the section entitled Neuro/Emotional/ Behavioral Status. MO560, MO570, MO580, and MO590 all seek information regarding the patient's mental status. Depression, confusion, altered cognitive functioning, and anxiety should be indicated here.

20. Prognosis MO260 asks for the best description of the patient's overall prognosis for recovery from this episode of illness. HCFA provides room for five responses; OASIS only provides poor and good/fair. Again, try to keep the 485 and the OASIS in agreement. If the patient has an excellent prognosis, he probably will need only very short-term home care.

21. Orders for Discipline and Treatments (Specify Amount/Frequency/Duration) Many of the OASIS items are of significance in this field. Items dealing with chronic or acute conditions or situations (urinary incontinence, intravenous or infusion therapy, parenteral nutrition, enteral nutrition, skin lesions or open wounds, ostomies, respiratory treatments, management of medications, treatments, and equipment) should be considered here. Any specific treatment or dressing, frequency of catheter change, care of new ostomy, etc., should be indicated in detail. Certain MO items may trigger referrals to other disciplines; orders for these disciplines can be included here along with care they will provide, frequency, duration, etc., of the same. Remember that all daily care, such as wound care, should have a finite and predictable end listed. Possible MO items include MO220, MO250, MO440, MO445, MO468, MO480, MO780, MO790, MO800, MO810, MO820, MO830, and MO840.

22. Goals/Rehabilitation Potential/Discharge Plans MO270 speaks to rehabilitative prognosis, the best description of a patient's overall prognosis for functional status. In addition, MO640 through MO820 are good indicators of the patient's current level of function and potential rehabilitation potential, which may affect the response documented here. Discharge planning may also be affected by the responses to these MO items.

23. Nurse's Signature and Date of Verbal SOC Where Applicable No OASIS items for this field.

24. Physician's Name and Address No OASIS items for this field.

25. Date HHA Received Signed POT No OASIS items for this field.

26. Certification of Medicare Compliance "I certify/recertify that this patient is confined to his/her home and needs intermittent skilled nursing care, physical therapy, and/or speech therapy or continues to need occupational therapy. The patient is under my care, and I have authorized the services on this plan of care and will periodically review the plan."

This field is to be completed by the physician and is not affected by the OASIS.

27. Attending Physician's Signature and Date Signed This field is not affected by the OASIS.

28. Antifraud Statement "Anyone who misrepresents, falsifies, or conceals essential information required for payment of Federal funds may be subject to fine, imprisonment, or civil penalty under applicable Federal laws."

The OASIS data fits well into the nursing assessment that must be performed to complete the HCFA-485 appropriately. Since the POC must be updated and reviewed by the physician every 60–62 days and the OASIS data must be collected every 57–62 days, care must be used to maintain consistency in responses across both documents. Reassessment, including the use of the OASIS items, can continue to assist in developing the most appropriate and effective plan of care for home care patients.

COP ALERT!

Check the most current Medicare COPs to determine the intervals for collection of the recertification information and the collection of follow-up OASIS data.

Using OASIS Data to Develop the Plan of Care

The OASIS data and other information on the assessment form are used along with the physician's orders to develop the patient's care plan. In the MEQA, criteria that could be used to assess documentation for accuracy and completeness were developed by the center. The 100 criteria that were developed are named Outcome Review Criteria (ORC). An example of an ORC can be found in Figure 6–2. While ORCs were originally intended for retrospective review, they can be incorporated into the agency's care plan forms and used as a guide for nursing actions, patient teaching, and documentation. By using them in this way, agencies can more easily identify care behaviors that are important variables in measuring processes and outcomes of care. Also, by identifying these areas an agency wants to measure and placing ORC information in the care plan, data can be more easily retrieved either by manual system or computer analysis up front rather than by conducting retrospective chart reviews.

Examples of How ORCs Relate to Patient Care Planning

Learning Exercise: Example Care Plan from Agency A

Let's say agency A chooses *lack of compliance with cardiac glycosides* as a problematic outcome of patients with a primary diagnosis of acute cardiac/peripheral vascular conditions e.g., congestive heart failure (CHF), angina, coronary artery disease, hypertension, myocardial infarction (MI), or atherosclerotic heart disease. The agency would then choose to use ORC Set Number 85 (see Figure 6–2) and integrate these characteristics, assessments, and care planning/interventions into their standardized care plans or clinical pathways. An example of the standardized care plan and the teaching guides that could be generated for Agency A is found in Figure 6–3. *Look carefully to identify the characteristics of ORC Set Number 85 integrated into this care plan.*

These care plans could be computer-generated, used from a point-of-care system, or be on manual, paper forms. At the process-of-care review (see Chapter 8), the review team conducts a retrospective chart review of the identified number of patients needed for the review. An ORC form is created for each record that is reviewed. The yes/no columns of the form are completed for each record, and the data on all forms are then aggregated into one report. This presents an overview of how the agency's care compares with the review criteria on the ORC. From this analysis, the agency analyzes in more depth the specific areas for remediation (a plan to address the deficiencies and problems) or reinforcement (a plan to encourage the continuation of a behavior or care process). Like the care plans, these reports can be computer-generated, manually prepared, or created through another process system the agency uses.

Figure 6-2 Example of Outcome Review Criteria (ORC).

OBJECTIVE REVIEW CRITERIA (ORC) SET NUMBER 85

OUTCOME: LACK OF COMPLIANCE WITH CARDIAC GLYCOSIDES

Relates specifically to patients with:
- Acute Cardiac/Peripheral Vascular Conditions (e.g., CHF, angina, coronary artery disease, hypertension, myocardial infarction, atherosclerotic heart disease)

Characteristic	Assessment	Assessment Documented Yes/No	Characteristic Present Yes/No	Care Planning/Intervention	In Plan of Care Yes/No/Not Applicable	Intervention Documented Yes/No/Not Applicable
Inadequate knowledge of cardiac glycoside regimen	**Record if the following assessment was done and if it indicates the presence of inadequate knowledge of cardiac glycoside regimen:** 1. Assess baseline knowledge of cardiac glycoside regimen. If knowledge is inadequate, Characteristic Present is "Yes." **If no inadequate knowledge of cardiac glycoside regimen is present, proceed to the next characteristic. If inadequate knowledge of cardiac glycoside regimen is indicated by any assessment activity, determine if the following detailed assessments were done:** 2. Assess knowledge of rationale for use of cardiac glycoside. 3. Assess knowledge of schedule for taking cardiac glycoside. 4. Assess knowledge of proper dosage of cardiac glycoside. **Proceed to Care Planning/Intervention.**			1. Insure that patient is seen by an RN. 2. If patient does not know rationale for taking cardiac glycoside, instruct in rationale for taking cardiac glycoside. 3. If patient does not know schedule for taking cardiac glycoside, instruct in schedule for taking cardiac glycoside. 4. If patient does not know proper dosage of cardiac glycoside, instruct in proper dosage of cardiac glycoside. 5. Provide teaching aids to reinforce teaching. 6. Determine if patient learned what was taught. 7. If patient did not learn, redesign the teaching plan to incorporate new teaching approaches. 8. If patient did not learn, reteach using the new teaching plan. 9. If patient did not learn and reteaching occurred, evaluate if patient learned what was taught.		
Side effects of cardiac glycoside therapy	**Record if the following assessments were done and if they indicate the presence of side effects of cardiac glycoside therapy:** 1. Assess for nausea, vomiting, diarrhea, or anorexia. 2. Assess for headache, weakness, apathy, drowsiness. 3. Assess for abnormal heart rhythm. 4. Assess heart rate. If heart rate is below 60, Characteristic Present is "Yes." **If the presence of side effects of cardiac glycoside therapy is indicated by any assessment activity, proceed to Care Planning/Intervention. If no side effects of cardiac glycoside therapy are present, proceed to the next characteristic.**			1. Insure that patient is seen by an RN. 2. If nausea, vomiting, diarrhea, or anorexia occur, instruct patient in measures to reduce symptoms. 3. If medications are producing side effects/adverse reactions, instruct patient to hold medication and consult with physician within same calendar day as visit. 4. If side effects/adverse reactions are documented as life threatening, advise patient to seek emergency care.		

Figure 6-2   Continued

Characteristic	Assessment	Assessment Documented Yes/No	Characteristic Present Yes/No	Care Planning/Intervention	In Plan of Care Yes/No/ Not Applicable	Intervention Documented Yes/No/ Not Applicable
Complexity of treatment regimen	**Record if the following assessments were done and if they indicate the presence of complexity of treatment regimen:** 1. Assess patient's compliance with the entire therapeutic regimen, including administration of other treatments and medications. 2. Assess impact of entire therapeutic regimen on usual lifestyle. **If complexity of treatment regimen is indicated by any assessment activity, proceed to Care Planning/Intervention. If no complexity of treatment regimen is present, proceed to the next characteristic.**			1. Insure that patient is seen by an RN. 2. Assist patient to develop a medication administration schedule designed to reduce complexity and accommodate lifestyle. 3. Consult with physician to determine if medications or treatments can be consolidated or eliminated.		
lack of cardiac symptom relief	**Record if the following assessments were done and if they indicate a lack of cardiac symptom relief:** 1. Assess patient's expectations regarding relief of cardiac symptoms. If expectations are inappropriate/unrealistic, Characteristic Present is "Yes." 2. Review cardiac symptom relief patient is experiencing to determine if medications are having desired effect. **If a lack of cardiac symptom relief is indicated by any assessment activity, proceed to Care Planning/Intervention. If no lack of cardiac symptom relief is present, proceed to the next characteristic.**			1. Insure that patient is seen by an RN. 2. If medications are not having desired effect, consult with physician. 3. If patient's expectations regarding cardiac symptom relief are not appropriate/realistic, instruct in likely symptom relief to be obtained form medication regimen.		

Centers for Health Policy and Services Research, Denver, CO. OUTCOME 85 ORC ABSTRACTING FORM 8/93; 85.1. Used with permission.

Figure 6-2 *Continued*

Characteristic	Assessment	Assessment Documented Yes/No	Charac-teristic Present Yes/No	Care Planning/Intervention	In Plan of Care Yes/No/ Not Applicable	Intervention Documented Yes/No/ Not Applicable
Altered cognitive functioning affecting ability to manage medications	**Record if the following assessments were done and if they indicate the presence of altered cognitive functioning affecting ability to manage medications:** 1. Assess for memory loss. 2. Assess for confusion (level of orientation). 3. Assess ability to differentiate time of day. 4. Assess ability to differentiate day of week. 5. Assess ability to count or pour proper dose of medication. 6. Assess use of medication causing alterations in mental status. 7. Assess alcohol use. 8. Assess substance abuse other than alcohol. **If altered cognitive functioning affecting ability to manage medications is indicated by any assessment activity, proceed to Care Planning/Intervention. If no altered cognitive functioning affecting ability to manage medications is present, proceed to the next characteristic.**			1. Insure that patient is seen by an RN. 2. Provide a medication reminder system (alarms, diary, etc.). 3. Insure that medications are correctly set up. 4. Consult with physician or pharmacist to provide medications of different size, color, or shape. 5. If patient is using medications causing altered mental status, consult with physician to determine if medications can be eliminated or substitutions made. 6. If patient's alcohol use is affecting mental status, encourage patient to decrease alcohol use or refer for counseling/support. 7. If substance abuse other than alcohol is causing altered mental status, report use to the appropriate care provider.		

Figure 6–2 *Continued*

Characteristic	Assessment	Assessment Documented Yes/No	Characteristic Present Yes/No	Care Planning/Intervention	In Plan of Care Yes/No/Not Applicable	Intervention Documented Yes/No/Not Applicable
Need for human assistance with medication administration	**Record if the following assessment was done and if it indicates the presence of need for human assistance with medication administration:** 1. Assess need for human assistance with medication administration. If assistance is needed, Characteristic Present is "Yes." **If no need for human assistance with medication administration is present, proceed to the next characteristic. If need for human assistance with medication administration is indicated by any assessment activity, determine if the following detailed assessments were done:** 2. Assess how often assistance with medication administration is needed. 3. Assess if there is a person available to assist with medication administration as often as needed (do not include services provided by the home health agency). 4. Assess if there is a person capable of assisting with medication administration as often as needed (do not include services provided by the home health agency). 5. Assess if there is a person willing to assist with medication administration as often as needed (do not include services provided by the home health agency). **Proceed to Care Planning/Intervention.**			1. Insure that patient is seen by an RN. 2. If there is a person who can provide assistance with medication administration, instruct that person how to provide assistance. 3. If the patient needs more assistance with medication administration than the person can provide, insure that the patient receives supplemental assistance. 4. If there is no one to provide assistance with medication administration, insure that assistance is provided as often as needed. 5. If home health agency services are the only source of assistance, refer to other community agencies for ongoing assistance. 6. If financial assistance/counseling is needed, insure that financial assistance/counseling is provided.		

Centers for Health Policy and Services Research, Denver, CO. OUTCOME 85 ORC ABSTRACTING FORM 8/93; 85.1. Used with permission.

Figure 6-2 *Continued*

Characteristic	Assessment	Assess-ment Docu-mented Yes/No	Charac-teristic Present Yes/No	Care Planning/Intervention	In Plan of Care Yes/No/ Not Applicable	Intervention Documented Yes/No/ Not Applicable
Inadequate environment for compliance with cardiac glycoside regimen	**Record if the following assessments were done and if they indicate the presence of an inadequate environment for compliance with cardiac glycoside regimen:** 1. Assess if patient has an adequate supply of cardiac glycoside. 2. Assess if patient has financial resources to insure an adequate supply of cardiac glycoside. **If an inadequate environment for compliance with cardiac glycoside regimen is indicated by any assessment activity, proceed to Care Planning/Intervention. If no inadequate environment for compliance with cardiac glycoside regimen is present, proceed to the next characteristic.**			1. Assist patient to procure cardiac glycosides. 2. If financial resources are not adequate, provide information regarding financial assistance.		

Centers for Health Policy and Services Research, Denver, CO. OUTCOME 85 ORC ABSTRACTING FORM 8/93; 85.1. Used with permission.

Figure 6–3 *Example of a care plan for a cardiac patient integrating ORCs.*

Patient Name: _____ SOC: _____

CARDIAC CONDITION/CIRCULATORY OVERLOAD

POTENTIAL MEDICAL DIAGNOSES AND ICD-9 CODES:
(Relates specifically to patients with acute cardiac/peripheral vascular conditions)

Congestive Heart Failure—428.0
Atrial Fibrillation—427.31
Angina—413.9
Cardiomyopathy—425.4
Coronary Atherosclerosis—414.00
Cardiac Dysrhythmia—427.9
Edema—782.3
Heart Block—426.9
Hypertension—401.9

Fluid and Electrolyte Imbalance—276.9
Myocardial Infarction—410.92
Peripheral Vascular Disease—443.9
Pulmonary Edema with Cardiac Disease—428.1
Left Heart Failure—428.1
Mitral Valve Disease—424.0
Pericardial Disease—423.9
Venous Thrombosis—453.9

ASSOCIATED NURSING DIAGNOSES:

Activity Intolerance
Anxiety
Body Image Disturbance
Breathing Pattern Disturbance
Caregiver Role Strain
Constipation
Coping, Ineffective family or individual
Decreased Cardiac Output
Denial, Ineffective
Family Processes, Altered
Fatigue

Fear
Fluid Volume Excess
Impaired Gas Exchange
Knowledge Deficit (specify)
Impaired Physical Mobility
Pain
Self-Care Deficit
Altered Tissue Perfusion
Altered Urinary Elimination
Energy Conservation (Inadequate)
Others

Characteristic 1:

Deterioration in the patient's cardiac status.

Assessments:

Record if the following assessments were done and if they indicate the presence of deterioration in the patient's cardiac status:

1. Assess for increased shortness of breath at rest.
2. Assess for increased shortness of breath during or immediately after activity.
3. Assess weight. ($\geq$ 2 # increase in 2 days)
4. Assess respirations for variations from norm.
5. Assess pulse for variations from norm.
6. Assess blood pressure for variations from norm.
7. Assess breath sounds for abnormalities.
8. Assess for peripheral edema. (Document 0–4+)
9. Assess for chest pain. (Amount, site, frequency, type, radiation, and duration)
10. Assess for cyanosis (Assess nail beds, skin, lip color, edema.)

If deterioration in the patient's cardiac status is indicated by any assessment activity, proceed to interventions appropriate to that condition. If no deterioration in the patient's cardiac status is present, proceed to the next characteristic.

Figure 6-3 *Continued*

Characteristic 2:

Patient/Caregiver's inability to manage cardiac therapy.

Assessments

1. Assess ability of patient/caregiver to manage oral medications.
2. Assess ability of patient/caregiver to manage activity level.
3. Assess ability of patient/caregiver to manage patient's anxiety level.
4. Assess ability of patient/caregiver to manage patient's dyspnea.
5. Assess for nitroglycerin use, frequency, amount, relief patterns.
6. Assess baseline knowledge of cardiac glycoside regimen.
7. Assess knowledge of schedule for taking cardiac glycosides.

If patient/caregiver's inability to manage cardiac therapy is indicated by any assessment activity, proceed to interventions appropriate to that condition. If no problem exists, proceed to the next characteristic.

Characteristic 3:

Patient/Caregiver's compliance with therapy.

Assessments

1. Assess if patient is taking medications as prescribed.
2. Assess if patient is taking fluids as prescribed.
3. Assess if patient is following dietary regimen.
4. Assess if patient is following protocol for other treatments (i.e. cardiac rehab, exercises).
5. Assess for presence of side effects of medications or treatments or fluids.
6. Assess expectations for symptom relief.
7. Assess complexity of medication or treatment regimen.
8. Assess patient safety in presence of noncompliance to avoid leaving patient in an unsafe environment.
9. Assess for confusion, nausea, vomiting, diarrhea, or anorexia.

Characteristic 4:

Inadequate environment for providing home care.

Assessments

1. Assess if patient's home has adequate heating.
2. Assess if patient's home environment has running water.
3. Assess if patient's home environment has adequate sanitation.
4. Assess if patient's home environment is safe.
5. Assess for substance and alcohol use.

DOCUMENT ALL VARIATIONS FROM THE NORM.

Assess for Risk Factors

· Heavy smoking
· Obesity
· Alcohol dependency
· Drug dependency

If OASIS assessment indicates deficiencies in any of the following, referral to the appropriate discipline is necessary. (MO150, MO160, MO220, MO300, MO310, MO320, MO330, MO350, MO360, MO370, MO390, MO400, MO560, MO590, MO610, MO620, MO640, MO650, MO660, MO670, MO680, MO690, MO700, MO710, MO720, MO740, MO750, MO760, MO770, MO810.)

Figure 6-3 *Continued*

Triggers for Referral To:

MSW:

MO150, MO160, MO170, MO220, MO300, MO310, MO320, MO330, MO340, MO360, MO370, MO380, MO390, MO400, MO560, MO570, MO580, MO590, MO600, MO610, MO620, MO760, MO770.

PT:

MO270, MO310, MO320, MO380, MO420, MO430, MO640, MO650, MO660, MO670, MO680, MO690, MO700, MO710, MO810.

OT:

MO380, MO720, MO730, MO740, MO750, MO760, MO770, MO780, MO790.

ST:

MO400, MO410.

Dietician:

MO250, MO290, MO710, MO720.

INTERVENTIONS

Visit number/date
i.e. #2/10-9-98

1. Explain patient rights and responsibilities. _____
2. Assess for home safety. _____
3. Assess vital signs _____
4. Assess hydration and nutrition. _____
5. Assess coping skills of caregiver. _____
6. Assess patient's need for personal care assistance and schedule home health aide as indicated. _____
7. Refer to PT, ST, OT, MSW as indicated. _____
8. Instruct patient/caregiver on home safety. _____
9. Instruct patient/caregiver on medication regimen. _____
10. Instruct patient/caregiver on home maintenance program. _____
11. Teach patient to report increased shortness of breath/seek emergency care. _____
12. If weight gain is >2 pounds within 1 week, consult with physician. _____
13. If respirations are outside patient's normal range, consult with physician, if indicated. _____
14. If pulse is outside patient's normal range, consult with physician, if indicated. _____
15. Teach patient/caregiver to take patient's pulse and report pulse outside specified parameters to skilled nurse or physician. _____
16. Instruct on blood pressure monitoring and safe parameters for patient. (___/___) _____
17. If blood pressure is outside patient's normal range, consult with physician. _____
18. If abnormal breath sounds occur, consult with physician, if indicated. _____
19. If peripheral edema occurs, monitor edema/consult with physician if indicated. _____
20. Teach patient to report chest pain/seek emergency care. _____
21. Instruct patient/caregiver on observing for pallor, cyanosis, or disphoresis and when to report same to physician. _____
22. Instruct patient/caregiver to report lethargy, confusion and anxiety to SN or physician. _____
23. Instruct patient to avoid activities that elicit a Vasalva response. _____
24. Teach patient to elevate lower extremities by ___ inches/feet and avoid pressure under knees. _____
25. Teach patient to alternate periods of rest with periods of activity to avoid undue stress. _____
26. Instruct on dietary restrictions (Low Na or other diet). _____

Figure 6-3 *Continued*

27. Teach to supplement potassium in the diet if indicated. (Specify what is to be taught.) _____
28. Teach patient ordered exercises, addressing issues of stair climbing, lifting, and daily rest periods as indicated. _____

29. Instruct on avoiding activities which can precipitate chest pain. _____
30. Teach energy conservation techniques to patient and caregiver. _____
31. Instruct on the appropriate use of medications (specify). _____
32. Instruct on the importance of obtaining frequent weights to assess fluid retention. _____
33. Teach to follow fluid restrictions as ordered. (Specify amt/24hr.) _____
34. Instruct on signs and symptoms of cardiac decompensation. (Specify) _____
35. If patient/caregiver are unable to manage oral medications, insure that assistance with managing medications is provided. _____
36. If patient/caregiver are unable to manage the patient's activity level, insure that assistance with management are provided. (Consider MSW referral.) _____
37. If patient is not taking medications as prescribed, instruct in medication regimen. _____ (Specify medications and teaching in documentation.)
38. If patient is not following dietary regimen, instruct as necessary. (Consider referral to dietician.) _____
39. If patient is not following protocol for other treatments, instruct as necessary. (Specify problem and teaching in documentation.) _____
40. Instruct patient/caregiver regarding care and safety with oxygen therapy at home. _____
41. If side effects of therapy are present, instruct in measures to relieve side effects and when to notify SN and physician. _____
42. Instruct patient/caregiver regarding possible side effects, schedule, function, and actions of multiple medications. _____
43. If medication/treatment regimen is complex, consult with physician for the possibility of simplification/consolidation. Consider drug/drug and drug/food interactions. _____
44. Instruct patient/caregiver regarding venipunctures and other labwork as indicated. _____
45. Instruct patient in the correct use of antiembolic stockings. _____
46. Teach patient signs and symptoms of pacemaker problems or failure, including SOB, dizziness, others. _____

47. Other interventions as necessary. (Specify.) _____

Exacerbation Summary

Exacerbation of characteristic # _____ and assessment(s) # _____ Date: _____

Interventions Chosen _____ Encounter Dates _____

Exacerbation of characteristic # _____ and assessment(s) # _____ Date: _____

Interventions Chosen _____ Encounter Dates _____

Exacerbation of characteristic # _____ and assessment(s) # _____ Date: _____

Interventions Chosen _____ Encounter Dates _____

Exacerbation of characteristic # _____ and assessment(s) # _____ Date: _____

Interventions Chosen _____ Encounter Dates _____

Figure 6-3 *Continued*

EXPECTED OUTCOMES (E.O.)

Variance codes: 1 **Patient related.**
2 **Situation related.**
3 **Systems related.**
N/A Not Applicable = No Variance

1. Stable cardiac status, as evidenced by cardiac assessment and BP between _____ and _____ .
2. Patient/caregiver demonstrates compliance with home therapeutic regimen/medication regimen.
3. Patient/caregiver demonstrates understanding of and compliance with dietary and hydration regimen as evidenced by clinical assessment and stabilization of weight.
4. Patient/caregiver demonstrates understanding of safe oxygen therapy as evidenced by return demonstration.
5. Patient/caregiver can define cardiac disease process.
6. Patient/caregiver can describe basic anatomy and physiology of the heart/circulatory system.
7. Patient/caregiver can list factors which increase risk of cardiac disease.
8. Patient/caregiver can recognize signs and symptoms of exacerbation of disease.
9. Patient/caregiver can report measures to prevent exacerbation of cardiac disease.
10. Patient/caregiver can demonstrate method of securing assistance during exacerbation of disease process. (Emergency call, etc.).

E.O.# ____   Date met: ____   Variance: ____   E.O.# ____   Date met: ____   Variance: ____
E.O.# ____   Date met: ____   Variance: ____   E.O.# ____   Date met: ____   Variance: ____
E.O.# ____   Date met: ____   Variance: ____   E.O.# ____   Date met: ____   Variance: ____
E.O.# ____   Date met: ____   Variance: ____   E.O.# ____   Date met: ____   Variance: ____
E.O.# ____   Date met: ____   Variance: ____   E.O.# ____   Date met: ____   Variance: ____

Management and Evaluation (M&E) of the Patients Plan of Care:

_____

Date M&E began

Projected Discharge Date: _____
Date discharge teaching initiated: (to begin 3 wks prior to d/c date): _____
Date discharge teaching completed: _____

SIGNATURE OF TEAM MEMBERS/SKILLED CARE PROVIDERS

Team Member Signature _____ Initials: _____
Team Member Signature _____ Initials: _____
Team Member Signature _____ Initials: _____
Team Member Signature _____ Initials: _____

Figure 6-4 *Cardiovascular Diseases Teaching Guides*

Patient Name: _____ SOC: _____

Date _____ **Encounter #** _____ **Specific Teaching** _____ **Initials** _____

I. PERIPHERAL VASCULAR DISEASE

*Instruct the patient/caregiver regarding peripheral vascular disease. _____

A. It is a diminished blood supply to the lower extremities, resulting in lack of oxygen and nutrients to the lower extremities.
B. It can be caused by heart failure or obstructed blood vessels.
C. May cause sharp or aching, cramp-like pain, depending upon cause.

*Explain the signs and symptoms of peripheral vascular disease. _____

A. Arterial insufficiency:
 1. Sharp pain, which increases after exercise.
 2. Cool, pale skin.
 3. Absent or diminished pulse in legs and feet.
 4. Reddish-blue color of skin.
 5. Delayed healing of extremities.

B. Venous insufficiency:
 1. Aching, cramping-type pain.
 2. Edema of affected extremities.
 3. Mottled and pigmented skin.
 4. Ulcers close to ankle.

*Teach patient/caregiver possible precipitating factors and appropriate measures to decrease risk. _____

A. Factor: Constriction of blood vessels
 Measures:
 1. Avoid smoking.
 2. Avoid constrictive clothing.
 3. Never cross legs.
 4. Avoid long periods of sitting or standing.
 5. Avoid exposing lower extremities to cold.

B. Factor: Sedentary life style
 Measures:
 1. Exercise as ordered by physician to promote circulation.
 2. Walking is an excellent exercise for this disease if patient can tolerate.

C. Factor: Poor nutrition
 Measures:
 1. Eat a well-balanced diet.
 2. Refer to dietician if needed.

D. Factor: Not taking medication or taking it incorrectly.
 Measures:
 1. Instruct patient to take medications as ordered.
 2. Instruct on benefits of medication and results of not taking it as ordered.
 3. Instruct in use of pill planner or other reminder if needed.

Figure 6-4 *Cardiovascular Diseases Teaching Guides—Continued*

Patient Name: _____ *SOC:* _____

Date _____ **Encounter #** _____ **Specific Teaching** _____ **Initials** _____

E. Factor: Inadequate hygiene
Measures:
  1. Wash feet carefully each day and pat dry.
  2. Wear clean cotton socks daily.
  3. Trim nails with caution or refer to podiatrist.
  4. Assess feet for infection, redness, others.
  5. Refer for Home Health Aide if necessary.

F. Factor: Injury to lower extremity
Measures:
  1. Never go barefooted.
  2. Cut toenails carefully straight across after soaking them for ten minutes.
  3. Wear well-fitting shoes; avoid open-toe sandals for outside use.
  4. Avoid scratching lower extremities. Use lotion as needed to relieve dry skin.
  5. Refer to podiatrist for corns, calluses, ingrown toenails, etc.

*Instruct the patient/caregiver regarding possible complications. _____

A. Stasis ulcers
B. Cellulitis
C. Gangrene
D. Thrombophlebitis

Figure 6-4 *Cardiovascular Diseases Teaching Guides—Continued*

Patient Name: _____ SOC: _____

Date _____ Encounter # _____ Specific Teaching _____ Initials _____

II. CONGESTIVE HEART FAILURE

*Instruct the patient/caregiver regarding the definition of Congestive Heart Failure. _____

A. It is a condition in which the heart is unable to pump an adequate supply of blood to meet the oxygen and nutritional needs of the body.
B. The decrease in amount of blood pumped with each heart contraction causes an increase in circulatory pressure.
C. This pressure can enlarge the heart and cause the muscle to weaken and fail.

*Describe the anatomy and physiology of the heart briefly to the patient/caregiver. _____

A. The heart consists of four chambers—the right and left ventricles, and the right and left atria.
B. The upper chambers, the atria, receive blood from various parts of the body and pump it into the ventricles.
C. The right ventricle pumps blood into the lungs, and the left ventricle pumps blood into all parts of the body.
D. When the heart weakens, this pump is ineffective and heart failure develops.

*List factors that may increase the risk of developing congestive heart failure. _____

A. Myocardial infarction.
B. Heart arrhythmias.
C. Hypertension.
D. Congenital heart defects.
E. Lung infections and diseases.
F. Anemia.
G. Obesity.

*Instruct in recognizing the signs and symptoms of congestive heart failure. _____

A. Fatigue.
B. Shortness of breath.
C. Rapid heart rate.
D. Edema (fluid retention).
E. Excessive urination at night.
F. Cold, sweaty skin.
G. Restlessness or confusion.
H. Dry cough, or a cough which produces frothy sputum.
I. Unexplained rapid weight gain.
J. Loss of appetite.

*Instruct patient/caregiver in measures to prevent Congestive Heart Failure episodes. _____

A. Avoid stress.
B. Avoid fatigue by gradually increasing activity, with planned rest periods, until a balance can be obtained between activity and precipitation of symptoms.
C. Eat a well-balanced, low-sodium diet if ordered by physician.
D. Avoid extremes in temperature.
E. Take medication exactly as prescribed. (Instruct on all aspects of medications.)
F. Restrict fluids, if ordered.
G. Weigh daily to assess weight gain and to detect fluid retention.

Figure 6-4   *Cardiovascular Diseases Teaching Guides—Continued*

Patient Name: _____   *SOC:* _____

Date _____ **Encounter #** _____ **Specific Teaching** _____ **Initials** _____

H. Report the following symptoms immediately:
  1. Weight gain.
  2. Loss of appetite.
  3. Increased shortness of breath.
  4. Edema.
  5. Persistent cough.
  6. Frequent urination at night.

*Instruct the patient/caregiver regarding possible complications of long-term, untreated CHF. _____

A. Acute pulmonary edema.
B. Damage to such organs as liver, kidney, or brain.
C. Pulmonary infections.

Figure 6-4 *Cardiovascular Diseases Teaching Guides—Continued*

Patient Name: _____   SOC: _____

Date _____ Encounter # _____ Specific Teaching _____ Initials _____

III. ANGINA PECTORIS

*Instruct patient/caregiver in definition of angina pectoris. _____

A. It is temporary pain without damage to the heart.
B. Pain is caused by insufficient oxygen to meet the demands of the heart.
C. Lack of oxygen occurs when insufficient blood flows through the coronary arteries due to constriction or blockage of vessels.
D. Stable angina usually has a precipitating cause, while unstable angina can occur while at rest.

*Teach the patient/caregiver to recognize signs and symptoms of angina pectoris and differentiate from pain of MI. _____

A. Chest pain (may range from mild to very severe).
B. Anxiety.
C. Indigestion.
D. Sweating.
E. Shortness of breath.
F. Relieved by rest.

*Instruct patient/caregiver regarding possible locations of anginal pain. _____

A. Mid-anterior chest.
B. Neck and/or jaw.
C. Inner aspects of arms (left arm more common).
D. Upper abdomen.
E. Shoulders and between shoulder blades.

*Discuss possible precipitating factors and appropriate measures to decrease risk. _____

A. Factor: Sudden physical exertion
   Measures:
   1. Exercise regularly.
   2. Take regular rest periods.
   3. Take nitroglycerin before increasing activity level, including sexual activity.

B. Factor: Emotional Stress
   Measures:
   1. Avoid stressful situations if possible.
   2. Practice stress management.

C. Factor: Consumption of a heavy meal.
   Measures:
   1. Eat small, frequent meals.
   2. Rest after eating.

D. Factor: Temperature extremes
   Measures:
   1. Dress warmly in cold weather.
   2. Avoid sleeping in cold rooms.
   3. Avoid becoming overheated.

Figure 6-4 *Cardiovascular Diseases Teaching Guides—Continued*

Patient Name: _____ SOC: _____

Date _____ Encounter # _____ Specific Teaching _____ Initials _____

4. Do not mow/garden during day/cooler evening temperatures are preferred.
5. Avoid inhaling extremely cold air.

E. Factor: Nicotine
Measures:
1. Avoid smoking, as this constricts blood vessels.
2. Do not use snuff or chewing tobacco as well.

F. Factor: Hypertension
Measures:
1. Take medications as prescribed.
2. Follow dietary restrictions.
3. Monitor blood pressure frequently or as ordered by physician.

G. Factor: Obesity
Measures:
1. Achieve and maintain ideal body weight.
2. Follow dietary restrictions.
3. Avoid foods high in cholesterol.
4. Dietary consult if needed.

H. Factor: Constipation accompanied by severe straining.
Measures:
1. Eat diet high in fiber.
2. Exercise regularly.
3. Take stool softeners as needed.
4. Increase intake of fruits and vegetables.

*Instruct patient/caregiver on actions to take if an anginal attack occurs. _____

A. Take nitroglycerin at the first sign of angina.
B. Rest in a lying or sitting position.
C. Maintain a quiet environment.
D. If the client feels no relief five minutes after taking nitroglycerin, repeat nitroglycerin again.
E. If another five minutes pass and the client feels no relief, take nitro a third time.
F. If the client feels no relief five minutes after the third dose of nitroglycerin, seek medical attention immediately.

Instruct patient/caregiver regarding possible complications of angina. _____
A. Cardiac dysrhythmias.
B. Myocardial infarction.
C. Others.

Figure 6-4   *Cardiovascular Diseases Teaching Guides—Continued*

Patient Name: _____   *SOC:* _____

Date _____ **Encounter #** _____ **Specific Teaching** _____ **Initials** _____

IV. THROMBOPHLEBITIS

*Instruct the patient/caregiver regarding the definition of thrombophlebitis _____

A. It is an inflammation of the vein with a clot formation.
B. It occurs most often in the veins of the legs, but may also occur in other areas of the body.
C. It breaks loose and travels through the bloodstream is known as embolis; can cause death, especially if it reaches the pulmonary tree.

*Teach the patient/caregiver factors that increase the risk of thrombophlebitis. _____

A. Long periods of immobility or lack of position changes.
B. Oral contraceptives.
C. Trauma.
D. Varicose veins or other vascular problems.
E. Intravenous therapy.
F. Advancing age.
G. Cardiac disease.
H. Cigarette smoking.
I. Obesity.
J. Surgery.

*Instruct patient/caregiver regarding the signs and symptoms of thrombophlebitis _____

A. **Superficial thrombophlebitis:**
   1. Increased firmness of the vein.
   2. Redness and warmth along the vein.
   3. Tenderness.
   4. Fever.
   5. Swelling.

B. **Deep vein thrombosis: (Note: occasionally may be asymptomatic)**
   1. Cramping leg pain aggravated by movement.
   2. Increased warmth of the skin.
   3. Fever.
   4. Tenderness.
   5. Edema.

*Teach the patient/caregiver measures to prevent or manage thrombophlebitis _____

A. Promote good circulation especially to extremities.
   1. Avoid constrictive clothing (garters, girdles, etc.).
   2. Avoid smoking (constricts blood bessels).
   3. Avoid crossing legs and sitting for long periods.
   4. Exercise regularly.
   5. Wear support hose when standing for long periods.
   6. Elevate legs periodically.
B. There has been a risk of thrombophlebitis associated with oral contraceptives. In patients with a history of clotting problems, OCP's should be avoided.

Figure 6-4 *Cardiovascular Diseases Teaching Guides—Continued*

Patient Name: _____ *SOC:* _____

Date _____ **Encounter #** _____ **Specific Teaching** _____ **Initials** _____

C. Eat a well-balanced diet (Calcium, vitamin E, and vitamin K all affect clotting mechanism).
D. Achieve and maintain ideal weight.
E. Follow post-operative teaching:
   1. Early ambulation.
   2. Passive and active exercise.
   3. Deep breathing exercise.

*Instruct patient/caregiver regarding treatments that may be ordered _____

A. Pain relief:
   1. Warm, a moist heat to affected area as ordered.
   2. Analgesics as ordered.
   3. Avoid rubbing painful extremity.

B. Anticoagulants as ordered. Tailor teaching to fit oral or injectable anticoagulants.
C. Bedrest or activity as ordered by physician.
D. Prevention of emboli:
   1. Fluids increased to at least 6–8 glasses per day.
   2. Antiembolism stockings.
   3. Activity as per physicians order.

*Instruct patient/caregiver regarding possible complications _____

A. Pulmonary embolism (blood clot to the lung).
B. Stroke (blood clot to the brain).
C. Death.

Figure 6-4   *Cardiovascular Diseases Teaching Guides—Continued*

Patient Name: _____   *SOC:* _____

Date _____ **Encounter #** _____ **Specific Teaching** _____ **Initials** _____

V. MYOCARDIAL INFARCTION

*Instruct patient/caregiver regarding definition of myocardial infarction _____

A. It is irreversible damage to the heart muscle.
B. An occlusion or narrowing of the coronary artery interrupts blood and oxygen flow to the heart.
C. An inadequate blood and oxygen supply to the heart causes damage to the heart muscle.

*Instruct patient/caregiver regarding risk factors _____

A. Smoking.
B. Stress.
C. Obesity.
D. Sedentary lifestyle.
E. Diet high in saturated fats.
F. Age.
G. History of heart disease, hypertension, or diabetes mellitus.

*Instruct patient/caregiver regarding signs and symptoms of a myocardial infarction _____

A. Difficulty breathing.
B. Palpitations.
C. Nausea or vomiting.
D. Weakness.
E. Perspiration.
F. Anxiety.
G. Chest pain:
    1. Can vary from mild discomfort to very severe, crushing pain.
    2. May radiate to neck, arms, shoulder, or jaw.
    3. Unrelieved by rest or nitroglycerin.

*Instruct patient/caregiver regarding action to take if a myocardial infarction occurs. _____

A. Stop activity and remain calm.
B. Call an ambulance and notify physician. Have these emergency numbers posted by the telephone.
C. Assume the least painful position, usually sitting or lying with head elevated.
D. If the client looses consciousness and no pulse is found, cardiopulmonary resuscitation should begin and continue until emergency help arrives.

*Review measures which can prevent a recurrence of myocardial infarction _____

A. Achieve and maintain ideal weight to decrease workload of the heart.
B. Eat diet low in saturated fat, cholesterol, and sodium.
C. Exercise regularly.
    1. Begin with a cardiac rehabilitation program under the guidance of a health professional.
    2. Stop exercise immediately if any pain, shortness of breath, or dizziness is noted.
    3. Progress activity gradually.
    4. Do not exercise 1–2 hours after eating.
D. Monitor and control blood pressure.
E. Learn stress management techniques.

Figure 6-4 *Cardiovascular Diseases Teaching Guides—Continued*

Patient Name: _____ *SOC:* _____

Date _____ **Encounter #** _____ **Specific Teaching** _____ **Initials** _____

F. Avoid tobacco and alcohol.

G. Avoid constipation to decrease strain on the heart.

H. Take medications as ordered and have regular medical checkups.

*Instruct patient/caregiver regarding possible complications of myocardial infarction _____

A. Arrhythmias.

B. Pulmonary Edema.

C. Congestive Heart Failure.

D. Shock.

E. Recurrent myocardial infarction.

F. Structural heart problems (aneurysm or rupture).

G. Thromboembolism.

H. Others.

Figure 6-4 *Cardiovascular Diseases Teaching Guides—Continued*

Patient Name: _____   *SOC:* _____

Date _____ **Encounter #** _____ **Specific Teaching** _____ **Initials** _____

VI. HYPERTENSION

*Instruct patient/caregiver regarding the definition of hypertension. _____

A. It is the occasional or continued elevation of diastolic or systolic blood pressure.
B. The systolic reading (the top number) represents the pressure exerted on the blood vessel wall when the heart is contracting.
C. The diastolic reading (the bottom number) represents the pressure on the blood vessel wall while the heart is at rest.

*Instruct the patient/caregiver regarding "normal" blood pressure values. While no absolute dividing line exists between normal and high blood pressure, the American Heart Association suggests the following guidelines: _____

A. Blood pressure readings for people age 50 or older should not consistently exceed 160/90.
B. Blood pressure readings for people ages 18–49 should not consistently exceed 140/90.

*Teach the patient/caregiver the signs and symptoms of high blood pressure. _____

A. Instruct that blood pressure elevations may not be symptomatic, so pressure should be checked at regular intervals.
B. Dizziness.
C. Headaches.
D. Palpitations.
E. Blurring of vision.
F. Fatigue.
G. Nosebleeds.

*Patient/caregiver can list risk factors for hypertension. _____

A. Age (hypertension typically affects men over 35 and women over 45).
B. Race (incidence rate is higher in African-Americans than Caucasians).
C. Family history.
D. Stress.
E. High sodium intake.
F. High cholesterol intake.
G. Oral contraceptives.
H. Cigarette smoking.
I. Obesity.
J. Sedentary lifestyle.

*Instruct patient/caregiver in measures to control hypertension _____

A. Monitor blood pressure frequently, and have regular medical checkups.
B. Take medication exactly as prescribed.
C. Avoid or control stress.
D. Decrease cholesterol to avoid atherosclerosis.
E. Avoid excessive sodium to decrease fluid retention.
F. Stop smoking (smoking constricts vessels and increases blood pressure).
G. Achieve and maintain ideal weight.

Figure 6-4 *Cardiovascular Diseases Teaching Guides—Continued*

Patient Name: _____ *SOC:* _____

Date _____ **Encounter #** _____ **Specific Teaching** _____ **Initials** _____

  H. Exercise regularly.
  I. Change from oral contraceptives to another form of birth control. (Be sure to discuss this with your physician.)

*Instruct patient/caregiver regarding possible complications of hypertension. _____

  A. Visual changes due to retinal damage.
  B. Heart disease.
  C. Stroke.
  D. Kidney damage/failure.
  E. Hypertensive crisis (sharp rise in blood pressure to greater than 200/120, severe headache, vomiting).

Figure 6-4   *Cardiovascular Diseases Teaching Guides—Continued*

Patient Name: _____   SOC: _____

Date _____ Encounter # _____ Specific Teaching _____ Initials _____

VII. CORONARY ARTERY DISEASE

*Instruct the patient/caregiver regarding coronary artery disease. _____

A. It is a narrowing or blockage of one or more of the coronary arteries causing a decreased blood and oxygen supply to the heart.
B. Lack of oxygen may cause damage to the heart muscle.
C. The disease develops very slowly and may be very advanced before symptoms develop.
D. The primary cause is atherosclerosis.
    1. Atherosclerosis is the buildup of fatty, fibrous plaques o the inner wall of the artery causing it to become narrowed and hardened.
    2. Stages of atherosclerosis can range from a fatty streak to a complicated lesion.

*Teach patient/caregiver to identify factors that may increase risk of coronary heart disease. _____

A. Controllable factors:
    1. Cigarette smoking.
    2. Elevated blood pressure.
    3. Stress.
    4. High cholesterol diet.
    5. Obesity.
    6. Sedentary lifestyle.
    7. Diabetes mellitus.

B. Noncontrollable factors:
    1. Age (risk increases with age).
    2. Sex (incidence rate in men is three times that of women).
    3. Race (incidence rate is higher in blacks than whites).
    4. Genetic predisposition.

*Instruct patient/caregiver regarding measures to prevent or manage coronary heart disease. _____

A. Avoid high-cholesterol foods.
B. Avoid food and drinks containing caffeine (e.,g. chocolate, coffee, and colas).
C. Avoid excess sodium.
D. Exercise regularly.
E. Avoid or decrease stress.
F. Achieve and maintain ideal weight. (May refer to dietician if needed.)
G. Avoid smoking.

*Discuss possible diseases which may result from untreated or inadequately treated coronary artery disease. _____

A. Myocardial infarction.
B. Angina pectoris.
C. Heart failure.
D. Dysrhythmias.
E. Cardiac arrest.

Part III

Data Interpretation and Measurement of Outcomes

Measuring Outcomes   7

Introduction

Now that your agency is collecting quality data, the question of what to do with this information arises. It is not enough to simply collect the data using the OASIS data set. The agency must be able to use these data to determine if the care is being provided in a sufficient or appropriate way. Although the proposed Medicare Conditions of Participation (COPs) of March 10, 1997, didn't address the data analysis being conducted by the demonstration agencies, these systems will most likely become part of the final or future regulations. Thus, this chapter and Chapter 8 will describe data interpretation and the measurement of outcomes, centering on the systems developed and used by the Center for Health Policy at Denver.

Measurement of Outcomes

The desired results of care always include positive outcomes, adherence to clinical standards, compliance with regulatory and accreditation guidelines, and outcomes as good as or better than those of other agencies on a local, regional, and national basis. Additionally, outcome data will also allow a home care organization to show payers the result of the care they have been able to pay for within their guidelines.

For home health organizations that have an ongoing system of performance improvement (PI) activities, integrating the OASIS data to measure outcomes will become a part of this process. Many agencies have computerized systems that collect and manage clinical and financial information but may not have data that can be used for program planning and evaluation as well as PI activities. It is clear from the proposed HCFA home health regulations mandating the collection of OASIS information that all home care organizations will need to become computerized to remain as providers in the Medicare program. Since the collection of OASIS and OBQI mandated data for the Medicare program and additional requirements from the Joint Commission on Healthcare Organizations (JCAHO) through the ORYX program are in the development process, the majority of computer systems will need adequate time to become fully integrated. Very small agencies, or those presently without computerization, may need to somewhat laboriously construct these outcomes with pencil and paper, calculator, and persistence until they can obtain computer assistance through their own vendor or through collaboration with others.

As discussed in Chapters 1 and 2, an outcome measure is the quantification (assignment of numerical values) of a change in health status between two or more time points *or* an event that represents a proxy (something that happens externally to the patient that affects a change in health status—i.e., hospitalization, transfer to inpatient facility). Outcomes can be positive, negative, or neutral. Chapter 1 presented an overview of what outcomes are and what they are not. The OASIS data set has been extensively tested for inter-rater reliability so that it doesn't matter if different nurses actually perform the series of data collection as long as they are trained in the same manner with the same content and have their assessments checked periodically by supervisory staff.

Implementing Outcomes Measurement in Your Agency

In order to compute outcome results, the following somewhat laborious process must occur:

1. It must be determined whether the outcomes are to be measured for all patients (i.e., global outcomes) or for a certain group of patients with the same primary diagnosis, such as those with CHF or COPD (i.e., focused outcomes).

2. When implementing the OASIS and OBQI process, initially it is desirable to look closely at only one or two outcomes of care. This will enable the individual(s) coordinating the process, the work team, management, and administration to become familiar with the process before attempting to look at numerous outcomes. In choosing your two outcomes, consider the definitions in Display 7–1, to determine the *types* of outcomes you want to analyze.

3. In the MEQA project, 25 Quality Indicator Groups (QUIGs) were described; of these, 16 focused on acute conditions and 9 on chronic conditions (see Display 7–2). QUIGs can be used to stratify patients into nonexclusive or nonoverlapping groups in order to examine within-condition outcome measures, or they can be used in case mix analysis and risk adjustment to adjust global or focused outcome measures. It is possible for patients to belong to three or four QUIGs, both acute and chronic.

4. Since these QUIGs were developed to be used with various patient groups, it is important to pay attention to sample sizes when determining the specific outcomes an agency desires to measure. When choosing focused outcome measures for conditions, the center recommended that an agency admit at *least* 60 patients with that condition in a nine-month period. For example, if there are too few patients within a category selected for study, it may be difficult to extrapolate the findings to larger groups of patients because too few subjects may skew the reliability of the processes or artificially inflate the numbers.

5. The most important outcomes to monitor must be determined. For example, if an agency chooses to focus on COPD patients, a change in a patient's functional ability to provide his/her own breathing treatments or to manage a required metered-dose inhaler may be critical health attributes. Also, it is usually best to use the measurement points of admission and discharge to analyze this outcome, since this will encompass an "episode of care."

6. Remember that the definition or criteria for start-of-care (SOC) and follow-up points must correspond to the same time periods for all patients being considered. To measure outcomes,

Display 7-1 *Definitions of Outcomes and Related Terms*

Dichotomous outcome measure The possibility of only two values; a commonly used dichotomous measure is that of gender—i.e., 0=male, 1=female. There are only two possible choices for this type of measure. If the patient can improve and does so, he will "earn" or be assigned the value of "1." If he does not improve, he is assigned the value of "0." So if the patient is rated at "2" for bathing at SOC but rated at "1" at discharge, he will be assigned the value of "1" since he didn't worsen but in fact got better.

End-Result Outcome (pure outcome) A change in patient health status between two or more time points.

Focused Outcome Restricted to a subgroup of patients—i.e., cardiac.

Global Outcome Pertaining to all patients. These results are projected to apply universally.

Health Status Attribute A measurement of some attribute of individual or aggregate health that is considered to reflect health status. Each attribute is given a numerical value, and a score is calculated for the individual or community from the aggregate of these values. To the extent possible, these attributes are objective—that is, they are facts for which various observers or investigators would each find the same value. These attributes can be determined by examination, function, quality of life, activities of daily living (ADL), emotional well-being, episodes of medical care, or diagnoses.

Improvement Outcome Measures Corresponding to a specific health status attribute such as ambulation or dyspnea. As is a dichotomous measure, takes on the value of either:

1 If the patient improves according to the scale for the health status attribute under consideration
0 If the patient does not improve.

An improvement measure cannot be computed if the patient's health is optimal for the attribute of interest at SOC (i.e., the patient cannot possibly improve or achieve a more optimal level of health status according to the scale being considered). Simply speaking, a number value will be applied to improvement or the lack thereof.

Intermediate-Result Outcome (instrumental outcome) A change in patient (or informal caregiver's) behavior, emotions, or knowledge that can influence the patient's end-result outcomes.

Stabilization Outcome Measures Corresponding to a specific health status attribute such as ambulation or dyspnea. As a dichotomous measure, takes on the value of either:

1 If the patient improves or does not worsen (i.e., remains the same) according to the scale for the health status attribute under consideration
0 If the patient worsens

A stabilization measure *cannot be computed* if the patient's health is at the most severely impaired level for the attribute of interest at SOC—i.e., the patient's condition cannot worsen according to the scale being conducted. Thus, the patient who is rated "2" for bathing at SOC and also at discharge would receive a stabilization value of "1."

If the patient changed from level "2" at SOC to level "3" at discharge, the stabilization measure would take on the value of "0" since the patient actually got worse. "Stabilization" means staying the same or not worsening—being consistent. This term is familiar to nurses from early clinical training. That is, if the patient doesn't get better or worse, he is considered stable.

Utilization Outcome (proxy outcome) A type of health care utilization that reflects (typically a substantial) change in patient health status over time.

Display 7-2 *Description of Quality Indicator Groups (QUIGs) and Examples*

Acute Conditions

1. Acute Orthopedic Conditions (*e.g., fracture, amputation, joint replacement, degenerative joint disease*)

2. Acute Neurologic Conditions (*e.g., cerebrovascular accident, multiple sclerosis, head injury*)

3. Open Wounds and Lesions (*e.g., pressure ulcers, surgical wounds, stasis ulcers*)

4. Terminal Conditions (*e.g., palliative care for malignant neoplasms, advanced cardiopulmonary disease, end-stage AIDS*)

5. Acute Cardiac/Peripheral Vascular Conditions (*e.g., congestive heart failure, angina, coronary artery disease, hypertension, myocardial infarction*)

6. Acute Pulmonary Conditions (*e.g., chronic obstructive pulmonary disease, pneumonia, pulmonary edema*)

7. Acute Diabetes Mellitus[a]

8. Acute Gastrointestinal Disorders (*e.g., gastric ulcer, diverticulitis, constipation with changing treatment approaches, ostomies, liver disease*)

9. Contagious/Communicable Conditions (*e.g., hepatitis, tuberculosis, AIDS, salmonella*)

10. Acute Urinary Incontinence/Catheter[a]

11. Acute Mental/Emotional Conditions (*e.g., anxiety disorder, depression, bipolar disorder*)

12. Oxygen Therapy[a]

13. IV/Infusion Therapy[a]

14. Enteral/Parenteral Nutrition (*e.g., total parenteral nutrition, gastrostomy/jejunostomy feeding*)

15. Ventilator Therapy[a]

16. Other Acute Conditions[a]

Chronic Conditions

17. Chronic Dependence in Living Skills (*e.g., meal preparation, housekeeping, laundry*)

18. Chronic Dependence in Personal Care (*e.g., bathing, dressing, grooming*)

19. Chronic Impaired Ambulation/Mobility (*e.g., ambulation, transferring, toileting*)

20. Chronic Eating Disability[a]

21. Chronic Urinary Incontinence/Catheter Use[a]

22. Chronic Dependence in Medication Administration[a]

23. Chronic Pain[a]

24. Chronic Cognitive/Mental/Behavioral Problems (*e.g., Alzheimer's, confusion, agitation, chronic brain syndrome*)

25. Chronic Patients with Caregiver Present[a]

[a]Example not given as QUIG name is sufficient to define condition.

Source: Shaughnessy, P.W. & Crisler, K.S. (1995). *Outcome-based quality improvement—A manual for home care agencies on how to use outcomes.* Washington, DC: National Association for Home Care.

the same time frame must be used, not only within the agency but between agencies that are comparing data for benchmarking. Start-of-care, follow-up, and discharge time periods must be *strictly defined* to avoid variations and impure data. For instance, a common definition of discharge must be determined. Currently, home health agencies use many time periods to determine when discharge will occur. Some may discharge all patients as soon as they go into the hospital, while others may wait 24 hours, 48 hours, several days, or even weeks. Prior to the collection of OASIS data, there has been no requirement to uniformly define a home care discharge. A variable definition of discharge simply won't work for computing outcomes (Shaughnessey & Crisler, 1995).

COP ALERT!

The proposed COPs require that a patient be reassessed within 48 hours after discharge from a facility, but they do not set a time frame for discharge to occur. In the MEQA study, a patient was discharged from the agency if he had been admitted to a facility for 48 hours or more.

The Process of Tallying the Outcome Data

If an agency has a computer vendor collecting the outcome information and producing reports, the team in charge of analyzing the data has the information at hand. Once the outcomes have been determined and data collection has begun, it would be prudent for the home care organization tabulating the information manually to begin tallying the data. The form that was used in the MEQA study is found in Figure 7–1 and includes space for:

1. The MOO numbers you wish to specifically examine (left column)
2. Case mix and related factors at start of care (top)
3. The SOC date and date of discharge when applicable

In Figure 7–1, MO490, MO700, and MO800 are combined to look at the outcome of dyspnea. This is meant as an example only; agencies *must* develop their own tally

sheets based on the exact outcomes they are measuring and the related MOO numbers.

It is recommended that agencies keep these sheets in a ring binder and complete the information when each patient being tracked is admitted, at follow-up, and at discharge. Whatever process is followed should be easy for the agency. Forms may be alphabetized by the patient's last name or arranged numerically. Only the OASIS information to be used in determining outcomes should be recorded.

In the example in Figure 7–1, the patient data was collected only at start of care and at discharge. Although outcomes are determined by comparing two time points, the most accurate reflection of the patient's outcome on an episode-of-care basis is obtained if those two time points are start of care and discharge (rather than start of care and re-certification).

Determining Improvement and Stabilization Measures

In Figure 7–1 under the SOC column for MO490, the patient was at level "3" at SOC. Thus, the number 3 is the numerical value of the description that *best* illustrates the patient's dyspnea at this time point (admission). When the patient was discharged, his status was reevaluated for MO490 and found to be a "1." Now compare the discharge result with that of the start of care and calculate the following:

1. An improvement outcome
2. A stabilization outcome (by determining if the patient improved, stabilized, or worsened)

In Figure 7–1, M0490 (dyspnea) at the start-of-care evaluation by the assessor was "3," meaning that the patient experienced dyspnea "with minimal exertion" (e.g., while eating, talking, or performing other ADLs) or "with agitation"; at discharge the response was "1," "when walking more than 20 feet, climbing stairs." Thus, the patient in this example had an *improvement outcome* of "1."

REMEMBER!

An *improvement outcome* is a dichotomous measure of a specific health status attribute, such as ambulation or dyspnea, which takes on one of the following values:

> **1**   If the patient improves according to the scale for the health status attribute under consideration
> **0**   If the patient does not improve
>
> Note that if the patient's health is optimal for the attribute of interest at SOC (i.e., the patient cannot possibly improve or achieve a more optimal level of health status according to the scale being considered), an improvement measure cannot be computed, and it then also takes the value of "0."

In this example, M0490 (dyspnea) at the start-of-care evaluation by the assessor was "3" that is, the patient experienced dyspnea "with minimal exertion" (e.g., while eating, talking, or performing other ADLs) or "with agitation." At discharge, the response was "1," when walking more than 20 feet, climbing stairs. Thus, the patient will have a stabilization value of "1" because he/she did not stay the same but improved significantly; the patient also did not worsen, even though that result was also possible.

REMEMBER!

A *stabilization outcome* corresponds to a specific health status attribute such as ambulation or dyspnea and is a dichotomous measure that takes on the value of:

> **1**   If the patient improves or does not worsen (i.e., remains the same) according to the scale for the health status attribute under consideration
> **0**   If the patient worsens

A stabilization measure *cannot be computed* if the patient's health is at the most severely impaired level for the attribute of interest at SOC—i.e., the patient's condition cannot worsen according to the scale being conducted.

In the second example in Figure 7–1 relative to MO700 (ambulation/locomotion), the patient changed from a level "2" at admission to a level "1" by discharge. In this case, the patient received the following:

> **1.** An improvement value of "1" because he improved

2. A stabilization value of "1" because he did not decrease in his function even though he could have

In the third example in Figure 7–1 relative to MO800 (management of injectable medications), the patient was scored at level "1" on admission and remained at level "1" at discharge. For this MOO number, the patient received:

1. An improvement score of 0
2. A stabilization score of 1

NURSING ALERT!

Exclude patients for whom the measures cannot be computed using the criteria given earlier with the measure definitions. In other words, improvement measures are not defined if patients cannot get better, and stabilization measures are not defined if patients cannot get worse. Improvement and stabilization values are dichotomous, meaning that they are capable of only two values, "0" or "1" (*di* = "two").

Developing an Agency Global Outcomes and Case Mix Report

After all tally sheets have been completed and the first round of data collection is finished, the PI manager can compute the outcome and case mix profiles for all patients being analyzed and develop an Agency-Level Global Outcomes and Case Mix Report (Figure 7–2).

With a total sample size of 100 patients whose outcomes are tracked on Figure 7–2, look first at the information in the upper left of Section A: Agency-Level Outcomes (Global Outcomes)

Number Improved   Fifteen improved in ambulation/locomotion, 7 improved in injectable medication administration, and 20 improved in dyspnea.

Number Who Could Improve at SOC   The number who could have improved at SOC was 31 for ambulation/location, 19 for injectable medication administration, and 50 for dyspnea.

Percentage Improved   The percentages of improvement were 48.3%, 36.8%, and 40%, respectively.

> **Figure 7-1** *Sample outcome and case mix tally sheet. (Adapted from Shaughnessy, PW, Crisler, KS [1995]. Outcome-Based Quality Improvement—A manual for home care agencies on how to use outcomes. Washington DC: National Association for Home Care.)*

Pt. name: _____ Pt. ID: _____

Data Collection Points: Soc _____ 60d _____ 120d _____ Other _____ D/C _____

Case Mix and Related Factors at Start of Care

No. 1 Birth Year _1_ _9_ _1_ _6_	No. 2 Gender 1—Male ②—Female	No. 3 Inpatient Discharge 1—Hospital 2—Rehab Facility 3—Nursing Home 4—Other NA—No Inpatient Discharge	No. 4 Overall Prognosis 0—Poor ①—Good/Fair	No. 5 Rehab Prognosis 0—Guarded 1—Good UK—Unknown

(0490) When is the patient dyspneic or noticeably Short of Breath?

0—Never, patient is not short of breath
1—When walking more than 20 feet, climbing stairs
2—With moderate exertion (e.g., while dressing, using commode or bedpan, walking distances less than 20 feet)
3—With minimal exertion (e.g., while eating, talking, or peforming other ADLs) or with agitation
4—At rest (during day or night)

60 SOC	120 Day	Day	Other	Discharge	Outcome 0 or 1
3				1	*Improvement* *1* *Stabilization* *1*

(M0700) Ambulation/Locomotion: Ability to <u>SAFELY</u> walk, once in a standing position, or use a wheelchair, once in a seated position, on a variety of surfaces.

0—Able to independently walk on even and uneven surfaces and climb stairs with or without railings (i.e., needs no human assistance or assistive device).
1—Requires use of a device (e.g., cane, walker) to walk alone or requires human supervision or assistance to negotiate stairs or steps or uneven surfaces.
2—Able to walk only with the supervision or assistance of another person at all times.
3—Chairfast, <u>unable</u> to ambulate but is able to wheel self independently
4—Chairfast, unable to ambulate and is <u>unable</u> to wheel self.
5—Bedfast, unable to ambulate or be up in a chair.
UK—Unknown

60 SOC	120 Day	Day	Other	Discharge	Outcome 0 or 1
2				1	*Improvement* *1* *Stabilization* *1*

(M0800) Management of Injectable Medications: <u>Patient's ability</u> to prepare and take all prescribed injectable medications reliably and safely, including administration of correct dosage at the appropriate times/intervals. **<u>Excludes</u> IV medications.**

0—Able to independently take the correct medication and proper dosage at the correct times.
1—Able to take injectable medication at correct times if:
(a) individual syringes are prepared in advance by another person, <u>OR</u>
(b) given daily reminders
2—<u>Unable</u> to take injectable medication unless administered by someone else.

60 SOC	120 Day	Day	Other	Discharge	Outcome 0 or 1
1				1	*Improvement* *0* *Stabilization* *1*

Figure 7-2 *Agency-Level Global Outcomes and Case Mix Reports. (Adapted from Shaughnessy, PW, Crisler, KS [1995]. Outcome-Based Quality Improvement—A manual for home care agencies on how to use outcomes. Washington, DC: National Association for Home Care.)*

REPORTING PERIOD: _01_ / _06_ / _98,_ through _07_ / _06_ / _98_ NUMBER OF PATIENTS = _100_

SECTION A: Agency-Level Outcomes (Global Outcomes)

Outcome	Improved			Stabilized		
	# Improved	# Who Could Improve at SOC	% Improved	# Stabilized	# Who Could Worsen at SOC	% Stabilized
Ambulation/ Locomotion	15	31	48.3%	92	98	93.8%
Management of Injectible Meds	7	19	36.8%	75	88	85.2%
Dyspnea	20	50	40%	70	80	87.5%

SECTION B: Agency-Level Case Mix (Global Outcomes)

Factor	Category	Number	Percent
Age:	21–40	0	0.0%
	41–60	0	0.0%
	61–70	30	30%
	71–80	50	50%
	81–90	18	18%
	>90	2	2%
	Average Age	73.69	
Gender:	Male	39	39%
	Female	61	61%
Inpatient Discharge:	Hospital	63	60.6%
	Rehab Facility	7	6.7%
	Nursing Home	2	1.9%
	Other	0	0.0%
	NA—No Inpatient Discharge	29	28%
Overall Prognosis:	Poor	26	26%
	Good/Fair	74	74%
Rehab Prognosis:	Guarded	16	16%
	Good	84	84%

Figure 7-2 *Continued*

Dependency in:*	No. Dependent at SOC*	% Dependent at SOC
Ambulation/Locomotion	31	67%
Bathing		
Management of Inj Meds	19	19%
Pain Interfering with Activity		
Dyspnea	50	50%

*Same as # who could improve at SOC.

Adapted from Shaughnessy, PW, Crisler KS (1995) Outcome based quality improvement—A manual for home care agencies on how to use outcomes. Washington DC, NAHC.

The next step is to compute the number of patients who stabilized, look first at the information in the upper right of Section A: Agency-Level Outcomes (Global Outcomes).

Number Stabilized Of these 100 patients, 92 stabilized in ambulation/locomotion, 75 stabilized in injectable medication administration, and 70 stabilized in dyspnea.

Number Who Could Worsen at SOC The highest number of patients who could worsen at SOC was 98 for ambulation/locomotion, 88 for injectable medication administration, and 80 for dyspnea.

Percent Stabilized The percentages came to 93.8%, 85.2%, and 87.5% respectively.

Now look at Section B: Agency-Level Case Mix (Global Outcomes). In this category the average age of agency patients can be determined, as well as gender, inpatient discharge point, overall prognosis, and rehabilitative prognosis. Since this looks at *all* agency patients, it is considered a *global outcome*. This information will be significant in interpreting the outcome and case mix reports.

The improvement percentages in Section A are all below 60% (48.3%, 36.8%, and 40%). According to Shaughnessey and Crisler (1995), this is typical for home care patients. (Remember that patients who are independent in function or who cannot improve at SOC have already been excluded. Stabilization percentages are high because they include not only the patients who improved but also those who did not worsen.

By maintaining this information and reviewing it from year to year, the agency can determine a profile of the patients in their caseload. Questions that can be asked are:

♦ Are these patients older than the average for the nation?

♦ Are they more often coming from a hospital or nursing home with more acute than chronic problems, or vice versa?

♦ How do our patients fit in the rehabilitation picture?

♦ Do we need to include more physical or occupational therapy?

♦ Would having this therapy input help improve outcomes for our patients with injectable medications who have difficulty with their psychomotor skills?

Currently, the Agency Level Global Outcomes and Case Mix Report is being analyzed further by the MEQA study to help the demonstration agencies clarify their outcomes and case mix reports. Until further use of this form is conducted with the demonstration agencies and until the intent of the new Medicare COPs is clear, the home care organization can use the data for its own internal PI, marketing, and organizational needs. On a regional, state, and national basis, this information may become increasingly usable.

An evaluation of outcome findings that compares an agency's global and focused outcomes with other agencies' standards, means, or benchmarks is called a **1st-stage screen** (Figure 7–3). Keep in mind that this is only the tip of the iceberg when collecting data for outcome reporting.

Figure 7-3 *Illustrative outcome findings and 2nd-stage screen focus. (Shaughnessy, P.W., & Crisler, K.S. [1995]. Outcome-based quality improvement—A manual for home care agencies on how to use outcomes. Washington, DC: National Association for Home Care, pp. 5–16.)*

1st-STAGE SCREEN

Outcomes	National Norm	Your Agency Mean
1. Cardiac Patients: Improved in Dyspnea	43%	30%
2. All Patients: Stabilization in Ambulation	89%	96%

TARGETED 2nd-STAGE SCREEN

Focus of Process-of-Care Review

1. (Cardiac) Patients with CHF
2. (Global) Patients who Stabilized or Declined in Ambulation

This section has dealt with only a few of the reports and outcome approaches identified in the MEQA study. More will come in future editions as the sophistication of outcome analysis increases. Chapter 8 will deal with process-of-care analysis, or **2nd-stage screen,** which may lead an agency into remediation or reward.

The Process-of-Care Analysis

8

Introduction

Once the home care organization has received the outcome reports from the computer vendor or has used the tally worksheet to compile the results of the current round of data collection, it is necessary to review the information to determine which outcomes will be chosen for reward or remediation. This is called a process-of-care analysis. This chapter presents the steps of the process-of-care analysis and discusses risk adjustment from a conceptual standpoint.

The Concept of Case Mix and Risk Adjustment

Outcome reports should be distributed periodically based on the needs of the agency, the specifics of the agency's PI program, and its adherence to any regulatory or accreditation standards. Usually outcome reports are published no more often than quarterly. It is important that the vendor or the system being used to develop outcome reports accommodates for case mix and risk adjustment. Teaching agencies how to perform case mix/risk adjustment is not within the scope of this book. Rather, this chapter presents an overview of the steps of the process-of-care review and discusses risk adjustment from a conceptual standpoint. For more information on statistical methods of case mix/risk adjustment, refer to a text that defines statistical methodology for this practice.

Risk adjustment is performed to eliminate or at least minimize the effects of risk-factor differences when comparing outcome findings between two samples of patients—i.e., patients from different agencies. For example, Agency A may receive outcome results that show their agency has far more patients admitted to the hospital with orthopedic injuries than does Agency B. At first glance it may seem that Agency A is not providing the quality of care or ensuring safety with as much success as Agency B. But closer review reveals that the average age of Agency A's patients is 80.7, and the average age of Agency B's patients is 72.2. This single factor can make a great difference in patient outcomes for this health attribute, since the agency with the more elderly clients will be more likely to have increased hospitalization rates from falls and subsequent orthopedic injuries than the agency with the younger population.

Risk adjusting for the OASIS/OBQI study included the development of Quality Indicator Groups, or QUIGs (see Chapter 7 for more information on QUIGs). Using QUIGs is a process of risk adjustment called *stratification* or *grouping*. Risk adjustment through stratification or grouping involves dividing the two (or more) samples being compared into subgroups or strata according to important risk factors. Patients will likely be different from agency to agency, and risk factors for some of the outcomes under consideration will also be different. To compensate at least partially for these differences, an agency can use the QUIGs as a guideline.

Conceptual analyses, expert clinical opinions, and empirical analyses have demonstrated that risk factors used to develop and define the QUIGs were useful for categorizing home care patients into like groupings useful for comparing outcomes from agency to agency. A variety of other characteristics such as nursing or med-

ical diagnoses can be used to group patients for comparing outcomes. While statistical methods of risk adjustment are available, use of the QUIGs will be the most practical for the agency beginning to use OASIS and OBQI.

In Chapter 7, it was suggested that an agency choose those outcomes that may have the most immediate effect upon the patient, such as medication administration or dyspnea with exertion. Initially the agency would be best advised to choose only *two or three outcomes* to review. This will allow the PI team to internalize the procedure of data analysis and process-of-care review required for thorough comprehension and utilization of the outcome information provided. Once everyone is familiar with the material, the agency may choose to look at more outcomes or to break the patients down into groupings by diagnosis or by age.

When reviewing outcomes, the team must become acquainted with certain terms. *Care behaviors,* sometimes called clinical actions or processes of care, consist of those activities that care providers undertake directly or indirectly on behalf of patients. Typically, care behaviors consist of assessment and reassessment, care planning, intervention or treatment, care coordination, and patient monitoring services. They can also include documentation and evaluation of care (Shaughnessey & Crisler, 1995). The 1st-stage screens were discussed in Chapter 7.

REMEMBER!

The 1st-stage screen involves activities associated with collection and analysis of data on patient outcomes resulting in outcome reports. The 2nd-stage screen consists of all actions undertaken in response to outcome reports by agency staff in the process-of-care analysis and preparing the plan of action (Shaughnessey & Crisler, 1995). Terms and activities associated with the 2nd-stage screen include the process-of-care analysis and the plan of action, both of which will be discussed in this chapter.

Process-of-Care Analysis

The process-of-care analysis (investigation) includes the following components:

1. Identifying which outcomes to examine further. These are called *target outcomes*.

2. Analyzing the care provided that produced the target outcomes.

3. Deciding which care behaviors to reinforce or remediate. These are called *target care behaviors*.

4. Specifying the care practices that should become *gold standards* for care, either as substitutions for or extensions of the target care behaviors. These are termed *best practices*.

Just specifying the care practices isn't enough. It is necessary to write a plan of action to implement the best practices that have been determined and then to actually implement these practices and monitor the results of the plan. This will result in improved or consistently exemplary outcomes. Discussing the performance improvement processes used to develop this plan of action is beyond the scope of this book. Tools and processes such as fishboning, PARETO charts, storyboarding, etc., are integral to a sound PI program and should be used as appropriate in developing the plan of action.

REMEMBER!

Without the 2nd-stage screening, any changes in outcomes that may transpire could be considered as happening by chance since no deliberate quality improvement activities would be directed at improving the outcomes.

Reviewing Outcome Reports

When the outcome reports are first reviewed, enough time must be taken to thoroughly understand what the results mean. Upon first glance, the outcomes may appear horrendous, and it may seem that the agency has been providing abysmal care. In fact, often professional staff haven't seen outcome results in such a clear fashion before. Bar graphs are brutally honest and can be visually devastating, especially if many of the agency results are on the low end of the scale.

The initial response to unfavorable outcomes by staff, management, and administration is usually denial. Defense mechanisms come into play, and many excuses and explanations are offered. Staff members may criticize the data as flawed and complain that errors were made in transcribing or entering the data. But these outcries should die down once staff has been assured that

no retaliation or finger pointing will be directed toward specific individuals and that the entire agency will work as a team to make the reports meaningful. Then the actual process of care investigation can begin.

It is also important not to be misled in the other direction. For example, if agency outcomes are consistently above the national average, a false sense of security may develop. The agency may believe there is no reason to complete the process-of-care component of this OBQI activity. This approach to positive outcomes is inconsistent with the OBQI goal of identifying, reinforcing, and extending exemplary care practices.

To determine which target outcomes to select for the process-of-care investigation, the following six criteria should be considered:

1. Statistically Significant Outcome Differences

If your agency is sophisticated enough to determine the statistical probabilities related to the outcomes, this should influence the choice of outcomes for remediation or reward. A significance level of $p \leq .10$ is appropriate for choosing outcomes. The significance level means there is a less than 10% confidence that the information you see before you is false and 90% confidence that it is true. In contrast, a .45 significance level means there is a 45% confidence level that the data results depicted are false and a 55% confidence level that the data results are true.

2. Magnitude of the Outcome Differences

The actual magnitude of the difference in outcomes should be taken into consideration as well. For example, if sample sizes are large, it is possible for a somewhat small outcome difference to be statistically significant. There may actually be only a difference of 2 or 3 percentage points between the outcome measures. However, an outcome with a difference of 3 percentage points should not be considered as important as one with a difference of 15 or more. Regardless of statistical significance, examining the percentage differences can result in the choice of totally different outcomes.

3. Actual Significance Levels of the Differences

If one outcome produces a significance level of .45 while another produces a significance level of .20, the lower number is most likely the appropriate choice. While neither approaches the .10 significance level, the larger percentage is more likely to have occurred by chance.

4. Importance or Relevance to Your Agency's Goals

What are your agency's goals? What needs to be examined relative to marketing tools? Do your wound care or diabetic education programs provide outcomes above the national average? It may be important to remedy or reinforce behaviors determined in the process-of-care investigation within these and other associated areas.

5. Clinical Significance

What are the majority of your patients admitted for? If many of them have wounds, focus on the wound section of the outcome report from the OASIS data set and the best practices in wound care. If many of the patients have COPD, focus on dyspnea and activities to decrease exertion. If many have functional limitations, the focus may need to be on ADL and IADL.

6. Your Ability to Influence the Outcome by Changing Care Behaviors

During the first year or so of implementing OBQI, this criterion will be less significant than the previous five. For instance, it may require some time and experience to determine which outcomes can actually be effected by the care being provided.

REMEMBER!

In order to achieve the best possible results from the process-of-care investigation, the *entire process should be completed as quickly as possible, generally within three to four weeks of the receipt of outcomes.* It is all too easy to push the process-of-care investigation to the side while addressing what appear to be more pressing issues. The longer the process-of-care investigation is delayed, the less impact changes will have on the next cycle of data collection.

For systems that provide quarterly outcome results, changes may not be seen for two to three data cycles under the best of circumstances; delaying remediation will only lengthen this process. In addition, quite a burden has been put on staff members to learn to record data using the OASIS data set, and failing to promptly review the outcomes may send the message that they really aren't all that important anyway. To maintain staff morale, assure consistency in OASIS data collection, and build agency confidence, review the outcomes and perform the process-of-care investigation immediately upon receiving the outcome reports.

It is recommended that the OBQI team present the selected outcomes to staff members and ask for their input regarding important care behaviors or clinical practices. As with all such undertakings, some staff members will be extremely interested in the process and eager to help, while others simply won't be interested, regardless of what is being done. The important opportunity to brainstorm about clinical actions that will affect the target outcomes and help staff feel part of the entire OBQI process is the benefit of getting everyone involved.

An agency may want separate QI teams to work with each of the two outcomes chosen. This may not be possible in small agencies; however, if it is possible, be sure to include pivotal persons in the appropriate team, such as ET (Enterostomal Therapy) nurses on the wound care team and physical and/or occupational therapists if the target outcome concerns ADL and IADL. If staff feel they "own" the outcome, they will be more interested in contributing to its improvement.

Analyzing Outcome Reports Using an Actual System

To help the reader better understand the process of choosing significant outcomes for closer observation and evaluating the reports that can be generated, this section will discuss each field in Figures 8–1, 8–2, and 8–3. These reports, composed of fictitious information, have been provided by Outcomes USA, a company affiliated with the Indiana Association for Home and Hospice Care. Outcomes USA is one of several companies that electronically collects OASIS data from home health agencies and provides outcome reports to those agencies.

Figure 8–1 is a case mix report for all patients at start of care (admission) for the ABC Home Health Agency. The data was collected over a period of three months, from 4/1/97 to 6/30/97. The total number of admissions during that period was 5,790 for *all* agencies involved in this study. Agency ABC had submitted information about 604 patients in the current data collection period. This number included not only admissions but also follow-ups (re-certifications) and discharges. There were 230 admissions to ABC Home Health during the three-month period.

Figure 8-1 *Case mix report: SOC patients for Agency ABC. (Used with permission of the Indiana Association for Home and Hospice Care and ERIS Incorporated, Indianapolis, In.)*

OUTCOMES USA

CASE MIX REPORT
Start of Care Patients
ABC Company (56789)

Aggregate Number of Admits in Current Period: **5,790**
Agency's Number of Cards in Current Period: **604**
Agency's Number of Admits in Current Period: **230**

Report Period: 4/1/97–6/30/97
Report Date: September 9, 1997

Demographic	Agency Average	Aggregate Average
Age (Years)	74.25	74.05
% Male	30.26%	34.35%
% Female	69.74%	65.65%
Inpatient Discharge Point		
Hospital	63.06%	61.79%
Rehabilitation	3.15%	5.57%
Nursing Home	9.46%	6.46%
Other	5.86%	6.18%
Not Applicable	18.47%	20.01%
Prognosis		
Good Overall Prognosis	51.74%	72.11%
Good Rehab Prognosis	35.53%	52.96%
ADL Disability Scales		
Ambulation (Note: 1)	1.21	1.22
Bathing (Note: 2)	1.88	1.76
Prevalence of Moderate ADL Disabilities		
Ambulation (Note: 3)	20.87%	21.52%
Bathing (Note: 4)	12.61%	11.40%
IADL Disability Scale		
Management of Oral Medications (Note: 5)	0.62	0.68
Prevalence of Severe IADL Disability		
Management of Oral Medications (Note: 6)	8.26%	14.87%
Health Status		
Pain Interfering with Activity (Note: 7)	1.14	1.08
Dyspnea (Note: 8)	1.99	1.52

1. Ambulation: the agency and aggregate averages for this area represent the total patient average on a scale from 0–5 (0 = independent, 5 = bedfast).
2. Bathing: the agency and aggregate averages for this area represent the total patient average on a scale form 0–5 (0 = able, 5 = unable/total).
3. Prevalence of Ambulation: represents the percent of patients on the scale that are at or above two (2) (i.e. patients that are coded as supervised or above).
4. Prevalence of Bathing: represents the percent of patients on the scale that are at or above four (4) (i.e. unable).
5. Management of Oral Medications: the agency and aggregate averages for this area represent the total patient average on a scale of 0–2 (0 = able, 2 = unable).
6. Prevalence of Oral Medications: represents the percent of patients on a scale that are at or above two (2) (i.e. unable).
7. Pain Interfering With Activity: the average profile of the total number of patients on a scale of 0–3 (0 = none, 3 = all).
8. Dyspnea: the average profile of the total number of patients on a scale of 0–4 (0 = never, 4 = at rest).

Figure 8–2 *Case mix report: All patients in current period for Agency ABC. (Used with permission of Indiana Association for Home and Hospice Care and ERIS Incorporated, Indianapolis, In.)*

OUTCOMES USA

CASE MIX REPORT
All Patients in Current Period
ABC Company (56789)

Aggregate Number of Patients in Current Period:	**10,147**	Report Period:	4/1/97–6/30/97
Agency's Number of Cards in Current Period:	**604**	Report Date:	September 9, 1997
Agency's Number of Patients in Current Period:	**400**		

Total Visits Per Discipline	Agency Total	Aggregate Total
RN	3,383	97,608
HHA	3,298	79,195
PT	329	19,382
OT	72	3,845
SLP	37	1,186
SW	123	3,221

Visit Timing		
Initial	230	5,790
60 days	70	1,747
120 days	46	848
180 days	28	404
240 days	4	119
More than 240 days	1	134
Discharge	225	4,684

Payment Source	Agency Total	Agency %	Aggregate %
None	2	0.50%	0.62%
Medicare	336	84.00%	87.70%
Traditional Insurance	54	13.50%	9.31%
Medicaid	24	6.00%	3.86%
Managed Care Insurance	13	3.25%	2.68%
Medicare/Managed Care	0	0.00%	0.33%
Medicaid/Managed Care	0	0.00%	0.02%
Other	4	1.00%	1.39%

<table>
<tr><th colspan="3">Top 5 Primary Diagnostic Codes
at Start of Care</th></tr>
<tr><th>Diagnostic Code</th><th>Count</th><th>Percentage</th></tr>
<tr><td>428.0</td><td>29</td><td>12.61%</td></tr>
<tr><td>496</td><td>12</td><td>5.22%</td></tr>
<tr><td>715.90</td><td>11</td><td>4.78%</td></tr>
<tr><td>250.01</td><td>9</td><td>3.91%</td></tr>
<tr><td>436</td><td>6</td><td>2.61%</td></tr>
</table>

<table>
<tr><th colspan="3">Top 5 Secondary Diagnostic Codes
at Start of Care</th></tr>
<tr><th>Diagnostic Code</th><th>Count</th><th>Percentage</th></tr>
<tr><td>401.9</td><td>25</td><td>10.87%</td></tr>
<tr><td>428.0</td><td>22</td><td>9.57%</td></tr>
<tr><td>496</td><td>13</td><td>5.65%</td></tr>
<tr><td>414.9</td><td>9</td><td>3.91%</td></tr>
<tr><td>250.01</td><td>8</td><td>3.48%</td></tr>
</table>

Figure 8-3 *Case mix report: All patients outcome report for Agency ABC. (Used with permission of Indiana Association for Home and Hospice Care and ERIS Incorporated, Indianapolis, In.)*

Agency: ABC

OUTCOMES USA
All Patients Outcome Report

Current Period: 1-Apr-97 30-Jun-97
Prior Period: 1-Jan-97 31-Mar-97

	State		Current Period		Prior Period	
	Cases	**Percent**	**Cases**	**Percent**	**Cases**	**Percent**
Improvement in Ambulation	2,767	23.53%	229	23.14%	163	26.99%
Stabilization in Ambulation	3,819	85.44%	286	87.06%	207	83.57%
Improvement in Bathing	2,813	39.10%	242	36.78%	174	32.18%
Stabilization in Bathing	3,901	86.18%	302	88.08%	214	85.51%
Improvement in Oral Meds	2,122	28.09%	167	29.34%	126	30.95%
Stabilization in Oral Meds	3,907	89.28%	299	88.96%	214	86.45%
Improvement in Pain Interference	2,877	35.77%	217	35.48%	134	32.84%
Stabilization in Pain Interference	3,871	81.63%	300	83.33%	214	85.98%
Improvement in Dyspnea	2,838	35.06%	236	29.24%	163	30.67%
Stabilization in Dyspnea	3,911	78.16%	299	80.94%	220	78.64%

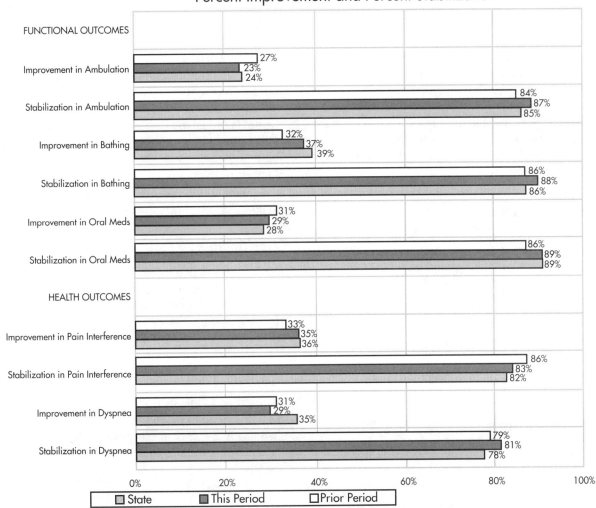

Demographic

A review of the demographics indicates that the agency average for patient age is very similar to the aggregate average from all agencies. Slightly over 30% of the agency admissions were male patients compared to 34.35% of the aggregate. Females comprised 69.74% of the total admissions compared to 65.65% of the aggregate.

Inpatient Discharge Point

The largest number of patients for both Agency ABC and the state aggregate were admitted after hospitalization. Agency ABC receives only 3.15% of its referrals from rehabilitation centers, while the state average is 5.57%. Three percent more nursing home referrals are given to Agency ABC than to the state aggregate. "Other" discharge points were nearly the same for both the agency and the aggregate. Agency ABC receives a little less than 2% fewer admissions identified as "not applicable," which probably means these patients were admitted after referral from physicians offices or exhausted caregivers.

Prognosis

Agency ABC is much lower in the areas of good overall prognosis (20.27% less than the state aggregate) and good rehabilitation prognosis (17.43%). This is an interesting difference since its patients are not older than the average and do not significantly differ from the average in sex or discharge point. It is possible that Agency ABC receives sicker referrals than the aggregate; perhaps there are no hospice services available and this agency serves that purpose. Further investigation into this observation would be recommended.

ADL Disability Scales

There is little variation between the agency average and the aggregate average in this category. Agency ABC's patients can ambulate a bit better than the aggregate average, but they have slightly more difficulty bathing than the average.

Prevalence of Moderate ADL Disabilities

This area is a percentage equivalent of the ADL disability scale.

IADL Disability Scale

For management of oral medications, the numbers are very similar, with both the agency and the aggregate hovering around "1." These patients can probably take their medications correctly if someone sets up individual doses (i.e., a pill planner), if they are given daily reminders, or if someone develops a drug diary or chart.

Prevalence of Severe IADL Disability

These numbers convert the previous category into percentages. Agency ABC has approximately 6.6% fewer patients with problems managing oral medications than the state aggregate.

Health Status

In the category of pain interfering with activity, Agency ABC has slightly more patients who complain of pain interfering with their activities than does the state aggregate. Agency ABC also has patients who are slightly more dyspneic than the aggregate.

Total Visits per Discipline

Figure 8–2 shows the total number of visits made by the agency per discipline *for all patients for whom data has been collected.* This information is valuable for agencies tracking resource consumption. The number of visits performed by various disciplines can be compared quarterly to assess trends.

Another possible use for this information is in determining causes of specific outcomes. For instance, if the agency consistently has lower than average outcomes in the areas of ADL/IADL, perhaps it is because physical or occupational therapy visits have been absent or limited. Better outcomes may be achieved by increasing the number of therapy visits, thus providing more range of motion exercises and manual dexterity training for the patients.

Visit Timing

This section indicates when the majority of the assessment visits took place. For Agency ABC it appears that the majority of visits occurred at SOC. The remaining data are useful in identifying cases that may be chronic or have simply continued too long.

Payment Source

By referring to this section, agencies can determine who their primary payers are. If the scales are tipped too heavily in favor of one or another payer, it may be wise for the agency to diversify, assuring income from several sources.

Top Diagnostic Codes (Primary and Secondary)

These two sections deal with the top five primary and top five secondary diagnoses by ICD-9 code. By determining what type of patient makes up the majority of the agency's caseload, priorities can be established for developing clinical pathways or standards of care.

Figure 8–3 represents a further breakdown of outcomes for all patients. The top two boxes present actual numbers of patients, which have been converted into percentages for use on the bar graph below. In the graph labeled "Percent Improvement and Percent Stabilization," the top bar for each outcome depicts the percentage from the prior period, the middle bar represents current percentages, and the bottom bar portrays the state aggregate. This chart shows results for both percent of improvement and percent of stabilization for each outcome. Stabilization rates are typically 75% or higher, while improvement rates at the agency level are usually from 25% to 60%.

REMEMBER!

A stabilization measure takes on the value of "1" if the patient does not worsen (stays the same or improves) and "0" if the patient worsens; it is not computed if the patient cannot worsen. An improvement measure takes on the value "1" if the patient improves and "0" if the patient does not improve; it is not computed if the patient cannot improve.

Agency ABC has 4% less improvement in ambulation than at its last report. This is really not a significant change unless certain factors enter in, such as the loss of a physical therapist or a decrease in physical therapy consults. Note also the stabilization in ambulation measurement, which indicates that 3% more patients have stabilized in ambulation compared to the last report time. Perhaps these patients have reached a plateau and won't progress further, or perhaps a change in care should be recommended. If these patients have stabilized, they haven't *worsened*, so this may not be an outcome an agency would be concerned about.

Agency ABC's patients have improved in bathing by 5% since the last report. Those who did not improve appear to have stabilized. This may not be an area the

agency wishes to investigate; however, it may be an area for reward due to the significant increase.

Improvement in oral medications decreased 2% from the prior period, and Agency ABC has a 1% advantage over the state aggregate. A slightly greater number of patients (3%) have stabilized in ability to manage oral medications than the state aggregate. This may be an area of concern since the ability to manage oral medications appears not to have changed greatly and this is a very necessary behavior in order for patients to live safely at home.

The agency's patients have improved in the area of pain interference with ADL and IADL. These numbers are very close to the state aggregate, and while possibly not significant by themselves, they may interrelate with the ability to manage oral medications and thus be an area of concern.

Agency ABC is 6% below the state aggregate in improvement in dyspnea and 2% lower than the previous report. Stabilization in dyspnea is 3% above the state aggregate and 2% above agency results at the last report. It is possible that pain is interfering with the patient's ability to take oral medications, which is then leading to more respiratory problems and increased or rebound dyspnea.

The two most important areas to consider are medication administration and dyspnea. Presence of pain and improvement in ambulation and bathing are important functional assessments. The agency then moves into the process-of-care analysis to determine what care behaviors will be changed.

Learning Exercise

Figures 8–4, 8–5, and 8–6 are presented to let you analyze the reports for yourself and become comfortable with understanding how they are presented. While looking at these reports, try to answer the following questions:

1. How does Agency XYZ compare with the state average in overall prognosis and rehabilitation prognosis?
2. Do patients at Agency XYZ demonstrate more or less disability than the state average (i.e., difficulty with ambulation or bathing)?
3. Is there any correlation between the IADL disability scale for Agency XYZ and the management of oral medications by patients?
4. How many home health aide visits were made by Agency XYZ during the report period? Physical therapist visits? Occupational therapist visits?

OUTCOMES USA
Case Mix Report

Indiana Home Care Agency: **XYZ Agency (999)**

State Total Number of Patients in Current Period:	**5,953**		Report Period:	10/01/96–12/31/96
Agency's Number of Cards in Current Period:	**547**		Report Date:	4/16/97
Agency's Number of Patients in Current Period:	**440**			

	Averages	
	Agency	**State**
Demographic		
Age (Years)	74.22	72.68
% Male	34.43%	36.71%
% Female	65.57%	63.29%
Inpatient Discharge Point		
Hospital	61.25%	76.49%
Rehabilitation	3.75%	6.97%
Nursing Home	25.42%	9.27%
Other	9.58%	7.28%
Prognosis		
Good Overall Prognosis	72.31%	74.55%
Good Rehab Prognosis	42.92%	55.96%
ADL Disability Scales		
Ambulation (Note: 1)	1.35	1.15
Bathing (Note: 2)	2.05	1.69
Prevalence of Moderate ADL Disabilities		
Ambulation (Note: 3)	25.5%	22.1%
Bathing (Note: 4)	14.5%	14.6%
IADL Disability Scale		
Management of Oral Medications (Note: 5)	0.71	0.70
Prevalence of Severe IADL Disability		
Management of Oral Medications (Note: 6)	15.7%	18.0%
Health Status		
Pain Interfering with Activity (Note: 7)	0.98	1.12
Dyspnea (Note: 8)	1.42	1.39

1. Ambulation: the agency and state average for this area represent the total patient average on a scale from 0–5 (0 = independent, 5 = bedfast.
2. Bathing: the agency and state averages for this area represent the total patient average on a scale form 0–5 (0 = Able, 5 = Unable/Total).
3. Prevalence of Ambulation: represents the percent of patients on the scale that are at or above two (2) (i.e. patients that are coded as supervised or above).
4. Prevalence of Bathing: represents the percent of patients on the scale that are at or above four (4).
5. Management of Oral Medications: the agency and state averages for this area represent the total patient average on a scale of 0–2 (0 = Able, 2 = Unable).
6. Prevalence of Oral Medications: represents the percent of patients on a scale that are at or above two (2) .
7. Pain Interfering With Activity: the average profile of the total number of patients on a scale of 0–3 (0 = None, 3 = All).
8. Dyspnea: the average profile of the total number of patients on a scale of 0–4 (0 = Never, 4 = At Rest).

Figure 8-5 *Case mix report: All patients for Agency XYZ. (Used with permission of Indiana Association for Home and Hospice Care and ERIS Incorporated, Indianapolis, In.)*

OUTCOMES USA
Case Mix Report

Indiana Home Care Agency: **XYZ Agency (999)**

State Total Number of Patients in Current Period:	**5,953**	Report Period:	10/01/96–12/31/96
Agency's Number of Cards in Current Period:	**547**	Report Date:	4/16/97
Agency's Number of Patients in Current Period:	**440**		

Total Visits Per Discipline	Agency	State
RN	431	5,890
HHA	65	925
PT	36	569
OT	5	154
SLP	2	45
SW	10	340

Visit Timing	Agency	State
Initial	312	3,711
60 days	30	524
120 days	2	59
180 days	0	24
240 days	1	4
More than 240 days	0	25
Discharge	95	1,640

Payment Source	Agency	Agency %	State %
None	0	0.00%	0.77%
Medicare	392	89.09%	83.42%
Traditional Insurance	11	2.50%	6.85%
Medicaid	30	6.82%	4.01%
Managed Care Insurance	42	9.55%	4.52%
Medicare/Managed CAre	32	7.27%	0.54%
Medicaid/Managed Care	7	1.59%	0.12%
Other	2	0.45%	1.44%

Top Primary Diagnostic Codes

Diagnostic Code	Count	Percentage
428.0	24	5.45%
496	17	3.86%
401.9	16	3.64%
436	16	3.64%
250.01	14	3.18%

Top Secondary Diagnostic Codes

Diagnostic Code	Count	Percentage
No ICD-9 Code	48	10.91%
401.9	32	7.27%
428.0	25	5.68%
496	12	2.73%
414.9	10	2.27%

Agency: XYZ

OUTCOMES USA
All Patients Outcome Report

Current Period: 1-Jan-97 31-Mar-97
Prior Period: 1-Oct-96 31-Dec-96

	State		Current Period		Prior Period	
	Cases	Percent	Cases	Percent	Cases	Percent
Improvement in Ambulation	426	18.78%	18	22.22%	16	25.00%
Stabilization in Ambulation	414	89.86%	18	94.44%	16	87.50%
Improvement in Bathing	430	24.65%	18	22.22%	18	22.22%
Stabilization in Bathing	398	86.43%	18	88.89%	17	88.24%
Improvement in Oral Meds	428	18.69%	15	20.00%	13	7.69%
Stabilization in Oral Meds	344	87.21%	12	83.33%	10	90.00%
Improvement in Pain Interference	428	18.22%	8	25.00%	8	25.00%
Stabilization in Pain Interference	398	86.43%	17	82.35%	10	90.00%
Improvement in Dyspnea	424	24.53%	17	23.53%	15	20.00%
Stabilization in Dyspnea	392	80.10%	16	68.75%	15	80.00%
Total # Patients Assessed	440		18		16	

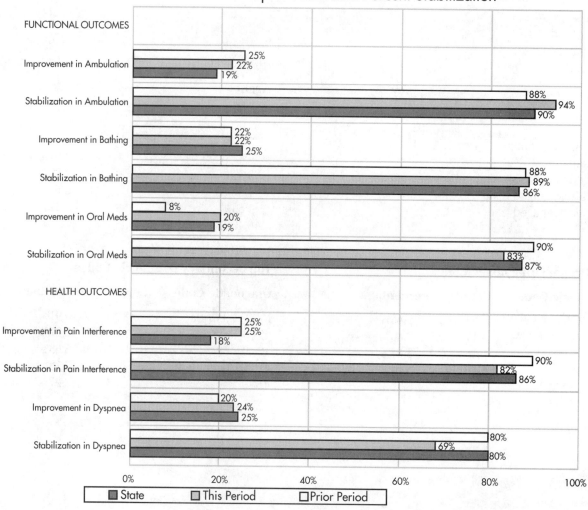

5. Could there be a correlation between the number of physical and occupational therapy visits and the prevalence of moderate ADL disabilities?
6. What percentages of Agency XYZ's patients have Medicare as a primary payment source? Traditional insurance? Medicaid/Managed Care?
7. What is the top primary diagnostic code for Agency XYZ?
8. How does Agency XYZ compare with the state regarding the functional outcome of improvement in ambulation? With prior period results?
9. What has occurred with the stabilization in ambulation results from this report? How do these results correlate with question 8?
10. What percentage of Agency XYZ's patients demonstrated improvement in dyspnea? How do these results compare with the state aggregate?

Determining Target Care Behaviors

At this point in the process, the agency is ready to begin brainstorming within the committee(s) regarding potential *target care behaviors*. Examine all care practices and add to or alter them as needed. Have everyone ask, "Why are outcomes being attained or not attained?" Now is the time to review clinical practice guidelines, agency standardized care plans, point-of-care systems, clinical pathways, policies and procedures, teaching guides, and any other agency documents being used to provide care. Additional resources from outside the agency may be reviewed as well.

If you have used fishbone diagrams, flow charts, or other established performance improvement methods now or in the past, review them for their relevance in determining target care behaviors. The CHPR suggests that the following process can assist a home care organization in forming a final set of target care behaviors:

1. Initial brainstorming
2. Documenting a first list of important care behaviors
3. Revising and expanding this list by examining other sources of information on optimal ways to provide care relative to the target outcome under consideration
4. Performing a clinical record review
5. Conducting a second round of brainstorming

In order to thoroughly assess the target care behaviors, a minimum of 15–20 charts should be selected for clinical record review. Large agencies may choose to randomly sample records, such as every fifth chart, while smaller agencies may need to include every record of patients with a particular diagnosis to reach the appropriate sample size. Agencies may also choose to select some charts that met the target outcome and some that did not. If a comparison is to be made between the last period and the current results, it may be helpful to choose an equal number of records from both reporting periods. If both outcomes are consistently above the norm, the agency may be consistently providing exemplary care to patients with the particular problem or diagnosis.

Certain patients fail to attain the outcome due to the natural progression of disease rather than inadequate or inappropriate care practices. However, when outcomes are attained by a certain number of patients and not attained by another significant number, it will be possible to review charts to determine who actually met the outcomes, who didn't, and why. Best care practices can be identified by retrospective chart review and gold standards or by best practices for care developed and implemented.

To determine if target behaviors are being attained, a clear, concise definition of the target behavior(s) must be developed. According to Shaughnessy and Crisler (1995), "Process-of-care problem and strength statements should have the following attributes:

♦ A clear focus on behavior that demonstrates either inadequacy or superiority (relative to problematic or exemplary outcomes, respectively)
♦ Specific and tangible wording using concrete terms to which your clinical staff can relate, rather than general concepts or somewhat vague terms
♦ Unqualified specification of the process-of-care problem or strength, without explanations or solutions"

It will be necessary for every member of the clinical practice field staff, regardless of discipline, to visualize the statement in the same way and be able to identify clinical areas where their input is necessary.

An example of appropriate *problem statements* follows:

♦ In patients with dyspnea, contributing factors such as anxiety are poorly assessed.
♦ In patients with inability to administer injectable medications, there is no indication of occupational therapy involvement to assess and improve manual dexterity.

Examples of specific *statements of strength* are:

♦ For patients with improvement in oral medications, teaching methods used to improve compliance are clearly documented.
♦ For patients with difficulty in ambulation, a thorough safety assessment of the area where the patient frequently ambulates is documented.

Once the problem and strength statements have been developed, it should be possible to complete the process-of-care investigation with a clear understanding of best practices for achieving the outcome required. These best practices then can be substituted, added as improvements, or continued as extensions of target care behaviors.

REMEMBER!

The thrust of activities is toward performance improvement rather than quality improvement or quality management. Performance improvement is based on the PDCA cycle (Plan, Do, Check, Act).

Team members should keep the following questions in mind when investigating target care behaviors:

♦ What are we trying to accomplish? What is our aim? What background information is available about this improvement?
♦ How will we know that a change is actually an improvement? How does the new process work? How does it vary from the current process?
♦ What changes can we make that we predict will lead to improvement?
♦ How shall we plan the pilot? Who is going to do what, by when, and why?
♦ What is being learned as we do the pilot?

After the current investigation is finished, the second data cycle continues. When results from this cycle are reported, the following two questions may be appropriate:

♦ As we check and study what happened, what have we learned?
♦ As we act to hold the gains or abandon unprofitable efforts, what have we learned?

Remember, the commitment to the organization by all levels of staff, managers, and leaders to embrace the challenge of performance improvement is paramount in successful performance improvement activities.

Figure 8–7 is a *plan of action form* for continuous quality improvement. Any format can be utilized as long as the plan of action is documented and the agency can demonstrate to surveyors that outcomes are being reviewed and remediated or reinforced.

Researchers at the University of Colorado Health Sciences Center created outcome review criteria (ORCs) for each of 100 conditions common to home care patients. These ORCs were discussed in Chapter 6. The specific criteria are regarded as key items that should be documented in patient records if proper care is being provided. The ORC sets were developed in a format to enhance record review. Agencies can use the ORCs as models for developing similar forms that include practices desired by or common to individual agencies. This type of record review focuses on care behaviors and care processes rather than on structural aspects of documentation such as completeness of record, timeliness of signatures, or other information a home health organization may want to track and monitor.

Once the process-of-care investigation has concluded, it becomes necessary for the agency to determine the plan for remediation or reward of care behaviors. The plan of action will correspond to a specific target outcome and best practices selected for remediation or reinforcement of the care provided. *Reinforcement* is the process of encouraging a positive behavior to be sustained so that a positive outcome can continue to be achieved. *Remediation* is using best practices for care provision to replace or supplement current practices to improve outcomes.

REMEMBER!

The plan of action should describe *all steps* involved in implementing and monitoring remediation or reinforcement activities.

Preparing the Plan of Action

There should be a plan of action for every target outcome. The target outcome as well as care behaviors or processes selected as best practices should be identified. Intervention actions should:

Figure 8-7   *Sample plan of action for Continuous Quality Improvement. (Used with permission of the Center for Health Policy Research, Denver, Colo.)*

Plan of Action for Continuous Quality Improvement

Quality Improvement Team Members

1. _____(Facilitator)_____   4. _____   7. _____

2. _____   5. _____   8. _____

3. _____   6. _____   9. _____

Outcome Report Date: _____   Plan of Action Date: _____

1. Target Outcome Addressed by Plan of Action:

2. Action Plan for (circle one):   a. Remediation   b. Reinforcement

3. Identified Problem or Strength:

4. Care Behaviors or Processes Selected as Best Practices (Prioritized):
   a.

   b.

   (etc. as needed)

5. Intervention Actions (Prioritized):

| | Time Frame | | | |
| Action | Start | Finish | Responsible Persons | Monitoring Approaches and Frequency |

   a. _____

   b. _____

   c. _____

   *

   *

   *

6. Evaluation:

   a. Review of Plan:

   Date: _____

   Responsible Person(s): _____

   Results:

   c. Monitoring Activities

   (1) Activity: _____

   Date Completed: _____

   Finding: _____

   Response: _____

   b. Next Outcome Report

   Date: _____

   Result: _____

   Next step(s):

   (2) Activity: _____

   Date Completed: _____

   Finding: _____

   Response: _____

♦ Be listed in order of priority
♦ Include a start and finish time
♦ Include the name of the person(s) responsible for implementing the actions
♦ Identify how the plan will be monitored
♦ Schedule the frequency of monitoring exercises

The action plan intervention, not to be confused with a clinical intervention, is that set of activities designed to increase care providers' familiarity with and use of best practices for care provision where the best practices are intended to replace or supplement current practices (for remediation) or extend current practices (for reinforcement applications). The action plan intervention is focused on changing or reinforcing agency staff behaviors, agency policies, or structure—that is, this type of intervention is not directly focused on patients or clients, although it is obviously intended to influence patient outcomes (Shaughnessy & Crisler, 1995).

Sharing the Plan of Action with Staff

Once the plan of action has been completed, it becomes necessary to provide group in-service education for the staff regarding the changes. A disadvantage of sharing the plan in in-services is that the process seems to be mostly lecture with little or no group interaction. Dividing the group into a series of smaller groups and allowing adequate time for questions and answers is optimal. In addition, combining the in-service with some other sort of pleasurable experience, such as a "Midnight at the OASIS" party, may help make the process less difficult.

Involving the staff ensures they understand that the entire process will not work without their cooperation and that the best approach and practices will be identified and carried through. Be certain that everything you say to them isn't negative, even if the outcomes look very poor or if the documentation seemed severely flawed during the chart reviews. Remember that OBQI is a movement *away* from traditional quality improvement and *toward* process improvement—from finger pointing to group responsibility.

This is an excellent time to develop new clinical policies, pathways, and competencies, and to acquire and distribute new learning or patient-teaching materials. It is a good idea to set up a mentoring program so that those with the most experience can help those with less. The home care organization may need to hire a consultant with experience in the area being remediated to provide assistance to management and staff. Designing new or revising existing patient screening tools or other documentation may also be effective. Be careful not to overlook new employees. Pairing them with a preceptor will make the transition to OBQI easier.

Remember that the primary focus of the plan of action and its designated interventions is to establish and reinforce excellence in care behaviors. Because old habits or processes are difficult to change, the monitoring function permits the OBQI team to determine whether what was proposed is actually happening, without passively waiting for the next outcome report.

Appendices

Appendix

A

OUTCOME AND
ASSESSMENT INFORMATION
SET (OASIS-B1 (6/98))

Introduction

The proposed Medicare Conditions of Participation (COPs), issued in March 1997, addressed the need for and mandate of a standardized set of home care patient information so that quality and appropriateness of home care services could be measured consistently across the United States. It appears the final regulations to mandate these changes will be issued in 1998 with an effective date specified at that time.

This patient information, collected on all patients in a Medicare certified home health agency who receive home health services (except for those exempt), is documented when home care starts, is collected again at certain time points (usually at recertification [every 60 days]), and then gathered again when the patient is discharged. The information collected at these times can be used to "paint a picture" of the patient's progress or lack of progress while receiving home care services. The data are to be used by home care organizations internally to measure the outcomes of patients with similar diagnoses and situations, as well as externally to show how services provided relate to other provider organizations on a local, regional, state and national scale.

The proposed data set to be mandated by Medicare is called the Outcome and Assessment Information Set (OASIS). This data set contains items that are designed to measure changes in adult clients' health status and allow home care organizations to statistically risk-adjust these outcomes for groups of patients. OASIS data are collected at the initiation of care (admission), at follow-up (recertification), and at discharge to determine the effectiveness of interventions and to document outcomes.

Some facts that are helpful in understanding OASIS and its use are:

♦ The OASIS data set was developed through the Center for Health Policy Research at the University of Colorado in Denver.

♦ Involved in the process were nurses, statisticians, and economists with input from physical, occupational, and speech therapists; social workers; and physicians. This interdisciplinary approach has resulted in a set of measurements capable of globally assessing the patient, indicating areas where referrals to social services or physical or occupational therapy may be required and then used to measure the patient's progression or lack of progress while receiving home care.

♦ Data collection using OASIS has been proven to be a valid and reliable way to measure the quality of home care services over several years by the 50 home health agencies who have been using it and reporting back to Colorado to refine the data set and the analysis.

♦ The specific content of the data elements assists in assessment and care planning. All home care staff can easily and quickly review a patient's levels of activities of daily living (ADLs) and instrumental ADLs (IADLs) from admission throughout the time on service. The information collected can assist in determining if a patient should be recertified after initial 60-day period of care, as well as measure progress from a baseline calculation (upon admission) to discharge.

♦ The OASIS data set is intended to be integrated into an agency's existing assessment form, not tagged on as an additional form or an extra activity to complete and document separately from the assessment. It is meant to become a permanent part of the patient's clinical record.

♦ The OASIS data set does not exist in isolation. This information must be used as a component of the home care organization's outcomes-based quality improvement program. Collection of data over a period of time and comparison of results with other home health providers of similar size and with a similar mix of patients will allow the measurement of quality care to be compared.

Outcome reports that come from the data are critical in indicating areas that have demonstrated improvement, areas that require continued monitoring, areas in need of remediation, as well as areas of practice that are exemplary. The outcome data used in process improvement activities can also assist in developing standards of practice within the agency and externally with other agencies.

As home care moves forward into managed care and prospective payment for services, the monitoring of outcomes will become increasingly important to justify the level of care provided and to demonstrate that an agency can provide the most positive outcomes possible. This appendix presents the entire OASIS-B1 in its most current form.

Outcome and Assessment Information Set (OASIS-B1)

> This data set should not be reviewed or used without first reading the accompanying narrative prologue that explains the purpose of the OASIS and its past and planned evolution.

Items to be Used at Specific Time Points

Start or Resumption of Care MOO10–MO820
   Start of care—further visits planned
   Start of care—no further visits planned
   Resumption of care (after inpatient stay)

Follow-Up MOO10–MO100, MO150, MO200–MO220, MO250,
                                                         MO280–MO380, MO410–MO840
   Recertification (follow-up) assessment
   Other follow-up assessment

Transfer to an Inpatient Facility MOO10–MO100, MO830–MO855, MO890–MO906
   Transferred to an inpatient facility—patient not discharged from an agency
   Transferred to an inpatient facility—patient discharged from agency

Discharge from Agency—Not to an Inpatient Facility
   Death at home MOO10–MO100, MO906
   Discharge from agency MOO10–MO100, MO150, MO200–MO220, MO250,
                                                         MO280–MO380, MO410–MO880, MO903–MO906
   Discharge from agency—no visitws completed
   after start/resumption of care assessment MOO10–MO100, MO830–MO880, MO903–MO906

Note: For items MO640-MO800, please note special instructions at the beginning of the section.

Demographics and Patient History

(MOO10) Agency Provider Number: __ __ __ __ __ __ __ __

(MOO20) Patient ID Number: _____

(MOO30) Start of Care Date: __ __/__ __/__ __ __ __
                          month   day   year

(MOO32) Resumption of Care Date: __ __/__ __/__ __ __ __   ❑ NA – Not Applicable
                          month   day   year

(MOO40) Patient's Name:

_____ ____ _____ _____

(First)   (MI) (Last)   (Suffix)

(MOO50) Patient State of Residence: __ __

(MOO60) Patient Zip Code: __ __ __ __ __

(MOO63) Medicare Number: _____ ❑ NA – No Medicare
               (including suffix if any)

(MOO64) Social Security Number: __ __ __-__ __-__ __ __ __   ❏ UK – Unknown or Not Available

(MOO65) Medicaid Number: __ __ __ __ __ __ __ __ __ __ __ __ __ __   ❏ NA – No Medicaid

(MOO66) Birth Date: __ __/__ __/__ __ __ __
                                month day   year

(MOO69) Gender:

❏ 1 – Male

❏ 1 – Female

(MOO72) Primary Referring Physician ID:

_____   ❏ UK – Unknown or Not Available

(MOO80) Discipline of Person Completing Assessment:

❏ 1 – RN   ❏ 2 – RPT   ❏ 3 – SLP/ST   ❏ 4 –OT

(MOO90) Date Assessment Information

Recorded: __ __/__ __/__ __ __ __
                month   day   year

(MO100) This Assessment is Currently Being Completed for the Following Reason:

❏ 1 – Start of care

❏ 2 – Resumption of care (after inpatient stay)

❏ 3 – Discharge from agency—not to an inpatient facility **[Go to MO150]**

❏ 4 – Transferred to an inpatient facility—discharged from agency **[Go to MO830]**

❏ 5 – Transferred to an inpatient facility—not discharged from agency **[Go to MO830]**

❏ 6 – Died at home **[Go to MO906]**

❏ 7 – Recertification reassessment (follow-up) **[Go to MO150]**

❏ 8 – Other follow-up **[Go to MO150]**

(MO140) Race/Ethnicity (as identified by patient): **(Mark all that apply.)**

❏ 1 – American Indian or Alaska Native

❏ 2 – Asian

❏ 3 – Black or African-American

❏ 4 – Hispanic or Latino

❏ 5 – Native Hawaiian or Pacific Islander

❏ 6 – White

❏ UK – Unknown

(MO150) Current Payment Sources for Home Care: (Mark all that apply.)

❏ 0 – None; no charge for current services

❏ 1 – Medicare (traditional fee-for-service)

❏ 2 – Medicare (HMO/managed care)

❏ 3 – Medicaid (traditional fee-for-service)

❏ 4 – Medicaid (HMO/managed care)

❏ 5 – Workers' compensation

❏ 6 – Title programs (e.g., Title III, V, or XX)

❏ 7 – Other government (e.g., CHAMPUS, VA, etc.)

❏ 8 – Private insurance

❏ 9 – Private HMO/managed care

❏ 10 – Self-pay

❏ 11 – Other (specify)

❏ UK – Unknown

(MO160) Financial Factors limiting the ability of the patient/family to meet basic health needs: (Mark all that apply.)

❏ 0 – None

❏ 1 – Unable to afford medicine or medical supplies

❏ 2 – Unable to afford medical expenses that are not covered by insurance/Medicare (e.g., copayments)

❏ 3 – Unable to afford rent/utility bills

❏ 4 – Unable to afford food

❏ 5 – Other (specify)

(MO170) From which of the following Inpatient Facilities was the patient discharged *during the past 14 days?* (Mark all that apply.)

❏ 1 – Hospital

❏ 2 – Rehabilitation facility

❏ 3 – Nursing home

❏ 4 – Other (specify) _____

❏ NA – Patient was not discharged from an inpatient facility **[if NA, go to MO200]**

(MO180) Inpatient Discharge Date (most recent): __ __/__ __/__ __ __ __
month   day   year

❏ UK – Unknown

(MO190) Inpatient Diagnoses and three-digit ICD code categories *for only those conditions treated during an inpatient facility stay within the last 14 days* (no surgical or V-codes):

Inpatient Facility Diagnosis   *ICD*

a._____   (__ __ __)

b._____   (__ __ __)

(MO200) Medical or Treatment Regimen Change Within Past 14 Days: Has this patient experienced a change in medical or treatment regimen (e.g., medication, treatment, or service change due to new or additional diagnosis, etc.) within the last 14 days?

❏ 0 – No **[If No, go to MO220]**

❏ 1 – Yes

(MO210) List the patient's Medical Diagnoses and three-digit ICD code categories for those conditions requiring changed medical or treatment regimen (no surgical or V-codes):

Changed Medical Regimen Diagnosis   *ICD*

a._____   (__ __ __)

b._____   (__ __ __)

c._____   (__ __ __)

d._____   (__ __ __)

(MO220) Conditions Prior to Medical or Treatment Regimen Change or Inpatient Stay Within Past 14 Days: If this patient experienced an inpatient facility discharge or change in medical or treatment regimen within the past 14 days, indicate any conditions which existed *prior to* the inpatient stay or change in medical or treatment regimen. (Mark all that apply.)

❏ 1 – Urinary incontinence

❏ 2 – Indwelling/suprapubic catheter

❏ 3 – Intractable pain

❏ 4 – Impaired decision-making

❏ 5 – Disruptive or socially inappropriate behavior

❏ 6 – Memory loss to the extent that supervision required

❏ 7 – None of the above

❏ NA – No inpatient facility discharge and no change in medical or treatment regimen in past 14 days

❏ UK – Unknown

(MO230/MO240) Diagnoses and Severity Index: List each medical diagnosis or problem for which the patient is receiving home care and ICD code category (no surgical or V-codes) and rate them using the following severity index. (Choose one value that represents the most severe rating appropriate for each diagnosis.)

❏ 0 – Asymptomatic, no treatment needed at this time

❏ 1 – Symptoms well controlled with current therapy

❏ 2 – Symptoms controlled with difficulty, affecting daily functioning; patient needs ongoing monitoring

❏ 3 – Symptoms poorly controlled, patient needs frequent adjustment in treatment and dose monitoring

❏ 4 – Symptoms poorly controlled, history of rehospitalizations

(MO230) Primary Diagnosis	ICD	Severity Rating
a._____	(__ __ __)	❏ 0 ❏ 1 ❏ 2 ❏ 3 ❏ 4

(MO240) Other Diagnoses	ICD	Severity Rating
b._____	(__ __ __)	❏ 0 ❏ 1 ❏ 2 ❏ 3 ❏ 4
c._____	(__ __ __)	❏ 0 ❏ 1 ❏ 2 ❏ 3 ❏ 4
d._____	(__ __ __)	❏ 0 ❏ 1 ❏ 2 ❏ 3 ❏ 4
e._____	(__ __ __)	❏ 0 ❏ 1 ❏ 2 ❏ 3 ❏ 4
f._____	(__ __ __)	❏ 0 ❏ 1 ❏ 2 ❏ 3 ❏ 4

(MO250) Therapies the patient receives at home: (Mark all that apply.)

❏ 1 – Intravenous or infusion therapy (excludes TPN)

❏ 2 – Parenteral nutrition (TPN or lipids)

❏ 3 – Enteral nutrition (nasogastric, gastrostomy, jejunostomy, or any other artificial entry into the alimentary canal)

❏ 4 – None of the above

(MO260) Overall Prognosis: BEST description of patient's overall prognosis for recovery from this episode of illness.

❏ 0 – Poor: little or no recovery is expected and/or further decline is imminent

❏ 1 – Good/Fair: partial to full recovery is expected

❏ UK – Unknown

(MO270) Rehabilitative Prognosis: BEST description of patient's prognosis for functional status.

❏ 0 – Guarded: minimal improvement in functional status is expected; decline is possible

❏ 1 – Good: marked improvement in functional status is expected

❏ UK – Unknown

(MO280) Life Expectancy: (Physician documentation is not required.)

0 – Life expectancy is greater than 6 months

1 – Life expectancy is 6 months or fewer

(MO290) High Risk Factors characterizing this patient: (Mark all that apply.)

❏ 1 – Heavy smoking

❏ 2 – Obesity

❏ 3 – Alcohol dependency

❏ 4 – Drug dependency

❏ 5 – None of the above

❏ UK – Unknown

Living Arrangements

(MO300) Current Residence:

❑ 1 – Patient's owned or rented residence (house, apartment, or mobile home or rented by patient/couple/significant other)

❑ 2 – Family member's residence

❑ 3 – Boarding home or rented room

❑ 4 – Board and care or assisted living facility

❑ 5 – Other (specify)

(MO310) Structural Barriers in the patient's environment limiting independent mobility: (Mark all that apply.)

❑ 0 – None

❑ 1 – Stairs inside home which must be used by the patient (e.g., to get to toileting, sleeping, eating areas)

❑ 2 – Stairs inside home which are used optionally (e.g., to get to laundry facilities)

❑ 3 – Stairs leading from inside house to outside

❑ 4 – Narrow or obstructed doorways

(MO320) Safety Hazards found in the patient's current place of residence: (Mark all that apply.)

❑ 0 – None

❑ 1 – Inadequate floor, roof, or windows

❑ 2 – Inadequate lighting

❑ 3 – Unsafe gas/electric appliance

❑ 4 – Inadequate heating

❑ 5 – Inadequate cooling

❑ 6 – Lack of fire safety devices

❑ 7 – Unsafe floor coverings

❑ 8 – Inadequate stair railings

❑ 9 – Improperly stored hazardous materials

❑ 10 – Lead-based paint

❑ 11 – Other (specify)

(MO330) Sanitation Hazards found in the patient's current place of residence: (Mark all that apply.)

❑ 0 – None

❑ 1 – No running water

❑ 2 – Contaminated water

❑ 3 – No toileting facilities

❑ 4 – Outdoor toileting facilities only

❑ 5 – Inadequate sewage disposal

❑ 6 – Inadequate/improper food storage

❑ 7 – No food refrigeration

❑ 8 – No cooking facilities

❑ 9 – Insects/rodents present

❑ 10 – No scheduled trash pickup

❑ 11 – Cluttered/soiled living area

❑ 12 – Other (specify)

(MO340) Patient Lives With: (Mark all that apply.)

❏ 1 – Lives alone
❏ 2 – With spouse or significant other
❏ 3 – With other family member
❏ 4 – With a friend
❏ 5 – With paid help (other than home care agency staff)
❏ 6 – With other than above

Supportive Assistance

(MO350) Assisting Person(s) Other than Home Care Agency Staff: (Mark all that apply.)

❏ 1 – Relatives, friends, or neighbors living outside the home
❏ 2 – Person residing in the home (EXCLUDING paid help)
❏ 3 – Paid help
❏ 4 – None of the above **[If None of the above, go to MO390]**
❏ UK – Unknown **[If Unknown, go to MO390]**

(MO360) Primary Caregiver taking lead responsibility for providing or managing the patient's care, providing the most frequent assistance, etc. (other than home care agency staff):

❏ 0 – No one person **[If No one person, go to MO390]**
❏ 1 – Spouse or significant other
❏ 2 – Daughter or son
❏ 3 – Other family member
❏ 4 – Friend or neighbor or community or church member
❏ 5 – Paid help
❏ UK – Unknown **[If Unknown go to MO390]**

(MO370) How Often does the patient receive assistance from the primary caregiver?

❏ 1 – Several times during day and night
❏ 2 – Several times during day
❏ 3 – Once daily
❏ 4 – Three or more times per week
❏ 5 – One to two times per week
❏ 6 – Less often than weekly
❏ UK – Unknown

(MO380) Type of Primary Caregiver Assistance: (Mark all that apply.)

❏ 1 – ADL assistance (e.g., bathing, dressing, toileting, bowel/bladder, eating/feeding)
❏ 2 – IADL assistance (e.g., meds, meals, housekeeping, laundry, telephone, shopping, finances)
❏ 3 – Environmental support (housing, home maintenance)
❏ 4 – Psychosocial support (socialization, companionship, recreation)
❏ 5 – Advocates or facilitates patient's participation in appropriate medical care
❏ 6 – Financial agent, power of attorney, or conservator of finance
❏ 7 – Health care agent, conservator of person, or medical power of attorney
❏ UK – Unknown

Sensory Status

(MO390) Vision with corrective lenses if the patient usually wears them:

❑ 0 – Normal vision: sees adequately in most situations; can see medication labels, newsprint.

❑ 1 – Partially impaired: cannot see medication labels or newsprint, but can see obstacles in path, and the surrounding layout; can count fingers at arm's length.

❑ 2 – Severely impaired: cannot locate objects without hearing or touching them or patient nonresponsive.

(MO400) Hearing and Ability to Understand Spoken Language in patient's own language (with hearing aids of the patient usually uses them):

❑ 0 – No observable impairment. Able to hear and understand complex or detailed instructions and extended or abstract conversation.

❑ 1 – With minimal difficulty, able to hear and understand most multi-step instructions and ordinary conversation. May need occasional repetition, extra time, or louder voice.

❑ 2 – Has moderate difficulty hearing and understanding simple, one-step instructions and brief conversation; needs frequent prompting or assistance.

❑ 3 – Has severe difficulty hearing and understanding simple greetings and short comments. Requires multiple repetitions, restatements, demonstrations, additional time.

❑ 4 – Unable to hear and understand familiar words or common expressions consistently, or patient nonresponsive.

(MO410) Speech and Oral (Verbal) Expression of Language (in patient's own language):

❑ 0 – Expresses complex ideas, feelings, and needs clearly, completely, and easily in all situations with no observable impairment.

❑ 1 – Minimal difficulty in expressing ideas and needs (may take extra time; makes occasional errors in word choice, grammar or speech intelligibility; needs minimal prompting or assistance).

❑ 2 – Expresses simple ideas or needs with moderate difficulty (needs prompting or assistance, errors in word choice, organization or speech intelligibility). Speaks in phrases or short sentences.

❑ 3 – Has severe difficulty expressing basic ideas or needs and requires maximal assistance or guessing by listener. Speech limited to single words or short phrases.

❑ 4 – Unable to express basic needs even with maximal prompting or assistance but is not comatose or unresponsive (e.g., speech is nonsensical or unintelligible).

❑ 5 – Patient nonresponsive or unable to speak.

(MO420) Frequency of Pain interfering with patient's activity or movement:

❑ 0 – Patient has no pain or pain does not interfere with activity or movement

❑ 1 – Less often than daily

❑ 2 – Daily, but not constantly

❑ 3 – All of the time

(MO430) Intractable Pain: Is the patient experiencing pain that is *not easily relieved,* occurs at least daily, and affects the patient's sleep, appetite, physical or emotional energy, concentration, personal relationships, emotions, or ability or desire to perform physical activity?

❑ 0 – No

❑ 1 – Yes

Integumentary Status

(MO440) Does this patient have a Skin Lesion or an Open Wound? This excludes "OSTOMIES."

❑ 0 – No **[If No, go to MO490]**

❑ 1 – Yes

(MO445) Does this patient have a Pressure Ulcer?

❑ 0 – No **[If No, go to MO468]**

❑ 1 – Yes

    a. **(MO450) Current Number of Pressure Ulcers at Each Stage:** (Circle one response for each stage.)

Pressure Ulcer Stages	Number of Pressure Ulcers				
a) Stage 1: Nonblanchable erythema of intact skin; the heralding of skin ulceration. In darker-pigmented skin, warmth, edema, hardness, or discolored skin may be indicators	0	1	2	3	4 or more
b) Stage 2: Partial thickness skin loss involving epidermis and/or dermis. The ulcer is superficial and presents clinically as an abrasion, blister, or shallow crater.	0	1	2	3	4 or more
c) Stage 3: Full-thickness skin loss involving damage or necrosis of subcutaneous tissue which may extend down to, but not through, underlying fascia. The ulcer presents clinically as a deep crater with or without undermining of adjacent tissue.	0	1	2	3	4 or more
d) Stage 4: Full-thickness skin loss with extensive destruction, tissue necrosis, or damage to muscle, bone, or supporting structures (e.g., tendon, joint capsule, etc.)	0	1	2	3	4 or more

e) In addition to the above, is there at least one pressure ulcer that cannot be observed due to the presence of eschar or a nonremovable dressing, including casts?
    0 – No
    1 – Yes					

    b. **(MO460) Stage of Most Problematic (Observable) Pressure Ulcer:**

        ❑ 1 – Stage 1

        ❑ 2 – Stage 2

        ❑ 3 – Stage 3

        ❑ 4 – Stage 4

        ❑ NA – No observable pressure ulcer

    c. **(MO464) Status of Most Problematic (Observable) Pressure Ulcer:**

        ❑ 1 – Fully granulating

        ❑ 2 – Early/partial granulation

        ❑ 3 – Not healing

        ❑ NA – No observable pressure ulcer

(MO468) Does this patient have a Stasis Ulcer?

❑ 0 – No **[If No, go to MO482]**

❑ 1 – Yes

    a. **(MO470) Current Number of Observable Stasis Ulcer(s):**

        ❑ 0 – Zero

        ❑ 1 – One

        ❑ 2 – Two

❑ 3 – Three

❑ 4 – Four or more

   b. **(MO474) Does this patient have at least one Stasis Ulcer that Cannot be Observed due to the presence of a nonremovable dressing?**

      ❑ 0 – No

      ❑ 1 – Yes

   c. **(MO476) Status of Most Problematic (Observable) Stasis Ulcer:**

      ❑ 1 – Fully granulating

      ❑ 2 – Early/partial granulation

      ❑ 3 – Not healing

      ❑ NA – No observable stasis ulcer

(MO482) Does this patient have a Surgical Wound?

❑ 0 – No **[If No, go to MO490]**

❑ 1 – Yes

   a. **(MO484) Current Number of (Observable) Surgical Wounds:** (If a wound is partially closed but has more than one opening, consider each opening as a separate wound.)

      ❑ 0 – Zero

      ❑ 1 – One

      ❑ 2 – Two

      ❑ 3 – Three

      ❑ 4 – Four or more

   b. **(MO486) Does this patient have at least one Surgical Wound that Cannot be Observed due to the presence of a nonremovable dressing?**

      ❑ 0 – No

      ❑ 1 – Yes

   c. **(MO488) Status of Most Problematic (Observable) Surgical Wound:**

      ❑ 1 – Fully granulating

      ❑ 2 – Early/partial granulation

      ❑ 3 – Not healing

      ❑ NA – No observable surgical wound

Respiratory Status

(MO490) When is the patient dyspneic or noticeable Short of Breath?

❑ 0 – Never, patient is not short of breath

❑ 1 – When walking more than 20 feet, climbing stairs

❑ 2 – With moderate exertion (e.g., while dressing, using commode or bedpan, walking distances less than 20 feet)

❑ 3 – With minimal exertion (e.g., while eating, talking, or performing other ADLs) or with agitation

❑ 4 – At rest (during day or night)

(MO500) Respiratory Treatments utilized at home: (Mark all that apply.)

❑ 1 – Oxygen (intermittent or continuous)

❑ 2 – Ventilator (continually or at night)

❑ 3 – Continuous positive airway pressure

❑ 4 – None of the above

Elimination Status

(MO510) Has this patient been treated for a Urinary Tract Infection in the past 14 days?

❏ 0 – No
❏ 1 – Yes
❏ NA – Patient on prophylactic treatment
❏ UK – Unknown

(MO520) Urinary Incontinence or Urinary Catheter Presence:

❏ 0 – No incontinence or catheter (includes anuria or ostomy for urinary drainage) **[If No, go to MO540]**
❏ 1 – Patient is incontinent
❏ 2 – Patient requires a urinary catheter (i.e., external, indwelling, intermittent, suprapubic) **[Go to MO540]**

(MO530) When does Urinary Incontinence occur?

❏ 0 – Timed-voiding defers incontinence
❏ 1 – During the night only
❏ 2 – During the day and night

(MO540) Bowel Incontinence Frequency:

❏ 0 – Very rarely or never has bowel incontinence
❏ 1 – Less than once weekly
❏ 2 – One to three times weekly
❏ 3 – Four to six times weekly
❏ 4 – On a daily basis
❏ 5 – More often than once daily
❏ NA – Patient has ostomy for bowel elimination
❏ UK – Unknown

(MO550) Ostomy for Bowel Elimination: Does this patient have an ostomy for bowel elimination that (within the last 14 days): a) was related to an inpatient facility stay, or b) necessitated a change in medical or treatment regimen?

❏ 0 – Patient does *not* have an ostomy for bowel elimination.
❏ 1 – Patient's ostomy was not related to an inpatient stay and did not necessitate change in medical or treatment regimen.
❏ 2 – The ostomy was related to an inpatient stay or did necessitate change in medical or treatment regimen.

Neuro/Emotional/Behavioral Status

(MO560) Cognitive Functioning: (Patient's current level of alertness, orientation, comprehension, concentration, and immediate memory for simple commands.)

❏ 0 – Alert/oriented, able to focus and shift attention, comprehends and recalls task directions independently.
❏ 1 – Requires prompting (cueing, repetition, reminders) only under stressful or unfamiliar conditions.
❏ 2 – Requires assistance and some direction in specific situations (e.g., on all tasks involving shifting of attention), or consistently requires low stimulus environment due to distractibility.
❏ 3 – Requires considerable assistance in routine situations. Is not alert and oriented or is unable to shift attention and recall directions more than half the time.
❏ 4 – Totally dependent due to disturbances such as constant disorientation, coma, persistent vegetative state, or delirium.

(MO570) When Confused (Reported or Observed):

❏ 0 – Never

❏ 1 – In new or complex situations only

❏ 2 – On awakening or at night only

❏ 3 – During the day and evening, but not constantly

❏ 4 – Constantly

❏ NA – Patient nonresponsive

(MO580) When Anxious (Reported or Observed):

❏ 0 – None of the time

❏ 1 – Less often than daily

❏ 2 – Daily, but not constantly

❏ 3 – All of the time

❏ NA – Patient nonresponsive

(MO590) Depressive Feelings Reported or Observed in Patient: (Mark all that apply.)

❏ 1 – Depressed mood (e.g., feeling sad, tearful)

❏ 2 – Sense of failure or self reproach

❏ 3 – Hopelessness

❏ 4 – Recurrent thoughts of death

❏ 5 – Thoughts of suicide

❏ 6 – None of the above feelings observed or reported

(MO600) Patient Behaviors (Reported or Observed): (Mark all that apply.)

❏ 1 – Indecisiveness, lack of concentration

❏ 2 – Diminished interest in most activities

❏ 3 – Sleep disturbances

❏ 4 – Recent change in appetite or weight

❏ 5 – Agitation

❏ 6 – A suicide attempt

❏ 7 – None of the above behaviors observed or reported

(MO610) Behaviors Demonstrated at Least Once a Week (Reported or Observed): (Mark all that apply.)

❏ 1 – Memory deficit: failure to recognize familiar persons/places, inability to recall events of past 24 hours, significant memory loss so that supervision is required

❏ 2 – Impaired decision-making: failure to perform usual ADLs or IADLs, inability to appropriately stop activities, jeopardizes safety through actions

❏ 3 – Verbal disruption: yelling, threatening, excessive profanity, sexual references, etc.

❏ 4 – Physical aggression: aggressive or combative to self and others (e.g., hits self, throws objects, punches, dangerous maneuvers with wheelchair or other objects)

❏ 5 – Disruptive, infantile, or socially inappropriate behavior (excludes verbal actions)

❏ 6 – Delusional, hallucinatory, or paranoid behavior

❏ 7 – None of the above behaviors demonstrated

(MO620) Frequency of Behavior Problems (Reported or Observed) (e.g., wandering episodes, self abuse, verbal disruption, physical aggression, etc.):

❏ 0 – Never

❏ 1 – Less than once a month

❏ 2 – Once a month

❏ 3 – Several times each month

❏ 4 – Several times a week

❏ 5 – At least daily

(MO630) Is this patient receiving Psychiatric Nursing Services at home provided by a qualified psychiatric nurse?

❑ 0 – No
❑ 1 – Yes

ADL/IADLS

(MO640) Grooming: Ability to tend to personal hygiene needs (i.e., washing face and hands, hair care, shaving or make-up, teeth or denture care, fingernail care).

> For MO640-MO800, complete the "current" column for all patients. For these same items, complete the "prior" column only at start of care; mark the level that corresponds to the patient's condition 14 days prior to start of care. In all cases, record what the patient is able to do.

Prior   Current
❑   ❑   0 – Able to groom self unaided, with or without the use of assistive devices or adapted methods.
❑   ❑   1 – Grooming utensils must be placed within reach before able to complete grooming activities.
❑   ❑   2 – Someone must assist the patient to groom self.
❑   ❑   3 – Patient depends entirely upon someone else for grooming needs.
         ❑   UK – Unknown

(MO650) Ability to Dress Upper Body (with or without dressing aids) including undergarments, pullovers, front-opening shirts and blouses, managing zippers, buttons, and snaps:

Prior   Current
❑   ❑   0 – Able to get clothes out of closets and drawers, put them on and remove them from the upper body without assistance.
❑   ❑   1 – Able to dress upper body without assistance if clothing is laid out or handed to the patient.
❑   ❑   2 – Someone must help the patient put on upper body clothing.
❑   ❑   3 – Patient depends entirely upon another person to dress the upper body.
         ❑   UK – Unknown

(MO660) Ability to Dress Lower Body (with or without dressing aids) including undergarments, slacks, socks or nylons, shoes:

Prior   Current
❑   ❑   0 – Able to obtain, put on, and remove clothing and shoes without assistance.
❑   ❑   1 – Able to dress lower body without assistance if clothing and shoes are laid out or handed to the patient.
❑   ❑   2 – Someone must help the patient put on undergarments, slacks, socks or nylons, and shoes.
❑   ❑   3 – Patient depends entirely upon another person to dress lower body.
         ❑   UK – Unknown

(MO670) Bathing: Ability to wash entire body. Excludes grooming (washing face and hands only).

Prior   Current
❑   ❑   0 – Able to bathe self in shower or tub independently.
❑   ❑   1 – With the use of devices, is able to bathe self in shower or tub independently.
❑   ❑   2 – Able to bathe in shower or tub with the assistance of another person:
              (a) for intermittent supervision or encouragement or reminders, OR
              (b) to get in and out of the shower or tub, OR
              (c) for washing difficult to reach areas.

Prior	Current	
❑	❑	3 – Participates in bathing self in shower or tub, but requires presence of another person throughout the bath for assistance or supervision.
❑	❑	4 – Unable to use the shower or tub and is bathed in bed or bedside chair.
❑	❑	5 – Unable to effectively participate in bathing and is totally bathed by another person.
	❑	UK – Unknown

(MO680) Toileting: Ability to get to and from the toilet or bedside commode.

Prior	Current	
❑	❑	0 – Able to get to and from the toilet independently with or without a device.
❑	❑	1 – When reminded, assisted, or supervised by another person, able to get to and from the toilet.
❑	❑	2 – Unable to get to and from the toilet but is able to use a bedside commode (with or without assistance).
❑	❑ 3 –	Unable to get to and from the toilet or bedside commode but is able to use a bedpan/urinal independently.
❑	❑	4 – Is totally dependent in toileting.
	❑	UK – Unknown

(MO690) Transferring: Ability to move from bed to chair, on and off toilet or commode, into and out of tub or shower, and ability to turn and position self in bed if patient is bedfast.

Prior	Current	
❑	❑	0 – Able to independently transfer.
❑	❑	1 – Transfers with minimal human assistance or with use of an assistive device.
❑	❑	2 – Unable to transfer self but is able to bear weight and pivot during the transfer process.
❑	❑	3 – Unable to transfer self and is unable to bear weight or pivot when transferred by another person.
❑	❑	4 – Bedfast, unable to transfer but is able to turn and position self in bed.
❑	❑	5 – Bedfast, unable to transfer and is unable to turn and position self.
	❑	UK – Unknown

(MO700) Ambulation/Locomotion: Ability to SAFELY walk, once in a standing position, or use a wheelchair, once in a seated position, on a variety of surfaces.

Prior	Current	
❑	❑	0 – Able to independently walk on even and uneven surfaces and climb stairs with or without railings (i.e., needs no human assistance or assistive device).
❑	❑	1 – Requires use of a device (e.g., cane, walker) to walk alone or requires human supervision or assistance to negotiate stairs or steps or uneven surfaces.
❑	❑	2 – Able to walk only with the supervision or assistance of another person at all times.
❑	❑	3 – Chairfast, unable to ambulate but is able to wheel self independently.
❑	❑	4 – Chairfast, unable to ambulate and is unable to wheel self.
❑	❑	5 – Bedfast, unable to ambulate or be up in a chair.
	❑	UK – Unknown

(MO710) Feeding or Eating: Ability to feed self meals and snacks.

Note: This refers only to the process of eating, chewing, and swallowing, not preparing the food to be eaten.

Prior	Current	
❑	❑	0 – Able to independently feed self.
❑	❑	1 – Able to feed self independently but requires:

        (a) meal set-up; OR

        (b) intermittent assistance or supervision from another person; OR

        (c) a liquid, pureed or ground meat diet.

Prior   Current

❏   ❏   2 – Unable to feed self and must be assisted or supervised throughout the meal/snack.

❏   ❏   3 – Able to take in nutrients orally and receives supplemental nutrients through a nasogastric tube or gastrostomy.

❏   ❏   4 – Unable to take in nutrients orally and is fed nutrients through a nasogastric tube or gastrostomy.

❏   ❏   5 – Unable to take in nutrients orally or by tube feeding.

            ❏   UK – Unknown

(MO720) Planning and Preparing Light Meals (e.g., cereal, sandwich) or reheat delivered meals:

Prior   Current

❏   ❏   0 – (a) Able to independently plan and prepare all light meals for self or reheat delivered meals; OR

                         (b) Is physically, cognitively, and mentally able to prepare light meals on a regular basis but has not routinely performed light meal preparation in the past (i.e., prior to this home care admission).

❏   ❏   1 – Unable to prepare light meals on a regular basis due to physical, cognitive, or mental limitations.

❏   ❏   2 – Unable to prepare any light meals or reheat any delivered meals.

            ❏   UK – Unknown

(MO730) Transportation: Physical and mental ability to safely use a car, taxi, or public transportation (bus, train, subway).

Prior   Current

❏   ❏   0 – Able to independently drive a regular or adapted car; OR uses a regular or handicap-accessible public bus.

❏   ❏   1 – Able to ride in a car only when driven by another person; OR able to use a bus or handicap van only when assisted or accompanied by another person.

❏   ❏   2 – Unable to ride in a car, taxi, bus, or van, and requires transportation by ambulance.

            ❏   UK – Unknown

(MO740) Laundry: Ability to do own laundry—to carry laundry to and from washing machine, to use washer and dryer, to wash small items by hand.

Prior   Current

❏   ❏   0 – (a) Able to independently take care of all laundry tasks; OR

                         (b) Physically, cognitively, and mentally able to do laundry and access facilities, but has not routinely performed laundry tasks in the past (i.e., prior to this home care admission).

❏   ❏   1 – Able to do only light laundry, such as minor hand wash or light washer loads. Due to physical, cognitive, or mental limitations, needs assistance with heavy laundry such as carrying large loads of laundry.

❏   ❏   2 – Unable to do any laundry due to physical limitation or needs continual supervision and assistance due to cognitive or mental limitation.

            ❏   UK – Unknown

(MO750) Housekeeping: Ability to safely and effectively perform light housekeeping and heavier cleaning tasks.

Prior   Current

❏   ❏   0 – (a) Able to independently perform all housekeeping tasks; OR

                         (b) Physically, cognitively, and mentally able to perform all housekeeping tasks but has not routinely participated in housekeeping tasks in the past (i.e., prior to this home care admission).

❏   ❏   1 – Able to perform only light housekeeping (e.g., dusting, wiping kitchen counters) tasks independently.

❏   ❏   2 – Able to perform housekeeping tasks with intermittent assistance or supervision from another person.

Prior	Current	
❏	❏	3 – Unable to consistently perform any housekeeping tasks unless assisted by another person throughout the process.
❏	❏	4 – Unable to effectively participate in any housekeeping tasks.
❏	❏	UK – Unknown

(MO760) Shopping: Ability to plan for, select, and purchase items in a store and to carry them home or arrange delivery.

Prior	Current	
❏	❏	0 – (a) Able to plan for shopping needs and independently perform shopping tasks, including carrying packages; OR (b) Physically, cognitively, and mentally able to take care of shopping, but has not done shopping in the past (i.e., prior to this home care admission).
❏	❏	1 – Able to go shopping, but needs some assistance: (a) By self is able to do only light shopping and carry small packages, but needs someone to do occasional major shopping; OR (b) Unable to go shopping alone, but can go with someone to assist.
❏	❏	2 – Unable to go shopping, but is able to identify items needed, place orders, and arrange home delivery.
❏	❏	3 – Needs someone to do all shopping and errands.
	❏	UK – Unknown

(MO770) Ability to Use Telephone: Ability to answer the phone, dial numbers, and effectively use the telephone to communicate.

Prior	Current	
❏	❏	0 – Able to dial numbers and answer calls appropriately and as desired.
❏	❏	1 – Able to use a specially adapted telephone (i.e., large numbers on the dial, teletype phone for the deaf) and call essential numbers.
❏	❏	2 – Able to answer the telephone and carry on a normal conversation but has difficulty with placing calls.
❏	❏	3 – Able to answer the telephone only some of the time or is able to carry on only a limited conversation.
❏	❏	4 – Unable to answer the telephone at all but can listen if assisted with equipment.
❏	❏	5 – Totally unable to use the telephone.
❏	❏	NA – Patient does not have a telephone.
	❏	UK – Unknown

Medications

(MO780) Management of Oral Medications: Patient's ability to prepare and take all prescribed oral medications reliably and safely, including administration of the correct dosage at the appropriate times/intervals. Excludes injectable and IV medications. (NOTE: This refers to ability, not compliance or willingness.)

Prior	Current	
❏	❏	0 – Able to independently take the correct oral medication(s) and proper dosage(s) at the correct times.
❏	❏	1 – Able to take medication(s) at the correct times if: (a) individual dosages are prepared in advance by another person; OR (b) given daily reminders; OR (c) someone develops a drug diary or chart.
❏	❏	2 – Unable to take medication unless administered by someone else.
	❏	NA – No oral medications prescribed.
	❏	UK – Unknown

(MO790) Management of Inhalant/Mist Medications: Patient's ability to prepare and take all prescribed inhalant/mist medications (nebulizers, metered dose devices) reliable and safely, including administration of the correct dosage at the appropriate times/intervals. Excludes all other forms of medication (oral tablets, injectable and IV medications).

Prior　　Current

❑　　　❑　　　0 – Able to independently take the correct medication and proper dosage at the correct times.

❑　　　❑　　　1 – Able to take medication at the correct times if:

　　　　　　　　　　(a) individual dosages are prepared in advance by another person, OR

　　　　　　　　　　(b) given daily reminders.

❑　　　❑　　　2 – Unable to take medication unless administered by someone else.

　　　　❑　　　NA – No inhalant/mist medications prescribed.

　　　　❑　　　UK – Unknown

(MO800) Management of Injectable Medications: Patient's ability to prepare and take all prescribed injectable medications reliably and safely, including administration of correct dosage at the appropriate times/intervals. Excludes IV medications.

Prior　　Current

❑　　　❑　　　0 – Able to independently take the correct medication and proper dosage at the correct times.

❑　　　❑　　　1 – Able to take injectable medication at correct times if:

　　　　　　　　　　(a) individual syringes are prepared in advance by another person, OR

　　　　　　　　　　(b) given daily reminders.

❑　　　❑　　　2 – Unable to take injectable medications unless administered by someone else.

　　　　❑　　　NA – No injectable medications prescribed.

　　　　❑　　　UK – Unknown

Equipment Management

(MO810) Patient Management of Equipment (includes ONLY oxygen, IV/infusion therapy, enteral/parenteral nutrition equipment or supplies): Patient's ability to set up, monitor and change equipment reliable and safely, add appropriate fluids or medication, clean/store/dispose of equipment or supplies using proper technique. (NOTE: This refers to ability, not compliance or willingness.)

❑ 0 – Patient manages all tasks related to equipment completely independently.

❑ 1 – If someone else sets up equipment (i.e., fills portable oxygen tank, provides patient with prepared solutions), patient is able to manage all other aspects of equipment.

❑ 2 – Patient requires considerable assistance from another person to manage equipment, but independently completes portions of the task.

❑ 3 – Patient is only able to monitor equipment (e.g., liter flow, fluid in bag) and must call someone else to manage the equipment.

❑ 4 – Patient is completely dependent on someone else to manage all equipment.

❑ NA – No equipment of this type used in care **[If NA, go to MO830]**

(MO820) Caregiver Management of Equipment (includes ONLY oxygen, IV/infusion equipment, enteral/parenteral nutrition, ventilator therapy equipment or supplies): Caregiver's ability to set up, monitor, and change equipment reliably and safely, add appropriate fluids or medication, clean/store/dispose of equipment or supplies using proper technique. (NOTE: This refers to ability, not compliance or willingness.)

❑ 0 – Caregiver manages all tasks related to equipment completely independently.

❑ 1 – If someone else sets up equipment, caregiver is able to manage all other aspects.

❑ 2 – Caregiver requires considerable assistance from another person to manage equipment, but independently completes significant portions of task.

❑ 3 – Caregiver is only able to complete small portions of task (e.g., administer nebulizer treatment, clean/store/dispose of equipment or supplies).

❑ 4 – Caregiver is completely dependent on someone else to manage all equipment.

❑ NA – No caregiver

❑ UK – Unknown

Emergent Care

(MO830) Emergent Care: Since the last time OASIS data were collected, has the patient utilized any of the following services for emergent care (other than home care agency services)? (Mark all that apply.)

❑ 0 – No emergent care services **[If No emergent care and patient discharged, go to MO855]**

❑ 1 – Hospital emergency room (includes 23-hour holding)

❑ 2 – Doctor's office emergency visit/house call

❑ 3 – Outpatient department/clinic emergency (includes urgicenter sites)

❑ UK – Unknown

(MO840) Emergent Care Reason: For what reason(s) did the patient/family seek emergent care? (Mark all that apply.)

❑ 1 – Improper medication administration, medication side effects, toxicity, anaphylaxis

❑ 2 – Nausea, dehydration, malnutrition, constipation, impaction

❑ 3 – Injury caused by fall or accident at home

❑ 4 – Respiratory problems (e.g., shortness of breath, respiratory infection, tracheobronchial obstruction)

❑ 5 – Wound infection, deteriorating wound status, new lesion/ulcer

❑ 6 – Cardiac problems (e.g., fluid overload, exacerbation of CHF, chest pain)

❑ 7 – Hypo/Hyperglycemia, diabetes out of control

❑ 8 – GI bleeding, obstruction

❑ 9 – Other than above reasons

❑ UK – Reason unknown

Data Items Collected at Inpatient Facility Admission or Discharge Only

(MO855) To which Inpatient Facility has the patient been admitted?

❑ 1 – Hospital **[Go to MO890]**

❑ 2 – Rehabilitation facility **[Go to MO903]**

❑ 3 – Nursing home **[Go to MO900]**

❑ 4 – Hospice **[Go to MO903]**

❑ NA – No inpatient facility admission

(MO870) Discharge Disposition: Where is the patient after discharge from your agency? (choose only one answer.)

❑ 1 – Patient remained in the community (not in hospital, nursing home, or rehab facility)

❑ 2 – Patient transferred to a noninstitutional hospice **[Go to MO903]**

❑ 3 – Unknown because patient moved to a geographic location not served by this agency **[Go to MO903]**

❑ UK – Other unknown **[Go to MO903]**

(MO880) After discharge, does the patient receive health, personal, or support Services or Assistance? (Mark all that apply.)

❑ 1 – No assistance or services received

❑ 2 – Yes, assistance or services provided by family or friends

❑ 3 – Yes, assistance or services provided by other community resources (e.g., meals-on-wheels, home health services, homemaker assistance, transportation assistance, assisted living, board and care) **[Go to MO903]**

(MO890) If the patient was admitted to an acute care Hospital, for what Reason was he/she admitted?

❑ 1 – Hospitalization for *emergent* (unscheduled) care

❑ 2 – Hospitalization for *urgent* (scheduled within 24 hours of admission) care

❑ 3 – Hospitalization for *elective* (scheduled more than 24 hours before admission) care

❑ UK – Unknown

(MO895) Reason for Hospitalization: (Mark all that apply.)

❑ 1 – Improper medication administration, medication side effects, toxicity, anaphylaxis

❑ 2 – Injury caused by fall or accident at home

❑ 3 – Respiratory problems (SOB, infection, obstruction)

❑ 4 – Wound or tube site infection, deteriorating wound status, new lesion/ulcer

❑ 5 – Hypo/Hyperglycemia, diabetes out of control

❑ 6 – GI bleeding, obstruction

❑ 7 – Exacerbation of CHF, fluid overload, heart failure

❑ 8 – Myocardial infarction, stroke

❑ 9 – Chemotherapy

❑ 10 – Scheduled surgical procedure

❑ 11 – Urinary tract infection

❑ 12 – IV catheter-related infection

❑ 13 – Deep vein thrombosis, pulmonary embolus

❑ 14 – Uncontrolled pain

❑ 15 – Psychotic episode

❑ 16 – Other than above reasons **[Go to MO903]**

(MO900) For what Reason(s) was the patient Admitted to a Nursing Home? (Mark all that apply.)

❑ 1 – Therapy services

❑ 2 – Respite care

❑ 3 – Hospice care

❑ 4 – Permanent placement

❑ 5 – Unsafe for care at home

❑ 6 – Other

❑ UK – Unknown

Go to MO903

(MO903) Date of Last (Most Recent) Home Visit: __ __/__ __/__ __ __ __
                                                         month day   year

(MO906) Discharge/Transfer/Death Date: Enter the date of the discharge, transfer, or death (at home) of the patient. __ __/__ __/__ __ __ __
                    month   day   year

❑ UK – Unknown

Appendix B

SAMPLE INITIAL ASSESSMENT FORM #1 WITH
OASIS ITEMS
(ALSO USED FOR RESUMPTION OF CARE
FOLLOWING INPATIENT STAY)

Demographics

(MOO10) Agency Number ID: __ __ __ __ __ __ __ __

(MOO20) Patient ID Number: _____

(MOO30) Start of Care Date: __ __ / __ __ / __ __ __ __
                                        month   day   year

(MOO32) Resumption of Care Date: __ __ / __ __ / __ __ __ __   ❑ NA – Not Applicable
                                               month   day   year

(MOO40) Patient's Name:

_____ _____ _____ _____

(First)   (MI)   (Last)   (Suffix)

(MOO50) Patient State of Residence: __ __

(MOO60) Patient Zip Code: __ __ __ __ __

(MOO63) Medicare Number: _____   ❑ NA – No Medicare
                                     (including suffix if any)

(MOO64) Social Security Number: __ __ __-__ __-__ __ __ __   ❑ UK – Unknown or Not Available

(MOO66) Birth Date: __ __ / __ __ / __ __ __ __
                              month day   year

(MOO69) Gender:

❑ 1 – Male

❑ 1 – Female

Emergency Contact

· Name _____   · Relationship _____

· Address _____

· Phone H _____   W _____

(MOO72) Primary Referring Physician ID:

_____   ❑ UK – Unknown or Not Available

(MOO80) Discipline of Person Completing Assessment:

❑ 1-RN   ❑ 2-PT   ❑ 3-SLP/ST   ❑ 4-OT

(MOO90) Date Assessment Information

Recorded: __ __ / __ __ / __ __ __ __
                month day   year

(MO100) This Assessment is Currently Being Completed for the Following Reason:

Start/Resumption of Care

❑ 1 – Start of care—further visits planned

❑ 2 – Start of care—no further visits planned

❑ 3 – Resumption of care (after inpatient stay)

Follow-Up

❑ 4 – Recertification (follow-up) reassessment **[Go to MO150]**

❑ 5 – Other follow-up **[Go to MO150]**

<u>Transfer to an Inpatient Facility</u>

❏ 6 – Transferred to an inpatient facility—patient not discharged from agency **[Go to MO830]**

❏ 7 – Transferred to an inpatient facility—patient discharged from agency **[Go to MO830]**

<u>Discharge from Agency—Not to an Inpatient Facility</u>

❏ 8 – Died at home **[Go to MO906]**

❏ 9 – Discharge from agency **[Go to MO150]**

❏ 10 – Discharge from agency—no visits completed after start/resumption of care assessment **[Go to MO380]**

(MO140) Race/Ethnicity (as identified by patient): **(Mark all that apply.)**

❏ 1 – American Indian or Alaska Native

❏ 2 – Asian

❏ 3 – Black or African-American

❏ 4 – Hispanic or Latino

❏ 5 – Native Hawaiian or Pacific Islander

❏ 6 – White

❏ UK – Unknown

(MO150) Current Payment Sources for Home Care: (Mark all that apply.)

❏ 0 – None; no change for current services

❏ 1 – Medicare (traditional fee-for-service)

❏ 2 – Medicare (HMO/managed care)

❏ 3 – Medicaid (traditional fee-for-service)

❏ 4 – Medicaid (HMO/managed care)

❏ 5 – Workers' compensation

❏ 6 – Title programs (e.g., Title III, V, or XX)

❏ 7 – Other government (e.g., CHAMPUS, VA, etc.)

❏ 8 – Private insurance

❏ 9 – Private HMO/managed care

❏ 10 – Self-pay

❏ 11 – Other (specify)_____

❏ UK – Unknown

(MO160) Financial Factors limiting the ability of the patient/family to meet basic health needs:
(Mark all that apply.)

❏ 0 – None

❏ 1 – Unable to afford medicine or medical supplies

❏ 2 – Unable to afford medical expenses that are not covered by insurance/Medicare (e.g., copayments)

❏ 3 – Unable to afford rent/utility bills

❏ 4 – Unable to afford food

❏ 5 – Other (specify) _____

(MO170) From which of the following Inpatient Facilities was the patient discharged *during the past 14 days?* **(Mark all that apply.)**

❏ 1 – Hospital

❏ 2 – Rehabilitation facility

❏ 3 – Nursing home

❏ 4 – Other (specify) _____

❏ NA – Patient was not discharged from an inpatient facility **[If NA, go toMO200]**

(MO180) Inpatient Discharge Date (most recent):

__ __ /__ __ / __ __ __ __

month day   year

❏ UK – Unknown

(MO190) Inpatient Diagnoses and three-digit ICD code categories *for only those conditions treated during an inpatient facility stay within the last 14 days* (no surgical or V-codes):

Inpatient Facility Diagnosis   ICD

a._____   (__ __ __)

b._____   (__ __ __)

(MO200) Medical or Treatment Regimen Change Within Past 14 Days: Has this patient experienced a change in medical or treatment regimen (e.g., medication, treatment, or service change due to new or additional diagnosis, etc.) within the last 14 days?

❏ 0 – NO **[If No, go to MO220]**

❏ 1 – Yes

(MO210) List the patient's **Medical Diagnoses** and three-digit ICD code categories *for those conditions requiring changed medical or treatment regimen* (no surgical or V- codes):

Changed Medical Regimen Diagnosis   ICD

a._____   (__ __ __)

b._____   (__ __ __)

c._____   (__ __ __)

d._____   (__ __ __)

(MO220) Conditions Prior to Medical or Treatment Regimen Change or Inpatient Stay Within Past 14 Days: If this patient experienced an inpatient facility discharge or change in medical or treatment regimen within the past 14 days, indicate any conditions which existed *prior to* the inpatient stay or change in medical or treatment regimen. (Mark all that apply.)

❏ 1 – Urinary incontinence

❏ 2 – Indwelling/suprapubic catheter

❏ 3 – Intractable pain

❏ 4 – Impaired decision-making

❏ 5 – Disruptive or socially inappropriate behavior

❏ 6 – Memory loss to the extent that supervision required

❏ 7 – None of the above

❏ NA – No inpatient facility discharge *and* no change in medical or treatment regimen in past 14 days

❏ UK – Unknown

(MO230/MO240) Diagnoses and Severity Index: List each medical diagnosis or problem for which the patient is receiving home care and ICD code category (no surgical or V-codes) and rate them using the following severity index. (Choose one value that represents the most severe rating appropriate for each diagnosis.)

0 – Asymptomatic, no treatment needed at this time

1 – Symptoms well controlled with current therapy

2 – Symptoms controlled with difficulty, affecting daily functioning; patient needs ongoing monitoring

3 – Symptoms poorly controlled, patient needs frequent adjustment in treatment and dose monitoring

4 – Symptoms poorly controlled, history of rehospitalization

(MO230) Primary Diagnosis	*ICD*	*Severity Rating*
a._____	(__ __ __)	0 1 2 3 4 5

(MO240) Other Diagnosis	*ICD*	*Severity Rating*
b. _____	(__ __ __)	0 1 2 3 4 5
c. _____	(__ __ __)	0 1 2 3 4 5
d. _____	(__ __ __)	0 1 2 3 4 5
e. _____	(__ __ __)	0 1 2 3 4 5
f. _____	(__ __ __)	0 1 2 3 4 5

(MO250) Therapies the patient receives *at home:* **(Mark all that apply.)**

❑ 1 – Intravenous or infusion therapy (excludes TPN)

❑ 2 – Parenteral nutrition (TPN or lipids)

❑ 3 – Enteral nutrition (nasogastric, gastrostomy, jejunostomy, or any other artificial entry into the alimentary canal)

❑ 4 – None of the above

(MO260) Overall Prognosis: BEST description of patient's overall prognosis for *recovery from this episode of illness.*

❑ 0 – Poor: little or no recovery is expected and/or further decline is imminent

❑ 1 – Good/Fair: partial to full recovery is expected

❑ UK – Unknown

(MO270) Rehabilitative Prognosis: BEST description of patient's prognosis for *functional status.*

❑ 0 – Guarded: minimal improvement in functional status is expected; decline is   possible

❑ 1 – Good: marked improvement in functional status is expected

❑ UK – Unknown

(MO280) Life Expectancy: (Physician documentation is not required.)

❑ 0 – Life expectancy is greater than 6 months

❑ 1 – Life expectancy is 6 months or fewer

(MO290) High Risk Factors characterizing this patient: **(Mark all that apply.)**

❑ 1 – Heavy smoking

❑ 2 – Obesity

❑ 3 – Alcohol dependency

❏ 4 – Drug dependency

❏ 5 – None of the above

❏ UK – Unknown

(MO300) Current Residence:

❏ 1 – Patient's owned or rented residence (house, apartment, or mobile home owned or rented by patient/couple/significant other)

❏ 2 – Family member's residence

❏ 3 – Boarding home or rented room

❏ 4 – Board and care or assisted living facility

❏ 5 – Other (specify) _____

(MO310) Structural Barriers in the patient's environment limiting independent mobility: **(Mark all that apply.)**

❏ 0 – None

❏ 1 – Stairs inside home which *must* be used by the patient (e.g., to get to toileting, sleeping, eating areas)

❏ 2 – Stairs inside home which are used optionally (e.g., to get to laundry facilities)

❏ 3 – Stairs leading from inside house to outside

❏ 4 – Narrow or obstructed doorways

(MO320) Safety Hazards found in the patient's current place of residence: **(Mark all that apply.)**

❏ 0 – None

❏ 1 – Inadequate floor, roof, or windows

❏ 2 – Inadequate lighting

❏ 3 – Unsafe gas/electric appliance

❏ 4 – Inadequate heating

❏ 5 – Inadequate cooling

❏ 6 – Lack of fire safety devices

❏ 7 – Unsafe floor coverings

❏ 8 – Inadequate stair railings

❏ 9 – Improperly stored hazardous materials

❏ 10 – Lead-based paint

❏ 11 – Other (specify) _____

(MO330) Sanitation Hazards found in the patient's current place of residence: **(Mark all that apply.)**

❏ 0 – None

❏ 1 – No running water

❏ 2 – Contaminated water

❏ 3 – No toileting facilities

❏ 4 – Outdoor toileting facilities only

❏ 5 – Inadequate sewage disposal

❏ 6 – Inadequate/improper food storage

❏ 7 – No food refrigeration

❏ 8 – No cooking facilities

❏ 9 – Insects/rodents present

❏ 10 – No scheduled trash pickup

❏ 11 – Cluttered/soiled living area

❏ 12 – Other (specify)_____

(MO340) Patient Lives With: (Mark all that apply.)

❏ 1 – Lives alone

❏ 2 – With spouse or significant other

❏ 3 – With other family member

❏ 4 – With a friend

❏ 5 – With paid help (other than home care agency staff)

❏ 6 – With other than above

SUPPORTIVE ASSISTANCE

(MO350) Assisting Person(s) Other than Home Care Agency Staff: (Mark all that apply.)

❏ 1 – Relatives, friends, or neighbors living outside the home

❏ 2 – Person residing in the home (EXCLUDING paid help)

❏ 3 – Paid help

❏ 4 – None of the above **[If None of the above, go to MO390]**

❏ UK - Unknown **[If Unknown, go to MO390]**

(MO360) Primary Caregiver taking *lead* responsibility for providing or managing the patient's care, providing the most frequent assistance, etc. (other than home care agency staff):

❏ 0 – No one person **[If No one person, go to MO390]**

❏ 1 – Spouse or significant other

❏ 2 – Daughter or son

❏ 3 – Other family member

❏ 4 – Friend or neighbor or community or church member

❏ 5 – Paid help

❏ UK – Unknown **[If Unknown, go to MO390]**

(MO370) How Often does the patient receive assistance from the primary caregiver?

❏ 1 – Several times during day and night

❏ 2 – Several times during day

❏ 3 – Once daily

❏ 4 – Three or more times per week

❏ 5 – One or two times per week

❏ 6 – Less often than weekly

❏ UK – Unknown

(MO380) Type of Primary Caregiver Assistance: (Mark all that apply.)

❏ 1 – ADL assistance (e.g., bathing, dressing, toileting, bowel/bladder, eating/feeding)

❏ 2 – IADL assistance (e.g., meds, meals, housekeeping, laundry, telephone, shopping, finances)

❏ 3 – Environmental support (housing, home maintenance)

❏ 4 – Psychosocial support (socialization, companionship, recreation)

❏ 5 – Advocates or facilitates patient's participation in appropriate medical care

❏ 6 – Financial agent, power of attorney, or conservator of finance

❏ 7 – Health care agent, conservator of person, or medical power of attorney

❏ UK – Unknown

(MO390) Vision with corrective lenses if the patient usually wears them:

❏ 0 – Normal vision: sees adequately in most situations; can see medication labels, newsprint.

❏ 1 – Partially impaired: cannot see medication labels or newsprint, but *can* see obstacles in path, and the surrounding layout; can count fingers at arm's length.

❏ 2 – Severely impaired: cannot locate objects without hearing or touching them *or* patient is nonresponsive.

(MO400) Hearing and Ability to Understand Spoken Language in patient's own language (with hearing aids if the patient usually uses them):

❏ 0 – No observable impairment. Able to hear and understand complex or detailed instructions and extended or abstract conversation.

❏ 1 – With minimal difficulty, able to hear and understand most multi-step instructions and ordinary conversation. May need occasional repetition, extra time, or louder voice.

❏ 2 – Has moderate difficulty hearing and understanding simple, one-step instructions and brief conversation; needs frequent prompting or assistance.

❏ 3 – Has severe difficulty hearing and understanding simple greeting and short comments. Requires multiple repetitions, restatements, demonstrations, additional time.

❏ 4 – *Unable* to hear and understand familiar words or common expressions consistently, *or* patient is nonresponsive.

(MO410) Speech and Oral (Verbal) Expression of Language (in patient's own language):

❏ 0 – Expresses complex ideas, feelings, and needs clearly, completely, and easily in all situations with no observable impairment.

❏ 1 – Minimal difficulty in expressing ideas and needs (may take extra time; makes occasional errors in word choice, grammar or speech intelligibility; needs minimal prompting or assistance).

❏ 2 – Expresses simple ideas or needs with moderate difficulty (needs prompting or assistance, errors in word choice, organization or speech intelligibility). Speaks in phrases or short sentences.

❏ 3 – Has severe difficulty expressing basic ideas or needs and requires maximal assistance or guessing by listener. Speech limited to single words or short phrases.

❏ 4 – *Unable* to express basic needs even with maximal prompting or assistance but is not comatose or unresponsive (e.g., speech is nonsensical or unintelligible).

❏ 5 – Patient nonresponsive or unable to speak.

(MO420) Frequency of Pain interfering with patient's activity or movement:

❏ 0 – Patient has no pain or pain does not interfere with activity or movement

❏ 1 – Less often than daily

❏ 2 – Daily, but not constantly

❏ 3 – All of the time

(MO430) Intractable Pain: Is the patient experiencing pain that is *not easily relieved,* occurs at least daily, and affects the patient's sleep, appetite, physical or emotional energy, concentration, personal relationships, emotions, or ability or desire to perform physical activity.

❏ 0 – No

❏ 1 – Yes

PHYSIOLOGICAL INTEGRITY

		Yes	No
Mucous membranes:	Pink/moist.	❏	❏
	Pale.	❏	❏
	Cyanotic.	❏	❏
	Dry.	❏	❏
	Cracked.	❏	❏
Skin warm/dry/usual color:		❏	❏
	Hot.	❏	❏
	Cool.	❏	❏
	Moist.	❏	❏
	Pale.	❏	❏
	Flushed.	❏	❏
	Cyanotic.	❏	❏
	Jaundiced.	❏	❏
Seborrheic or senile keratoses present:		❏	❏
	Age spots:	❏	❏
	Cherry angiomas:	❏	❏
	Bruising:	❏	❏
	Location_____		
	Suspicious lesions:	❏	❏
	Location_____		
Skin and Mucous Membranes Intact:		❏	❏
	Pain or sores in mouth:	❏	❏
	Persistent hoarseness:	❏	❏
	Lips symmetrical:	❏	❏
	Fullness/pain in thyroid region:	❏	❏
Nails intact:		❏	❏
	Brittle:	❏	❏
	Thick:	❏	❏

	Yes	No
Yellow:	❏	❏
Clubbing:	❏	❏
Capillary refill adequate:	❏	❏

Skin Risk: Rate Categories A-E each with a score of 1, 2, 3, 4; add the 5 scores for total and determine skin risk.

    A. Sensory Perception: 1-Completely limited, 2-Very limited, 3-Slightly limited, 4-No impairment.

    B. Moisture: 1-Constantly Moist, 2-Moist, 3-Occasionally moist, 4-Rarely moist

    C. Mobility: 1-Completely immobile, 2-Very Limited, 3-Slightly limited, 4-No limitations.

    D. Nutritional: 1-Very Poor, 2-Probably inadequate, 3-Adequate, 4-Excellent

    E. Friction: 1-Problem, 2-Potential problem, 3-No problem

    Skin Risk is Evaluated AEB: _____ Total

    NO or LOW SKIN RISK Score ≥ 15

    MODERATE SKIN RISK Score 13–14

    HIGH SKIN RISK Score ≤ 12 or Skin Ulcer/Disruption

Fall Risk: Each condition below results in one score point (Add all points to obtain total and determine fall risk.)

	Y	N
· Blackouts in Past 6 Months	❏	❏
· Communication Barrier	❏	❏
· Impaired motor/sensory function	❏	❏
· Uncorrected impaired vision	❏	❏
· Hypotension	❏	❏
· Assistive Devices/Multiple equipment use	❏	❏
· Bowel/Bladder Problems	❏	❏

FALL RISK is Evaluated AEB:

LOW FALL – Level I, Score of 0.

Low Fall Risk interventions

| · Remove rugs from floor or apply non-skid backing. | ❏ | ❏ |
| · Encourage use of nonslip footwear. | ❏ | ❏ |

MODERATE FALL RISK – Level II, Score 1- 4.

Moderate Fall Risk Interventions:

· Level 1 interventions AND:

· Instruct to be up only with help	❏	❏
· Offer help q1–2 hr.	❏	❏
· Use night light.	❏	❏

HIGH FALL RISK – Level III, Score > 4 OR altered mentation, history of falls, noncomplaint with instructions.

	Y	N
High Fall Risk Interventions:		
· Level I and II interventions AND:		
· Check and/or offer help qhr	❏	❏
· Other interventions as effective.	❏	❏

OTHER SAFETY INTERVENTIONS:

	Y	N
· Reorient to activity and environment	❏	❏
· Reposition as necessary	❏	❏
· Up in chair	❏	❏
· Decrease environmental stimuli	❏	❏
· Apply motion alarm (if needed and if available)	❏	❏
· Review meds for mental status effect.	❏	❏

(MO440) Does this patient have a Skin Lesion or an Open Wound? This excludes "OSTOMIES."

❏ 0 – No **[If No, go to MO490]**

❏ 1 – Yes

(MO445) Does this patient have a **Pressure Ulcer?**

❏ 0 – No **[If No, go to MO468]**

❏ 1 – Yes

(MO450) Current Number of Pressure Ulcers at Each Stage: (Circle one response for each stage.)

Pressure Ulcer Stages	Number of Pressure Ulcers				
a) Stage 1: Nonblanchable erythema of intact skin; the heralding of skin ulceration. In darker-pigmented skin, warmth, edema, hardness, or discolored skin may be indicators	0	1	2	3	4 or more
b) Stage 2: Partial thickness skin loss involving epidermis and/or dermis. The ulcer is superficial and presents clinically as an abrasion, blister, or shallow crater.	0	1		3	4 or more
c) Stage 3: Full-thickness skin loss involving damage or necrosis of subcutaneous tissue which may extend down to, but not through, underlying fascia. The ulcer presents clinically as a deep crater with or without undermining of adjacent tissue.	0	1	2	3	4 or more
d) Stage 4: Full-thickness skin loss with extensive destruction, tissue necrosis, or damage to muscle, bone, or supporting structures (e.g., tendon, joint capsule, etc.)	0	1	2	3	4 or more
e) In addition to the above, is there at least one pressure ulcer that cannot be observed due to the presence of eschar or a nonremovable dressing, including casts? ❏ 0 – No ❏ 1 – Yes					

(MO460) Stage of Most Problematic (Observable) Pressure Ulcer:

❏ 1 – Stage 1

❏ 2 – Stage 2

❏ 3 – Stage 3

❏ 4 – Stage 4

❏ NA – No observable pressure ulcer

(MO464) Status of Most Problematic (Observable) Pressure Ulcer:

❏ 1 – Fully granulating

❏ 2 – Early/partial granulation

❏ 3 – Not healing

❏ NA – No observable pressure ulcer

(MO468) Does this patient have a **Stasis Ulcer?**

❏ 0 – No **[If No, go to MO482]**

❏ 1 – Yes

(MO470) Current Number of Observable Stasis Ulcer(s):

❏ 0 – Zero

❏ 1 – One

❏ 2 – Two

❏ 3 – Three

❏ 4 – Four or more

(MO474) Does this patient have at least one **Stasis Ulcer that Cannot be Observed** due to the presence of a nonremovable dressing?

❏ 0 – No

❏ 1 – Yes

(MO476) Status of Most Problematic (Observable) Stasis Ulcer:

❏ 1 – Fully granulating

❏ 2 – Early/partial granulation

❏ 3 – Not healing

❏ 4 – No observable stasis ulcer

(MO482) Does this patient have a **Surgical Wound?**

❏ 0 – No [If No, go to MO490]

❏ 1 – Yes

(MO484) Current Number of (Observable) Surgical Wounds: (If a wound is partially closed but has *more* than one opening, consider each opening as a separate wound.)

❏ 0 – Zero

❏ 1 – One

❏ 2 – Two

❏ 3 – Three

❏ 4 – Four or more

(MO486) Does this patient have at least one **Surgical Wound that Cannot be Observed** due to the presence of a nonremovable dressing?

❏ 0 – No

❏ 1 – Yes

(MO488) Status of Most Problematic (Observable) Surgical Wound:

❏ 1 – Fully granulating

❏ 2 – Early/partial granulation

❏ 3 – Not healing

❏ NA – No observable surgical wound

Indicate lesion # on the corresponding areas affected on the body figure

1. Bruise

2. Laceration

3. Abrasion

4. Rash

5. Ulcer

6. Blister

7. Swelling

8. Drainage

9. Radiation TX

10. Stoma

11. Incision

12. Suture(s)

13. Staple(s)

14. Drugs

15. Steri Strips

16. Masses

17. Scars

18. Stasis ulcer

19. Pressure ulcer

	Y	N	
Sero-Sanguineous drainage	❏	❏	
Purulent drainage	❏	❏	
Wound edges well approximated	❏	❏	Size: _____
Edges not well approximated	❏	❏	Depth: _____
Wound exhibits redness	❏	❏	
Wound exhibits swelling	❏	❏	

	Y	N
If dressed, wound dressing intact	❏	❏
If present, sutures/staples steri strips intact	❏	❏
If present, Drainage Tube(s) secure & functioning properly:	❏	❏

Location: _____

Type: _____

RESPIRATORY FUNCTION

	Y	N	
Resp regular	❏	❏	
Resp irregular	❏	❏	
Resp unlabored	❏	❏	
Resp labored	❏	❏	
No c/o dyspnea/SOB	❏	❏	
c/o dyspnea/SOB	❏	❏	
Orthopnea	❏	❏	
No cough	❏	❏	
Non-productive cough	❏	❏	
Productive cough	❏	❏	
Sputum color	❏	❏	
Sputum viscosity	❏	❏	
Sputum amount	❏	❏	
Nailbeds pink	❏	❏	
Nailbeds pale	❏	❏	
Nailbeds cyanotic	❏	❏	
Oxygenation adequate	❏	❏	Pulse oximetry: _____

Bilateral breath sounds clear

	Right	Left
Crackles	❏	❏
Diminished	❏	❏
Wheezing	❏	❏
Rhonchi	❏	❏
Pleural Friction Rub	❏	❏

	Y	N
Scoliosis:	❏	❏
Kyphosis:	❏	❏
Increased AP diameter:	❏	❏
Tenderness in spine:	❏	❏

(MO490) When is the patient dyspneic or noticeably Short of Breath?

❏ 0 – Never, patient is not short of breath

❏ 1 – When walking more than 20 feet, climbing stairs

❏ 2 – With moderate exertion (e.g., while dressing, using commode or bedpan, walking distances less than 20 feet)

❏ 3 – With minimal exertion (e.g., while eating, talking, or performing other ADLs) or with agitation

❏ 4 – At rest (during day or night)

(MO500) Respiratory Treatments utilized at home: **(Mark all that apply.)**

❏ 1 – Oxygen (intermittent or continuous)

❏ 2 – Ventilator (continually or at night)

❏ 3 – Continuous positive airway pressure

❏ 4 – None of the above

	Y	N
Safety Measures Taught:	❏	❏

T:_____ Ax, oral, tympanic

P:_____ radial _____ apical

R: _____

B/Psystolic

_____/_____   _____   _____   _____
  diastolic   standing   sitting   lying

CARDIOVASCULAR FUNCTION

	Y	N	
Pulse regular:	❏	❏	
irregular:	❏	❏	
pacemaker:	❏	❏	Rate:_____ Model:_____
No chest pain/discomfort:	❏	❏	
Chest pain/discomfort	❏	❏	
Known heart disease: ❏	❏		
CHF:	❏	❏	
HX MI	❏	❏	
Hx Angina:	❏	❏	
frequency of attacks: _____			
Relieved by nitros	❏	❏	
Claudication:	❏	❏	
Cold extremities:	❏	❏	
Hypertension:	❏	❏	

	Y	N
Venous disease:	❑	❑
Varicose veins:	❑	❑
Ankle swelling:	❑	❑
Phlebitis:	❑	❑
Hx of clot:	❑	❑
Peripheral Vascular System:	❑	❑
Arterial occlusion:		
Decreased Perfusion:	❑	❑
Condition of skin of lower extremities:		
Pale:	❑	❑
Shiny:	❑	❑
Atrophic skin:	❑	❑
Hair loss:	❑	❑
Cyanosis:	❑	❑
Pedal Pulses Palpable:	❑	❑
Post tibial:	❑	❑
Dorsalis pedis:	❑	❑

NUTRITIONAL ASSESSMENT

Appetite: _____

Diet: _____

	Y	N
Nausea:	❑	❑
Vomiting:	❑	❑
Chewing difficulties:	❑	❑
Swallowing difficulties:	❑	❑
Food intolerance:	❑	❑	_____
Increased gas (flatus or belching):	❑	❑
Feeding tube:	❑	❑

    If yes, Type:_____

Dietitian needed: if ≥ 2 of the following, consider dietitian consult:

❑ Age > 75

❑ Chewing/Swallowing problems

❑ Pressure ulcers

❑ Surgical wounds

❑ Clear liquids > 2 days

❑ Recent weight loss

❑ Decreased appetite > 3 days (50% or less eaten)

❑ Newly diagnosed diabetic

❑ Special diet requirements: _____

❑ End Stage Renal Disease

❑ TPN/enteral nutrition: _____

BOWEL AND BLADDER ASSESSMENT

Urine:

Clear ❑

Color ❑   ❑   ❑   ❑   ❑

     Amber   Pale Yellow   Red (blood)   Brown   Other _____

	Y	N
Bladder distention:	❑	❑
c/o incomplete emptying:	❑	❑
Burning:	❑	❑
Frequency:	❑	❑
Urgency:	❑	❑
Hesitancy:	❑	❑

(MO510) Has this patient been treated for a **Urinary Tract Infection** in the past 14 days?

❑ 0 – No

❑ 1 – Yes

❑ NA – Patient on prophylactic treatment

❑ UK – Unknown

(MO520) Urinary Incontinence or Urinary Catheter Presence:

❑ 0 – No incontinence or catheter (including anuria or ostomy for urinary drainage) [If No, go to MO540]

❑ 1 – Patient is incontinent

❑ 2 – Patient requires a urinary catheter (i.e., external, indwelling, intermittent, suprapubic) [Go to MO540]

(MO530) When does **Urinary incontinence** occur?

❑ 0 – Timed-voiding defers incontinence

❑ 1 – During the night only

❑ 2 – During the day and night

	Y	N
Urostomy present:	❑	❑

Catheter type, if present: _____

Frequency of catheter changes: _____

Date due: _____

Bowel sounds present X 4: ☐ ☐

Abdomen

     Soft: ☐ ☐

     Firm: ☐ ☐

     Distended: ☐ ☐

		Y	N
Last BM _____	Usual for patient:	☐	☐
Constipation:		☐	☐
Diarrhea:		☐	☐

(MO540) Bowel Incontinence Frequency:

☐ 0 – Very rarely or never has bowel incontinence

☐ 1 – Less than once weekly

☐ 2 – One to three times weekly

☐ 3 – Four to six times weekly

☐ 4 – On a daily basis

☐ 5 – More often than once daily

☐ NA – Patient has ostomy for bowel elimination

☐ UK – Unknown

(MO550) Ostomy for Bowel Elimination: Does this patient have an ostomy for bowel elimination that (within the last 14 days): a) was related to an inpatient facility stay, *or* b) necessitated a change in medical or treatment regimen?

☐ 0 – Patient does *not* have an ostomy for bowel elimination.

☐ 1 – Patient's ostomy was *not* related to an inpatient stay and did not necessitate change in medical or treatment regimen.

☐ 2 – The ostomy *was* related to an inpatient stay or *did* necessitate change in medical or treatment regimen.

NEUROLOGICAL FUNCTION

	Y	N	
Pain site:	☐	☐	
Perceived pain level (0-5): _____			
(0 = no pain)			
Dizziness:	☐	☐	
Headache:	☐	☐	Location:_____
Sleeping/resting without problem:	☐	☐	
Eyes:			
Pupils equal:	☐	☐	
Pupils reactive to light:	☐	☐	
Glasses:	☐	☐	

	Y	N	
Contact Lenses:	❏	❏	
Blurred vision:	❏	❏	
Double vision:	❏	❏	
Glaucoma:	❏	❏	Treatment:_____
	Y	N	
Discharge/itching:	❏	❏	
Vision changes:	❏	❏	

Ears:

	Y	N	
Hearing aid present:	❏	❏	
Deafness or Hard of Hearing:	Left	Right	
Drainage:	❏	❏	_____
Redness/inflamation of pinna:	❏	❏	

Speech:

	Y	N
Clear:	❏	❏
Aphasic:	❏	❏
Slurred:	❏	❏
Nonverbal:	❏	❏
Inappropriate:	❏	❏

Extremities:

	Y / UE	N / LE	
HX CVA	❏	❏	
Moves all extremities:	❏	❏	
Weakness:	UE	LE	
Paralysis:	UE	LE	
Parasthesia:	UE	LE	
Tremor:	UE	LE	
Unequal grasp:	❏	❏	_____>_____

Pediatric:

	Y	N	
Age appropriate:	❏	❏	
Delayed:	❏	❏	
107. Lack of coordination:	❏	❏	
108. Vertigo:	❏	❏	
109. Syncope:	❏	❏	
110. Seizures:	❏	❏	Recent onset: ❏ ❏
111. Asymetry of face:	❏	❏	

PSYCHOLOGICAL INTEGRITY

	Y	N
Appropriate anxiety/coping behaviors	❏	❏
Inappropriate anxiety		
Patient:	❏	❏
Family:	❏	❏

	Y	N
Ineffective coping behaviors		
Patient:	❏	❏
Family:	❏	❏
Effective interactions	❏	❏
Interactions ineffective		
Patient:	❏	❏
Family:	❏	❏
States/demonstrates understanding of Plan of Care	❏	❏
Unable to state/demonstrate plan		
Patient:	❏	❏
Family:	❏	❏
Communicates spiritual/cultural needs if any	❏	❏
Unable to communicate needs		
Patient:	❏	❏
Family:	❏	❏
Appropriate Growth/Development	❏	❏
Inappropriate Growth/Development		
Patient:	❏	❏
Family:	❏	❏

(MO560) Cognitive Functioning: (Patient's current level of alertness, orientation, comprehension, concentration, and immediate memory for simple commands.)

❏ 0 – Alert/oriented, able to focus and shift attention, comprehends and recalls task directions independently.

❏ 1 – Requires prompting (cuing, repetition, reminders) only under stressful or unfamiliar conditions.

❏ 2 – Requires assistance and some direction in specific situations (e.g., on all tasks involving shifting of attention), or consistently requires low stimulus environment due to distractibility.

❏ 3 – Requires considerable assistance in routine situations. Is not alert and oriented or is unable to shift attention and recall directions more than half the time.

❏ 4 – Totally dependent due to disturbances such as constant disorientation, coma, persistent vegetative state, or delirium.

(MO570) When Confused (Reported or Observed):

❑ 0 – Never

❑ 1 – In new or complex situations only

❑ 2 – On awakening or at night only

❑ 3 – During the day and evening, but not constantly

❑ 4 – Constantly

❑ NA – Patient nonresponsive

(MO580) When Anxious (Reported or Observed):

❑ 0 – None of the time

❑ 1 – Less often than daily

❑ 2 – Daily, but not constantly

❑ 3 – All of the time

❑ NA – Patient nonresponsive

(MO590) Depressive Feelings Reported or Observed in Patient: (Mark all that apply.)

❑ 1 – Depressed MOOd (e.g., feeling sad, tearful)

❑ 2 – Sense of failure or self repoach

❑ 3 – Hopelessness

❑ 4 – Recurrent thoughts of death

❑ 5 – Thoughts of suicide

❑ 6 – None of the above feelings observed or reported

(MO600) Patient Behaviors (Reported or Observed): (Mark all that apply.)

❑ 1 – Indecisiveness, lack of concentration

❑ 2 – Diminished interest in most activities

❑ 3 – Sleep disturbances

❑ 4 – Recent change in appetite or weight

❑ 5 – Agitation

❑ 6 – A suicide attempt

❑ 7 – None of the above behaviors observed or reported

(MO610) Behaviors Demonstrated *at Least Once a Week* (Reported or Observed): (Mark all that apply.)

❑ 1 – Memory deficit: failure to recognize familiar persons/places, inability to recall events of past 24 hours, significant memory loss so that supervising is required

❑ 2 – Impaired decision-making: failure to perform usual ADLs or IADLs, inability to appropriately stop activities, jeopardizes safety through actions

❑ 3 – Verbal disruption: yelling, threatening, excessive profanity, sexual references, etc.

❑ 4 – Physical aggression: aggressive or combative to self and others (e.g., hits self, throws objects, punches, dangerous maneuvers with wheelchair or other objects)

❑ 5 – Disruptive, infantile, or socially inappropriate behavior (excludes verbal actions)

❑ 6 – Delusional, hallucinatory, or paranoid behavior

❑ 7 – None of the above behaviors demonstrated

(MO620) Frequency of Behavior Problems (Reported or Observed) (e.g., wandering episodes, self abuse, verbal disruption, physical aggression, etc):

❑ 0 – Never

❑ 1 – Less than once a month

❑ 2 – Once a month

❑ 3 – Several times each month

❑ 4 – Several times a week

❑ 5 – At least daily

(MO630) Is this patient receiving **Psychiatric Nursing Services** at home provided by a qualified psychiatric nurse?

❑ 0 – No

❑ 1 – Yes

Other comments regarding psychological integrity: _____

_____

_____

_____

ADL/IADLs

For MO640-MO800, complete the "current" column for all patients. For these same items, complete the "prior" column only at start of care; mark the level that corresponds to the patient's condition 14 days prior to start of care. In all cases, record what the patient is able to do.

(MO640) Grooming: Ability to tend to personal hygiene needs (i.e., washing face and hands, hair care, shaving or make up, teeth or denture care, fingernail care).

Prior	Current	
❑	❑	0 – Able to groom self unaided, with or without the use of assistive devices or adapted methods.
❑	❑	1 – Grooming utensils must be placed within reach before able to complete grooming activities.
❑	❑	2 – Someone must assist the patient to groom self.
❑	❑	3 – Patient depends entirely upon someone else for grooming needs.
❑		UK – Unknown

(MO650) Ability to Dress *Upper* Body (with or without dressing aids) including undergarments, pullovers, front-opening shirts and blouses, managing zippers, buttons, and snaps:

Prior	Current	
❑	❑	0 – Able to get clothes out of closets and drawers, put them on and remove them from the upper body without assistance.
❑	❑	1 – Able to dress upper body without assistance if clothing is laid out or handed to the patient.
❑	❑	2 – Someone must help the patient put on upper body clothing.
❑	❑	3 – Patient depends entirely upon another person to dress the upper body.
❑		UK – Unknown

(MO660) Ability to Dress *Lower Body* (with or without dressing aids) including undergarments, slacks, socks or nylons, shoes:

Prior   *Current*

❏   ❏   0 – Able to obtain, put on, and remove clothing and shoes without assistance.

Prior   *Current*

❏   ❏   1 – Able to dress lower body without assistance if clothing and shoes are laid out or handed to the patient.

❏   ❏   2 – Someone must help the patient put on undergarments, slacks, socks or nylons, and shoes.

❏   ❏   3 – Patient depends entirely upon another person to dress lower body.

❏   UK – Unknown

(MO670) Bathing: Ability to wash entire body. ***Excludes* grooming (washing face and hands only).**

Prior   *Current*

❏   ❏   0 – Able to bathe self in *shower or tub* independently.

❏   ❏   1 – With the use of devices, is able to bathe self in shower or tub independently.

❏   ❏   2 – Able to bathe in shower or tub with the assistance of another person:

                                    (a) for intermittent supervision or encouragement or reminders, *OR*

                                    (b) to get in and out of the shower or tub, *OR*

                                    (c) for washing difficult to reach areas.

❏   ❏   3 – Participates in bathing self in shower or tub, *but* requires presence of another person throughout the bath for assistance or supervision.

❏   ❏   4 – *Unable* to use the shower or tub and is bathed in *bed or bedside chair.*

❏   ❏   5 – Unable to effectively participate in bathing and is totally bathed by another person.

❏   UK – Unknown

(MO680) Toileting: Ability to get to and from the toilet or bedside commode.

Prior   *Current*

❏   ❏   0 – Able to get to and from the toilet independently with or without a device.

❏   ❏   1 – When reminded, assisted, or supervised by another person, able to get to and from the toilet.

❏   ❏   2 – *Unable* to get to and from the toilet but is able to use bedside commode (with or without assistance).

❏   ❏   3 – *Unable* to get to and from the toilet or bedside commode but is able to use a bedpan/urinal independently.

❏   ❏   4 – Is totally dependent in toileting.

❏   UK – Unknown

(MO690) Transferring: Ability to move from bed to chair, on and off toilet or commode, into and out of tub or shower, and ability to turn and position self in bed if patient is bedfast.

Prior   *Current*

❏   ❏   0 – Able to independently transfer.

❏   ❏   1 – Transfers with minimal human assistance or with use of an assistive device.

❏   ❏   2 – *Unable* to transfer self but is able to bear weight and pivot during the transfer process.

Prior	Current	
❑	❑	3 – Unable to transfer self and is *unable* to bear weight or pivot when transferred by another person.
❑	❑	4 – Bedfast, unable to transfer but is able to turn and position self in bed.
❑	❑	5 – Bedfast, unable to transfer and is *unable* to turn and position self.
❑		UK – Unknown

(MO700) Ambulation/Locomotion: Ability to *SAFELY* walk, once in a standing position, or use a wheelchair, once in a seated position, on a variety of surfaces.

Prior	Current	
❑	❑	0 – Able to independently walk on even and uneven surfaces and climb stairs with or without railings (i.e., needs no human assistance or assistive device).
❑	❑	1 – Requires use of a device (e.g., cane, walker) to walk alone *or* requires human supervision or assistance to negotiate stairs or steps or uneven surfaces.
❑	❑	2 – Able to walk only with the supervision or assistance of another person at all times.
❑	❑	3 – Chairfast, *unable* to ambulate but is able to wheel self independently.
❑	❑	4 – Chairfast, unable to ambulate and is *unable* to wheel self.
❑	❑	5 – Bedfast, unable to ambulate or be up in a chair.
	❑	UK – Unknown

(MO710) Feeding or Eating: Ability to feed self meals and snacks. **Note: This refers only to the process of *eating, chewing,* and *swallowing, not preparing* the food to be eaten**.

Prior	Current	
❑	❑	0 – Able to independently feed self.
❑	❑	1 - Able to feed self independently but requires:
		(a) meal set-up; *OR*
		(b) intermittent assistance or supervision from another person; *OR*
		(c) a liquid, pureed or ground meat diet.
❑	❑	2 – *Unable* to feed self and must be assisted or supervised throughout the meal/snack.
❑	❑	3 – Able to take in nutrients orally *and* receives supplemental nutrients though a nasogastric tube or gastrostomy.
❑	❑	4 – *Unable* to take in nutrients orally and is fed nutrients though a nasogastric tube or gastrostomy.
❑	❑	5 – Unable to take in nutrients orally or by tube feeding.
❑		UK – Unknown

(MO720) Planning and Preparing Light Meals (e.g., cereal, sandwich) or reheat delivered meals:

Prior	Current	
❑	❑	0 – (a) Able to independently plan and prepare all light meals for self or reheat delivered meals; *OR*
		(b) is physically, cognitively, and mentally able to prepare light meals on a regular basis but has not routinely performed light meal preparation in the past (i.e., prior to this home care admission).
❑	❑	1 – *Unable* to prepare light meals on a regular basis due to physical, cognitive, or mental limitations.
❑	❑	2 – Unable to prepare any light meals or reheat any delivered meals.
❑		UK – Unknown

(MO730) Transportation: Physical and mental ability to *safely* use a car, taxi, or public transportation (bus, train, subway).

Prior   *Current*

❏   ❏   0 – Able to independently drive a regular or adapted car; *OR* uses a regular or handicap-accessible public bus.

❏   ❏   1 – Able to ride in a car only when driven by another person; *OR* able to use a bus or handicap van only when assisted or accompanied by another person.

❏   ❏   2 – *Unable* to ride in a car, taxi, bus, or van, and requires transportation by ambulance.

❏   UK – Unknown

(MO740) Laundry: Ability to do own laundry — to carry laundry to and from washing machine, to use washer and dryer, to wash small items by hand.

Prior   *Current*

❏   ❏   0 – (a) Able to independently take care of all laundry tasks; *OR*

                          (b) Physically, cognitively, and mentally able to do laundry and access facilities, *but* has not routinely performed laundry tasks in the past (i.e., prior to this home care admission).

❏   ❏   1 – Able to do only light laundry, such as minor hand wash or light washer loads. Due to physical, cognitive, or mental limitation, needs assistance with heavy laundry such as carrying large loads of laundry.

❏   ❏   2 – *Unable* to do any laundry due to physical limitation or needs continual supervision and assistance due to cognitive or mental limitation.

❏   UK – Unknown

(MO750) Houskeeping: Ability to safely and effectively perform light housekeeping and heavier cleaning tasks.

Prior   *Current*

❏   ❏   0 – (a) Able to independently perform all housekeeping tasks; *OR*

                          (b) Physically, cognitively, and mentally able to perform *all* housekeeping tasks but has not routinely participated in housekeeping tasks in the past (i.e., prior to this home care admission).

❏   ❏   1 – Able to perform only *light* housekeeping (e.g., dusting, wiping kitchen counters) tasks independently.

❏   ❏   2 – Able to perform housekeeping tasks with intermittent assistance or supervision from another person.

❏   ❏   3 – *Unable* to consistently perform any housekeeping tasks unless assisted by another person thoughout the process.

❏   ❏   4 – Unable to effectively participate in any housekeeping tasks.

❏   UK – Unknown

(MO760) Shopping: Ability to plan for, select, and purchase items in a store and to carry them home or arrange delivery.

Prior   *Current*

❏   ❏   0 – (a) Able to plan for shopping needs and independently perform shopping tasks, including carrying packages; *OR*

                          (b) Physically, cognitively, and mentally able to take care of shopping, but has not done shopping in the past (i.e., prior to this home care admission).

Prior	Current
❏	❏

Prior   *Current*

❏   ❏   1 – Able to go shopping, but needs some assistance:

           (a) By self is able to do only light shopping and carry small packages, but needs someone to do occasional major shopping; *OR*

           (b) *Unable* to go shopping alone, but can go with someone to assist.

❏   ❏   2 – *Unable* to go shopping, but is able to identify items needed, place orders, and arrange home delivery.

❏   ❏   3 – Needs someone to do all shopping and errands.

❏   ❏   UK – Unknown

(MO770) Ability to Use Telephones: Ability to answer the phone, dial numbers, and *effectively* use the telephone to communicate.

Prior   *Current*

❏   ❏   0 – Able to dial numbers and answer calls appropriately and as desired.

❏   ❏   1 – Able to use a specially adapted telephone (i.e., large numbers on the dial, teletype phone for the deaf) and call essential numbers.

❏   ❏   2 – Able to answer the telephone and carry on a normal conversation but has difficulty with placing calls.

❏   ❏   3 – Able to answer the telephone only some of the time or is able to carry on only a limited conversation.

❏   ❏   4 – *Unable* to answer the telephone at all but can listen if assisted with equipment.

❏   ❏   5 – Totally unable to use the telephone.

❏   ❏   NA – Patient does not have a telephone.

❏   ❏   UK – Unknown

MEDICATIONS

(MO780) Management of Oral Medications: *Patient's ability* to prepare and take *all* prescribed oral medications reliably and safely, including administration of the correct dosage at the appropriate times/intervals. ***Excludes* injectable and IV medications. (NOTE: This refers to ablity, not compliance or willingness.)**

Prior   *Current*

❏   ❏   0 – Able to independently take the correct oral medication(s) and proper dosage(s) at the correct times.

❏   ❏   1 – Able to take medication(s) at the correct time if:

           (a) individual dosages are prepared in advance by another person; *OR*

           (b) given daily reminders; *OR*

           (c) someone develops a drug diary or chart.

❏   ❏   2 – *Unable* to take medication unless administered by someone else.

❏   ❏   NA – No oral medications prescribed.

❏   ❏   UK – Unknown

(MO790) Management of Inhalant/Mist Medications: *Patient's ability* to prepare and take *all* prescribed inhalant/mist medication (nebulizers, metered dose devices) reliably and safely, including administration of the correct dosage at the appropriate times/intervals. *Excludes* **all other forms of medication (oral tablets, injectable and IV medications).**

Prior   *Current*

❏   ❏   0 – Able to independently take the correct medication and proper dosage at the correct times.

❏   ❏   1 – Able to take medication at the correct times if:

        (a) individual dosages are prepared in advance by another person, *OR*

        (b) given daily reminders.

❏   ❏   2 – *Unable* to take medication unless administered by someone else.

❏   ❏   NA – No inhalant/mist medications prescribed.

❏   UK – Unknown

(MO800) Management of Injectable Medications: *Patient's ability* to prepare and take *all* prescribed injectable medications reliably and safely, including administration of correct dosage at the appropriate times/intervals. *Excludes* **IV medications.**

Prior   *Current*

❏   ❏   0 – Able to independently take the correct medication and proper dosage at the correct times.

❏   ❏   1 – Able to take injectable medication at correct times if:

        (a) individual syringes are prepared in advance by another person, *OR*

        (b) given daily reminders.

❏   ❏   2 – *Unable* to take injectable medication unless administered by someone else.

❏   ❏   NA – No injectable medications prescribed.

❏   UK – Unknown

EQUIPMENT MANAGEMENT

(MO810) Patient Management of Equipment (Includes only oxygen, IV/infusion therapy, enteral/parenteral nutrition equipment or supplies): *Patient's ability* to set up, monitor and change equipment reliably and safely, add appropriate fluids or medication, clean/store/dispose of equipment or supplies using proper technique.

(NOTE: This refers to ablility, not compliance or willingness.)

❏ 0 – Patient manages all tasks related to equipment completely independently.

❏ 1 – If someone else sets up equipment (i.e., fills portable oxygen tank, provides patient with prepared solutions), patient is able to manage all other aspects of equipment.

❏ 2 – Patient requires considerable assistance from another person to manage equipment, but independently completes portions of the task.

❏ 3 – Patient is only able to monitor equipment (e.g., liter flow, fluid in bag) and must call someone else to manage the equipment.

❏ 4 – Patient is completely dependent on someone else to manage all equipment.

❏ NA – No equipment of this type used in care [If NA, STOP here]

(MO820) Caregiver Management of Equipment (Includes *ONLY* oxygen, IV/Infusion equipment, enteral/parenteral nutrition, ventilator therapy equipment or supplies): *Caregiver's ability* to set up, monitor, and change equipment reliably and safely, add appropriate fluids or medication, clean/store/ dispose of equipment or supplies using proper technique. **(NOTE: This refers to ability, not compliance or willingness.)**

❑ 0 – Caregiver manages all tasks related to equipment completely independently.

❑ 1 – If someone else sets up equipment, caregiver is able to manage all other aspects.

❑ 2 – Caregiver requires considerable assistance from another person to manage equipment, but independently completes significant portions of task.

❑ 3 – Caregiver is only able to complete small portions of task (e.g., administer nebulizer treatment, clean/store/dispose of equipment or supplies).

❑ 4 – Caregiver is completely dependent on someone else to manage all equipment.

❑ NA – No caregiver

❑ UK – Unknown

Skilled interventions performed this date:

_____

_____

_____

_____

_____

_____

Safety Hazards identified:

_____

Measures to protect patient taught to patient and caregiver:

_____

_____

_____

_____

	Y	N
Plans for emergencies:	❑	❑

_____

_____

_____

Patient/Caregiver informed about advance directive

(Durable Power of Attorney, Living Will, etc):	❑	❑
Has copy on chart:	❑	❑

Physician: Primary _____   Phone number:_____

      Secondary_____   Phone number:_____

      Pharmacy of Choice:_____   Phone number: _____

      Discharge Planning: _____

_____

_____

Signature of Assessor: **Date of Assessment:**

_____   _____

DATA ITEMS COLLECTED AT REASSESSMENT

EMERGENT CARE

(MO830) Emergent Care: Since the last time OASIS data were collected, has the patient utilized any of the following services for emergent care (other than home care agency services)? **(Mark all that apply.)**

❏ 0 – No emergent care services **[If No emergent care, STOP here]**

❏ 1 – Hospital emergency room (includes 23-hour holding)

❏ 2 – Doctor's office emergency visit/house call

❏ 3 – Outpatient department/clinic emergency (including urgicenter sites)

❏ UK – Unknown **[If UK, STOP here]**

(MO840) Emergent Care Reason: For what reason(s) did the patient/family seek emergent care? **(Mark all that apply.)**

❏ 1 – Improper medication administration, medication side effects, toxicity, anaphylaxis

❏ 2 – Nausea, dehydration, malnutrition, constipation, impaction

❏ 3 – Injury caused by fall or accident at home

❏ 4 – Respiratory problems (e.g., shortness of breath, respiratory infection, tracheobronchial obstruction)

❏ 5 – Wound infection, deteriorating wound status, new lesion/ulcer

❏ 6 – Cardiac problems (e.g., fluid overload, exacerbation of CHF, chest pain)

❏ 7 – Hypo/Hyperglycemia, diabetes out of control

❏ 8 – Gl bleeding, obstruction

❏ 9 – Other than above reasons

❏ UK – Unknown

DATA ITEMS COLLECTED AT INPATIENT FACILITY ADMISSION OR DISCHARGE ONLY

(MO855) To which Inpatient Facility has the patient been admitted?

❏ 1 – Hospital **[Go to MO890]**

❏ 2 – Rehabilitation facility **[Go to MO903]**

❏ 3 – Nursing home **[Go to MO900]**

❏ 4 – Hospice **[Go to MO903]**

❏ NA – No inpatient facility admission

(MO870) Discharge Disposition: Where is the patient after discharge from your agency? (Choose only one answer.)

❏ 1 – Patient remained in the community (not in hospital, nursing, or rehab facility)

❏ 2 – Patient transferred to a noninstitutional hospice **[Go to MO903]**

❏ 3 – Unknown because patient moved to a geographic location not served by this agency **[Go to MO903]**

❏ UK – Other unknown **[Go to MO903]**

(MO880) After discharge, does the patient receive health, personal, or support Services or Assistance? (Mark all that apply.)

❏ 1 – No assistance or services received

❏ 2 – Yes, assistance or services provided by family or friends

❏ 3 – Yes, assistance or services provided by other community resources (e.g., meals-on-wheels, home health services, homemaker assistance, transportation assistance, assisted living, board and care)

[Go to MO903]

(MO890) If the patient was admitted to an acute care Hospital, for what Reason was he/she admitted?

❏ 1 – Hospitalization for *emergent* (unscheduled) care

❏ 2 – Hospitalization for *urgent* (scheduled within of admission) care

❏ 3 – Hospitalization for *elective* (scheduled more than 24 hours before admission) care

❏ UK – Unknown

(MO895) Reason for Hospitalization: (Mark all that apply.)

❏ 1 – Improper medication administration, medication side effects, toxicity, anaphylaxis

❏ 2 – Injury caused by fall or accident at home

❏ 3 – Respiratory problems (SOB, infection, obstruction)

❏ 4 – Wound or tube site infection, deteriorating wound status, new lesion/ulcer

❏ 5 – Hypo/Hyperglycemia, diabetes out of control

❏ 6 – Gl bleeding, obstruction

❏ 7 – Exacerbation of CHF, fluid overload, heart failure

❏ 8 – Myocardial infarction, stroke

❏ 9 – Chemotherapy

❏ 10 – Scheduled surgical procedure

❏ 11 – Urinary tract infection

❏ 12 – IV catheter-related infection

❏ 13 – Deep vein thrombosis, pulmonary embolus

❏ 14 – Uncontrolled pain

❏ 15 – Psychotic episode

❏ 16 – Other than above reasons

[Go to MO903]

(MO900) For what Reason(s) was the patient Admitted to a Nursing Home? (Mark all that apply.)

❏ 1 – Therapy services

❏ 2 – Respite care

❏ 3 – Hospice care

❏ 4 – Permanent placement

❏ 5 – Unsafe for care at home

❏ 6 – Other

❏ UK – Unknown

[Go to MO903]

(MO903) Date of Last (Most Recent) Home Visit:

         __ __ / __ __ / __ __ __ __

         month day   year

(MO906) Discharge/Transfer/Death Date: Enter the date of the discharge, transfer, or death (at home) of the patient.

         __ __ / __ __ / __ __ __ __

         month day   year

UK – Unknown

OASIS ITEMS TO USE FOR FOLLOW-UP, DISCHARGE, TRANSFER, AND DEATH AT HOME

Note: For follow-up, mark only current column. Record what the patient **is able to do.**

FOLLOW-UP:

MOO10, MOO20, MOO3O, MOO40, MOO50, MOO60, MOO63, MOO64, MOO66, MOO80, MOO90, MO100, MO150, MO200, MO210, MO220, MO250, MO260, MO270, MO280, MO290, MO300, MO310, MO320, MO330, MO340, MO350, MO360, MO370, MO380, MO410 to MO840.

DISCHARGE (Not to Inpatient Facility)

MOO10 up to and including MO100, MO150, MO200 up to and including MO220, MO250, MO280 up to and including MO380, MO410 up to and including MO880, MO903, MO906.

TRANSFER TO INPATIENT FACILITY (with or without agency discharge)

MOO10 up to and including MO100, MO830, MO840, MO855, MO890 up to and including MO906.

DEATH AT HOME

MOO10 UP TO AND INCLUDING MO100, MO906

Appendix

C

SAMPLE ASSESSMENT FORM #2
START OF CARE VERSION

DEMOGRAPHIC/GENERAL INFORMATION

(MO010) Agency Provider number	(MO020) Patient ID Number	(MO030) Start of Care Date
		— — — — — — mm dd yy

(MO032) Resumption of Care Date
— — — — — —   ❑ NA – Not applicable
mm   dd   yy

(MO063) Medicare Number
— — — — — — — — — — — —   ❑ NA – No Medicare
(including suffix if any)

(MO040) Patient Name/Address/Phone

First   MI   Last   Suffix

Street, Route, Apt.   County

City   **(MO050) State**   **(MO060) Zip**

Patient Phone(   ) _____ — _____

(MO064) Social Security Number
❑ UK – Unknown or Not Available
— — — — — — — — —

(MO065) Medicaid number
❑ No Medicaid
— — — — — — — — — — —

(MO066) Birthdate
— — — — — —
mm   dd   yy

(MO069) Gender:

    ❑ 1 – Male

    ❑ 2 – Female

(MO072) Primary Referring Physician ID:

— — — — — — — — — — — —   ❑ UK–Unknown or Not Available

(MO080) Discipline of Person Completing Assessment:

    ❑ 1–RN   ❑ 2–PT   ❑ 3–SLP/ST   ❑ 4–OT

(MO090) Date Assessment Completed:

    — — — — — —
    month   day   year

(MO100) This Assessment is Currently Being Completed for the Following Reason:

    Start/Resumption of Care

    ❑ 1 – Start of care—further visits planned

    ❑ 2 – Start of care—no further visits planned

    ❑ 3 – Resumption of care (after inpatient stay)

    Follow-Up

    ❑ 4 – Recertification (follow-up) reassessment **(Go to MO150)**

    ❑ 5 – Other follow-up **(Go to MO150)**

    Transfer to an Inpatient Facility

    ❑ 6 – Transferred to an inpatient facility—patient not discharged from agency **(Go to MO830)**

    ❑ 7 – Transferred to an inpatient facility—patient discharged from agency **(Go to MO830)**

Discharge from Agency—Not to an Inpatient Facility

❏ 8 – Death at home **(Go to MO906)**

❏ 9 – Discharge from agency **(Go to MO150)**

❏ 10 – Discharge from agency—no visits completed after start/resumption of care assessment **(Go to MO830)**

DEMOGRAPHICS AND PATIENT HISTORY

(MO140) Race/Ethnicity (as identified by patient): **(Mark all that apply.)**

❏ 1 – American Indian or Alaska Native

❏ 2 – Asian

❏ 3 – Black or African-American

❏ 4 – Hispanic or Latino

❏ 5 – Native Hawaiian or Pacific Islander

❏ 6 – White

❏ 7 – UK – Unknown

Emergency Contact/Address/Phone

Name	Relationship

Street, Route, Apt.	County

City	State	Zip

Phone (   ) _____ – _____

(MO150) Current Payment Sources for Home Care: **(Mark all that apply.)**

❏ 0 – None; no charge for current services

❏ 1 – Medicare (traditional fee-for-service)

❏ 2 – Medicare (HMO/managed care)

❏ 3 – Medicaid (traditional fee-for-service)

❏ 4 – Medicaid (HMO/managed care)

❏ 5 – Worker's compensation

❏ 6 – Title programs (e.g., Title III, V, or XX)

❏ 7 – Other government (e.g., CHAMPUS, VA, etc.)

❏ 8 – Private insurance

❏ 9 – Private HMO/managed care

❏ 10 – Self-pay

❏ 11 – Other (specify) _____

❏ UK – Unknown

Marital Status

❏ Married

❏ Not Married

❏ Widowed

❏ Divorced

❏ Separated

❏ Unknown

(MO160) Financial Factors limiting the ability of the patient/family to meet basic health needs: **(Mark all that apply.)**

❏ 0 – None

❏ 1 – Unable to afford medicine or medical supplies

❏ 2 – Unable to afford medical expenses that are not covered by insurance/Medicare (e.g., copayments)

❏ 3 – Unable to afford rent/utility bills

❏ 4 – Unable to afford food

❏ 5 – Other (specify) _____

(MO170) From which of the following **inpatient facilities** was the patient discharged <u>during the past 14 days.</u> *(Mark all that apply.)*

❑ 1 — Hospital

❑ 2 — Rehabilitation facility

❑ 3 — Nursing home

❑ 4 — Other (specify) _____

❑ NA — Patient was not discharged from an inpatient facility. *[If NA, go to M0200]*

(MO180) Inpatient Discharge Date *(most recent):*

    __ __ / __ __ / __ __ __ __
     month   day   year

❑ UK - Unknown

(MO190) Inpatient Diagnoses and three-digit ICD code categories <u>for only those conditions treated during an inpatient facility stay within the last 14 days</u> (no surgical or V-codes):

<u>Inpatient Facility Diagnosis</u>	<u>ICD</u>
a. _____	(__ __ __)
b. _____	(__ __ __)

(MO200) Medical or Treatment Regimen Change Within Past 14 Days: Has this patient experienced a change in medical or treatment regimen (e.g., medication, treatment, or service change due to new or additional diagnosis, etc.) within the last 14 days?

❑ 0 — No *[If No, go to M0220]*

❑ 1 — Yes

(MO210) List the patient's **Medical Diagnoses** and three-digit ICD code categories <u>for those conditions requiring changed medical or treatment regimen</u> (no surgical or V-codes);

<u>Changed Medical Regimen Diagnosis</u>	<u>ICD</u>
a. _____	(__ __ __)
b. _____	(__ __ __)
c. _____	(__ __ __)
d. _____	(__ __ __)

(MO220) Conditions Prior to Medical or Treatment Regimen Change or Inpatient Stay Within Past 14 Days: If this patient experienced inpatient facility discharge or change in medical or treatment regimen within the past 14 days, indicate any conditions which existed <u>prior to</u> the inpatient stay or change in medical or treatment regimen. *(Mark all that apply).*

❑ 1 — Urinary incontinence

❑ 2 — Indwelling/suprapubic catheter

❑ 3 — Intractable pain

❑ 4 — Impaired decision-making

❑ 5 — Disruptive or socially inappropriate behavior

❑ 6 — Memory loss to the extent that supervision required

❑ 7 — None of the above

❑ NA — No inpatient facility discharge and no change in medical or treatment regimen in past 14 days

❑ UK — Unknown

(MO230/MO240) Diagnoses and Severity Index: List each medical diagnosis or problem for which the patient is receiving home care and ICD code category (**no surgical or V-codes**) and rate them using the following severity index. (Choose one value that represents the most severe rating appropriate for each diagnosis.)

0 — Asymptomatic, no treatment needed at this time

1 — Symptoms well controlled with current therapy

2 — Symptoms controlled with difficulty, affecting daily functioning; patient needs ongoing monitoring

3 — Symptoms poorly controlled, patient needs frequent adjustment in treatment and dose monitoring

4 — Symptoms poorly controlled, history of rehospitalizations

(MO230) Primary Diagnosis	ICD	Severity Rating				
a. _____	(_ _ _)	❏ 0	❏ 1	❏ 2	❏ 3	❏ 4

(MO240) Other Diagnoses	ICD	Severity Rating				
b. _____	(_ _ _)	❏ 0	❏ 1	❏ 2	❏ 3	❏ 4
c. _____	(_ _ _)	❏ 0	❏ 1	❏ 2	❏ 3	❏ 4
d. _____	(_ _ _)	❏ 0	❏ 1	❏ 2	❏ 3	❏ 4
e. _____	(_ _ _)	❏ 0	❏ 1	❏ 2	❏ 3	❏ 4
f. _____	(_ _ _)	❏ 0	❏ 1	❏ 2	❏ 3	❏ 4

Does patient/family demonstrate understanding of present illness: ❏ Yes ❏ No

SIGNIFICANT OR CONTRIBUTING PAST HEALTH HISTORY:

Allergies *(list if present):*

Environmental: _____   *Food:* _____

Drugs: _____   *Other:* _____

(MO250) Therapies the patient receives <u>at home:</u> (**Mark all that apply.**)

❏ 1 — Intravenous or infusion therapy (excludes TPN)

❏ 2 — Parenteral nutrition (TPN or lipids)

❏ 3 — Enteral nutrition (nasogastric, gastrostomy, jejunostomy, or any other artificial entry into the alimentary canal)

❏ 4 — None of the above

(MO260) Overall Prognosis: BEST description of patient's overall prognosis for <u>recovery from this episode of illness.</u>

❏ 0 — Poor: little or no recovery is expected and/or further decline is imminent

❏ 1 — Good/Fair: partial to full recovery is expected

❏ UK — Unknown

(MO270) Rehabilitative Prognosis: BEST description of patient's overall prognosis for <u>functional status.</u>

❏ 0 — Guarded: minimal improvement in functional status is expected; decline is possible

❏ 1 — Good: marked improvement in functional status is expected

❏ UK — Unknown

(MO280) Life Expectancy: (Physician documentation is not required.)

❏ 0 — Life expectancy is greater than 6 months

❏ 1 — Life expectancy is 6 months or fewer

(MO290) High Risk Factors characterizing this patient: **(Mark all that apply.)**

❑ 1 — Heavy smoking
❑ 2 — Obesity
❑ 3 — Alcohol dependency
❑ 4 — Drug dependency
❑ 5 — None of the above
❑ UK

LIVING ARRANGEMENTS

(MO300) Current Residence:

❑ 1 — Patient's owned or rented residence (house, apartment, or mobile home owned or rented by patient/couple/significant other)
❑ 2 — Family member's residence
❑ 3 — Boarding home or rented room
❑ 4 — Board and care or assisted living facility
❑ 5 — Other (specify) _____

(MO310) Structural Barriers in the patient's environment limiting independent mobility: **(Mark all that apply.)**

❑ 0 — None
❑ 1 — Stairs inside home which must be used by the patient (e.g., to get to toileting, sleeping, eating areas.)
❑ 2 — Stairs inside home which are used optionally (e.g., to get to laundry facilities)
❑ 3 — Stairs leading from inside house to outside
❑ 4 — Narrow or obstructed doorways

(MO320) Safety Hazards found in the patient's current place of residence: **(Mark all that apply.)**

❑ 0 — None
❑ 1 — Inadequate floor, roof, or windows
❑ 2 — Inadequate lighting
❑ 3 — Unsafe gas/electric appliance
❑ 4 — Inadequate heating
❑ 5 — Inadequate cooling
❑ 6 — Lack of fire safety devices
❑ 7 — Unsafe floor coverings
❑ 8 — Inadequate stair railings
❑ 9 — Improperly stored hazardous materials
❑ 10 — Lead-based paint
❑ 11 — Other (specify) _____

(MO330) Sanitation Hazards found in the patient's current place of residence: **(Mark all that apply.)**

❑ 0 — None
❑ 1 — No running water
❑ 2 — Contaminated water
❑ 3 — No toileting facilities
❑ 4 — Outdoor toileting facilities only
❑ 5 — Inadequate sewage disposal
❑ 6 — Inadequate/improper food storage
❑ 7 — No food refrigeration
❑ 8 — No cooking facilities
❑ 9 — Insects / rodents present
❑ 10 — No scheduled trash pickup
❑ 11 — Cluttered / soiled living area
❑ 12 — Other (specify) _____

(MO340) Patient Lives With: (Mark all that apply.)

❑ 1 — Lives alone
❑ 2 — With spouse or significant other   Name: _____
❑ 3 — With other family member   Relationship: _____
❑ 4 — With a friend
❑ 5 — With paid help (other than home care agency staff)
❑ 6 — With other than above

SUPPORT SYSTEMS

(MO350) Assisting Person(s) Other Than Home Care Agency Staff: (Mark all that apply.)

❑ 1 — Relatives, friends, or neighbors living outside the home
❑ 2 — Person residing in the home (EXCLUDING paid help)
❑ 3 — Paid help
❑ 4 — None of the above **[If None of the above, go to Systems Review: Neurosensory]**
❑ UK — Unknown **[If unknown, go to Systems Review: Neurosensory]**

(MO360) Primary Caregiver taking **lead responsibility** for providing or managing the patient's care, providing the most frequent assistance, etc. (other than home care agency staff.)

❑ 0 — No one person **[If unknown, go to Systems Review: Neurosensory]**
❑ 1 — Spouse or significant other
❑ 2 — Daughter or son
❑ 3 — Other family member
❑ 4 — Friend or neighbor or community or church member
❑ 5 — Paid help
❑ UK — Unknown **[If unknown, go to Systems Review: Neurosensory]**

(MO370) How Often does the patient receive assistance from the primary caregiver?

❑ 1 — Several times during day and night
❑ 2 — Several times during day
❑ 3 — Once daily
❑ 4 — Three or more times per week
❑ 5 — One or two times per week
❑ 6 — Less often than weekly
❑ UK — Unknown

(MO380)Type of Primary Caregiver Assistance: (Mark all that apply.)

❑ 1 — ADL assistance (e.g., bathing, dressing, toileting, bowel/bladder, eating/feeding)
❑ 2 — IADL assistance (eg.. meds, meals, housekeeping, laundry, telephone, shopping, finances)
❑ 3 — Environmental support (housing, home maintenance)
❑ 4 — Psychological support (socialization, companionship, recreation)
❑ 5 — Advocates or facilitates patient's participation in appropriate medical care
❑ 6 — Financial agent, power of attorney, or conservator of finance
❑ 7 — Health care agent, conservator of person, or medical power of attorney
❑ UK — Unknown

Client's Name:

Client Record No.

SYSTEMS REVIEW

NEUROSENSORY:

HEAD: Dizziness ❑   Headache ❑ (describe location, duration) _____

EYES: Glasses ❑   Blurred/double vision ❑   Glaucoma ❑
              Cataracts ❑   PERRL ❑   Other (specify) _____

(MO390) Vision with corrective lenses if the patient usually wears them:

❑ 0 — Normal vision: sees adequately in most situations; can see medication labels, newsprint.

❑ 1 — Partially impaired: cannot see medication labels or newsprint, but can see obstacles in path, and the surrounding layout; can count fingers at arm's length.

❑ 2 — Severely impaired: cannot locate objects without hearing or touching them or patient nonresponsive

EARS: Hearing Aid ❑   Tinnitus ❑   Other (specify) _____

(MO400) Hearing and ability to understand spoken language in patient's own language (with hearing aids if the patient usually uses them):

❑ 0 — No observable impairment. Able to hear and understand complex or detailed instructions and extended or abstract conversation

❑ 1 — With minimal difficulty, able to hear and understand most multi-step instructions and ordinary conversation. May need occasional repetition, extra time, or louder voice.

❑ 2 — Has moderate difficulty hearing and understanding simple, one-step instructions and brief conversation; needs frequent prompting or assistance.

❑ 3 — Has severe difficulty hearing and understanding simple greetings and short comments. Requires multiple repetitions. restatements, demonstrations, additional time.

❑ 4 — Unable to hear and understand familiar words or common expressions consistently, or patient nonresponsive.

(MO410) Speech and Oral (Verbal) Expression of Language (in patient's own language):

❑ 0 — Expresses complex ideas. feelings. and needs clearly, completely, and easily in all situations with no observable impairment.

❑ 1 — Minimal difficulty in expressing ideas and needs (may take extra time; makes occasional errors in word choice, grammar or speech intelligibility; needs minimal prompting or assistance).

❑ 2 — Expresses simple ideas or needs with moderate difficulty (needs prompting or assistance, errors in word choice, organization or speech intelligibility). Speaks in phrases or short sentences.

❑ 3 — Has severe difficulty expressing basic ideas or needs and requires maximal assistance or guessing by listener. Speech limited to single words or short phrases.

❑ 4 — Unable to express basic needs even with maximal prompting or assistance but is not comatose or unresponsive (e.g., speech is nonsensical or unintelligible.)

❑ 5 — Patient nonresponsive or unable to speak.

ADDITIONAL NEURO SIGNS:

❑ unequal grasp   ❑ vertigo   ❑ paralysis (where: _____)

❑ gait disturbance   ❑ syncope   ❑ frequent falls _____

❑ lack of coordination (balance)   ❑ seizure   ❑ tremor

❑ numbness   ❑ L.O.C.   ❑ aphasia / inarticulate speech

Patient's Perceived Pain Level _____ (Scale 1-10)

(MO420) Frequency of pain interfering with patient's activity or movement:

❑ 0 — Patient has no pain or pain does not interfere with activity or movement
❑ 1 — Less often than daily
❑ 2 — Daily, but not constantly
❑ 3 — All of the time

(MO430) Intractable Pain: Is the patient experiencing pain that is <u>not easily relieved,</u> occurs at least daily, and affects the patient's sleep, appetite, physical or emotional energy, concentration, personal relationships, emotions, or ability or desire to perform physical activity?

❑ 0 — No
❑ 1 — Yes

INTEGUMENTARY:

(MO440) Does this patient have a **Skin Lesion** or an **Open Wound**? This excludes "OSTOMIES."

❑ 0 — No **[If No, go to Integumentary Status Assessment Tool]**
❑ 1 — Yes

(MO445) Does this patient have a **Pressure Ulcer?**

❑ 0 — No **[If No, go to M0468]**
❑ 1 — Yes

(MO450) Current Number of Pressure Ulcers at Each Stage: (Circle one response for each stage.)

	Pressure Ulcer Stages	Number of Pressure Ulcers				
a)	**Stage 1:** Nonblanchable erythema of intact skin; the heralding of skin ulceration. In darker-pigmented skin, warmth, edema, hardness. or discolored skin may be indicators.	0	1	2	3	4 or more
b)	**Stage 2:** Partial thickness skin loss involving epidermis and/or dermis. The ulcer is superficial and presents clinically as an abrasion. blister. or shallow crater.	0	1	2	3	4 or more
c)	**Stage 3:** Full-thickness skin loss involving damage or necrosis of subcutaneous tissue which may extend down to, but not through, underlying fascia. The ulcer presents clinically as a deep crater with or without undermining of adjacent tissue.	0	1	2	3	4 or more
d)	**Stage 4:** Full-thickness skin loss with extensive destruction, tissue necrosis, or damage to muscle, bone, or supporting structures (e.g., tendon, joint capsule, etc.)	0	1	2	3	4 or more
e)	In addition to the above, is there at least one pressure ulcer that cannot be observed due to the presence of eschar or a nonremovable dressing, including casts? ❑ 0 — No ❑ 1 — Yes					

(MO460) Stage of Most Problematic (Observable) Pressure Ulcer:

❏ 1 — Stage 1
❏ 2 — Stage 2
❏ 3 — Stage 3
❏ 4 — Stage 4
❏ NA — No observable pressure ulcer

(MO464) Status of Most Problematic (Observable) Pressure Ulcer:

❏ 1 — Fully granulating   ❏ 3 — Not Healing
❏ 2 — Early / partial granulation   ❏ NA — No observable pressure ulcer

PRESSURE SORE STATUS TOOL

ITEM	ASSESSMENT	DATE
		Score
1. Size	1 = Length x width < 4 sq. cm. 2 = Length x width 4 to 16 sq. cm. 3 = Length x width 16.1 to 36 sq. cm. 4 = Length x width 36.1 to 80 sq. cm. 5 = Length x width > 80 sq. cm.	
2. Depth	1 = Non-blanchable erythema of intact skin 2 = Partial-thickness skin loss involving epidermis &/or dermis 3 = Full-thickness skin loss involving damage or necrosis of subcutaneous tissue; may extend down to but not through underlying fascia; &/or mixed partial- or full-thickness &/or tissue layers obscured by granulation tissue. 4 = Obscured by necrosis 5 = Full-thickness skin loss with extensive destruction, tissue necrosis or damage to muscle, bone, or supporting structures	
3. Edges	1 = Indistinct, diffuse, none clearly visible 2 = Distinct, outline clearly visible, attached, even with wound base 3 = Well-defined, not attached to wound base 4 = Well-defined, not attached to base, rolled under, thickened 5 = Well-defined, fibrotic, scarred, or hyperkeratotic	
4. Under-mining	1 = Undermining < 2 cm. in any area 2 = Undermining 2 to 4 cm. involving < 50% wound margins 3 = Undermining 2 to 4 cm. involving > 50% wound margins 4 = Undermining > 4 cm. in any area 5 = Tunneling &/or sinus tract formation	
5. Necrotic Tissue Type	1 = None visible 2 = White/gray non-viable tissue &/or non-adherent yellow slough 3 = Loosely adherent yellow slough 4 = Adherent, soft black eschar 5 = Firmly adherent, hard black eschar	
6. Necrotic Tissue Amount	1 = None visible 2 = < 25% of wound bed covered 3 = 25% to 50% of wound covered 4 = > 50% and < 75% of wound covered 5 = 75% to 100% of wound covered	

ITEM	ASSESSMENT	DATE
		Score
7. Exudate Type	1 = None or bloody 2 = Serosanguineous: thin, watery, pale red/pink 3 = Serous: thin, watery, clear 4 = Purulent: thin or thick, opaque, tan/yellow 5 = Foul purulent: thick, opaque, yellow/green with odor	
8. Exudate Amount	1 = None 2 = Scant 3 = Small 4 = Moderate 5 = Large	
9. Skin Color Surrounding Wound	1 = Pink or normal for ethnic group 2 = Bright red &/or blanches to touch 3 = White or gray pallor or hypopigmented 4 = Dark red or purple &/or non-blanchable 5 = Black or hyperpigmented	
10. Peripheral Tissue Edema	1 = Minimal firmness around wound 2 = Non-pitting edema extends < 4 cm. around wound 3 = Non-pitting edema extends ≥ 4 cm. around wound 4 = Pitting edema extends < 4 cm. around wound 5 = Crepitus &/or pitting edema extends ≥ 4 cm.	
11. Peripheral Tissue Induration	1 = Minimal firmness around wound 2 = Induration < 2 cm. around wound 3 = Induration 2 to 4 cm. extending < 50% around wound 4 = Induration 2 to 4 cm. extending ≥ 50% around wound 5 = Induration > 4 cm. in any area	
12. Granulation Tissue	1 = Skin intact or partial-thickness wound 2 = Bright, beefy red; 75% to 100% of wound filled &/or tissue overgrowth 3 = Bright, beefy red; < 75% & > 25% of wound filled 4 = Pink, &/ or dull, dusky red &/ or fills ≤ 25% wound 5 = No granulation tissue present	
13. Epithelializ-ation	1 = 100% of wound covered, surface intact 2 = 75% to < 100% of wound covered &/or epithelial tissue extends > 0.5 cm. into wound bed 3 = 50% to < 75% of wound covered &/or epithelial tissue extends to < 0.5 cm. into wound bed 4 = 25% to < 50% of wound covered 5 = < 25% of wound covered	

TOTAL SCORE:

PRESSURE STATUS CONTINUUM

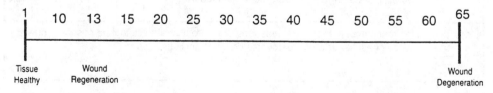

1   10   13   15   20   25   30   35   40   45   50   55   60   65

Tissue Healthy   Wound Regeneration   Wound Degeneration

Plot the total score on the Pressure Sore Status Continuum by putting an "X" on the line and the date beneath the line.

Used with permission.

Protocol for Care

VENOUS LEG ULCER ASSESSMENT   Venous   Arterial

Patient Name _____ **Age:** _____ **Date:** _____

I.   Medical History:

☐ Severe leg trauma (Date: _____)	☐ Obesity
☐ Blood clot [DVT] (Date: _____)	☐ Frequent leg swelling
☐ Heart disease/Congestive heart failure	☐ Pregnancy
☐ Family history of leg ulcers	

☐ Heart disease/Heart attack	☐ Diabetes: ☐ Type I ☐ Type II
☐ Stroke	

☐ Recurrent leg ulcers	Immune status: ☐ Good ☐ Compromised

II. Pertinent Surgeries:

☐ Vein surgery (Date: _____)

☐ Cardiac bypass (Date: _____)   ☐ Neck/Carotid artery (Date: _____)

☐ Skin graft (Date: _____)

III. Social Assessment:

Occupation: _____

Hobbies/Activities: _____

Approximate hours per day spent: Standing: _____ hrs.   Sitting: _____ hrs.

Is someone available at home to assist with treatments?   ☐ Yes (_____) ☐ No

IV. Allergies: (Include previous reactions to topical treatments):

_____

V.   Ankle/Brachial Index _____

VI. Physical Examination	Left Leg		Right Leg	
Ulcer Location:	☐ Medial lower leg and/or ankle	☐ Foot and/or lateral ankle	☐ Medial lower leg and/or ankle	☐ Foot and/or lateral ankle
Edema:	☐ Present	☐ Absent	☐ Present	☐ Absent
Dorsalis Pedis Pulse: • Palpation • Doppler	☐ Present ☐ Present	☐ Absent ☐ Absent	☐ Present ☐ Present	☐ Absent ☐ Absent
Posterior Tibial Pulse: • Palpation • Doppler	☐ Present ☐ Present	☐ Absent ☐ Absent	☐ Present ☐ Present	☐ Absent ☐ Absent
Pain:	☐ Absent ☐ Decreased w/elevation	☐ Constant ☐ Increased w/elevation	☐ Absent ☐ Decreased w/elevation	☐ Constant ☐ Decreased w/elevation
Ulcer Appearance: • Ulcer Borders • Exudate • Wound Depth • Wound Base • Peri-wound Skin	☐ Irregular ☐ Present ☐ Shallow ☐ Ruddy & granular ☐ Yellow fibrous tissue ☐ Dilated veins ☐ Dermatitis (Dry/ scaly or weeping) ☐ Indurated/ hardened ☐ Hyperpigmented	☐ Even/smooth ☐ Absent ☐ Deep ☐ Pale & dry ☐ Thick black eschar ☐ Thin & shiny ☐ Hair loss ☐ Cool to touch ☐ Pallor on elevation	☐ Irregular ☐ Present ☐ Shallow ☐ Ruddy & granular ☐ Yellow fibrous tissue ☐ Dilated veins ☐ Dermatitis (Dry/ scaly or weeping) ☐ Indurated/ hardened ☐ Hyperpigmented	☐ Even/smooth ☐ Absent ☐ Deep ☐ Pale & dry ☐ Thick black eschar ☐ Thin & shiny ☐ Hair loss ☐ Cool to touch ☐ Pallor on elevation

(MO482) Does this patient have a Surgical Wound?

❑ 0 — No **[If No, go to Integumentary Status Assessment Tool]**
❑ 1 — Yes

(MO484) Current Number of (Observable) Surgical Wounds: (If a wound is partially closed but has <u>more</u> than one opening, consider each opening as a separate wound.)

❑ 0 — Zero
❑ 1 — One
❑ 2 — Two
❑ 3 — Three
❑ 4 — Four or more

(MO486) Does this patient have at least one Surgical Wound that Cannot be Observed due to the presence of a nonremovable dressing?

❑ 0 — No
❑ 1 — Yes

(MO488) Status of Most Problematic (Observable) Surgical Wound:

❑ 1 — Fully granulating
❑ 2 — Early / partial granulation
❑ 3 — Not healing
❑ NA — No observable surgical wound

INTEGUMENTARY STATUS ASSESSMENT TOOL

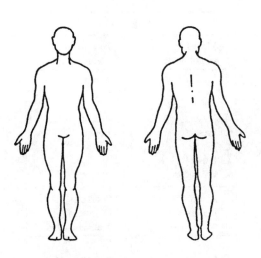

Indicate location of integumentary
problem on figure above

*** Please indicate size & depth
as applicable**

Type	Yes	No
* 1. Lesions, Rashes	❑	❑
* 2. Bruises	❑	❑
* 3. Masses	❑	❑
* 4. Scars	❑	❑
* 5. Stasis Ulcers	❑	❑
* 6. Pressure Ulcers	❑	❑
* 7. Incisions	❑	❑
8. Excessive dryness, pruritus	❑	❑
* 9. Areas of excoriation, redness, trauma	❑	❑
10. Temperature changes in skin (coolness, warmth)	❑	❑
11. Changes in hair distribution	❑	❑
12. Nails: ridges, thickening, color bands, texture changes	❑	❑
* Past skin diseases (eczema, etc.)	❑	❑
* Healing time increased	❑	❑
* Chronic long-term sun exposure	❑	❑
* Recent changes in a wart or mole	❑	❑
* Turgor: good, fair, poor (circle)	❑	❑

COMMENTS: *(If it is noted above, comment please.)* _____
_____
_____
_____

MUSCULOSKELETAL:

❑ Hx. arthritis

❑ gout

❑ stiffness

❑ swollen joints / joint pain

❑ weakness

❑ muscle cramps / spasms

❑ leg cramps

❑ deformities

❑ amputation

❑ prostheses

❑ appliances

❑ other_____

❑ Hx. of osteoporosis

❑ Hx. of fractures

❑ R.O.M.

Active: _____

Passive: _____

❑ Crepitus

❑ Kyphosis

❑ Scoliosis

❑ Lordosis

Comments:

CARDIOPULMONARY:

Temperature _____   Method Taken: O   A   R

PULSE: Apical Rate _____   Radial Rate _____

Rhythm _____   Quality _____

Respirations _____

BLOOD PRESSURE: Lying _____   Sitting _____

Standing _____ L.A. _____   R.A. _____

CARDIOVASCULAR:

❑ Palpitations

❑ Claudication

❑ Fatigues easily

❑ Pacemaker Date of

last battery change _____

❑ Angina

❑ Dyspnea on exertion

❑ Paroxysmal nocturnal dyspnea

❑ Orthopnea (# of pillows _____)

❑ Bradycardia, tachycardia, arrythmias

❑ "BP Problems", hypertension, hypotension

❑ Chest pain, pressure, tightness

❑ Neck vein distention

❑ "Heart" problems

(specify) _____

❑ Other (specify) _____

❑ Peripheral vascular complaints:
Coldness. pain sensation,
exaggerated response to cold

❑ Calf tenderness

❑ Murmurs, bruits

❑ Edem a _____ (O to +4)

❑ Cyanosis

❑ Varicosities

❑ Homan's sign

COMMENTS:

RESPIRATORY:

History of:

❑ Bronchitis ❑ Pneumonia ❑ Asthma ❑ TB ❑ Pleurisy ❑ Emphysema

❑ Other (specify) _____

Present Condition:

❑ Cough (describe) _____ ❑ Sputum (character & amount) _____

❑ SOB ❑ Tachypnea ❑ Dyspnea ❑ Cheyne-Stokes ❑ Kussmaul

❑ Symmetry of chest configuration: (normal, barrel chest, pigeon chest, funnel chest) _____

❑ Breath Sounds (describe) _____

❑ Tracheostomy ❑ Other (specify) _____

(MO490) When is the patient dyspneic or noticeably **Short of Breath?**

❑ 0 — Never, patient is not short of breath

❑ 1 — When walking more than 20 feet, climbing stairs

❑ 2 — With moderate exertion (e.g., while dressing, using commode or bedpan, walking distances less than 20 feet)

❑ 3 — With minimal exertion (e.g., while eating, talking, or performing other ADLs) or with agitation

❑ 4 — At rest (during day or night)

(MO500) **Respiratory Treatments** utilized at home: (**Mark all that apply.**)

❑ 1 — Oxygen (intermittent or continuous)

❑ 2 — Ventilator (continually or at night)

❑ 3 — Continuous positive airway pressure

❑ 4 — None of the above

COMMENTS:

Client's Name:

Client Record No.

GENITOURINARY

❑ Frequency   ❑ Nocturia   ❑ dribbling

❑ Pain   ❑ Urgency   ❑ anuria

❑ Hematuria   ❑ Prostate disorder   ❑ dialysis _____ times per week _____

❑ Stress incontinence   ❑ Other (specify) _____

(MO510) Has this patient been treated for a Urinary Tract Infection in the past 14 days?

❑ 0 — No

❑ 1 — Yes

❑ NA — Patient on prophylactic treatment

❑ UK — Unknown

(MO520) Urinary Incontinence or Urinary Catheter Presence:

❑ 0 — No incontinence or catheter (includes anuria or ostomy for urinary drainage) **[If no, go to M0540]**

❑ 1 — Patient is incontinent

❑ 2 — Patient requires a urinary catheter (i.e. external, indwelling, intermittent, suprapubic) **[Go to M0540]**

(M0530) When does Urinary Incontinence occur?

❑ 0 — Timed-voiding defers incontinence

❑ 1 — During the night only

❑ 2 — During the day and night

GASTROINTESTINAL

❑ Indigestion, heartburn   ❑ Hernias (where)_____   ❑ Hemorrhoids   ❑ Other (specify): _____

❑ Nausea, vomiting   ❑ Diarrhea/constipation   ❑ Gallbladder problems   _____

❑ Ulcers   ❑ Recent Δ in bowel habits   ❑ Jaundice   _____

❑ Flatulence, eructation   ❑ Ascites   ❑ Tenderness/distention   ❑ Date of last BM _____

❑ Pain   ❑ Rectal bleeding   ❑ Diverticulitis

(MO540) Bowel Incontinence Frequency:

❑ 0 — Very rarely or never has bowel incontinence

❑ 1 — Less than once weekly

❑ 2 — One to three times weekly

❑ 3 — Four to six times weekly

❑ 4 — On a daily basis

❑ 5 — More often than once daily

❑ NA — Patient has ostomy for bowel elimination

❑ UK — Unknown

(MO550) Ostomy for Bowel Elimination: Does this patient have an ostomy for bowel elimination that (within the last 14 days): a) was related to an inpatient facility stay, or b) necessitated a change in medical or treatment regimen?

❑ 0 — Patient does not have an ostomy for bowel elimination.

❑ 1 — Patient's ostomy was not related to an inpatient stay and did not necessitate change in medical or treatment regimen.

❑ 2 — The ostomy was related to an inpatient stay or did necessitate change in medical or treatment regimen.

NUTRITIONAL STATUS:

❑ Dysphagia

❑ Anorexia

Diet Order _____

Supplements _____

Typical 24° fluid intake _____

Appetite For Meals (%) _____

Weight_____ ❑ actual ❑ reported

Patient appears: ❑ normal weight   ❑ under weight   ❑ slightly under weight   ❑ overweight

Feeding ability: ❑ self   ❑ assisted   ❑ spoon   ❑ syringe   ❑ tube

Usually dines alone: ❑ Yes   ❑ No

Nutrition Consult: _____

COMMENTS:

REPRODUCTIVE

❑ dysmenorrhea   ❑ gravida/para   ❑ vag discharge/bleeding

❑ hx hysterectomy   Date of last pap _____   ❑ hx BPH

❑ hx of abnormal pap   Date of last mammogram _____   ❑ penile discharge

BREASTS (Both male and female)

❑ Lumps   ❑ Tenderness   ❑ Symmetry   ❑ Dimpling   ❑ Discharge   ❑ Other (specify) _____

Hx of breast lump(s) _____

Comments _____

ENDOCRINE AND HEMATOPOIETIC:

❑ Polyuria   ❑ Polydipsia   Coumadin: _____ Heparin: _____

❑ IDDM   ❑ NIDDM   Pallor: _____

Hx hyperthyroidism: _____   Excessive Bleeding or Bruising: _____

Hx hypothyroidism: _____   Hx Leukemia: _____ Type: _____

Current laboratory orders: _____   Hx Thrombocytopenia: _____ Hx Sickle Cell: _____

_____   Pernicious Anemia: _____ Polycythemia: _____

_____   ❑ Intolerance to heat and cold   ❑ Enlarged lymph nodes

                                   ❑ Family hx of endocrine/hematopoietic disorders

                                   ❑ Other (specify) _____

EMOTIONAL / BEHAVIORAL

☐ Hx of previous psych. illness
☐ Memory loss-short term / long-term
☐ Disorientation time / place / person
☐ Depression
☐ Labile moods

☐ Mania
☐ Poor judgement / impaired judgement
☐ Hallucination / delusions

☐ Other (specify) _____

(MO560) Cognitive Functioning: (Patient's current level of alertness, orientation, comprehension, concentration, and immediate memory for simple commands).

☐ 0 — Alert / oriented, able to focus and shift attention, comprehends and recalls task directions independently.

☐ 1 — Requires prompting (cuing, repetition, reminders) only under stressful or unfamiliar conditions.

☐ 2 — Requires assistance and some direction in specific situations (e.g. on all tasks involving shifting of attention), or consistently requires low stimulus environment due to distractibility.

☐ 3 — Requires considerable assistance in routine situations. Is not alert and oriented or is unable to shift attention and recall directions more than half the time.

☐ 4 — Totally dependent due to disturbances such as constant disorientation, coma, persistent vegetative state, or delirium.

(M0570) When Confused (Reported or Observed):

☐ 0 — Never

☐ 1 — In new or complex situations only

☐ 2 — On awakening or at night only

☐ 3 — During the day and evening, but not constantly

☐ 4 — Constantly

☐ NA — Patient nonresponsive

(M0580) When Anxious (Reported or Observed):

☐ 0 — None of the time

☐ 1 — Less often than daily

☐ 2 — Daily, but not constantly

☐ 3 — All of the time

☐ NA — Patient nonresponsive

(M0590) Depressive Feelings Reported or Observed in Patient: (Mark all that apply.)

☐ 1 — Depressed mood (e.g. feeling sad. tearful)

☐ 2 — Sense of failure or self reproach

☐ 3 — Hopelessness

☐ 4 — Recurrent thoughts of death

☐ 5 — Thoughts of suicide

☐ 6 — None of the above feelings observed or reported

(MO600) Patient Behaviors (Reported or Observed): (Mark all that apply.)

❑ 1 — Indecisiveness, lack of concentration
❑ 2 — Diminished interest in most activities
❑ 3 — Sleep disturbances
❑ 4 — Recent change in appetite or weight
❑ 5 — Agitation
❑ 6 — A suicide attempt
❑ 7 — None of the above behaviors observed or reported

(MO610) Behaviors <u>Demonstrated at Least Once A Week</u> (Reported or Observed): (Mark all that apply.)

❑ 1 — Memory deficit: failure to recognize familiar persons/places, inability to recall events of past 24 hours, significant memory loss so that supervision is required.
❑ 2 — Impaired decision-making: failure to perform usual ADLs or IADLs, inability to appropriately stop activities, jeopardizes safety through actions
❑ 3 — Verbal disruption: yelling, threatening, excessive profanity, sexual references, etc.
❑ 4 — Physical aggression: aggressive or combative to self and others (e.g., hits self, throws objects, punches, dangerous maneuvers with wheelchair or other objects)
❑ 5 — Disruptive, infantile, or socially inappropriate behavior (excludes verbal actions)
❑ 6 — Delusional, hallucinatory, or paranoid behavior
❑ 7 — None of the above behaviors demonstrated

(MO620) Frequency of Behavior Problems (Reported or Observed) (e.g. wandering episodes, self abuse, verbal disruption, physical aggression, etc.):

❑ 0 — Never
❑ 1 — Less than once a month
❑ 2 — Once a month
❑ 3 — Several times each month
❑ 4 — Several times a week
❑ 5 — At least daily

(MO630) Is this patient receiving **Psychiatric Nursing Services** at home provided by a qualified psychiatric nurse?

❑ 0 — No
❑ 1 — Yes

ADL/IADLs

> For M0640-M0800 complete the "current" column for all patients. For the same items, complete the "prior" column only at start of care; mark the level that corresponds to the patient's condition 14 days prior to start of care. In all cases, record what the patient is *able to do.*

(MO640) Grooming: Ability to tend to personal hygiene needs (i.e., washing face and hands, hair care, shaving or make up, teeth or denture care, fingernail care).

Prior	Current	
❑	❑	0 — Able to groom self unaided, with or without the use of assistive devices or adapted methods.
❑	❑	1 — Grooming utensils must be placed within reach before able to complete grooming activities.
❑	❑	2 — Someone must assist the patient to groom self.
❑	❑	3 — Patient depends entirely upon someone else for grooming needs.
❑		UK — Unknown

(MO650) Ability to Dress Upper Body (with or without dressing aids) including undergarments, pullovers, front-opening shirts and blouses, managing zippers, buttons, and snaps:

Prior   Current

☐   ☐   0 — Able to get clothes out of closets and drawers, put them on and remove them from the upper body without assistance

☐   ☐   1 — Able to dress upper body without assistance if clothing is laid out or handed to the patient.

☐   ☐   2 — Someone must help the patient put on upper body clothing

☐   ☐   3 — Patient depends entirely upon another person to dress the upper body.

☐   UK — Unknown

(MO660) Ability to Dress Lower Body (with or without dressing aids) including undergarments, slacks, socks or nylons, shoes:

Prior   Current

☐   ☐   0 — Able to obtain, put on, and remove clothing and shoes without assistance.

☐   ☐   1 — Able to dress lower body without assistance if clothing and shoes are laid out or handed to the patient.

☐   ☐   2 — Someone must help the patient put on undergarments, slacks, socks or nylons, and shoes.

☐   ☐   3 — Patient depends entirely upon another person to dress lower body.

☐   UK — Unknown

(MO670) Bathing: Ability to wash entire body. Excludes grooming (washing face and hands only):

Prior   Current

☐   ☐   0 — Able to bathe self in shower or tub independently.

☐   ☐   1 — With the use of devices, is able to bathe self in shower or tub independently.

☐   ☐   2 — Able to bathe in shower or tub with the assistance of another person:

        (a) for intermittent supervision or encouragement or reminders, OR

        (b) to get in and out of the shower or tub, OR,

        (c) for washing difficult to reach areas

☐   ☐   3 — Participates in bathing self in shower or tub, but requires presence of another person throughout the bath for assistance or supervision.

☐   ☐   4 — Unable to use the shower or tub and is bathed in bed or bedside chair.

☐   ☐   5 — Unable to effectively participate in bathing and is totally bathed by another person.

☐   UK — Unknown

(MO680) Toileting: Ability to get to and from the toilet or bedside commode.

Prior   Current

☐   ☐   0 — Able to get to and from the toilet independently with or without a device.

☐   ☐   1 — When reminded, assisted, or supervised by another person, able to get to and from the toilet

☐   ☐   2 — Unable to get to and from the toilet but is able to use a bedside commode (with or without assistance)

☐   ☐   3 — Unable to get to and from the toilet or bedside commode but is able to use a bedpan/urinal independently.

☐   ☐   4 — Is totally dependent in toileting.

☐   UK — Unknown.

(MO690) Transferring: Ability to move from bed to chair, on and off toilet or commode, into and out of tub or shower, and ability to turn and position self in bed if patient is bedfast.

Prior   Current

❑   ❑   0 — Able to independently transfer

❑   ❑   1 — Transfers with minimal human assistance or with use of an assistive device.

❑   ❑   2 — Unable to transfer self but is able to bear weight and pivot during the transfer process.

❑   ❑   3 — Unable to transfer self and is unable to bear weight or pivot when transferred by another person.

❑   ❑   4 — Bedfast, unable to transfer but is able to turn and position self in bed.

❑   ❑   5 — Bedfast, unable to transfer but is unable to turn and position self.

❑   UK — Unknown

(MO700) Ambulation / Locomotion: Ability to SAFELY walk, once in a standing position, or use a wheelchair, once in a seated position, on a variety of surfaces.

Prior   Current

❑   ❑   0 — Able to independently walk on even and uneven surfaces and climb stairs with or without railings (i.e., needs no human assistance or assistive device).

❑   ❑   1 — Requires use of a device (e.g., cane, walker) to walk alone or requires human supervision or assistance to negotiate stairs or steps or uneven surfaces.

❑   ❑   2 — Able to walk only with the supervision or assistance of another person at all times.

❑   ❑   3 — Chairfast, unable to ambulate but is able to wheel self independently.

❑   ❑   4 — Chairfast, unable to ambulate and is unable to wheel self.

❑   ❑   5— Bedfast, unable to ambulate or be up in a chair.

❑   UK — Unknown

(MO710) Feeding or Eating: Ability to feed self meals and snacks. This refers only to the process of eating, chewing, and swallowing, not preparing the food to be eaten.

Prior   Current

❑   ❑   0 — Able to independently feed self.

❑   ❑   1 — Able to feed self independently but requires:

                  (a) meal set-up; OR
                  (b) intermittent assistance or supervision from another person; OR
                  (c) a liquid, pureed or ground meat diet.

❑   ❑   2 — Unable to feed self and must be assisted or supervised throughout the meal/snack.

❑   ❑   3 — Able to take in nutrients orally and receives supplemental nutrients through a nasogastric tube or gastrostomy.

❑   ❑   4 — Unable to take in nutrients orally and is fed nutrients through a nasogastric tube or gastrostomy.

❑   ❑   5 — Unable to take in nutrients orally or by tube feeding.

❑   UK — Unknown

(MO720) Planning and Preparing Light Meal: (e.g., cereal, sandwich) or reheat delivered meals.

Prior   Current

❑   ❑   0 — (a) Able to independently plan and prepare all light meals for self or reheat delivered meals;

                     OR
                     (b) Is physically, cognitively, and mentally able to prepare light meals on a regular basis but has not routinely performed light meal preparation in the past (i.e., prior to this home care admission).

❑   ❑   1 — Unable to prepare light meals on a regular basis due to physical, cognitive, or mental limitations.

❑   ❑   2 — Unable to prepare any light meals or reheat any delivered meals.

❑   UK — Unknown

(MO730) Transportation: Physical and mental ability to safely use a car, taxi, or public transportation (bus, train, subway).

Prior   Current

❑   ❑   0 — Able to independently drive a regular or adapted car; OR use a regular or handicap-accessible public bus.

❑   ❑   1 — Able to ride in a car only when driven by another person; OR able to use a bus or handicap van only when
            assisted or accompanied by another person.

❑   ❑   2 — Unable to ride in a car, taxi, bus, or van, and requires transportation by ambulance.

❑   UK — Unknown

(MO740) Laundry: Ability to do own laundry — to carry laundry to and from washing machine, to use washer and dryer, to wash small items by hand.

Prior   Current

❑   ❑   0 — (a) Able to independently take care of all laundry tasks; OR
            (b) Physically, cognitively, and mentally able to do laundry and access facilities, but has not
                routinely performed laundry tasks in the past (i.e., prior to this home care admission).

❑   ❑   1 — Able to do only light laundry, such as minor hand wash or light washer loads. Due to physical, cognitive, or
            mental limitations, needs assistance with heavy laundry such as carrying large loads of laundry.

❑   ❑   2 — Unable to do any laundry due to physical limitation or needs continual supervision and assistance due to
            cognitive or mental limitation.

❑   UK — Unknown

(MO750) Housekeeping: Ability to safely and effectively perform light housekeeping and heavier cleaning tasks.

Prior   Current

❑   ❑   0 — (a) Able to independently perform all housekeeping tasks: OR
            (b) Physically, cognitively, and mentally able to perform all housekeeping tasks but has not routinely partici-
                pated in housekeeping tasks in the past (i.e., prior to this home care admission).

❑   ❑   1 — Able to perform only light housekeeping (e.g., dusting, wiping kitchen counters) tasks independently.

❑   ❑   2 — Able to perform housekeeping tasks with intermittent assistance or supervision from another person.

❑   ❑   3 — Unable to consistently perform any housekeeping tasks unless assisted by another person
            throughout the process.

❑   ❑   4 — Unable to effectively participate in any housekeeping tasks.

❑   UK — Unknown

(MO760) Shopping: Ability to plan for, select, and purchase items in a store and to carry them home or arrange delivery.

Prior   Current

❑   ❑   0 — (a) Able to plan for shopping needs and independently perform shopping tasks, including carrying pack-
                ages; OR
            (b) Physically, cognitively, and mentally able to take care of shopping, but has not done shopping in the
                past (i.e., prior this home care admission).

❑   ❑   1 — Able to go shopping, but needs some assistance:
            (a) By self is able to do only light shopping and carry small packages, but needs someone to do
                occasional major shopping; OR
            (b) Unable to go shopping alone, but can go with someone to assist.

❑   ❑   2 — Unable to go shopping, but is able to identify items needed, place orders, and arrange home delivery.

❑   ❑   3 — Needs someone to do all shopping and errands.

❑   UK — Unknown

(MO770) Ability to Use Telephone: Ability to answer the phone, dial numbers, and <u>effectively</u> use the telephone to communicate.

<u>Prior</u>   <u>Current</u>

❑   ❑   0 — Able to dial numbers and answer calls appropriately and as desired.

❑   ❑   1 — Able to use a specially adapted telephone (i.e., large numbers on the dial, teletype phone for the deaf) and call essential numbers.

❑   ❑   2 — Able to answer the telephone and carry on a normal conversation but has difficulty with placing calls.

❑   ❑   3 — Able to answer the telephone only some of the time or is able to carry on only a limited conversation.

❑   ❑   4— <u>Unable</u> to answer the telephone at all but can listen if assisted with equipment.

❑   ❑   5— Totally unable to use the telephone.

❑   ❑   NA— Patient does not have a telephone

❑   UK— Unknown

(MO780) Management of Oral Medications: <u>Patient's ability</u> to prepare and take <u>all</u> prescribed oral medications reliably and safely, including administration of the correct dosage at the appropriate times / intervals. <u>Excludes</u> injectable and IV medications. (NOTE: This refers to ability, not compliance or willingness.)

<u>Prior</u>   <u>Current</u>

❑   ❑   0 — Able to independently take the correct oral medication(s) and proper dosage(s) at the correct times.

❑   ❑   1 — Able to take medication(s) at the correct time if:
  (a) individual dosages are prepared in advance by another person; <u>OR</u>
  (b) given daily reminders; <u>OR</u>
  (c) someone develops a drug diary or chart

❑   ❑   2 — <u>Unable</u> to take medication unless administered by someone else.

❑   ❑   NA — No oral medications prescribed.

❑   UK — Unknown

(MO790) Management of Inhalant / Mist Medications: <u>Patient's ability</u> to prepare and take <u>all</u> prescribed inhalant / mist medications (nebulizers, metered dose devices) reliably and safely, including administration of the correct dosage at the appropriate times / intervals. <u>Excludes</u> all other forms of medication (oral tablets, injectable and IV medications).

<u>Prior</u>   <u>Current</u>

❑   ❑   0 — Able to independently take the correct medication and proper dosage at the correct times.

❑   ❑   1 — Able to take medication at the correct times if:
  (a) individual dosages are prepared in advance by another person, <u>OR</u>
  (b) given daily reminders.

❑   ❑   2 — <u>Unable</u> to take medication unless administered by someone else

❑   ❑   NA — No inhalant / mist medications prescribed.

❑   UK — Unknown

(MO800) Management of injectable Medications: <u>Patient's ability</u> to prepare and take <u>all</u> prescribed injectable medications reliably and safely, including administration of correct dosage at the appropriate times / intervals. <u>Excludes</u> IV medications.

<u>Prior</u>	<u>Current</u>	
❑	❑	0 — Able to independently take the correct medication and proper dosage at the correct times.
❑	❑	1 — Able to take injectable medication at correct times if:
❑	❑	(a) individual syringes are prepared in advance by another person, <u>OR</u>
		(b) given daily reminders.
❑	❑	2 —<u>Unable</u> to take injectable medications unless administered by someone else.
❑	❑	NA — No injectable medications prescribed.
❑		UK— Unknown

EQUIPMENT MANAGEMENT:

(MO810) Patient Management of Equipment (Includes <u>ONLY</u> oxygen, IV / infusion therapy, enteral / parenteral nutrition equipment or supplies): <u>Patient's ability</u> to set up, monitor and change equipment reliably and safely, add appropriate fluids or medication, clean / store / dispose of equipment or supplies using proper technique. **(NOTE: This refers to ability, not compliance or willingness.)**

❑ 0 — Patient manages all tasks related to equipment completely independently.

❑ 1 — If someone else sets up equipment (i.e. fills portable oxygen tank, provides patient with prepared solutions), patient is able to manage all other aspects of equipment.

❑ 2 — Patient requires considerable assistance from another person to manage equipment, but independently completes portions of the task.

❑ 3 — Patient is only able to monitor equipment (e.g., liter flow, fluid in bag) and must call someone else to manage the equipment.

❑ 4 — Patient is completely dependent on someone else to manage all equipment.

❑ NA — No equipment of this type used in care **[if NA, go to Equipment and Supplies.]**

(MO820) Caregiver Management of Equipment (Includes <u>ONLY</u> oxygen, IV/Infusion equipment, enteral / parenteral nutrition, ventilator therapy equipment or supplies): <u>Caregivers ability</u> to set up, monitor, and change equipment reliably and safely, add appropriate fluids or medication, clean / store / dispose of equipment or supplies using proper technique. **(NOTE: This refers to ability, not compliance or willingness.)**

❑ 0 — Caregiver manages all tasks related to equipment completely independently.

❑ 1 — If someone else sets up equipment, caregiver is able to manage all other aspects.

❑ 2 — Caregiver requires considerable assistance from another person to manage equipment, but independently completes significant portions of task.

❑ 3 — Caregiver is only able to complete small portions of task (e.g., administer nebulizer treatment, clean / store / dispose of equipment or supplies).

❑ 4 — Caregiver is completely dependent on someone else to manage all equipment.

❑ NA — No caregiver

❑ UK — Unknown

EQUIPMENT & SUPPLIES:

Equipment Needs (check appropriate box)

	Has	Needs
a. Oxygen / Respiratory Equip.		
b. Wheelchair		
c. Hospital Bed		
d. Walker		

2. Supplies Needed and Comments Regarding Equipment Needs

_____

3. Financial Problems / Needs / MSW Consult

SAFETY MEASURES RECOMMENDED TO PROTECT PATIENT FROM INJURY:_____

_____

_____

EMERGENCY PLANS: (Describe) _____

_____

_____

PATIENT PARTICIPATED IN DEVELOPING PLANS OF CARE: ❑ Yes   ❑ No

PHYSICIAN: Primary: _____

                       Secondary: _____

PHARMACY OF CHOICE: _____ Ph. _____

Does Patient Have Advance Directive? ❑ Yes   ❑ No   Copy on Chart?   ❑ Yes   ❑ No

Does Patient Have Living Will? ❑ Yes   ❑ No   Copy on Chart?   ❑ Yes   ❑ No

Skilled Interventions Performed This Visit: _____

_____

_____

Discharge Plans: _____

_____

_____

Signature of Assessor: _____   **Date of Assessment:** _____

Time In _____   **Out** _____

Appendix **D**

SAMPLE ASSESSMENT FORM #2
FOLLOW-UP VERSION

| **FOLLOW-UP ASSESSMENT** | Client's Name: |
| | Client Record No. |

DEMOGRAPHIC/GENERAL INFORMATION

(MO010) Agency Provider Number	**(MO020) Patient ID Number**	**(MO030) Start of Care Date**
		_ _ – _ _ – _ _
		mm dd yy

(MO032) Resumption of Care Date

_ _ – _ _ – _ _   ☐ NA – Not Applicable
mm   dd   yy

(MO040) Patient Name:

_ _
(First)   (MI) (Last)   (Suffix)

	Patient Phone ( ) _____ – _____
Street, Route, Apt. County	**(MO063) Medicare Number**
	_ _ _ _ _ _ _ _ _ _ _ ☐ NA – No Medicare
	(including suffix if any)
City **(MO050) State** **(MO060) Zip**	

(MO064) Social Security Number	**(MO066) Birthdate**
☐ UK – Unknown or Not Available	
_ _ _ – _ _ – _ _ _ _	_ _ – _ _ – _ _ _ _
	month day year
(MO065) Medicaid number	
☐ No Medicaid	
_ _ _ _ _ _ _ _ _ _ _	

(MO069) Gender:
    ☐ 1 – Male
    ☐ 2 – Female

(MO072) Primary Referring Physician ID:

_ _ _ _ _ _ _ _ _ _ _ _   ☐ UK – Unknown or Not Available

(MO080) Discipline of Person Completing Assessment:
    ☐ 1–RN   ☐ 2–PT   ☐ 3–SLP/ST   ☐ 4–OT

(MO090) Date Assessment Completed:

_ _ – _ _ – _ _
month   day   year

(MO100) This Assessment is Currently Being Completed for the Following Reason:

Start/Resumption of Care
☐ 1 – Start of care—further visits planned
☐ 2 – Start of care—no further visits planned
☐ 3 – Resumption of care (after inpatient stay)

Follow-Up
☐ 4 – Recertification (follow-up) reassessment **(Go to MO150)**
☐ 5 – Other follow-up **(Go to MO150)**

Transfer to an Inpatient Facility
☐ 6 – Transferred to an inpatient facility—patient not discharged from agency **(Go to MO830)**
☐ 7 – Transferred to an inpatient facility—patient discharged from agency **(Go to MO830)**

Discharge from Agency—Not to an Inpatient Facility
☐ 8 – Death at home **(Go to MO906)**
☐ 9 – Discharge from agency **(Go to MO150)**
☐ 10 – Discharge from agency—no visits completed after start/resumption of care assessment **(Go to MO830)**

(MO150) Current Payment Sources for Home Care:
(Mark all that apply.)
☐ 0 – None; no charge for current services
☐ 1 – Medicare (traditional fee-for-service)
☐ 2 – Medicare (HMO/managed care)
☐ 3 – Medicaid (traditional fee-for-service)
☐ 4 – Medicaid (HMO/managed care)
☐ 5 – Worker's compensation
☐ 6 – Title programs (e.g., Title III, V, or XX)
☐ 7 – Other government (e.g., CHAMPUS, VA, etc.)
☐ 8 – Private insurance
☐ 9 – Private HMO/managed care
☐ 10 – Self-pay
☐ 11 – Other (specify) _____

(MO200) Medical or Treatment Regimen Change Within Past 14 Days: Has this patient experienced a change in medical or treatment regimen (e.g., medication, treatment, or service change due to new or additional diagnosis, etc.) within the last 14 days?

❑ 0 — No *[If No, go to M0250]*

❑ 1 — Yes

(MO210) List the patient's **Medical Diagnose**s and three-digit ICD code categories <u>for those conditions requiring changed medical or treatment regimen</u> (no surgical or V-codes);

<u>Changed Medical Regimen Diagnosis</u>   <u>ICD</u>

a. _____   (__ __ __)

b. _____   (__ __ __)

c. _____   (__ __ __)

d. _____   (__ __ __)

(MO220) Conditions Prior to Medical or Treatment Regimen Change or Inpatient Stay Within Past 14 Days: If this patient experienced a change in medical or treatment regimen within the past 14 days, indicate any conditions which existed <u>prior to</u> the change in medical or treatment regimen. *(Mark all that apply)*.

❑ 1 — Urinary incontinence

❑ 2 — Indwelling/suprapubic catheter

❑ 3 — Intractable pain

❑ 4 — Impaired decision-making

❑ 5 — Disruptive or socially inappropriate behavior

❑ 6 — Memory loss to the extent that supervision required

❑ 7 — None of the above

(MO250) Therapies the patient receives <u>at home:</u> **(Mark all that apply.)**

❑ 1 — Intravenous or infusion therapy (excludes TPN)

❑ 2 — Parenteral nutrition (TPN or lipids)

❑ 3 — Enteral nutrition (nasogastric, gastrostomy, jejunostomy, or any other artificial entry into the alimentary canal)

❑ 4 — None of the above

(MO280) Life Expectancy: (Physician documentation is not required.)

❑ 0 — Life expectancy is greater than 6 months

❑ 1 — Life expectancy is 6 months or fewer

(MO290) High Risk Factors characterizing this patient: **(Mark all that apply.)**

❑ 1 — Heavy smoking

❑ 2 — Obesity

❑ 3 — Alcohol dependency

❑ 4 — Drug dependency

❑ 5 — None of the above

LIVING ARRANGEMENTS

(MO300) Current Residence:

❑ 1 — Patient's owned or rented residence (house, apartment, or mobile home owned or rented by patient/couple/significant other)
❑ 2 — Family member's residence
❑ 3 — Boarding home or rented room
❑ 4 — Board and care or assisted living facility
❑ 5 — Other (specify) _____

(MO310) Structural Barriers in the patient's environment limiting independent mobility: **(Mark all that apply.)**

❑ 0 — None
❑ 1 — Stairs inside home which must be used by the patient (e.g., to get to toileting, sleeping, eating areas.)
❑ 2 — Stairs inside home which are used optionally (e.g., to get to laundry facilities)
❑ 3 — Stairs leading from inside house to outside
❑ 4 — Narrow or obstructed doorways

(MO320) Safety Hazards found in the patient's current place of residence: **(Mark all that apply.)**

❑ 0 — None
❑ 1 — Inadequate floor, roof, or windows
❑ 2 — Inadequate lighting
❑ 3 — Unsafe gas/electric appliance
❑ 4 — Inadequate heating
❑ 5 — Inadequate cooling
❑ 6 — Lack of fire safety devices
❑ 7 — Unsafe floor coverings
❑ 8 — Inadequate stair railings
❑ 9 — Improperly stored hazardous materials
❑ 10 — Lead-based paint
❑ 11 — Other (specify) _____

(MO330) Sanitation Hazards found in the patient's current place of residence: **(Mark all that apply.)**

❑ 0 — None
❑ 1 — No running water
❑ 2 — Contaminated water
❑ 3 — No toileting facilities
❑ 4 — Outdoor toileting facilities only
❑ 5 — Inadequate sewage disposal
❑ 6 — Inadequate/improper food storage
❑ 7 — No food refrigeration
❑ 8 — No cooking facilities
❑ 9 — Insects / rodents present
❑ 10 — No scheduled trash pickup
❑ 11 — Cluttered / soiled living area
❑ 12 — Other (specify) _____

(MO340) Patient Lives With: (Mark all that apply.)

❏ 1 — Lives alone
❏ 2 — With spouse or significant other   Name: _____
❏ 3 — With other family member   Relationship: _____
❏ 4 — With a friend
❏ 5 — With paid help (other than home care agency staff)
❏ 6 — With other than above

SUPPORT SYSTEMS

(MO350) Assisting Person(s) Other Than Home Care Agency Staff: (Mark all that apply.)

❏ 1 — Relatives, friends, or neighbors living outside the home
❏ 2 — Person residing in the home (EXCLUDING paid help)
❏ 3 — Paid help
❏ 4 — None of the above **[If None of the above, go to Systems Review: Neurosensory]**

(MO360) Primary Caregiver taking **lead responsibility** for providing or managing the patient's care, providing the most frequent assistance, etc. (other than home care agency staff.)

❏ 0 — No one person **[If unknown, go to Systems Review: Neurosensory]**
❏ 1 — Spouse or significant other
❏ 2 — Daughter or son
❏ 3 — Other family member
❏ 4 — Friend or neighbor or community or church member
❏ 5 — Paid help

(MO370) How Often does the patient receive assistance from the primary caregiver?

❏ 1 — Several times during day and night
❏ 2 — Several times during day
❏ 3 — Once daily
❏ 4 — Three or more times per week
❏ 5 — One or two times per week
❏ 6 — Less often than weekly

(MO380)Type of Primary Caregiver Assistance: (Mark all that apply.)

❏ 1 — ADL assistance (e.g., bathing, dressing, toileting, bowel/bladder, eating/feeding)
❏ 2 — IADL assistance (eg., meds, meals, housekeeping, laundry, telephone, shopping, finances)
❏ 3 — Environmental support (housing, home maintenance)
❏ 4 — Psychological support (socialization, companionship, recreation)
❏ 5 — Advocates or facilitates patient's participation in appropriate medical care
❏ 6 — Financial agent, power of attorney, or conservator of finance
❏ 7 — Health care agent, conservator of person, or medical power of attorney

Client's Name:

Client Record No.

SYSTEMS REVIEW

NEUROSENSORY:

HEAD: Dizziness ❑   Headache ❑   (describe location, duration) _____

EYES: Glasses ❑   Blurred/double vision ❑   Glaucoma ❑

           Cataracts ❑   PERRL ❑   Other *(specify)* _____

EARS: Hearing Aid ❑   Tinnitus ❑   Other *(specify)* _____

(MO410) Speech and Oral (Verbal) Expression of Language (in patient's own language):

❑   0 — Expresses complex ideas, feelings, and needs clearly, completely, and easily in all situations with no observable impairment.

❑   1 — Minimal difficulty in expressing ideas and needs (may take extra time; makes occasional errors in word choice, grammar or speech intelligibility; needs minimal prompting or assistance).

❑   2 — Expresses simple ideas or needs with moderate difficulty (needs prompting or assistance, errors in word choice, organization or speech intelligibility). Speaks in phrases or short sentences.

❑   3 — Has severe difficulty expressing basic ideas or needs and requires maximal assistance or guessing by listener. Speech limited to single words or short phrases.

❑   4 — <u>Unable</u> to express basic needs even with maximal prompting or assistance but is not comatose or unresponsive (e.g., speech is nonsensical or unintelligible.)

❑   5 — Patient nonresponsive or unable to speak.

ADDITIONAL NEURO SIGNS:

❑ unequal grasp   ❑ vertigo   ❑ paralysis (where): _____)

❑ gait disturbance   ❑ syncope   ❑ frequent falls _____

❑ lack of coordination (balance)   ❑ seizure   ❑ tremor

❑ numbness   ❑ L.O.C.   ❑ aphasia / inarticulate speech

Patient's Perceived Pain Level _____ (Scale 1-10)

(MO420) Frequency of pain interfering with patient's activity or movement:

❑   0 — Patient has no pain or pain does not interfere with activity or movement

❑   1 — Less often than daily

❑   2 — Daily, but not constantly

❑   3 — All of the time

(MO430) Intractable Pain: Is the patient experiencing pain that is <u>not easily relieved,</u> occurs at least daily, and affects the patient's sleep, appetite, physical or emotional energy, concentration, personal relationships, emotions, or ability or desire to perform physical activity?

❑   0 — No

❑   1 — Yes

INTEGUMENTARY:

(MO440) Does this patient have a **Skin Lesion** or an **Open Wound**? This excludes "OSTOMIES."

❑ 0 — No [**If No, go to Integumentary Status Assessment Tool**]
❑ 1 — Yes

(MO445) Does this patient have a **Pressure Ulcer?**

❑ 0 — No [**If No, go to M0468**]
❑ 1 — Yes

(MO450) Current Number of Pressure Ulcers at Each Stage: (Circle one response for each stage.)

Pressure Ulcer Stages		Number of Pressure Ulcers				
a)	**Stage 1:** Nonblanchable erythema of intact skin; the heralding of skin ulceration. In darker-pigmented skin, warmth, edema, hardness, or discolored skin may be indicators.	0	1	2	3	4 or more
b)	**Stage 2:** Partial thickness skin loss involving epidermis and/or dermis. The ulcer is superficial and presents clinically as an abrasion, blister, or shallow crater.	0	1	2	3	4 or more
c)	**Stage 3:** Full-thickness skin loss involving damage or necrosis of subcutaneous tissue which may extend down to, but not through, underlying fascia. The ulcer presents clinically as a deep crater with or without undermining of adjacent tissue.	0	1	2	3	4 or more
d)	**Stage 4:** Full-thickness skin loss with extensive destruction, tissue necrosis, or damage to muscle. bone, or supporting structures (e.g., tendon, joint capsule. etc.)	0	1	2	3	4 or more
e)	In addition to the above. is there at least one pressure ulcer that cannot be observed due to the presence of eschar or a nonremovable dressing, including casts? ❑ 0 — No ❑ 1 — Yes					

(MO460) Stage of Most Problematic (Observable) Pressure Ulcer:

❑ 1 — Stage 1
❑ 2 — Stage 2
❑ 3 — Stage 3
❑ 4 — Stage 4
❑ NA — No observable pressure ulcer

(MO464) Status of Most Problematic (Observable) Pressure Ulcer:

❑ 1 — Fully granulating
❑ 2 — Early / partial granulation

❑ 3 — Not Healing
❑ NA — No observable pressure ulcer

PRESSURE SORE STATUS TOOL (BARBARA BATES-JENSEN)

ITEM	ASSESSMENT	DATE
		Score
1. Size	1 = Length x width < 4 sq. cm. 2 = Length x width 4 to 16 sq. cm. 3 = Length x width 16.1 to 36 sq. cm. 4 = Length x width 36.1 to 80 sq. cm. 5 = Length x width > 80 sq. cm.	
2. Depth	1 = Non-blanchable erythema of intact skin 2 = Partial-thickness skin loss involving epidermis &/or dermis 3 = Full-thickness skin loss involving damage or necrosis of subcutaneous tissue; may extend down to but not through underlying fascia: &/or mixed partial- or full-thickness &/or tissue layers obscured by granulation tissue. 4 = Obscured by necrosis 5 = Full-thickness skin loss with extensive destruction, tissue necrosis or damage to muscle, bone, or supporting structures	
3. Edges	1 = Indistinct, diffuse, none clearly visible 2 = Distinct, outline clearly visible, attached, even with wound base 3 = Well-defined, not attached to wound base 4 = Well-defined, not attached to base, rolled under, thickened 5 = Well-defined, fibrotic, scarred, or hyperkeratotic	
4. Under-mining	1 = Undermining < 2 cm. in any area 2 = Undermining 2 to 4 cm. involving < 50% wound margins 3 = Undermining 2 to 4 cm. involving > 50% wound margins 4 = Undermining > 4 cm. in any area 5 = Tunneling &/or sinus tract formation	
5. Necrotic Tissue Type	1 = None visible 2 = White/gray non-viable tissue &/or non-adherent yellow slough 3 = Loosely adherent yellow slough 4 = Adherent, soft black eschar 5 = Firmly adherent, hard black eschar	
6. Necrotic Tissue Amount	1 = None visible 2 = < 25% of wound bed covered 3 = 25% to 50% of wound covered 4 = > 50% and < 75% of wound covered 5 = 75% to 100% of wound covered	

ITEM	ASSESSMENT	DATE
		Score
7. Exudate Type	1 = None or bloody 2 = Serosanguineous: thin, watery, pale red/pink 3 = Serous: thin, watery, clear 4 = Purulent: thin or thick, opaque. tan/yellow 5 = Foul purulent: thick, opaque. yellow/green with odor	
8. Exudate Amount	1 = None 2 = Scant 3 = Small 4 = Moderate 5 = Large	
9. Skin Color Surrounding Wound	1 = Pink or normal for ethnic group 2 = Bright red &/or blanches to touch 3 = White or gray pallor or hypopigmented 4 = Dark red or purple &/or non-blanchable 5 = Black or hyperpigmented	
10. Peripheral Tissue Edema	1 = Minimal firmness around wound 2 = Non-pitting edema extends < 4 cm. around wound 3 = Non-pitting edema extends≥ 4 cm. around wound 4 = Pitting edema extends < 4 cm. around wound 5 = Crepitus &/or pitting edema extends ≥ 4 cm.	
11. Peripheral Tissue Induration	1 = Minimal firmness around wound 2 = Induration < 2 cm. around wound 3 = Induration 2 to 4 cm. extending < 50° around wound 4 = Induration 2 to 4 cm. extending ≥ 50° around wound 5 = Induration > 4 cm. in any area	
12. Granulation Tissue	1 = Skin intact or partial-thickness wound 2 = Bright, beefy red: 75% to 100% of wound filled &/or tissue overgrowth 3 = Bright, beefy red: < 75% & > 25% of wound filled 4 = Pink, &/ or dull, dusky red &/or fills ≤ 25% wound 5 = No granulation tissue present	
13. Epithelializ-ation	1 = 100% of wound covered, surface intact 2 = 75% to < 100% of wound covered & or epithelial tissue extends > 0.5 cm. into wound bed 3 = 50% to < 75% of wound covered &/or epithelial tissue extends to < 0.5 cm. into wound bed 4 = 25% to < 50% of wound covered 5 = < 25% of wound covered	
TOTAL SCORE:		

PRESSURE STATUS CONTINUUM

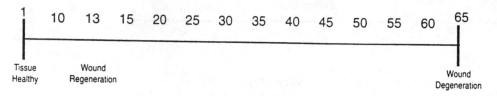

1   10   13   15   20   25   30   35   40   45   50   55   60   65

Tissue Healthy   Wound Regeneration   Wound Degeneration

Used with permission.

Plot the total score on the Pressure Sore Status Continuum by putting an "X" on the line and the date beneath the line.

(MO468) Does this patient have a Stasis Ulcer?

❑ 0 — No **[If No, go to MO482]**

❑ 1 —Yes

(MO470) Current Number of Observable Stasis Ulcer(s):

❏ 0 — Zero

❏ 1 — One

❏ 2 — Two

❏ 3 — Three

❏ 4 — Four or more

(MO474) Does this patient have at least one Stasis Ulcer that Cannot Be Observed due to the presence of a nonremovable dressing?

❏ 0 — No

❏ 1 — Yes

(MO476) Status of Most Problematic (Observable) Stasis Ulcer:

❏ 1 — Fully granulating

❏ 2 — Early/partial granulation

❏ 3 — Not healing

❏ NA — No observable stasis ulcer

Protocol for Care

VENOUS LEG ULCER ASSESSMENT

Venous   Arterial

Patient Name _____   Age: _____   Date: _____

I. Medical History:

☐ Severe leg trauma (Date: _____)
☐ Blood clot [DVT] (Date: _____)
☐ Heart disease/Congestive heart failure
☐ Family history of leg ulcers

☐ Obesity
☐ Frequent leg swelling
☐ Pregnancy

☐ Heart disease/Heart attack
☐ Stroke

☐ Diabetes: ☐ Type I   ☐ Type II

☐ Recurrent leg ulcers

Immune status: ☐ Good   ☐ Compromised

II. Pertinent Surgeries:

☐ Vein surgery (Date: _____)

☐ Cardiac bypass (Date: _____)   ☐ Neck/Carotid artery (Date: _____)

☐ Skin graft (Date: _____)

III. Social Assessment:

Occupation: _____

Hobbies/Activities: _____

Approximate hours per day spent: Standing: _____ hrs.   Sitting: _____ hrs.

Is someone available at home to assist with treatments?   ☐ Yes (_____)   ☐ No

IV. Allergies: (Include previous reactions to topical treatments): _____

V. Ankle/Brachial Index _____

VI. Physical Examination	Left Leg		Right Leg	
Ulcer Location:	☐ Medial lower leg and/or ankle	☐ Foot and/or lateral ankle	☐ Medial lower leg and/or ankle	☐ Foot and/or lateral ankle
Edema:	☐ Present	☐ Absent	☐ Present	☐ Absent
Dorsalis Pedis Pulse: • Palpation • Doppler	☐ Present ☐ Present	☐ Absent ☐ Absent	☐ Present ☐ Present	☐ Absent ☐ Absent
Posterior Tibial Pulse: • Palpation • Doppler	☐ Present ☐ Present	☐ Absent ☐ Absent	☐ Present ☐ Present	☐ Absent ☐ Absent
Pain:	☐ Absent ☐ Decreased w/elevation	☐ Constant ☐ Increased w/elevation	☐ Absent ☐ Decreased w/elevation	☐ Constant ☐ Decreased w/elevation
Ulcer Appearance: • Ulcer Borders • Exudate • Wound Depth • Wound Base • Peri-wound Skin	☐ Irregular ☐ Present ☐ Shallow ☐ Ruddy & granular ☐ Yellow fibrous tissue ☐ Dilated veins ☐ Dermatitis (Dry/ scaly or weeping) ☐ Indurated/ hardened ☐ Hyperpigmented	☐ Even/smooth ☐ Absent ☐ Deep ☐ Pale & dry ☐ Thick black eschar ☐ Thin & shiny ☐ Hair loss ☐ Cool to touch ☐ Pallor on elevation	☐ Irregular ☐ Present ☐ Shallow ☐ Ruddy & granular ☐ Yellow fibrous tissue ☐ Dilated veins ☐ Dermatitis (Dry/ scaly or weeping) ☐ Indurated/ hardened ☐ Hyperpigmented	☐ Even/smooth ☐ Absent ☐ Deep ☐ Pale & dry ☐ Thick black eschar ☐ Thin & shiny ☐ Hair loss ☐ Cool to touch ☐ Pallor on elevation

(MO482) Does this patient have a Surgical Wound?

☐ 0 — No **[If No, go to Integumentary Status Assessment Tool]**
☐ 1 — Yes

(MO484) Current Number of (Observable) Surgical Wounds: (If a wound is partially closed but has <u>more</u> than one opening, consider each opening as a separate wound.)

☐ 0 — Zero
☐ 1 — One
☐ 2 — Two
☐ 3 — Three
☐ 4 — Four or more

(MO486) Does this patient have at least one Surgical Wound that Cannot be Observed due to the presence of a nonremovable dressing?

☐ 0 — No
☐ 1 — Yes

(MO488) Status of Most Problematic (Observable) Surgical Wound:

☐ 1 — Fully granulating
☐ 2 — Early / partial granulation
☐ 3 — Not healing
☐ NA — No observable surgical wound

INTEGUMENTARY STATUS ASSESSMENT TOOL

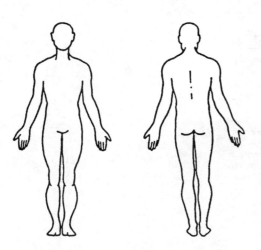

Indicate location of integumentary
problem on figure above

*** Please indicate size & depth
as applicable**

Type	Yes	No
* 1. Lesions, Rashes	☐	☐
* 2. Bruises	☐	☐
* 3. Masses	☐	☐
* 4. Scars	☐	☐
* 5. Stasis Ulcers	☐	☐
* 6. Pressure Ulcers	☐	☐
* 7. Incisions	☐	☐
8. Excessive dryness, pruritus	☐	☐
* 9. Areas of excoriation, redness, trauma	☐	☐
10. Temperature changes in skin (coolness, warmth)	☐	☐
11. Changes in hair distribution	☐	☐
12. Nails: ridges, thickening, color bands, texture changes	☐	☐
* Past skin diseases (eczema, etc.)	☐	☐
* Healing time increased	☐	☐
* Chronic long-term sun exposure	☐	☐
* Recent changes in a wart or mole	☐	☐
* Turgor: good, fair, poor (circle)	☐	☐

COMMENTS: *(If it is noted above, comment please.)* _____

_____

_____

_____

MUSCULOSKELETAL:

❑ Hx. arthritis

❑ gout

❑ stiffness

❑ swollen joints / joint pain

❑ weakness

❑ muscle cramps / spasms

❑ leg cramps

❑ deformities

❑ amputation

❑ prostheses

❑ appliances

❑ other_____

❑ Hx. of osteoporosis

❑ Hx. of fractures

❑ R.O.M.

    Active: _____

    Passive: _____

❑ Crepitus

❑ Kyphosis

❑ Scoliosis

❑ Lordosis

Comments:

CARDIOPULMONARY:

Temperature _____   Method Taken: O   A   R

PULSE: Apical Rate _____   Radial Rate _____

          Rhythm _____   Quality _____

Respirations _____

BLOOD PRESSURE: Lying _____   Sitting _____

          Standing _____   L.A. _____   R.A. _____

CARDIOVASCULAR:

❑ Palpitations

❑ Claudication

❑ Fatigues easily

❑ Pacemaker Date of

last battery change _____

❑ Angina

❑ Dyspnea on exertion

❑ Paroxysmal nocturnal dyspnea

❑ Orthopnea (# of pillows _____)

❑ Bradycardia, tachycardia, arrythmias

❑ "BP Problems", hypertension, hypotension

❑ Chest pain, pressure, tightness

❑ Neck vein distention

❑ "Heart" problems

  (specify) _____

❑ Other (specify) _____

❑ Peripheral vascular complaints:
  Coldness, pain sensation,
  exaggerated response to cold

❑ Calf tenderness

❑ Murmurs, bruits

❑ Edema ____ (O to +4)

❑ Cyanosis

❑ Varicosities

❑ Homan's sign

COMMENTS:

RESPIRATORY:

Present Condition:

❑ Cough *(describe)* _____   ❑ Sputum *(character & amount)* _____

❑ SOB   ❑ Tachypnea   ❑ Dyspnea   ❑ Cheyne-Stokes   ❑ Kussmaul

❑ Symmetry of chest configuration: (normal, barrel chest, pigeon chest, funnel chest) _____

❑ Breath Sounds *(describe)* _____

❑ Tracheostomy   ❑ Other *(specify)* _____

(MO490) When is the patient dyspneic or noticeably **Short of Breath?**

❑ 0 — Never, patient is not short of breath
❑ 1 — When walking more than 20 feet, climbing stairs
❑ 2 — With moderate exertion (e.g., while dressing, using commode or bedpan, walking distances less than 20 feet)
❑ 3 — With minimal exertion (e.g., while eating, talking, or performing other ADLs) or with agitation
❑ 4 — At rest (during day or night)

(MO500) Respiratory Treatments utilized at home: **(Mark all that apply.)**

❑ 1 — Oxygen (intermittent or continuous)
❑ 2 — Ventilator (continually or at night)
❑ 3 — Continuous positive airway pressure
❑ 4 — None of the above

COMMENTS:

GENITOURINARY

❑ Frequency   ❑ Nocturia   ❑ Dribbling
❑ Pain   ❑ Urgency   ❑ Anuria
❑ Hematuria   ❑ Prostate disorder   ❑ Dialysis _____ times per week _____
❑ Stress incontinence   ❑ Other (specify) _____

(MO510) Has this patient been treated for a Urinary Tract Infection in the past 14 days?

❑ 0 — No
❑ 1 — Yes
❑ NA — Patient on prophylactic treatment

(MO520) Urinary Incontinence or Urinary Catheter Presence:

❑ 0 — No incontinence or catheter (includes anuria or ostomy for urinary drainage) **[If no, go to Gastrointestinal]**
❑ 1 — Patient is incontinent
❑ 2 — Patient requires a urinary catheter (i.e. external, indwelling, intermittent, suprapubic) **[Go to MO540]**

(M0530) When does Urinary Incontinence occur?

❑ 0 — Timed-voiding defers incontinence
❑ 1 — During the night only
❑ 2 — During the day and night

Client's Name:

Client Record No.

GASTROINTESTINAL

❏ Indigestion, heartburn ❏ Hernias (where)_____ ❏ Hemorrhoids ❏ Other (specify): _____

❏ Nausea, vomiting ❏ Diarrhea/constipation ❏ Gallbladder problems _____

❏ Ulcers ❏ Recent Δ in bowel habits ❏ Jaundice _____

❏ Flatulence, eructation ❏ Ascites ❏ Tenderness/distention ❏ Date of last BM _____

❏ Pain ❏ Rectal bleeding ❏ Diverticulitis

(MO540) Bowel Incontinence Frequency:

❏ 0 — Very rarely or never has bowel incontinence

❏ 1 — Less than once weekly

❏ 2 — One to three times weekly

❏ 3 — Four to six times weekly

❏ 4 — On a daily basis

❏ 5 — More often than once daily

❏ NA — Patient has ostomy for bowel elimination

(MO550) Ostomy for Bowel Elimination: Does this patient have an ostomy for bowel elimination that (within the last 14 days) necessitated a change in medical or treatment regimen?

❏ 0 — Patient does not have an ostomy for bowel elimination.

❏ 1 — Patient's ostomy did not necessitate change in medical or treatment regimen.

❏ 2 — The ostomy did necessitate change in medical or treatment regimen.

NUTRITIONAL STATUS:

❏ Dysphagia

❏ Anorexia

Diet Order _____

Supplements _____

Typical 24˚ fluid intake _____

Appetite For Meals (%) _____

Weight_____ ❏ actual ❏ reported

Patient appears: ❏ normal weight ❏ under weight ❏ slightly under weight ❏ overweight

Feeding ability: ❏ self ❏ assisted ❏ spoon ❏ syringe ❏ tube

Usually dines alone: ❏ Yes ❏ No

Nutrition Consult: _____

COMMENTS:

REPRODUCTIVE

❑ dysmenorrhea   ❑ gravida/para   ❑ vag discharge/bleeding

❑ hx hysterectomy   Date of last pap _____   ❑ hx BPH

❑ hx of abnormal pap   Date of last mammogram _____   ❑ penile discharge

BREASTS (Both male and female)

❑ Lumps   ❑ Tenderness   ❑ Symmetry   ❑ Dimpling   ❑ Discharge   ❑ Other (specify) _____

Hx of breast lump(s) _____

Comments _____

ENDOCRINE AND HEMATOPOIETIC:

❑ Polyuria   ❑ Polydipsia   Coumadin: _____ Heparin: _____

❑ IDDM   ❑ NIDDM   Pallor: _____

Hx hyperthyroidism: _____   Excessive Bleeding or Bruising: _____

Hx hypothyroidism: _____   Hx Leukemia: _____ Type: _____

Current laboratory orders: _____   Hx Thrombocytopenia: _____ Hx Sickle Cell: _____

_____   Pernicious Anemia: _____ Polycythemia: _____

_____   ❑ Intolerance to heat and cold   ❑ Enlarged lymph nodes

                                        ❑ Family hx of endocrine/hematopoietic disorders

                                        ❑ Other (specify) _____

EMOTIONAL / BEHAVIORAL

❑ Hx of previous psych. illness   ❑ Mania

❑ Memory loss-short term / long-term   ❑ Poor judgement / impaired judgement

❑ Disorientation time / place / person   ❑ Hallucination / delusions

❑ Depression   ❑ Other (specify) _____

❑ Labile moods

(MO560) Cognitive Functioning: (Patient's current level of alertness, orientation, comprehension, concentration, and immediate memory for simple commands).

❑ 0 — Alert / oriented, able to focus and shift attention, comprehends and recalls task directions independently.

❑ 1 — Requires prompting (cuing, repetition, reminders) only under stressful or unfamiliar conditions.

❑ 2 — Requires assistance and some direction in specific situations (e.g. on all tasks involving shifting of attention), or consistently requires low stimulus environment due to distractibility.

❑ 3 — Requires considerable assistance in routine situations. Is not alert and oriented or is unable to shift attention and recall directions more than half the time.

❑ 4 — Totally dependent due to disturbances such as constant disorientation, coma, persistent vegetative state, or delirium.

(M0570) When Confused (Reported or Observed):

❑ 0 — Never

❑ 1 — In new or complex situations only

❑ 2 — On awakening or at night only

❑ 3 — During the day and evening, but not constantly

❑ 4 — Constantly

❑ NA — Patient nonresponsive

(M0580) When Anxious (Reported or Observed):

❑ 0 — None of the time

❑ 1 — Less often than daily

❑ 2 — Daily, but not constantly

❑ 3 — All of the time

❑ NA — Patient nonresponsive

(M0590) Depressive Feelings Reported or Observed in Patient: (Mark all that apply.)

❑ 1 — Depressed mood (e.g. feeling sad, tearful)

❑ 2 — Sense of failure or self reproach

❑ 3 — Hopelessness

❑ 4 — Recurrent thoughts of death

❑ 5 — Thoughts of suicide

❑ 6 — None of the above feelings observed or reported

(MO600) Patient Behaviors (Reported or Observed): (Mark all that apply.)

❑ 1 — Indecisiveness, lack of concentration

❑ 2 — Diminished interest in most activities

❑ 3 — Sleep disturbances

❑ 4 — Recent change in appetite or weight

❑ 5 — Agitation

❑ 6 — A suicide attempt

❑ 7 — None of the above behaviors observed or reported

(MO610) Behaviors <u>Demonstrated at Least Once A Week</u> (Reported or Observed): (Mark all that apply.)

❑ 1 — Memory deficit: failure to recognize familiar persons/places, inability to recall events of past 24 hours, significant memory loss so that supervision is required.

❑ 2 — Impaired decision-making: failure to perform usual ADLs or IADLs, inability to appropriately stop activities, jeopardizes safety through actions

❑ 3 — Verbal disruption: yelling, threatening, excessive profanity, sexual references, etc.

❑ 4 — Physical aggression: aggressive or combative to self and others (e.g., hits self, throws objects, punches, dangerous maneuvers with wheelchair or other objects)

❑ 5 — Disruptive, infantile, or socially inappropriate behavior (excludes verbal actions)

❑ 6 — Delusional, hallucinatory, or paranoid behavior

❑ 7 — None of the above behaviors demonstrated

(MO620) Frequency of Behavior Problems (Reported or Observed) (e.g. wandering episodes, self abuse, verbal disruption, physical aggression, etc.):

❑ 0 — Never
❑ 1 — Less than once a month
❑ 2 — Once a month
❑ 3 — Several times each month
❑ 4 — Several times a week
❑ 5 — At least daily

(MO630) Is this patient receiving **Psychiatric Nursing Services** at home provided by a qualified psychiatric nurse?

❑ 0 — No
❑ 1 — Yes

ADL/IADLs

┌──┐
│   — *RECORD WHAT THE PATIENT IS ABLE TO DO* —   │
└──┘

(MO640) Grooming: Ability to tend to personal hygiene needs (i.e., washing face and hands, hair care, shaving or make up, teeth or denture care, fingernail care).

❑ 0 — Able to groom self unaided, with or without the use of assistive devices or adapted methods.

❑ 1 — Grooming utensils must be placed within reach before able to complete grooming activities.

❑ 2 — Someone must assist the patient to groom self.

❑ 3 — Patient depends entirely upon someone else for grooming needs.

(MO650) Ability to Dress Upper Body (with or without dressing aids) including undergarments, pullovers, front-opening shirts and blouses, managing zippers, buttons, and snaps:

❑ 0 — Able to get clothes out of closets and drawers, put them on and remove them from the upper body without assistance

❑ 1 — Able to dress upper body without assistance if clothing is laid out or handed to the patient.

❑ 2 — Someone must help the patient put on upper body clothing

❑ 3 — Patient depends entirely upon another person to dress the upper body.

(MO660) Ability to Dress Lower Body (with or without dressing aids) including undergarments, slacks, socks or nylons, shoes:

❑ 0 — Able to obtain, put on, and remove clothing and shoes without assistance.

❑ 1 — Able to dress lower body without assistance if clothing and shoes are laid out or handed to the patient.

❑ 2 — Someone must help the patient put on undergarments, slacks, socks or nylons, and shoes.

❑ 3 — Patient depends entirely upon another person to dress lower body.

(MO670) Bathing: Ability to wash entire body. <u>Excludes</u> grooming (washing face and hands only):

❑ 0 — Able to bathe self in <u>shower or tub</u> independently.

❑ 1 — With the use of devices, is able to bathe self in shower or tub independently.

❑ 2 — Able to bathe in shower or tub with the assistance of another person:
    (a) for intermittent supervision or encouragement or reminders, <u>OR</u>
    (b) to get in and out of the shower or tub, <u>OR,</u>
    (c) for washing difficult to reach areas

❑ 3 — Participates in bathing self in shower or tub, <u>but</u> requires presence of another person throughout the bath for assistance or supervision.

❑ 4 — <u>Unable</u> to use the shower or tub and is bathed in <u>bed or bedside chair</u>.

❑ 5 — Unable to effectively participate in bathing and is totally bathed by another person.

(MO680) Toileting: Ability to get to and from the toilet or bedside commode.

❑ 0 — Able to get to and from the toilet independently with or without a device.

❑ 1 — When reminded, assisted, or supervised by another person, able to get to and from the toilet

❑ 2 — <u>Unable</u> to get to and from the toilet but is able to use a bedside commode (with or without assistance)

❑ 3 — <u>Unable</u> to get to and from the toilet or bedside commode but is able to use a bedpan/urinal independently.

❑ 4 — Is totally dependent in toileting.

(MO690) Transferring: Ability to move from bed to chair, on and off toilet or commode, into and out of tub or shower, and ability to turn and position self in bed if patient is bedfast.

❑ 0 — Able to independently transfer

❑ 1 — Transfers with minimal human assistance or with use of an assistive device.

❑ 2 — <u>Unable</u> to transfer self but is able to bear weight and pivot during the transfer process.

❑ 3 — Unable to transfer self and is <u>unable</u> to bear weight or pivot when transferred by another person.

❑ 4 — Bedfast, unable to transfer but is able to turn and position self in bed.

❑ 5 — Bedfast, unable to transfer but is <u>unable</u> to turn and position self.

(MO700) Ambulation / Locomotion: Ability to <u>SAFELY</u> walk, once in a standing position, or use a wheelchair, once in a seated position, on a variety of surfaces.

❑ 0 –– Able to independently walk on even and uneven surfaces and climb stairs with or without railings (i.e., needs no human assistance or assistive device).

❑ 1 — Requires use of a device (e.g., cane, walker) to walk alone <u>or</u> requires human supervision or assistance to negotiate stairs or steps or uneven surfaces.

❑ 2 — Able to walk only with the supervision or assistance of another person at all times.

❑ 3 — Chairfast, <u>unable</u> to ambulate but is able to wheel self independently.

❑ 4 — Chairfast, unable to ambulate and is <u>unable</u> to wheel self.

❑ 5— Bedfast, unable to ambulate or be up in a chair.

(MO710) Feeding or Eating: Ability to feed self meals and snacks. Note: This refers only to the process of <u>eating</u>, <u>chewing</u>, and <u>swallowing</u>, <u>not preparing</u> the food to be eaten.

❑ 0 — Able to independently feed self.

❑ 1 — Able to feed self independently but requires:
    (a) meal set-up; <u>OR</u>
    (b) intermittent assistance or supervision from another person; <u>OR</u>
    (c) a liquid, pureed or ground meat diet.

❑ 2 — <u>Unable</u> to feed self and must be assisted or supervised throughout the meal/snack.

❑ 3 — Able to take in nutrients orally <u>and</u> receives supplemental nutrients through a nasogastric tube or gastrostomy.

❑ 4 — <u>Unable</u> to take in nutrients orally and is fed nutrients through a nasogastric tube or gastrostomy.

❑ 5 — Unable to take in nutrients orally or by tube feeding.

(MO720) Planning and Preparing Light Meal: (e.g., cereal, sandwich) or reheat delivered meals.

❏ 0 — (a) Able to independently plan and prepare all light meals for self or reheat delivered meals;
     OR
     (b) Is physically, cognitively, and mentally able to prepare light meals on a regular basis but has not
     routinely performed light meal preparation in the past (i.e., prior to this home care admission).
❏ 1 — Unable to prepare light meals on a regular basis due to physical, cognitive, or mental limitations.
❏ 2 — Unable to prepare any light meals or reheat any delivered meals.

(MO730) Transportation: Physical and mental ability to safely use a car, taxi, or public transportation (bus, train, subway).

❏ 0 — Able to independently drive a regular or adapted car; OR use a regular or handicap-accessible public bus.
❏ 1 — Able to ride in a car only when driven by another person; OR able to use a bus or handicap van only when
     assisted or accompanied by another person.
❏ 2 — Unable to ride in a car, taxi, bus, or van, and requires transportation by ambulance.

(MO740) Laundry: Ability to do own laundry — to carry laundry to and from washing machine, to use washer and dryer, to wash small items by hand.

❏ 0 — (a) Able to independently take care of all laundry tasks; OR
     (b) Physically, cognitively, and mentally able to do laundry and access facilities, but has not
     routinely performed laundry tasks in the past (i.e., prior to this home care admission).
❏ 1 — Able to do only light laundry, such as minor hand wash or light washer loads. Due to physical, cognitive, or
     mental limitations, needs assistance with heavy laundry such as carrying large loads of laundry.
❏ 2— Unable to do any laundry due to physical limitation or needs continual supervision and assistance due to
     cognitive or mental limitation.

(MO750) Housekeeping: Ability to safely and effectively perform light housekeeping and heavier cleaning tasks.

❏ 0 — (a) Able to independently perform all housekeeping tasks: OR
     (b) Physically, cognitively, and mentally able to perform all housekeeping tasks but has not routinely participated in
     housekeeping tasks in the past (i.e., prior to this home care admission).
❏ 1 — Able to perform only light housekeeping (e.g., dusting, wiping kitchen counters) tasks independently.
❏ 2 — Able to perform housekeeping tasks with intermittent assistance or supervision from another person.
❏ 3 — Unable to consistently perform any housekeeping tasks unless assisted by another person throughout the process.
❏ 4 — Unable to effectively participate in any housekeeping tasks.

(MO760) Shopping: Ability to plan for, select, and purchase items in a store and to carry them home or arrange delivery.

❏ 0 — (a) Able to plan for shopping needs and independently perform shopping tasks, including carrying packages; OR
     (b) Physically, cognitively, and mentally able to take care of shopping, but has not done shopping in the
     past (i.e., prior this home care admission).
❏ 1 — Able to go shopping, but needs some assistance:
     (a) By self is able to do only light shopping and carry small packages, but needs someone to do occasional major shopping; OR
     (b) Unable to go shopping alone, but can go with someone to assist.
❏ 2 — Unable to go shopping, but is able to identify items needed, place orders, and arrange home delivery.
❏ 3 — Needs someone to do all shopping and errands.

(MO770) Ability to Use Telephone: Ability to answer the phone, dial numbers, and effectively use the telephone to communicate.

❏ 0 — Able to dial numbers and answer calls appropriately and as desired.
❏ 1 — Able to use a specially adapted telephone (i.e., large numbers on the dial, teletype phone for the deaf) and
     call essential numbers.
❏ 2 — Able to answer the telephone and carry on a normal conversation but has difficulty with placing calls.
❏ 3 — Able to answer the telephone only some of the time or is able to carry on only a limited conversation.
❏ 4— Unable to answer the telephone at all but can listen if assisted with equipment.
❏ 5— Totally unable to use the telephone.
❏ NA— Patient does not have a telephone

(MO780) Management of Oral Medications: <u>Patient's ability</u> to prepare and take <u>all</u> prescribed oral medications reliably and safely, including administration of the correct dosage at the appropriate times / intervals. <u>Excludes</u> injectable and IV medications. (NOTE: This refers to ability, not compliance or willingness.)

❏ 0 — Able to independently take the correct oral medication(s) and proper dosage(s) at the correct times.

❏ 1 — Able to take medication(s) at the correct time if:

    (a) individual dosages are prepared in advance by another person; <u>OR</u>

    ((b) given daily reminders; <u>OR</u>

    (c) someone develops a drug diary or chart

❏ 2 — <u>Unable</u> to take medication unless administered by someone else.

❏ NA — No oral medications prescribed.

(MO790) Management of Inhalant / Mist Medications: <u>Patient's ability</u> to prepare and take <u>all</u> prescribed inhalant / mist medications (nebulizers, metered dose devices) reliably and safely, including administration of the correct dosage at the appropriate times / intervals. <u>Excludes</u> all other forms of medication (oral tablets, injectable and IV medications).

❏ 0 — Able to independently take the correct medication and proper dosage at the correct times.

❏ 1 — Able to take medication at the correct times if:

    (a) individual dosages are prepared in advance by another person, <u>OR</u>

    (b) given daily reminders.

❏ 2 — <u>Unable</u> to take medication unless administered by someone else

❏ NA — No inhalant / mist medications prescribed.

(MO800) Management of injectable Medications: <u>Patient's ability</u> to prepare and take <u>all</u> prescribed injectable medications reliably and safely, including administration of correct dosage at the appropriate times / intervals. <u>Excludes</u> IV medications.

❏ 0 — Able to independently take the correct medication and proper dosage at the correct times.

❏ 1 — Able to take injectable medication at correct times if:

    (a) individual syringes are prepared in advance by another person, <u>OR</u>

    (b) given daily reminders.

❏ 2 — <u>Unable</u> to take injectable medications unless administered by someone else.

❏ NA — No injectable medications prescribed.

EQUIPMENT MANAGEMENT:

(MO810) Patient Management of Equipment (Includes <u>ONLY</u> oxygen, IV / infusion therapy, enteral / parenteral nutrition equipment or supplies): <u>Patient's ability</u> to set up, monitor and change equipment reliably and safely, add appropriate fluids or medication, clean / store / dispose of equipment or supplies using proper technique. **(NOTE: This refers to ability, not compliance or willingness.)**

❏ 0 — Patient manages all tasks related to equipment completely independently.

❏ 1 — If someone else sets up equipment (i.e. fills portable oxygen tank, provides patient with prepared solutions), patient is able to manage all other aspects of equipment.

❏ 2 — Patient requires considerable assistance from another person to manage equipment, but independently completes portions of the task.

❏ 3 — Patient is only able to monitor equipment (e.g., liter flow, fluid in bag) and must call someone else to manage the equipment.

❏ 4 — Patient is completely dependent on someone else to manage all equipment.

❏ NA — No equipment of this type used in care **[if NA, go to M0830.]**

(MO820) Caregiver Management of Equipment (Includes ONLY oxygen, IV/Infusion equipment, enteral / parenteral nutrition, ventilator therapy equipment or supplies): Caregivers ability to set up, monitor, and change equipment reliably and safely, add appropriate fluids or medication, clean / store / dispose of equipment or supplies using proper technique. **(NOTE: This refers to ability, not compliance or willingness.)**

- ❑ 0 — Caregiver manages all tasks related to equipment completely independently.
- ❑ 1 — If someone else sets up equipment, caregiver is able to manage all other aspects.
- ❑ 2 — Caregiver requires considerable assistance from another person to manage equipment, but independently completes significant portions of task.
- ❑ 3 — Caregiver is only able to complete small portions of task (e.g., administer nebulizer treatment, clean / store / dispose of equipment or supplies).
- ❑ 4 — Caregiver is completely dependent on someone else to manage all equipment.
- ❑ NA — No caregiver

EMERGENT CARE:

(MO830) Emergent Care: Since the last time OASIS data were collected, has the patient utilized any of the following services for emergent care (other than home care agency services)? **(Mark all that apply.)**

- ❑ 0 — No emergent care services. **[If No emergent care, STOP here]**
- ❑ 1 — Hospital emergency room (includes 23-hour holding)
- ❑ 2 — Doctor's office emergency visit/house call
- ❑ 3 — Outpatient department / clinic emergency (includes urgicenter sites)
- ❑ UK — Unknown **[If UK, STOP here]**

(MO840) Emergent Care Reason: For what reason(s) did the patient/family seek emergent care? **(Mark all that apply.)**

- ❑ 1 — Improper medication administration, medication side effects, toxicity, anaphylaxis
- ❑ 2 — Nausea, dehydration, malnutrition, constipation, impaction
- ❑ 3 — Injury caused by fall or accident at home
- ❑ 4 — Respiratory problems (e.g., shortness of breath, respiratory infection, tracheobronchial obstruction)
- ❑ 5 — Wound infection. deteriorating wound status, new lesion/ulcer
- ❑ 6 — Cardiac problems (e.g., fluid overload, exacerbation of CHF, chest pain)
- ❑ 7 — Hypo/Hyperglycemia. diabetes out of control
- ❑ 8 — GI bleeding, obstruction
- ❑ 9 — Other than above reasons
- ❑ UK — Reason unknown

Patient participated in reviewing plan of care: ❑ Yes   ❑ No

New problem / diagnosis added to care plan: ❑ Yes   ❑ No

Date of Assessment: _____   Signature of Assessor: _____

Copy of 60 Day Assessment sent to MD ❑

Appendix   **E**

SAMPLE ASSESSMENT FORM #2
DISCHARGE VERSION

DISCHARGE ASSESSMENT

DEMOGRAPHIC/GENERAL INFORMATION

(MO010) Agency Provider Number

(MO020) Patient ID Number

(MO030) Start of Care Date

— — — — — —
mm   dd   yy

(MO032) Resumption of Care Date

— — — — — —
mm   dd   yy

☐ NA – Not applicable

(MO040) Patient Name:

— —
(First)   (MI) (Last)   (Suffix)

Patient Phone (   ) _____ – _____

Street, Route, Apt.   County

(MO063) Medicare Number

— — — — — — — — — — — — ☐ NA – No Medicare
(including suffix if any)

City   **(MO050) State**   **(MO060) Zip**

(MO064) Social Security Number

— — — – — — – — — — — ☐ UK – Unknown or Not Available

(MO065) Medicaid number

— — — — — — — — — — — — ☐ No Medicaid

(MO066) Birthdate

— — – — — – — — — —
month   day   year

(MO069) Gender:

☐ 1 – Male

☐ 2 – Female

(MO072) Primary Referring Physician ID:

— — — — — — — — — —   ☐ UK – Unknown or Not Available

(MO080) Discipline of Person Completing Assessment:

☐ 1–RN   ☐ 2–PT   ☐ 3–SLP/ST   ☐ 4–OT

(MO090) Date Assessment Information Recorded:

— — – — — – — — — —
month   day   year

(MO100) This Assessment Is Currently Being Completed for the Following Reason:

Start/Resumption of Care

☐ 1 – Start of care—further visits planned

☐ 2 – Start of care—no further visits planned

☐ 3 – Resumption of care (after inpatient stay)

Follow-Up

☐ 4 – Recertification (follow-up) reassessment **(Go to MO150)**

☐ 5 – Other follow-up **(Go to MO150)**

Transfer to an Inpatient Facility

☐ 6 – Transferred to an inpatient facility—patient not discharged from agency **(Go to MO830)**

☐ 7 – Transferred to an inpatient facility—patient discharged from agency **(Go to MO830)**

Discharge from Agency - Not to an Inpatient Facility

☐ 8 – Death at home **(Go to MO906)**

☐ 9 – Discharge from agency **(Go to MO150)**

☐ 10 – Discharge from agency—no visits completed after start/resumption of care assessment **(Go to MO830)**

(MO150) Current Payment Sources for Home Care:
(Mark all that apply.)

☐ 0 – None; no charge for current services

☐ 1 – Medicare (traditional fee-for-service)

☐ 2 – Medicare (HMO/managed care)

☐ 3 – Medicaid (traditional fee-for-service)

☐ 4 – Medicaid (HMO/managed care)

☐ 5 – Worker's compensation

☐ 6 – Title programs (e.g., Title III, V, or XX)

☐ 7 – Other government (e.g., CHAMPUS, VA, etc.)

☐ 8 – Private insurance

☐ 9 – Private HMO/managed care

☐ 10 – Self-pay

☐ 11 – Other (specify) _____

☐ UK – Unknown

(MO200) Medical or Treatment Regimen Change Within Past 14 Days: Has this patient experienced a change in medical or treatment regimen (e.g., medication, treatment, or service change due to new or additional diagnosis, etc.) within the last 14 days?

❑ 0 — No *[If No, go to M0250]*
❑ 1 — Yes

(MO210) List the patient's **Medical Diagnose**s and three-digit ICD code categories <u>for those conditions requiring changed medical or treatment regimen</u> (no surgical or V-codes);

<u>Changed Medical Regimen Diagnosis</u>   <u>ICD</u>

a. _____   (___ ___ ___)

b. _____   (___ ___ ___)

c. _____   (___ ___ ___)

d. _____   (___ ___ ___)

(MO220) Conditions Prior to Medical or Treatment Regimen Change or Inpatient Stay Within Past 14 Days: If this patient experienced inpatient facility discharge or change in medical or treatment regimen within the past 14 days, indicate any conditions which existed <u>prior to</u> the inpatient stay or change in medical or treatment regimen. *(Mark all that apply).*

❑ 1 — Urinary incontinence
❑ 2 — Indwelling/suprapubic catheter
❑ 3 — Intractable pain
❑ 4 — Impaired decision-making
❑ 5 — Disruptive or socially inappropriate behavior
❑ 6 — Memory loss to the extent that supervision required
❑ 7 — None of the above
❑ NA — No inpatient facility discharge and no change in medical or treatment regimen in past 14 days
❑ UK — Unknown

(MO250) Therapies the patient receives <u>at home:</u> **(Mark all that apply.)**

❑ 1 — Intravenous or infusion therapy (excludes TPN)
❑ 2 — Parenteral nutrition (TPN or lipids)
❑ 3 — Enteral nutrition (nasogastric, gastrostomy, jejunostomy, or any other artificial entry into the alimentary canal)
❑ 4 — None of the above

(MO280) Life Expectancy: (Physician documentation is not required.)

❑ 0 — Life expectancy is greater than 6 months
❑ 1 — Life expectancy is 6 months or fewer

(MO290) High Risk Factors characterizing this patient: **(Mark all that apply.)**

❑ 1 — Heavy smoking
❑ 2 — Obesity
❑ 3 — Alcohol dependency
❑ 4 — Drug dependency
❑ 5 — None of the above
❑ UK

LIVING ARRANGEMENTS

(MO300) Current Residence:

❑ 1 — Patient's owned or rented residence (house, apartment, or mobile home owned or rented by patient/couple/significant other)
❑ 2 — Family member's residence
❑ 3 — Boarding home or rented room
❑ 4 — Board and care or assisted living facility
❑ 5 — Other (specify) _____

(MO310) Structural Barriers in the patient's environment limiting independent mobility: **(Mark all that apply.)**

❑ 0 — None
❑ 1 — Stairs inside home which must be used by the patient (e.g., to get to toileting, sleeping, eating areas.)
❑ 2 — Stairs inside home which are used optionally (e.g., to get to laundry facilities)
❑ 3 — Stairs leading from inside house to outside
❑ 4 — Narrow or obstructed doorways

(MO320) Safety Hazards found in the patient's current place of residence: **(Mark all that apply.)**

❑ 0 — None
❑ 1 — Inadequate floor, roof, or windows
❑ 2 — Inadequate lighting
❑ 3 — Unsafe gas/electric appliance
❑ 4 — Inadequate heating
❑ 5 — Inadequate cooling
❑ 6 — Lack of fire safety devices
❑ 7 — Unsafe floor coverings
❑ 8 — Inadequate stair railings
❑ 9 — Improperly stored hazardous materials
❑ 10 — Lead-based paint
❑ 11 — Other (specify) _____

(MO330) Sanitation Hazards found in the patient's current place of residence: **(Mark all that apply.)**

❑ 0 — None
❑ 1 — No running water
❑ 2 — Contaminated water
❑ 3 — No toileting facilities
❑ 4 — Outdoor toileting facilities only
❑ 5 — Inadequate sewage disposal
❑ 6 — Inadequate/improper food storage
❑ 7 — No food refrigeration
❑ 8 — No cooking facilities
❑ 9 — Insects / rodents present
❑ 10 — No scheduled trash pickup
❑ 11 — Cluttered / soiled living area
❑ 12 — Other (specify) _____

(MO340) Patient Lives With: (Mark all that apply.)

❑ 1 — Lives alone
❑ 2 — With spouse or significant other   Name: _____
❑ 3 — With other family member   Relationship: _____
❑ 4 — With a friend
❑ 5 — With paid help (other than home care agency staff)
❑ 6 — With other than above

SUPPORT SYSTEMS

(MO350) Assisting Person(s) Other Than Home Care Agency Staff: (Mark all that apply.)

❑ 1 — Relatives, friends, or neighbors living outside the home
❑ 2 — Person residing in the home (EXCLUDING paid help)
❑ 3 — Paid help
❑ 4 — None of the above **[If None of the above, go to Systems Review: Neurosensory]**
❑ UK — Unknown **[If unknown, go to Systems Review: Neurosensory]**

(MO360) Primary Caregiver taking **lead responsibility** for providing or managing the patient's care, providing the most frequent assistance, etc. (other than home care agency staff.)

❑ 0 — No one person **[If unknown, go to Systems Review: Neurosensory]**
❑ 1 — Spouse or significant other
❑ 2 — Daughter or son
❑ 3 — Other family member
❑ 4 — Friend or neighbor or community or church member
❑ 5 — Paid help
❑ UK — Unknown **[If unknown, go to Systems Review: Neurosensory]**

(MO370) How Often does the patient receive assistance from the primary caregiver?

❑ 1 — Several times during day and night
❑ 2 — Several times during day
❑ 3 — Once daily
❑ 4 — Three or more times per week
❑ 5 — One or two times per week
❑ 6 — Less often than weekly
❑ UK — Unknown

(MO380)Type of Primary Caregiver Assistance: (Mark all that apply.)

❑ 1 — ADL assistance (e.g., bathing, dressing, toileting, bowel/bladder, eating/feeding)
❑ 2 — IADL assistance (eg., meds, meals, housekeeping, laundry, telephone, shopping, finances)
❑ 3 — Environmental support (housing, home maintenance)
❑ 4 — Psychological support (socialization, companionship, recreation)
❑ 5 — Advocates or facilitates patient's participation in appropriate medical care
❑ 6 — Financial agent, power of attorney, or conservator of finance
❑ 7 — Health care agent, conservator of person, or medical power of attorney
❑ UK — Unknown

Client's Name:

Client Record No.

SYSTEMS REVIEW

NEUROSENSORY:

HEAD: Dizziness ❑   Headache ❑ (describe location, duration) _____

EYES: Glasses ❑   Blurred/double vision ❑   Glaucoma ❑
              Cataracts ❑   PERRL ❑   Other (specify) _____

EARS: Hearing Aid ❑   Tinnitus ❑   Other (specify) _____

(MO410) Speech and Oral (Verbal) Expression of Language (in patient's own language):

❑ 0 — Expresses complex ideas, feelings, and needs clearly, completely, and easily in all situations with no observable impairment.

❑ 1 — Minimal difficulty in expressing ideas and needs (may take extra time; makes occasional errors in word choice, grammar or speech intelligibility; needs minimal prompting or assistance).

❑ 2 — Expresses simple ideas or needs with moderate difficulty (needs prompting or assistance, errors in word choice, organization or speech intelligibility). Speaks in phrases or short sentences.

❑ 3 — Has severe difficulty expressing basic ideas or needs and requires maximal assistance or guessing by listener. Speech limited to single words or short phrases.

❑ 4 — Unable to express basic needs even with maximal prompting or assistance but is not comatose or unresponsive (e.g., speech is nonsensical or unintelligible.)

❑ 5 — Patient nonresponsive or unable to speak.

ADDITIONAL NEURO SIGNS:

❑ unequal grasp   ❑ vertigo   ❑ paralysis (where: _____)

❑ gait disturbance   ❑ syncope   ❑ frequent falls _____

❑ lack of coordination (balance) ❑ seizure   ❑ tremor

❑ numbness   ❑ L.O.C.   ❑ aphasia / inarticulate speech

Patient's Perceived Pain Level _____ (Scale 1-10)

(MO420) Frequency of pain interfering with patient's activity or movement:

❑ 0 — Patient has no pain or pain does not interfere with activity or movement
❑ 1 — Less often than daily
❑ 2 — Daily, but not constantly
❑ 3 — All of the time

(MO430) Intractable Pain: Is the patient experiencing pain that is not easily relieved, occurs at least daily, and affects the patient's sleep, appetite, physical or emotional energy, concentration, personal relationships, emotions, or ability or desire to perform physical activity?

❑ 0 — No
❑ 1 — Yes

INTEGUMENTARY:

(MO440) Does this patient have a **Skin Lesion** or an **Open Wound**? This excludes "OSTOMIES."

❑ 0 — No
❑ 1 — Yes

(MO445) Does this patient have a **Pressure Ulcer?**

❑ 0 — No **[If No, go to M0468]**
❑ 1 — Yes

(MO450) Current Number of Pressure Ulcers at Each Stage: (Circle one response for each stage.)

Pressure Ulcer Stages		Number of Pressure Ulcers				
a)	**Stage 1:** Nonblanchable erythema of intact skin: the heralding of skin ulceration. In darker-pigmented skin, warmth, edema, hardness, or discolored skin may be indicators.	0	1	2	3	4 or more
b)	**Stage 2:** Partial thickness skin loss involving epidermis and/or dermis. The ulcer is superficial and presents clinically as an abrasion, blister, or shallow crater.	0	1	2	3	4 or more
c)	**Stage 3:** Full-thickness skin loss involving damage or necrosis of subcutaneous tissue which may extend down to, but not through, underlying fascia. The ulcer presents clinically as a deep crater with or without undermining of adjacent tissue.	0	1	2	3	4 or more
d)	**Stage 4:** Full-thickness skin loss with extensive destruction, tissue necrosis, or damage to muscle, bone, or supporting structures (e.g., tendon, joint capsule, etc.)	0	1	2	3	4 or more
e)	In addition to the above, is there at least one pressure ulcer that cannot be observed due to the presence of eschar or a nonremovable dressing, including casts? ❑ 0 — No ❑ 1 — Yes					

(MO460) Stage of Most Problematic (Observable) Pressure Ulcer:

❑ 1 — Stage 1
❑ 2 — Stage 2
❑ 3 — Stage 3
❑ 4 — Stage 4
❑ NA — No observable pressure ulcer

(MO464) Status of Most Problematic (Observable) Pressure Ulcer:

❑ 1 — Fully granulating   ❑ 3 — Not Healing
❑ 2 — Early / partial granulation   ❑ NA — No observable pressure ulcer

PRESSURE SORE STATUS TOOL (BARBARA BATES-JENSEN)

ITEM	ASSESSMENT	DATE
		Score
1. Size	1 = Length x width < 4 sq. cm. 2 = Length x width 4 to 16 sq. cm. 3 = Length x width 16.1 to 36 sq. cm. 4 = Length x width 36.1 to 80 sq. cm. 5 = Length x width > 80 sq. cm.	
2. Depth	1 = Non-blanchable erythema of intact skin 2 = Partial-thickness skin loss involving epidermis &/or dermis 3 = Full-thickness skin loss involving damage or necrosis of subcutaneous tissue; may extend down to but not through underlying fascia: &/or mixed partial- or full-thickness &/or tissue layers obscured by granulation tissue. 4 = Obscured by necrosis 5 = Full-thickness skin loss with extensive destruction, tissue necrosis or damage to muscle, bone, or supporting structures	
3. Edges	1 = Indistinct, diffuse. none clearly visible 2 = Distinct, outline clearly visible, attached, even with wound base 3 = Well-defined. not attached to wound base 4 = Well-defined. not attached to base, rolled under, thickened 5 = Well-defined. fibrotic, scarred, or hyperkeratotic	
4. Under-mining	1 = Undermining < 2 cm. in any area 2 = Undermining 2 to 4 cm. involving < 50% wound margins 3 = Undermining 2 to 4 cm. involving > 50% wound margins 4 = Undermining > 4 cm. in any area 5 = Tunneling &/or sinus tract formation	
5. Necrotic Tissue Type	1 = None visible 2 = White/gray non-viable tissue &/or non-adherent yellow slough 3 = Loosely adherent yellow slough 4 = Adherent, soft black eschar 5 = Firmly adherent. hard black eschar	
6. Necrotic Tissue Amount	1 = None visible 2 = < 25% of wound bed covered 3 = 25% to 50% of wound covered 4 = > 50% and < 75% of wound covered 5 = 75% to 100% of wound covered	

ITEM	ASSESSMENT	DATE
		Score
7. Exudate Type	1 = None or bloody 2 = Serosanguineous: thin, watery, pale red/pink 3 = Serous: thin, watery, clear 4 = Purulent: thin or thick, opaque, tan/yellow 5 = Foul purulent: thick, opaque, yellow/green with odor	
8. Exudate Amount	1 = None 2 = Scant 3 = Small 4 = Moderate 5 = Large	
9. Skin Color Surrounding Wound	1 = Pink or normal for ethnic group 2 = Bright red &/or blanches to touch 3 = White or gray pallor or hypopigmented 4 = Dark red or purple &/or non-blanchable 5 = Black or hyperpigmented	
10. Peripheral Tissue Edema	1 = Minimal firmness around wound 2 = Non-pitting edema extends < 4 cm. around wound 3 = Non-pitting edema extends ≥ 4 cm. around wound 4 = Pitting edema extends < 4 cm. around wound 5 = Crepitus &/or pitting edema extends ≥ 4 cm.	
11. Peripheral Tissue Induration	1 = Minimal firmness around wound 2 = Induration < 2 cm. around wound 3 = Induration 2 to 4 cm. extending < 50% around wound 4 = Induration 2 to 4 cm. extending ≥ 50% around wound 5 = Induration > 4 cm. in any area	
12. Granulation Tissue	1 = Skin intact or partial-thickness wound 2 = Bright. beefy red: 75% to 100% of wound filled &/or tissue overgrowth 3 = Bright. beefy red, < 75% & > 25% of wound filled 4 = Pink. &/ or dull, dusky red &/or fills ≤ 25% wound 5 = No granulation tissue present	
13. Epithelializ-ation	1 = 100% of wound covered. surface intact 2 = 75% to < 100% of wound covered &/or epithelial tissue extends > 0.5 cm. into wound bed 3 = 50% to < 75% of wound covered &/or epithelial tissue extends to < 0.5 cm. into wound bed 4 = 25% to < 50% of wound covered 5 = < 25% of wound covered	

TOTAL SCORE:

PRESSURE STATUS CONTINUUM

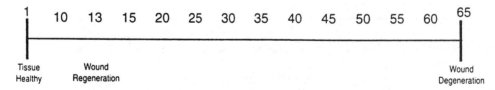

1   10   13   15   20   25   30   35   40   45   50   55   60   65

Tissue Healthy   Wound Regeneration   Wound Degeneration

Plot the total score on the Pressure Sore Status Continuum by putting an "X" on the line and the date beneath the line.

Used with permission.

(MO468) Does this patient have a Stasis Ulcer?

❏ 0 — No [If No, go to MO482]

❏ 1 —Yes

(MO470) Current Number of Observable Stasis Ulcer(s):

❑ 0 — Zero

❑ 1 — One

❑ 2 — Two

❑ 3 — Three

❑ 4 — Four or more

(MO474) Does this patient have at least one Stasis Ulcer that Cannot Be Observed due to the presence of a nonremovable dressing?

❑ 0 — No

❑ 1 — Yes

(MO476) Status of Most Problematic (Observable) Stasis Ulcer:

❑ 1 — Fully granulating

❑ 2 — Early/partial granulation

❑ 3 — Not healing

❑ NA — No observable stasis ulcer

Protocol for Care

VENOUS LEG ULCER ASSESSMENT   Venous   Arterial

Patient Name _____ Age: _____ Date: _____

I. Medical History:

☐ Severe leg trauma (Date: _____)   ☐ Obesity
☐ Blood clot [DVT] (Date: _____)   ☐ Frequent leg swelling
☐ Heart disease/Congestive heart failure   ☐ Pregnancy
☐ Family history of leg ulcers

☐ Heart disease/Heart attack   ☐ Diabetes: ☐ Type I ☐ Type II
☐ Stroke

☐ Recurrent leg ulcers   Immune status: ☐ Good ☐ Compromised

II. Pertinent Surgeries:

☐ Vein surgery (Date: _____)

☐ Cardiac bypass (Date: _____)   ☐ Neck/Carotid artery (Date: _____)

☐ Skin graft (Date: _____)

III. Social Assessment:

Occupation: _____

Hobbies/Activities: _____

Approximate hours per day spent: Standing: _____ hrs.   Sitting: _____ hrs.

Is someone available at home to assist with treatments?   ☐ Yes (_____) ☐ No

IV. Allergies: (Include previous reactions to topical treatments):

_____

V. Ankle/Brachial Index _____

VI. Physical Examination	Left Leg		Right Leg	
Ulcer Location:	☐ Medial lower leg and/or ankle	☐ Foot and/or lateral ankle	☐ Medial lower leg and/or ankle	☐ Foot and/or lateral ankle
Edema:	☐ Present	☐ Absent	☐ Present	☐ Absent
Dorsalis Pedis Pulse: • Palpation • Doppler	☐ Present ☐ Present	☐ Absent ☐ Absent	☐ Present ☐ Present	☐ Absent ☐ Absent
Posterior Tibial Pulse: • Palpation • Doppler	☐ Present ☐ Present	☐ Absent ☐ Absent	☐ Present ☐ Present	☐ Absent ☐ Absent
Pain:	☐ Absent ☐ Decreased w/elevation	☐ Constant ☐ Increased w/elevation	☐ Absent ☐ Decreased w/elevation	☐ Constant ☐ Decreased w/elevation
Ulcer Appearance: • Ulcer Borders • Exudate • Wound Depth • Wound Base	☐ Irregular ☐ Present ☐ Shallow ☐ Ruddy & granular ☐ Yellow fibrous tissue	☐ Even/smooth ☐ Absent ☐ Deep ☐ Pale & dry ☐ Thick black eschar	☐ Irregular ☐ Present ☐ Shallow ☐ Ruddy & granular ☐ Yellow fibrous tissue	☐ Even/smooth ☐ Absent ☐ Deep ☐ Pale & dry ☐ Thick black eschar
• Peri-wound Skin	☐ Dilated veins ☐ Dermatitis (Dry/ scaly or weeping) ☐ Indurated/ hardened ☐ Hyperpigmented	☐ Thin & shiny ☐ Hair loss ☐ Cool to touch ☐ Pallor on elevation	☐ Dilated veins ☐ Dermatitis (Dry/ scaly or weeping) ☐ Indurated/ hardened ☐ Hyperpigmented	☐ Thin & shiny ☐ Hair loss ☐ Cool to touch ☐ Pallor on elevation

(MO482) Does this patient have a Surgical Wound?

❑ 0 — No **[If No, go to Integumentary Status Assessment Tool]**
❑ 1 — Yes

(MO484) Current Number of (Observable) Surgical Wounds: (If a wound is partially closed but has <u>more</u> than one opening, consider each opening as a separate wound.)

❑ 0 — Zero
❑ 1 — One
❑ 2 — Two
❑ 3 — Three
❑ 4 — Four or more

(MO486) Does this patient have at least one Surgical Wound that Cannot be Observed due to the presence of a nonremovable dressing?

❑ 0 — No
❑ 1 — Yes

(MO488) Status of Most Problematic (Observable) Surgical Wound:

❑ 1 — Fully granulating
❑ 2 — Early / partial granulation
❑ 3 — Not healing
❑ NA — No observable surgical wound

INTEGUMENTARY STATUS ASSESSMENT TOOL

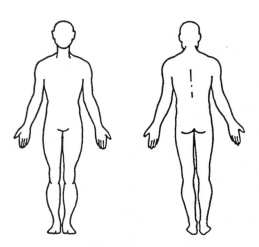

Indicate location of integumentary problem on figure above

* Please indicate size & depth as applicable

<u>Type</u>	Yes	No
* 1. Lesions, Rashes	❑	❑
* 2. Bruises	❑	❑
* 3. Masses	❑	❑
* 4. Scars	❑	❑
* 5. Stasis Ulcers	❑	❑
* 6. Pressure Ulcers	❑	❑
* 7. Incisions	❑	❑
8. Excessive dryness, pruritus	❑	❑
* 9. Areas of excoriation, redness, trauma	❑	❑
10. Temperature changes in skin (coolness, warmth)	❑	❑
11. Changes in hair distribution	❑	❑
12. Nails: ridges, thickening, color bands, texture changes	❑	❑
* Past skin diseases (eczema, etc.)	❑	❑
* Healing time increased	❑	❑
* Chronic long-term sun exposure	❑	❑
* Recent changes in a wart or mole	❑	❑
* Turgor: good, fair, poor (circle)	❑	❑

COMMENTS: *(If it is noted above, comment please.)* _____
_____
_____
_____

MUSCULOSKELETAL:

☐ Hx. arthritis   ☐ leg cramps   ☐ Hx. of osteoporosis   ☐ Kyphosis

☐ gout   ☐ deformities   ☐ Hx. of fractures   ☐ Scoliosis

☐ stiffness   ☐ amputation   ☐ R.O.M.   ☐ Lordosis

☐ swollen joints / joint pain   ☐ prostheses   Active: _____

☐ weakness   ☐ appliances   Passive: _____

☐ muscle cramps / spasms   ☐ other_____   ☐ Crepitus

Comments:

CARDIOPULMONARY:

Temperature _____   Method Taken: O   A   R

PULSE: Apical Rate _____   Radial Rate _____

Rhythm _____   Quality _____

Respirations _____

BLOOD PRESSURE: Lying _____   Sitting _____

Standing _____   L.A. _____   R.A. _____

CARDIOVASCULAR:

☐ Palpitations   ☐ Paroxysmal nocturnal dyspnea   ☐ "Heart" problems   ☐ Murmurs, bruits

☐ Claudication   ☐ Orthopnea (# of pillows _____)   (specify) _____   ☐ Edema ____ (O to +4

☐ Fatigues easily   ☐ Bradycardia, tachycardia, arrythmias   ☐ Other (specify) _____   ☐ Cyanosis

☐ Pacemaker Date of   ☐ "BP Problems", hypertension, hypotension   ☐ Peripheral vascular complaints: ☐ Varicosities
                                                                      Coldness, pain sensation,
last battery change _____   ☐ Chest pain, pressure, tightness   exaggerated response to cold   ☐ Homan's sign

☐ Angina   ☐ Neck vein distention   ☐ Calf tenderness

☐ Dyspnea on exertion

COMMENTS:

RESPIRATORY:

Condition at Discharge:

❑ Cough *(describe)* _____   ❑ Sputum *(character & amount)* _____

❑ SOB   ❑ Tachypnea   ❑ Dyspnea   ❑ Cheyne-Stokes   ❑ Kussmaul

❑ Symmetry of chest configuration: (normal, barrel chest, pigeon chest, funnel chest) _____

❑ Breath Sounds *(describe)* _____

❑ Tracheostomy   ❑ Other *(specify)* _____

(MO490) When is the patient dyspneic or noticeably **Short of Breath?**

❑ 0 — Never, patient is not short of breath

❑ 1 — When walking more than 20 feet, climbing stairs

❑ 2 — With moderate exertion (e.g., while dressing, using commode or bedpan, walking distances less than 20 feet)

❑ 3 — With minimal exertion (e.g., while eating, talking, or performing other ADLs) or with agitation

❑ 4 — At rest (during day or night)

(MO500) Respiratory Treatments utilized at home: **(Mark all that apply.)**

❑ 1 — Oxygen (intermittent or continuous)

❑ 2 — Ventilator (continually or at night)

❑ 3 — Continuous positive airway pressure

❑ 4 — None of the above

COMMENTS:

GENITOURINARY

❑ Frequency   ❑ Nocturia   ❑ dribbling

❑ Pain   ❑ Urgency   ❑ anuria

❑ Hematuria   ❑ Prostate disorder   ❑ dialysis _____ times per week _____

❑ Stress incontinence   ❑ Other (specify) _____

(MO510) Has this patient been treated for a Urinary Tract Infection in the past 14 days?

❑ 0 — No

❑ 1 — Yes

❑ NA — Patient on prophylactic treatment

❑ UK — Unknown

(MO520) Urinary Incontinence or Urinary Catheter Presence:

❑ 0 — No incontinence or catheter (includes anuria or ostomy for urinary drainage) **[If no, go to Gastrointestinal]**

❑ 1 — Patient is incontinent

❑ 2 — Patient requires a urinary catheter (i.e. external, indwelling, intermittent, suprapubic) **[Go to Gastrointestinal]**

(M0530) When does Urinary Incontinence occur?

❑ 0 — Timed-voiding defers incontinence

❑ 1 — During the night only

❑ 2 — During the day and night

Client's Name:

Client Record No.

GASTROINTESTINAL

❑ Indigestion, heartburn   ❑ Hernias (where)_____   ❑ Hemorrhoids   ❑ Other (specify): _____

❑ Nausea, vomiting   ❑ Diarrhea/constipation   ❑ Gallbladder problems   _____

❑ Ulcers   ❑ Recent Δ in bowel habits   ❑ Jaundice   _____

❑ Flatulence, eructation   ❑ Ascites   ❑ Tenderness/distention   ❑ Date of last BM _____

❑ Pain   ❑ Rectal bleeding   ❑ Diverticulitis

(MO540) Bowel Incontinence Frequency:

❑ 0 — Very rarely or never has bowel incontinence

❑ 1 — Less than once weekly

❑ 2 — One to three times weekly

❑ 3 — Four to six times weekly

❑ 4 — On a daily basis

❑ 5 — More often than once daily

❑ NA — Patient has ostomy for bowel elimination

❑ UK — Unknown

(MO550) Ostomy for Bowel Elimination: Does this patient have an ostomy for bowel elimination that necessitated a change in medical or treatment regimen?

❑ 0 — Patient does not have an ostomy for bowel elimination.

❑ 1 — Patient's ostomy did not necessitate change in medical or treatment regimen.

❑ 2 — The ostomy did necessitate change in medical or treatment regimen.

NUTRITIONAL STATUS:

❑ Dysphagia

❑ Anorexia

Diet Order _____

Supplements _____

Typical 24˙ fluid intake _____

Appetite For Meals (%) _____

Weight_____   ❑ actual ❑ reported

Patient appears: ❑ normal weight   ❑ under weight   ❑ slightly under weight   ❑ overweight

Feeding ability: ❑ self   ❑ assisted   ❑ spoon   ❑ syringe ❑ tube

Usually dines alone: ❑ Yes   ❑ No

Nutrition Consult: _____

COMMENTS:

REPRODUCTIVE

❑ dysmenorrhea   ❑ gravida/para   ❑ vag discharge/bleeding

❑ hx hysterectomy   Date of last pap _____   ❑ hx BPH

❑ hx of abnormal pap   Date of last mammogram _____   ❑ penile discharge

BREASTS (Both male and female)

❑ Lumps   ❑ Tenderness   ❑ Symmetry   ❑ Dimpling   ❑ Discharge   ❑ Other (specify) _____

Hx of breast lump(s) _____

Comments _____

ENDOCRINE AND HEMATOPOIETIC:

❑ Polyuria   ❑ Polydipsia   Coumadin: _____   Heparin: _____

❑ IDDM   ❑ NIDDM   Pallor: _____

Hx hyperthyroidism: _____   Excessive Bleeding or Bruising: _____

Hx hypothyroidism: _____   Hx Leukemia: _____   Type: _____

Current laboratory orders: _____   Hx Thrombocytopenia: _____   Hx Sickle Cell: _____

_____   Pernicious Anemia: _____   Polycythemia: _____

_____   ❑ Intolerance to heat and cold   ❑ Enlarged lymph nodes

❑ Family hx of endocrine/hematopoietic disorders

❑ Other (specify) _____

EMOTIONAL / BEHAVIORAL

❑ Hx of previous psych. illness   ❑ Mania

❑ Memory loss-short term / long-term   ❑ Poor judgement / impaired judgement

❑ Disorientation time / place / person   ❑ Hallucination / delusions

❑ Depression

❑ Labile moods   ❑ Other (specify) _____

(MO560) Cognitive Functioning: (Patient's current level of alertness, orientation, comprehension, concentration, and immediate memory for simple commands).

❑ 0 — Alert / oriented, able to focus and shift attention, comprehends and recalls task directions independently.

❑ 1 — Requires prompting (cuing, repetition, reminders) only under stressful or unfamiliar conditions.

❑ 2 — Requires assistance and some direction in specific situations (e.g. on all tasks involving shifting of attention), or consistently requires low stimulus environment due to distractibility.

❑ 3 — Requires considerable assistance in routine situations. Is not alert and oriented or is unable to shift attention and recall directions more than half the time.

❑ 4 — Totally dependent due to disturbances such as constant disorientation, coma, persistent vegetative state, or delirium.

(M0570) When Confused (Reported or Observed):

❏ 0 — Never

❏ 1 — In new or complex situations only

❏ 2 — On awakening or at night only

❏ 3 — During the day and evening, but not constantly

❏ 4 — Constantly

❏ NA — Patient nonresponsive

(M0580) When Anxious (Reported or Observed):

❏ 0 — None of the time

❏ 1 — Less often than daily

❏ 2 — Daily, but not constantly

❏ 3 — All of the time

❏ NA — Patient nonresponsive

(M0590) Depressive Feelings Reported or Observed in Patient: (Mark all that apply.)

❏ 1 — Depressed mood (e.g. feeling sad, tearful)

❏ 2 — Sense of failure or self reproach

❏ 3 — Hopelessness

❏ 4 — Recurrent thoughts of death

❏ 5 — Thoughts of suicide

❏ 6 — None of the above feelings observed or reported

(MO600) Patient Behaviors (Reported or Observed): (Mark all that apply.)

❏ 1 — Indecisiveness, lack of concentration
❏ 2 — Diminished interest in most activities
❏ 3 — Sleep disturbances
❏ 4 — Recent change in appetite or weight
❏ 5 — Agitation
❏ 6 — A suicide attempt
❏ 7 — None of the above behaviors observed or reported

(MO610) Behaviors <u>Demonstrated at Least Once A Week</u> (Reported or Observed): (Mark all that apply.)

❏ 1 — Memory deficit: failure to recognize familiar persons/places, inability to recall events of past 24 hours, significant memory loss so that supervision is required.
❏ 2 — Impaired decision-making: failure to perform usual ADLs or IADLs, inability to appropriately stop activities, jeopardizes safety through actions
❏ 3 — Verbal disruption: yelling, threatening, excessive profanity, sexual references, etc.
❏ 4 — Physical aggression: aggressive or combative to self and others (e.g., hits self, throws objects, punches, dangerous maneuvers with wheelchair or other objects)
❏ 5 — Disruptive, infantile, or socially inappropriate behavior (excludes verbal actions)
❏ 6 — Delusional, hallucinatory, or paranoid behavior
❏ 7 — None of the above behaviors demonstrated

(MO620) Frequency of Behavior Problems (Reported or Observed) (e.g. wandering episodes, self abuse, verbal disruption, physical aggression, etc.):

☐ 0 — Never
☐ 1 — Less than once a month
☐ 2 — Once a month
☐ 3 — Several times each month
☐ 4 — Several times a week
☐ 5 — At least daily

(MO630) Is this patient receiving **Psychiatric Nursing Services** at home provided by a qualified psychiatric nurse?

☐ 0 — No
☐ 1 — Yes

ADL/IADLs

— RECORD WHAT THE PATIENT IS ABLE TO DO —

(MO640) Grooming: Ability to tend to personal hygiene needs (i.e., washing face and hands, hair care, shaving or make up, teeth or denture care, fingernail care).

☐ 0 — Able to groom self unaided, with or without the use of assistive devices or adapted methods.

☐ 1 — Grooming utensils must be placed within reach before able to complete grooming activities.

☐ 2 — Someone must assist the patient to groom self.

☐ 3 — Patient depends entirely upon someone else for grooming needs.

(MO650) Ability to Dress Upper Body (with or without dressing aids) including undergarments, pullovers, front-opening shirts and blouses, managing zippers, buttons, and snaps:

☐ 0 — Able to get clothes out of closets and drawers, put them on and remove them from the upper body without assistance

☐ 1 — Able to dress upper body without assistance if clothing is laid out or handed to the patient.

☐ 2 — Someone must help the patient put on upper body clothing

☐ 3 — Patient depends entirely upon another person to dress the upper body.

(MO660) Ability to Dress Lower Body (with or without dressing aids) including undergarments, slacks, socks or nylons, shoes:

☐ 0 — Able to obtain, put on, and remove clothing and shoes without assistance.

☐ 1 — Able to dress lower body without assistance if clothing and shoes are laid out or handed to the patient.

☐ 2 — Someone must help the patient put on undergarments, slacks, socks or nylons, and shoes.

☐ 3 — Patient depends entirely upon another person to dress lower body.

(MO670) Bathing: Ability to wash entire body. <u>Excludes</u> grooming (washing face and hands only):

☐ 0 — Able to bathe self in <u>shower or tub</u> independently.

☐ 1 — With the use of devices, is able to bathe self in shower or tub independently.

☐ 2 — Able to bathe in shower or tub with the assistance of another person:
   (a) for intermittent supervision or encouragement or reminders, <u>OR</u>
   (b) to get in and out of the shower or tub, <u>OR,</u>
   (c) for washing difficult to reach areas

☐ 3 — Participates in bathing self in shower or tub, <u>but</u> requires presence of another person throughout the bath for assistance or supervision.

☐ 4 — <u>Unable</u> to use the shower or tub and is bathed in <u>bed or bedside chair</u>.

☐ 5 — Unable to effectively participate in bathing and is totally bathed by another person.

(MO680) Toileting: Ability to get to and from the toilet or bedside commode.

☐ 0 — Able to get to and from the toilet independently with or without a device.

☐ 1 — When reminded, assisted, or supervised by another person, able to get to and from the toilet

☐ 2 — <u>Unable</u> to get to and from the toilet but is able to use a bedside commode (with or without assistance)

☐ 3 — <u>Unable</u> to get to and from the toilet or bedside commode but is able to use a bedpan/urinal independently.

☐ 4 — Is totally dependent in toileting.

(MO690) Transferring: Ability to move from bed to chair, on and off toilet or commode, into and out of tub or shower, and ability to turn and position self in bed if patient is bedfast.

☐ 0 — Able to independently transfer

☐ 1 — Transfers with minimal human assistance or with use of an assistive device.

☐ 2 — <u>Unable </u>to transfer self but is able to bear weight and pivot during the transfer process.

☐ 3 — Unable to transfer self and is <u>unable</u> to bear weight or pivot when transferred by another person.

☐ 4 — Bedfast, unable to transfer but is able to turn and position self in bed.

☐ 5 — Bedfast, unable to transfer but is <u>unable</u> to turn and position self.

(MO700) Ambulation / Locomotion: Ability to <u>SAFELY</u> walk, once in a standing position, or use a wheelchair, once in a seated position, on a variety of surfaces.

☐ 0 — Able to independently walk on even and uneven surfaces and climb stairs with or without railings (i.e., needs no human assistance or assistive device).

☐ 1 — Requires use of a device (e.g., cane, walker) to walk alone <u>or</u> requires human supervision or assistance to negotiate stairs or steps or uneven surfaces

☐ 2 — Able to walk only with the supervision or assistance of another person at all times.

☐ 3 — Chairfast, <u>unable</u> to ambulate but is able to wheel self independently.

☐ 4 — Chairfast, unable to ambulate and is <u>unable</u> to wheel self.

☐ 5— Bedfast, unable to ambulate or be up in a chair.

(MO710) Feeding or Eating: Ability to feed self meals and snacks. This refers only to the process of <u>eating</u>, <u>chewing</u>, and <u>swallowing</u>, <u>not preparing</u> the food to be eaten.

☐ 0 — Able to independently feed self.

☐ 1 — Able to feed self independently but requires:
   (a) meal set-up; <u>OR</u>
   (b) intermittent assistance or supervision from another person; <u>OR</u>
   (c) a liquid, pureed or ground meat diet.

☐ 2 — <u>Unable</u> to feed self and must be assisted or supervised throughout the meal/snack.

☐ 3 — Able to take in nutrients orally <u>and</u> receives supplemental nutrients through a nasogastric tube or gastrostomy.

☐ 4 — <u>Unable</u> to take in nutrients orally and is fed nutrients through a nasogastric tube or gastrostomy.

☐ 5 — Unable to take in nutrients orally or by tube feeding.

(MO720) Planning and Preparing Light Meal: (e.g., cereal, sandwich) or reheat delivered meals.

❑ 0 — (a) Able to independently plan and prepare all light meals for self or reheat delivered meals;
    <u>OR</u>
    (b) Is physically, cognitively, and mentally able to prepare light meals on a regular basis but has not
    routinely performed light meal preparation in the past (i.e., prior to this home care admission).

❑ 1 — <u>Unable</u> to prepare light meals on a regular basis due to physical, cognitive, or mental limitations.

❑ 2 — Unable to prepare any light meals or reheat any delivered meals.

(MO730) Transportation: Physical and mental ability to safely use a car, taxi, or public transportation (bus, train, subway).

❑ 0 — Able to independently drive a regular or adapted car; OR use a regular or handicap-accessible public bus.

❑ 1 — Able to ride in a car only when driven by another person; OR able to use a bus or handicap van only when
    assisted or accompanied by another person.

❑ 2 — <u>Unable</u> to ride in a car, taxi, bus, or van, and requires transportation by ambulance.

(MO740) Laundry: Ability to do own laundry — to carry laundry to and from washing machine, to use washer and dryer, to wash small items by hand.

❑ 0 — (a) Able to independently take care of all laundry tasks; <u>OR</u>
    (b) Physically, cognitively, and mentally able to do laundry and access facilities, <u>but</u> has not
    routinely performed laundry tasks in the past (i.e., prior to this home care admission).

❑ 1 — Able to do only light laundry, such as minor hand wash or light washer loads. Due to physical, cognitive, or
    mental limitations, needs assistance with heavy laundry such as carrying large loads of laundry.

❑ 2— <u>Unable</u> to do any laundry due to physical limitation or needs continual supervision and assistance due to
    cognitive or mental limitation.

(MO750) Housekeeping: Ability to safely and effectively perform light housekeeping and heavier cleaning tasks.

❑ 0 — (a) Able to independently perform all housekeeping tasks: <u>OR</u>
    (b) Physically, cognitively, and mentally able to perform <u>all</u> housekeeping tasks but has not routinely participated in
    housekeeping tasks in the past (i.e., prior to this home care admission).

❑ 1 — Able to perform only <u>light</u> housekeeping (e.g., dusting, wiping kitchen counters) tasks independently.

❑ 2 — Able to perform housekeeping tasks with intermittent assistance or supervision from another person.

❑ 3 — <u>Unable</u> to consistently perform any housekeeping tasks unless assisted by another person throughout the process.

❑ 4 — Unable to effectively participate in any housekeeping tasks.

(MO760) Shopping: Ability to plan for, select, and purchase items in a store and to carry them home or arrange delivery.

❑ 0 — (a) Able to plan for shopping needs and independently perform shopping tasks, including carrying packages; <u>OR</u>
    (b) Physically, cognitively, and mentally able to take care of shopping, but has not done shopping in the
    past (i.e., prior this home care admission).

❑ 1 — Able to go shopping, but needs some assistance:
    (a) By self is able to do only light shopping and carry small packages, but needs someone to do occasional major shopping; <u>OR</u>
    (b) <u>Unable</u> to go shopping alone, but can go with someone to assist.

❑ 2 — <u>Unable</u> to go shopping, but is able to identify items needed, place orders, and arrange home delivery.

❑ 3 — Needs someone to do all shopping and errands.

(MO770) Ability to Use Telephone: Ability to answer the phone, dial numbers, and <u>effectively</u> use the telephone to communicate.

❑ 0 — Able to dial numbers and answer calls appropriately and as desired.

❑ 1 — Able to use a specially adapted telephone (i.e., large numbers on the dial, teletype phone for the deaf) and
    call essential numbers.

❑ 2 — Able to answer the telephone and carry on a normal conversation but has difficulty with placing calls.

❑ 3 — Able to answer the telephone only some of the time or is able to carry on only a limited conversation.

❑ 4— <u>Unable</u> to answer the telephone at all but can listen if assisted with equipment.

❑ 5— Totally unable to use the telephone.

❑ NA— Patient does not have a telephone

(MO780) Management of Oral Medications: <u>Patient's ability</u> to prepare and take <u>all</u> prescribed oral medications reliably and safely, including administration of the correct dosage at the appropriate times / intervals. <u>Excludes</u> injectable and IV medications. (NOTE: This refers to ability, not compliance or willingness.)

❑ 0 —   Able to independently take the correct oral medication(s) and proper dosage(s) at the correct times.

❑ 1 —   Able to take medication(s) at the correct time if:

    (a) individual dosages are prepared in advance by another person; <u>OR</u>

    ((b) given daily reminders; <u>OR</u>

    (c) someone develops a drug diary or chart

❑ 2 —   <u>Unable</u> to take medication unless administered by someone else.

❑ NA — No oral medications prescribed.

(MO790) Management of Inhalant / Mist Medications: <u>Patient's ability</u> to prepare and take <u>all</u> prescribed inhalant / mist medications (nebulizers, metered dose devices) reliably and safely, including administration of the correct dosage at the appropriate times / intervals. <u>Excludes</u> all other forms of medication (oral tablets, injectable and IV medications).

❑ 0 —   Able to independently take the correct medication and proper dosage at the correct times.

❑ 1 —   Able to take medication at the correct times if:

    (a) individual dosages are prepared in advance by another person, <u>OR</u>

    (b) given daily reminders.

❑ 2 —   <u>Unable</u> to take medication unless administered by someone else

❑ NA —   No inhalant / mist medications prescribed.

(MO800) Management of injectable Medications: <u>Patient's ability</u> to prepare and take <u>all</u> prescribed injectable medications reliably and safely, including administration of correct dosage at the appropriate times / intervals. <u>Excludes</u> IV medications.

❑ 0 —   Able to independently take the correct medication and proper dosage at the correct times.

❑ 1 —   Able to take injectable medication at correct times if:

    (a) individual syringes are prepared in advance by another person, <u>OR</u>

    (b) given daily reminders.

❑ 2 —   <u>Unable</u> to take injectable medications unless administered by someone else.

❑ NA — No injectable medications prescribed.

EQUIPMENT MANAGEMENT:

(MO810) Patient Management of Equipment (Includes ONLY oxygen, IV / infusion therapy, enteral / parenteral nutrition equipment or supplies): <u>Patient's ability</u> to set up, monitor and change equipment reliably and safely, add appropriate fluids or medication, clean / store / dispose of equipment or supplies using proper technique. (NOTE: **This refers to ability, not compliance or willingness.**)

❑ 0 — Patient manages all tasks related to equipment completely independently.

❑ 1 — If someone else sets up equipment (i.e. fills portable oxygen tank, provides patient with prepared solutions), patient is able to manage all other aspects of equipment.

❑ 2 — Patient requires considerable assistance from another person to manage equipment, but independently completes portions of the task.

❑ 3 — Patient is only able to monitor equipment (e.g., liter flow, fluid in bag) and must call someone else to manage the equipment.

❑ 4 — Patient is completely dependent on someone else to manage all equipment.

❑ NA — No equipment of this type used in care **[if NA, go to M0830.]**

(MO820) Caregiver Management of Equipment (Includes ONLY oxygen, IV/Infusion equipment, enteral / parenteral nutrition, ventilator therapy equipment or supplies): Caregivers ability to set up, monitor, and change equipment reliably and safely, add appropriate fluids or medication, clean / store / dispose of equipment or supplies using proper technique. **(NOTE: This refers to ability, not compliance or willingness.)**

☐   0 — Caregiver manages all tasks related to equipment completely independently.

☐   1 — If someone else sets up equipment, caregiver is able to manage all other aspects.

☐   2 — Caregiver requires considerable assistance from another person to manage equipment, but independently completes significant portions of task.

☐   3 — Caregiver is only able to complete small portions of task (e.g., administer nebulizer treatment, clean / store / dispose of equipment or supplies).

☐   4 — Caregiver is completely dependent on someone else to manage all equipment.

☐ NA — No caregiver

EMERGENT CARE:

(MO830) Emergent Care: Since the last time OASIS data were collected, has the patient utilized any of the following services for emergent care (other than home care agency services)? **(Mark all that apply.)**

☐   0 — No emergent care services. **[If No emergent care and patient discharged, go to M0855]**

☐   1 — Hospital emergency room (includes 23-hour holding)

☐   2 — Doctor's office emergency visit/house call

☐   3 — Outpatient department / clinic emergency (includes urgicenter sites)

☐ UK — Unknown **[If UK, go to M0855]**

(MO840) Emergent Care Reason: For what reason(s) did the patient/family seek emergent care? **(Mark all that apply.)**

☐   1 — Improper medication administration, medication side effects, toxicity, anaphylaxis

☐   2 — Nausea, dehydration, malnutrition, constipation, impaction

☐   3 — Injury caused by fall or accident at home

☐   4 — Respiratory problems (e.g., shortness of breath, respiratory infection, tracheobronchial obstruction)

☐   5 — Wound infection, deteriorating wound status, new lesion/ulcer

☐   6 — Cardiac problems (e.g., fluid overload, exacerbation of CHF, chest pain)

☐   7 — Hypo/Hyperglycemia, diabetes out of control

☐   8 — GI bleeding, obstruction

☐   9 — Other than above reasons

☐ UK — Reason unknown

DATA ITEMS COLLECTED AT INPATIENT FACILITY ADMISSION OR DISCHARGE ONLY

(MO855) To which **Inpatient Facility** has the patient been admitted?

☐   1 — Hospital **[Go to M0890]**

☐   2 — Rehabilitation facility **[Go to M0903]**

☐   3 — Nursing home **[Go to M0900]**

☐   4 — Hospice **[Go to M0903]**

☐ NA — No inpatient facility admission

(MO870) Discharge Disposition: Where is the patient after discharge from your agency? **(Choose only one answer.)**

☐   1 — Patient remained in the community (not in hospital, nursing home, or rehab facility)

☐   2 — Patient transferred to a noninstitutional hospice **[Go to M0903]**

☐   3 — Unknown because patient moved to a geographic location not served by this agency **[Go to M0903]**

☐ UK — Other unknown **[Go to M0903]**

(MO880) After discharge, does the patient receive health, personal, or support **Services Assistance? (Mark all that apply.)**

❑ 1 — No assistance or services received.

❑ 2 — Yes, assistance or services provided by family and friends

❑ 3 — Yes, assistance or services provided by other community resources (e.g., meals-on-wheels, home health services, home-maker assistance transportation assistance, assisted living, board and care)

[Go to M0903]

(MO890) If the patient was admitted to an acute care **Hospital,** for what **Reason** was he/she admitted?

❑ 1 — Hospitalization for <u>emergent</u> (unscheduled) care

❑ 2 — Hospitalization for <u>urgent</u> (scheduled within 24 hours of admission) care

❑ 3 — Hospitalization for <u>elective</u> (scheduled more than 24 hours before admission) care

❑ UK — Unknown

(MO895) Reason for Hospitalization: (Mark all that apply.)

❑ 1 — Improper medication administration, medication side effects, toxicity, anaphylaxis

❑ 2 — Injury caused by fall or accidental at home

❑ 3 — Respiratory problems (SOB, infection, obstruction)

❑ 4 — Wound or tube site infection, deteriorating wound status, new lesion/ulcer

❑ 5 — Hypo/Hyperglycemia, diabetes out of control

❑ 6 — GI bleeding, obstruction

❑ 7 — Exacerbation of CHF, fluid overload, heart failure

❑ 8 — Myocardial infarction, stroke

❑ 9 — Chemotherapy

❑ 10 — Scheduled surgical procedure

❑ 11 — Urinary tract infection

❑ 12 — IV catheter-related infection

❑ 13 — Deep vein thrombosis, pulmonary embolus

❑ 14— Uncontrolled pain

❑ 15 — Psychotic episode

❑ 16 — Other than above reasons   [Go to M0903]

(MO900) For what **Reason(s)** was the patient **Admitted to a Nursing Home? (Mark all that apply.)**

❑ 1 — Therapy services

❑ 2 — Respite care

❑ 3 — Hospice care

❑ 4 — Permanent placement

❑ 5 — Unsafe for care at home

❑ 6 — Other

❑ UK — Unknown

[Go to M0903]

(M0903) Date of Last (Most Recent) Home Visit:

__ __ - __ __ - __ __ __ __
Month   Day   Year

(M0906) Discharge / Transfer / Death Date: Enter the date of the discharge, transfer, or death (at home) of the patient.

__ __ - __ __ - __ __ __ __   ❑ UK — Unknown
Month   Day   Year

SUMMARY OF CARE PROVIDED DURING HOME CARE EPISODE:

1. Identified Problem	Interventions	Current Status
2. Overall Status at Discharge		

Copy of Summary to: ❑ Referral Source   ❑ Attending Physician

Date of Assessment: _____   **Signature of Assessor**_____

Appendix **F**

FREQUENTLY ASKED QUESTIONS ABOUT OASIS AND OBQI

What does OASIS stand for?

Answer: Outcome and Assessment Information Set.

What is the first step in implementing OASIS?

Answer: Learn as much about it as possible. Read, attend seminars, talk to colleagues in other agencies, and network with others who have used it or are also in the process of learning about it.

How do you suggest we begin to use the OASIS data set?

Answer: The most conducive way to implement the OASIS is to begin with a positive outlook. It will be very difficult to motivate staff if management is not enthusiastic about the task. While integrating OASIS into agency processes, keep in mind that the intent is to improve patient outcomes, thus improving the process of patient care.

Answer: Thoroughly in-service staff members in the process of data collection.

Answer: Ensure understanding of each item prior to beginning data collection. Allow adequate time for staff to learn the process prior to expecting perfection.

What is a good way to summarize for staff what OASIS is?

Answer: The OASIS is a data collection system that helps you organize your assessment information clearly and consistently. This uniform set of questions includes a variety of information relative to the patient's status at specified time points. This information is then used to show how the health care you provide affects the health status of the patient at discharge (outcomes). Most agencies who have learned OASIS and used it for a while find that it only takes an average of 10 minutes longer to conduct an initial assessment visit using OASIS than previously.

How were nurses involved in the development of the program, and how are they involved on an ongoing basis?

Answer: The research project was begun in 1988 with two nurses; one, Kathryn Crisler, is the Senior Research Associate still working with the project. Continuous input has also come from clinical panels that included a significant number of nurses, a technical advisory panel consisting of home care clinicians and managers, and various sources who are clinically based and work in patients' homes every day. Currently, there are several nurses on the project staff, all of whom have field and managerial experience in home care and quality improvement.

How do I complete yet *more* paperwork with all these questions?

Answer: The most efficient way to complete the assessment form with the OASIS items is to do the documentation in the home while you are on the visit. In this way, you can make the most of the checklist format of the OASIS questions and more accurately record the information while it is fresh in your mind. It can be overwhelming to try to remember the details at a later time.

How will using OASIS affect the way I document care?

Answer: *OASIS very much changes the way you document care.* The demonstration agencies have reported that their nurses and therapists like the checklist format and find that it has made their documentation easier. The specificity of the data elements helps in assessment and care planning, and they can quickly review the patient's level of activities of daily living (ADL) and instrumental ADL (IADL) to determine whether additional disciplines are needed and if the patient needs to be re-certified.

Can the OASIS data be collected over the phone without making a home visit?

Answer: No. To collect meaningful data, there *must* be a combination of interview, professional assessment information that can only be collected by directly observing the patient, and clinical decision-making by the assessor to determine the exact scoring for the various items.

The OASIS data set requires asking many questions, some of which include information about financial and personal support systems. Is it necessary to obtain patient permission to ask these rather lengthy questions?

Answer: It is not necessary to obtain permission beyond that which is always obtained in order to provide services to the patient. Remember that the OASIS data set is to be incorporated into the agency assessment, not used as an attachment or separate form. Incorporation ensures that questions are not repeated or information requested more than once. A combination of interview and assessment is used to obtain the information, and once the assessor becomes comfortable with the new form, the questions will not seem any more invasive than those on the previous assessment.

Should we incorporate the questions into our own assessment or purchase a preprinted or computerized form?

Answer: The process of incorporating the OASIS data set into an agency's assessment form seems a laborious one. Actually, this is the time to change the old assessment tool—to streamline it and delete information that will be collected by the OASIS items. Of course, there will be a cost for printing these documents, and they will need to be changed if and when the OASIS data set is altered.

Answer: If you choose to use a preprinted form, have it reviewed by someone familiar with the OASIS data set and the process of data collection using the OASIS prior to purchase. The market has been "buyer beware" up to this point, and there are forms out there that do not meet the specifications as defined by the CHPR. Be sure the skip patterns are correct and that no items are deleted. The alpha-numerical identifiers must be intact in order to maintain data integrity.

Answer: Computerized forms should be compatible with current software. If software is purchased, be sure you have the option to upgrade as necessary without tremendous expense. The OASIS items should be incorporated into the computerized assessment just as they are on paper; if it is necessary to have two separate assessment forms, valuable time will be lost in the assessment process or in data retrieval.

As a staff nurse working in home health, how involved am I in collecting this information?

Answer: The OASIS data set has been tested to be used exclusively by professional nurses or physical therapists. It is important to point out that the OASIS items are intended for use by these professional disciplines but are *not* meant to be used by other home care providers (i.e., assistive personnel).

What is OBQI?

Answer: OBQI stands for Outcome-Based Quality Improvement. It is the performance improvement system that is being mandated by Medicare through the Conditions of Participation, which govern home health agencies that provide services to Medicare beneficiaries. The difference between OBQI and the quality assurance approach taken in the past is the focus on outcomes. In other words, payers, providers, professionals, and consumers want to know how the home care affects patients in the short and long term. Focusing on outcomes asks, "What difference in the patient's health did home health services make, and additionally, how much were the costs for the patient to reach a certain outcome?"

I hear a lot about benchmarking. How does this fit in with OBQI and OASIS?

Answer: The goal of comparing data (or benchmarking) is to provide essential information to health care agencies, patients, referral sources, and payers about the outcomes of home health care provided and the costs involved in achieving them. First the OASIS data is collected on patients at start of care, follow-up timepoints, and discharge.

Answer: In the performance improvement phase of the process, the collected data are analyzed to make decisions about the quality of care. Many of these decisions are made by comparing the data from one agency to another or to a standard in the industry or other benchmarks established as quality indicators.

Answer: The OASIS data are important in this way because they are uniform, collected from all home health organizations throughout the country, and useful for benchmarking, not only with Medicare patients, but with managed care clients as well.

Not all agencies will continue to be Medicare certified—and may choose to be just JCAHO/ CHAP/CARF certified. How will OASIS fit into their needs?

Answer: Having a uniform data set that has been proven valid and reliable and has been consistently collected in all types of home health agencies throughout the country provides a strong database for many uses across payer and accreditation sources. Additionally, the fact that the data will be adjusted for risk allows agencies to compare themselves to other providers, even if their case mix and demographics are much different. Home health has long had difficulty providing accurate and consistent data on a regional, state, and national basis due to the lack of a sound database.

Answer: The OASIS data set and the OBQI evaluation that follows, being constantly monitored, will provide the opportunity to prove the value of home health and give us more power in the marketplace as we have sound data and cost figures to prove our worth, not just ancedotal evidence.

Where do JCAHO/CHAP/CARF regulations fit in, especially their requirement that agencies have an outcome management system of which OASIS is one of those recommended?

Answer: This is an excellent question, but one that is still in the process of being answered. Obviously, the integration of numerous PI requirements mandates that all providers and accreditors work closely together to assure there is minimal redundancy in this area so agencies can collect quality data information, yet not be bogged down with time-consuming collection of data that is overlapping. It will call on HCFA, JCAHO, and other accrediting bodies to work together to assist agencies in reaching this goal. The years 1998 to 2000 should prove instrumental in seeing how these regulations can be complimentary, not punitive.

How do we decide which outcome(s) to focus on?

Answer: HCFA has mandated collection of OASIS data on all Medicare patients. The agency can, however, focus on outcomes for patients with particular diagnoses rather than on global outcomes for all patients until the process has become internalized for all participants and the overall goals of the program are clear.

You were employed by an agency that was chosen for the OASIS pilot project. Did this prove beneficial?

Answer: Absolutely. The Center for Health Policy Research and Development provided unlimited support during this process. Experts were always available to discuss both clinical and data processing. The project managers never failed to give "positive strokes" to agencies at each encounter. In one instance, Jill Byers, the nursing contact assigned to our agency during the pilot project, set up a conference call with staff at the monthly meeting to personally answer questions and decrease frustration. When staff learned that one-on-one support was available through the Center in Denver as well as through administration at the agency, they really took ownership of the project and determined to do their best. Our data entry clerk

"loaded" the program, learned the data entry process, and worked out the "bugs" in the process over the phone with representatives from the pilot program. The Center will continue to be a valuable support.

How long does it take for the care provider to actually complete the assessment for agencies throughout this process?

Answer: Once the assessment form is internalized and the peak of the learning curve has passed, the actual data collection process will increase by approximately five minutes. Of course this is just an average; as with any other learning process, some assessors will pick up on the process quickly and some will be much slower to internalize it.

Answer: Agencies can provide maximum assistance by always being available and accessible for questions from staff. Too often changes are not fully understood by managers as well as by staff, and questions are discouraged in order to avoid "looking stupid" or "giving the wrong answer." Management should thoroughly understand the OASIS data set, data collection regulations, and critical time frames in order to maximize the learning process.

Answer: Remember to maintain a positive outlook during initial data assessment training—if staff feel that management isn't supportive of the project, they will quickly mirror negative behaviors.

What is the opinion of professional caregivers about the assessment tools?

Answer: Much has been said about the use of the OASIS data collection tool by those other than registered nurses. Since nurses see the majority of home care patients, they will have the main responsibility of collecting this information.

Answer: Remember that the OASIS data set was never intended as a complete assessment but rather to be assimilated into the agency's current assessment form. Such factors as vital signs, weight, and other *specific* assessment items must be added. This is the time to upgrade your assessment form and include areas that may have been somewhat "skimpy" before.

Answer: Agencies who have followed instructions from the Center have included physical therapists as well as nurses on the forms development committee. Some agencies have chosen to revise their physical therapy assessment forms to include the OASIS so the physical therapist could continue to use their own assessment forms when opening and discharging "therapy only" cases.

Do you recommend a "trial run" of data collection prior to actually making changes in agency processes and procedures?

Answer: Yes. By working with the data, even for a little while, before actually making decisions about policy and procedure changes, all staff can get accustomed to collecting the data, analyzing the reports, and addressing areas that need clarification. Even though the time for mandatory inclusion of the OASIS data set into an agency's assessment forms is here, it is still important to take it relatively slow, getting all staff trained and comfortable with the content and process of OASIS before determining that the information you are collecting is reliable and valid.

My agency doesn't think the OASIS questions will fit into their assessment as written and want to modify them. Is this allowed?

Answer: No. The Center for Health Care Policy Research at the University of Colorado has been emphatic that the OASIS questions are *not* to be modified in any way. As in all data collection, it is critically important that the questions be consistently asked the same way each time. Although the assessor doesn't have to read the questions off verbatim during a home visit, the question and the responses must remain constant so the data collected will be consistent over time. Additionally, since the data collected in each agency will be compared on a regional, state, and national basis, *everyone* collecting the information must use the same questions, or else we will be comparing apples and oranges.

Answer: The demonstration agencies that have integrated OASIS data into their existing assessment forms have found that many of the items are repetitive of what they are currently collecting. The result has been that their assessment forms have not expanded much in size, just rearranged to include the OASIS questions that organize their assessment findings more clearly.

Do you recommend checking the responses before entering them into the system?

Answer: All assessment forms should be reviewed by a professional staff member prior to entering information into the system for storage or transmission. Errors that may wreak havoc with agency outcomes can often be detected at this stage. The individual who actually performs this review should be a nurse who is familiar enough with the data set to identify inconsistencies and incorrect responses with a minimum of effort. Even after staff members are comfortable using the OASIS, it will be necessary to review the forms for incorrect skip patterns or missed questions.

Appendix G

Common Terms Used in Outcome-Based Quality Improvement and OASIS

analysis The systematic organization and examination of data to determine the results of a study.

applied research Research intended to address specific practical problems and questions.

assessor The professional who collects the OASIS data directly from assessment of the patient. This can be a registered nurse or a physical therapist.

benchmark With respect to a given attribute, the performance of an organization or individual that is considered to be the goal of others. In the context of health care reform, benchmark performance would be that which delivers the best combination of results and cost; that is, the "best" possible outcome may cost so much that it cannot be taken as a benchmark. When someone has the ability to gather meaningful data, compile it, and display results, setting benchmarks can occur.

benchmarking A system of comparing data whereby health care assessment measures its performance against "best-practice" standards. Best-practice standards can reflect:

evidenced-based practice

Practice supported by current investigative studies of like patient populations.

knowledge- and data-based systems

Explicit in benchmarking is movement away from anecdotal and single-practitioner experience based practice.

As a continuous process of comparison, projection, and implementation, benchmarking involves comparing an organization with others, discovering and projecting best trends in practices, and meeting and exceeding the expectations of internal administration, internal and external evaluators, and payers. The goal of benchmarking is to provide essential information to health care agencies, patients, referral sources, and payers about the outcomes of home health care and the costs involved in achieving them. Types of benchmarking include:

external benchmarking A comparison with a local, state, regional, or national database or with another organization(s) of similar size, case mix, or types of services.

internal benchmarking A comparison within an organization over time or against like groups within the organization such as departments, teams, or other branche offices.

operational benchmarking Looks at the differences between the organization's operational methods and those of others. It focuses on rating and comparing operational methods such as work teams, district management, and activity-based costing.

organizational benchmarking Rates and compares organizational processes with those of another organization to replicate the best processes. An example could be turnaround time for admitting patients, the time taken to get signed physician orders, etc.

strategic benchmarking Compares the organization's best performance based on strategies selected for growth and comparative achievement of the results.

bias Any influence introduced by the researcher, subjects, instrumentation, data collection, or analysis of data that distorts the results of a study.

case mix The mix of cases, defined by age, sex, diagnoses, treatments, and severity of illness, as well as other variables an agency may want to analyze. Case mix is defined by

(1) grouping patients (classification) according to these factors and then

(2) determining the proportion of the total falling into each group. Home health revenues are based on how many "items" an agency "sells" and of what kind—that is, the number of patients cared for and the diagnosis and payer of each. The revenue, therefore, is based on the agency's case mix.

checklist A format for written questionnaires in which the subject uses a checkmark to indicate which items on a list are applicable.

CHPR Center for Health Policy Research (Denver, Colorado).

clinical relevance The degree to which the purpose or findings of a study apply to or guide clinical practice.

clinical research Research studies that involve clients or have potential application to clinical practice.

COP Conditions of Participation The rules home health agencies must adhere to to participate in Medicare.

core data set Related data gathered from several sources that together allow agencies to look at numerous aspects of their operations. For example, OASIS data, additional assessment items, visit data, and cost-per-visit information can be used for various data analysis functions, not just for OBQI.

data collection The process of gathering information relevant to the purpose of the study.

data elements The individual items of information systematically collected in the course of a study.

data entry The process of entering data into the computer to create a database for analysis.

data set   A specific set of items of information. *Or:* The total of all responses obtained during a study—that is, all responses to OASIS questions collected over a nine-month period.

dichotomous   A dichotomous outcome measure indicates the possibility of only two values; for example, a commonly used dichotomous measure is gender, where there are only two possible choices (0=male; 1=female). For example, if the patient can improve and does so, he will "earn" or be assigned the value of "1." If he does not improve, he is assigned the value of "0. So if the patient is rated "2" for bathing at SOC but "1" at discharge, he will be assigned the value of "1" since he didn't worsen but in fact got better.

drift   The tendency to code differently over time.

empirical data (evidence)   Objective evidence or data collected through one of the senses.

exemplary   Commendable; to be used as an example or model.

follow-up   Another word for a time period when OASIS data is to be collected—for example, assessments performed between day 57 and day 62 of the initial assessment, assessments performed at readmission after a hospitalization discharge, etc.

HAVEN: The computer program for OASIS developed and supported by HCFA.

health status attribute   A measurement of some attribute of individual or aggregate health that is considered to reflect health status. Each attribute is given a numerical value, and a score is calculated for the individual or community from the aggregate of these values. To the extent possible, these attributes are objective—that is, they are facts for which various observers or investigators would each find the same value. These attributes can be determined by examination, function, quality of life, activities of daily living (ADL), emotional well-being, episodes of medical care or diagnoses.

ICD-9 code   The *International Classification of Diseases (ICD-9)* is maintained by the World Health Organization. In the United States, this coding system is adapted by the National Center for Health Statistics and the Health Care Financing Administration (HCFA). The ICD-9 coding system was originally designed to keep a statistical record of morbidity (disease) but has also been adapted for use with reimbursement mechanisms. Every ICD-9 code describes and denotes a different diagnosis, symptom, service, or procedure.

instruments   Tools or devices the researcher uses to measure phenomena in a research study, such as a questionnaire, survey, interview guide, thermometer, or scale. Also called research instruments or research tools.

interrater reliability   The degree of agreement among different persons (raters) expressing judgments (ratings) on the same data or observations.

Or:

The degree of agreement among judgments (ratings) by the same person (rater) made on the same data or on the same observations at different times.

interview   A method of data collection in which the researcher asks questions to obtain information from the participant. The researcher may use a written guide or follow a protocol for questions and may conduct the interview face-to-face or over the telephone.

JCAHO   Joint Commission on Accreditation of Healthcare Organizations. A health care accreditation organization that provides standards to meet for accreditation of hospitals, ambulatory care facilities, long-term care facilities, home health, hospice, and home medical equipment organizations.

knowledge   A group of facts, information, or perceptions accepted as true.

longitudinal study   A nonexperimental research study with data collection from the same sample at repeated points in time.

mean   A measure of central tendency; the descriptive statistic that is the arithmetic average of the observations.

measurement   The assignment of specified numerical values to an amount of some attribute of an event or object.

measures   Types of measures include the following

   structural measures   Reflect adequacy/qualifications of staffing, equipment, technology, care setting, etc.

   process measures   Reflect nature/excellence of treatments, care planning, assessment, services, etc.

   outcome measures   Reflect what actually happens to patients and their health during and after the time care is provided.

   aggregate measure   A measure based on a collection or aggregation of data about many events or phenomena.

   continuous measure   A measure that can take any value along a continuous scale.

   discrete measure   A measure that takes one of a fixed number of values.

median   The middle number in a set of observations; half the observations are above the number and half below.

MEQA   National Medicare Quality Assurance and Improvement Demonstration Project (1994–99).

> MEQA is funded by the Health Care Financing Administration (HCFA), the Office of Research and Demonstrations (ORD), and the Robert Wood Johnson Foundation (RWJF).

> National sample of 50 home health agencies (HHAs) are being used in the project called demonstration agencies.

> The purpose was to find a way to implement Implement Outcome-Based Quality Improvement (OBQI) on a national level.

mode   The most frequently occurring value or category in a set of data; a measure of central tendency.

OASIS   Outcome and Assessment Information Set.

objectivity   The process of remaining without judgment and bias in the conduct of scientific research to the extent that another independent researcher would obtain similar results concurrently.

OBQI   Outcome-Based Quality Improvement.

outcome   A change in patient health status between two or more time points. Types of outcomes include:

> ***end-result outcome (pure outcome)***   A change in patient health status between two or more time points.

> ***intermediate-result outcome (instrumental outcome)***   A change in patient (or informal caregiver's) behavior, emotions, or knowledge that can influence the patient's end-result outcomes.

> ***utilization outcome (proxy outcome)***   A type of health care utilization that reflects change (typically substantial) in patient health status over time.

> ***global outcome***   Pertains to all patients. These results are projected to apply universally.

> **focused outcome**   Restricted to a subgroup of patients—for example, cardiac patients.

patient tally report   A document that enumerates outcome measures and possibly other patient attributes at the start of care (SOC). The patient tally report can be useful for selecting individual patients for record review or further investigation on the basis of whether specific outcomes were attained or on the basis of specific patient attributes (case mix factors) at SOC.

pilot study/project   A trial run with a small-scale study prior to conducting a major study to test and refine procedures or to obtain preliminary information.

prevalence   The number of cases of a disease or other condition in a specified population at a particular point or period of time.

process-of-care analysis (investigation)   A process that consists of four steps:

> Identifying which outcomes to investigate further, termed *target outcomes*.

> Determining and undertaking activities to analyze the care that produced the target outcomes.

> As a result of the analysis in item 2, specifying the care behaviors that should be changed or reinforced, termed *target care behaviors*.

> Specifying the precise care behaviors that should be enacted as substitutes for, improvements on, or extensions of the target care behaviors. These are termed "best practices."

process measures   The series of events or the way in which tasks occur.

> These measurements can be reassessment, clinical pathways, or service treatment regimens.

proxy   Something that happens externally to the patient that affects a change in health status, such as hospitalization or transfer to an inpatient facility.

quality   The degree of excellence something possesses—the characteristics that make it either good or bad (JCAHO). *Or:* Continuously meeting customers' needs and expectations at a price they are willing to pay.

quantification   A way of measuring what happens to the patient as a result of the care provided. Instead of saying the patient is "better" or "worse" (using words that have relative meanings and may be different to different people), numbers are assigned to patient outcomes. The outcome is measured based on the difference or similarity between the patient's condition upon entry into home care and upon discharge from home care. The number can also mean the patient was hospitalized or moved to an inpatient facility. The number used has meaning when compared to other numbers within a range or system. For example, if "5" means the patient is completely independent and does not need the assistance of another person and "1" means he/she is completely dependent on another person, numbers falling in between that range would give you an idea of how dependent the patient actually is. Think of the number as a very finite way of naming the patient's current condition. These numbers simply help us define a standard that everyone can understand instead of using words that have different meanings depending upon your viewpoint.

QUIGs (Quality Indicatory Groups)   Can be used to stratify patients into nonexclusive or nonoverlapping groups for examining within-condition outcome measures or as case mix variables/risk factors to be employed in adjusting global outcome measures that pertain to all patients or larger groups of patients. QUIGs are divided into two broad types of conditions or care needs: acute and chronic. It is possible for patients to belong to three or four QUIGs, both acute and chronic.

reinforcement   The process of encouraging a positive behavior to be sustained so that a positive outcome can continue to be achieved.

reliable (reliability)   The degree of accuracy of results over a period of time, a number of trials, or among different observers or investigators. Also, the probability that a system will perform its function properly for a given period of time.

remediation   Using best practices for care provision to replace or supplement current practices and thus improve outcomes.

screen   Term used in the context of OBQI in two stages:

1st-stage screen   The first level of screening uses outcome reports to identify those particular outcomes for which process-of-care investigations will be done. The global and focused outcomes can be identified by comparing the data with national norms and standards or with local, regional, state, or national benchmarks and means.

2nd-stage screen   All actions undertaken in response to outcome reports by an agency staff in conducting the process-of-care analysis and preparing the plan of action.

sentinel event   A negative or untoward event that potentially reflects a relatively serious health problem or a decline in health status for an individual patient. Sentinel events are low-frequency events and therefore do not lend themselves readily to risk adjustment as other outcome measures do. Examples of sentinel events that an organization might want to monitor for a quality assurance and improvement program would be: (1) emergent care for falls or accidents, (2) emergent care for wounds or infections, (3) development of urinary tract infections, (4) increase in the number of pressure ulcers, and (5) deterioration in the status of surgical wounds (Center for Health Policy Research).

Or:

An unexpected occurrence involving death or serious physical or psychological injury or the risk thereof. A serious injury includes the loss of limb or function. The phrase "or the risk thereof" includes any process variation for which a recurrence would carry a significant chance of a serious adverse outcome. The event is called "sentinel" because it sends a signal or warning that requires immediate attention (Friedman, 1998).

TIQ   Telephone Interview Questionnaire. The tool used in the National Medicare Quality Assurance and Improvement Demonstration project to measure consumer response and satisfaction. The TIQ was administered to patients, or if the patient was unable to respond, it was administered to the caregivers.

trigger   An event that forces another event to happen.

valid (validity)   The degree to which an instrument measures what it is intended to measure.

website   HCFA OASIS website

http://www.hcfa.gov/medicare/hsqb/oasis/oasishmp.htm

Selected References

Adams, C., & Anthony, A. (Eds.). (1997). *Home health outcomes and resource utilization: Integrating today's critical priorities.* (Publication No. 19-7246.) New York: National League for Nursing.

Agency streamlines admissions to add OASIS . . . outcomes and assessment information set. (1996). *Home Care Quality Management, 2*(6) 64.

Benson, D. S. (1992). *Measuring outcomes in ambulatory care.* Chicago: American Hospital Publishing.

Bogan, C. E., and English, M. J. (1994). *Benchmarking for best practices.* New York: McGraw-Hill.

Carr, P. (1996). Clinicians' forum. Get ready for OASIS . . . the outcome and assessment information set. *Home Healthcare Nurse, 14*(1) 61–62.

Case managers collect OASIS data . . . outcome and assessment information set. (1997). *Home Care Quality Management, 3*(3)30–31.

Catching the wave: How to stay ahead of OASIS trend with your own project . . . outcome and assessment information set. (1996). *Home Care Quality Management 2*(8) 85–87.

Creating an OASIS: Hot topics—cool solutions. . . . Oncology Nursing Society 7th annual fall institute, Phoenix, AZ: November 8–10, 1996 (1996) *Oncology Nursing Forum 23*(7), 1001–1004.

Crisler, K. S., Campbell, B. M., & Shaughnessy, P. W. (1997). *OASIS basics.* Denver, CO: Center for Health Services and Policy Research.

Crisler, K. S., Kramer, A. M., Jenkins, J., Bauman, M. K., Bostrom, S. G., and Shaughnessy, P. W. (1994, September). *Objective review criteria for abstracting data for clinical record review of home health care. Vol. 3: Final report.* Denver, CO: University of Colorado Health Sciences Center, Center for Health Services Research.

Department of Health and Human Services. (1996). Health Care Financing Administration. *Medicare home health agency manual,* Section 205 .1, Rev. 277.

Donabedian, A. (1985). *The methods and findings of quality assessment and monitoring: An illustrated analysis* (Vol. 3). Ann Arbor, MI: Health Administration Press.

Expect Medicare to require OASIS as a part of COP. (1996). *Home Care Quality Management, 2*(6) 62.

Friedman, M. M. (1998). To Tell the Truth: The Joint Commission's Sentinel Event Policy. Home Healthcare Nurse, 16(10), 701–705.

Friedman, M. M. (1998). ORYX: The next evolution in accreditation. *Home Healthcare Nurse, 16*(4), 236–239.

Harrington, H. J., & Harrington, J. S. (1996). *High performance benchmarking: 20 steps to success.* New York: McGraw-Hill.

Health Care Financing Administration, Department of Health and Human Services. Medicare and Medicaid programs: Revision of conditions of participation for home health agencies and use of outcome assessment information set (OASIS). Proposed rules (42 CFR Part 484). (1997). *Federal Register, 62*(46) 11003–11064.

Hoeman, S. P. (1996). *Rehabilitation Nursing (2nd ed.)* St. Louis: C. V. Mosby Co.

Home Care 101: OASIS update from the field . . . outcomes and assessment sets (OASIS). (1977). *Home Care Nurse News, 4*(5) 1–3.

Hulley, D., Scribner K., & Siegel, H. (1997). OASIS: A case study by the home and health care association of Massachusetts. *The Remington Report, 5*(5) 49–55.

Humphrey, C. (1998). *Home care nursing handbook* 3rd Edition. Gaithersburg, MD: Aspen Publishers.

Humphrey, C., & Milone-Nuzzo, P. (1998). *Manual of home care orientation.* Gaithersburg, MD: Aspen Publishers.

Joint Commission on Accreditation of Healthcare Organizations. (1997). *Comprehensive accreditation manual for home care,* p. 9. Oakbrook Terrace, IL: Author.

Joint Commission on Accreditation of Health Care Organizations. (1997). ORYX: Performance measurement systems: Evaluation and selection. Oakbrook Terrace, IL: Author.

Joint Commission announces ORX: The next evolution in accreditation. (1997, February 18). *JCAHO News Release.*

Koch, L. A. (1997). Using OASIS (outcomes and assessment information set) to reach OBQI (outcome-based quality improvement). *Caring, 16*(8), 34–36, 38, 40–46.

Koch, L. A. (1997). Using OASIS to reach OBQI. *Caring, 16*(8), 34–46.

Mahoney, F. I., & Barthel, D. W. (1965). Functional evaluation: The Barthel Index. *Maryland State Medical Journal, 14*(2), 61–65.

Mann, M., Edwards, D., & Baum, C. M. (1986). OASIS: A new concept for promoting the quality of life for older adults. *American Journal of Occupational Therapy, 40*(11) 784–786.

Morris, J. N., Hawes, C., Fries, B. E., Phillips, C. D., (1990). Designing the national resident assessment instrument for nursing homes. *Gerontologist, 30*(3) 293–307.

Moskowitz, E., & McCann, C. B. (1957). Classification of disability in the chronically ill and aging. *Journal of Chronic Disease, 5,* 342–346.

Mosqueda, L. (1994). Geriatric rehabilitation. *Journal of Home Health Care Practice, 6*(3), 37–44.

Nathan, L., & Hartnett, M. (1998). *Implementing OASIS: Part 1. White Paper 98-001*. Seattle, WA: Outcome Concept Systems, Inc.

Nathan, L., & Hartnett, M. (1998). *Implementing OASIS: Part 2. White Paper 98–002*. Seattle, WA: Outcome Concept Systems, Inc.

OASIS Implementation: One Year Later, What's the Story? . . . Outcome and Assessment Information Set. (1997). *Home Care Quality Management, 3*(2) 13–15.

Outcome-based quality improvement and the OASIS data set. (1997). *Home Healthcare Nurse, 15*(3) 203–206.

Outcomes-based quality improvement: OASIS update. (1996). *Home Care Nurse News, 3*(7) 1, 3.

Pollack, N., Rheault, W., & Stoeker, J. L. (1996). Reliability and validity of the FIM for persons aged 80 years and above from a multilevel continuing care retirement community. *Archives of Physical Medicine and Rehabilitation, 77*(10), 1056–1061.

Prepare to revamp your patient assessment, data collection tools . . .some form of OASIS assessment tool. (1996). *Home Care Quality Management, 2*(6) 61–65.

Schlenker, R. E. (1996). *Home health payment legislation: Review and recommendations*. Washington, DC: American Association of Retired Persons, Public Policy Institute: 1996:9611.

Schlenker, R. E., Shaughnessy, P. W., & Crisler K. S. (1995). Outcome-based quality improvement as a financial strategy for home health care agencies. *Journal of Home Health Care Practice, 7*(4), 1–15.

Schlenker, R. E., Shaughnessy, P. W., Hittle, D. F. (1995). Patient-level cost of home health care under capitated and fee-for-service payment. *Inquiry, 32*(3) 252–270.

Shaughnessy, P. W., & Crisler, K. S. (1995). *Outcome-based quality improvement: A manual for home care agencies on how to use outcomes*. Washington, D.C., National Association for Home Care.

Shaughnessy, P. W., Crisler, K. S., & Schlenker, R. E. (1997). Medicare's OASIS: Standardized outcome and assessment information set for home health care. Denver, CO: *Center for Health Services and Policy Research* (distributed by the National Association for Home Care.

Shaughnessy, P. W., Crisler, K. S., & Schlenker, R. E. (1998). Outcome-based quality improvement in the information age. *Home Health Care Management & Practice, 10*(2) 11–19.

Shaughnessy, P. W., Crisler, K. S., Schlenker, R. E., Arnold, A. G. (1994). Measuring and assuring the quality of home health care. *Health Care Financial Review, 16*(1) 35–67.

Shaughnessy, P. W., Schlenker, R. E., Hittle, D. F. (1994). Home health care outcomes under capitated and fee-for-service payment. *Health Care Financial Review, 16*(1) 187–222.

Shaughnessy, P. W., Schlenker, R. E., & Hittle, D. F. (1994). Case mix of home health patients under capitated and fee-for-service payment. *Health Services Research, 30*(1) 79–113.

Slee, V. N., Slee, D. A., & Schmidt, H. J. (1996). *Slee's health care terms (third comprehensive ed.)*. St. Paul, MN: Trianga Press.

Sperling, R. (1997). Ask home healthcare nurse. Frequently asked questions about OASIS: Answers from a rural agency participant . . . outcome and assessment information set. *Home Healthcare Nurse, 15*(5), 340–342.

Sperling, R. (1996). Outcomes-based quality improvement: OASIS update (part three of three articles). *Home Care Nurse News 3*(11), 5–6.

Sperling, R. (1997). Management strategies for implementing OASIS. *Home Care Manager, 1*(2), 18–20.

Spotlight on . . .outcome-based quality improvement and the OASIS data set. Interview with Katheryn S. Crisler. *Home Healthcare Nurse, 15*(3), 203–206.

Steinbach, P. J., & Zuber, R. F. (1997). Tips for using OASIS now. *Home Healthcare Nurse, 15*(4), 261–264.

Vladeck, B. C., & Miller, N. A. (1994). The Medicare home health initiative. *Health Care Financial Review, 16*(1) 7–16.

Wilson, A. (1997). *Home care outcomes and OASIS*. Gig Harbor, WA: Wilson and Associates.

Wilson, A., and Nathan, L. (1997). *Understanding benchmarks*. White Paper 97-001, Seattle, WA.: Outcome concept Systems, Inc.

Index

Note: Page numbers in *italics* indicate illustrations; those followed by t indicate tables; and those followed by d indicate display material.